Offensive Marketing

An Action Guide to Gaining
Competitive Advantage

Offensive Marketing

An Action Guide to Gaining
Competitive Advantage

Hugh Davidson and
Warren J. Keegan

with Elyse Arnow Brill

ELSEVIER
BUTTERWORTH
HEINEMANN

AMSTERDAM • BOSTON • HEIDELBERG • LONDON • NEW YORK • OXFORD
PARIS • SAN DIEGO • SAN FRANCISCO • SINGAPORE • SYDNEY • TOKYO

Elsevier Butterworth–Heinemann
200 Wheeler Road, Burlington, MA 01803, USA
Linacre House, Jordan Hill, Oxford OX2 8DP, UK

 Recognizing the importance of preserving what has been written, Elsevier prints its books on acid-free paper whenever possible.

Library of Congress Cataloging-in-Publication Data

Keegan, Warren J.
   Offensive marketing: an action guide to gaining competitive advantage/Warren
  J. Keegan and Hugh Davidson; with Elyse Arno Brill.
     p. cm.
  Includes index.
  ISBN 0-7506-7459-8
   1. Marketing. I. Davidson, J. H. (J. Hugh), 1935–II. Brill, Elyse Arno. III. Title.

HF5415.K427 2003
658.8–dc22
                                                  2003057940

British Library Cataloguing-in-Publication Data
A catalogue record for this book is available from the British Library.

ISBN: 0-7506-7459-8

For information on all Butterworth–Heinemann publications visit our website at www.bh.com

03 04 05 06 07 08 09 10 9 8 7 6 5 4 3 2 1

Printed in the United States of America

Contents

Foreword

With *Offensive Marketing: An Action Guide to Gaining Competitive Advantage*, we have at last a well-written, insightful book about marketing that grasps that marketing is more than just a way to squeeze a few marginal increases out of a business model. Instead, Warren Keegan and Hugh Davidson challenge us to use marketing to drive an offensive, systematic, and long-term approach to business growth. This book is a road map to twenty-first-century strategic marketing, which focuses on creating unique value for customers and superior return for investors and all stakeholders of the enterprise.

With the thousands of books on marketing, why should busy business leaders read this one? The reason is simple—marketing is placed in today's challenging business environment. As other disciplines have changed, so too must marketing.

Offensive Marketing takes a critical look at the narrowness of many professional marketers and the growing bureaucracy of marketing departments. Professional marketers have often failed to prevent the erosion of long-term consumer value by focusing on short-term profit and have failed to realize that market-driven strategy is an investment that can deliver unique value to customers and superior return to the company.

Offensive marketing is an approach to building long-term, sustainable shareholder value. The use of offensive marketing enables the customer to drive demand and business systems, offering an aligned approach to creating an effective and sustainable business offering. Examples throughout the book, starting with Harley Davidson, document the success that commercial enterprises can have being "offensive."

This book offers us one of the first truly comprehensive looks into using marketing not only tactically, but also strategically. From the first chapter, which highlights the five elements of the offensive marketing approach—summarized by the mnemonic, POISE—Keegan and Davidson describe the road map and necessary rules of engagement for the "offensive" organization.

The goal of any commercial enterprise should be above-average, long-term profitability—the "P" of POISE. The authors challenge the purely financial view of profit, understanding that profitability is the reward for meeting customers' needs. They rightly assert that profitability cannot be viewed in isolation from other related goals of the enterprise, and they propose a marketing alignment process that matches markets, customers, and channels with competencies and assets of the organization.

An offensive attitude—the "O" of POISE—is an imperative ingredient of the offensive marketing approach. Despite many recent popular treatises on the topics of organizational culture and leadership, *Offensive Marketing* recognizes that many companies continue to lack an effective offensive attitude. Instead they cut costs, undertake "initiatives" and housekeeping efficiency, over-reward top executives, and think more about their share price than their customers.

Integrated marketing—the "I" of POISE—is fundamental to Keegan and Davidson's enterprise-wide approach to marketing. Integrated marketing means that every component of the business combines to deliver superior customer value at minimum cost. The integrated marketing concept and program formulated here is broader than the application of the term to describe a more narrow approach of combining various marketing communications. By using the original, broader use of the term, Keegan and Davidson challenge senior managers to use marketing as an approach to business rather than solely as a specialist discipline.

It is under this topic that the authors discuss integrated strategic planning, a concept that is inherently different from the conventional approach consisting of revenue, cost, and profit objectives. Marketing-driven planning focuses instead on the future needs of markets, customers, and consumers. Marketers rightly take the lead in facilitating and bringing their knowledge base to this interdepartmental dialogue.

Under the "S" of POISE, the authors discuss the strategic elements that go into the crucial analysis that comes before determining winning strategies. Under the first of four chapters, Keegan and Davidson offer an in-depth discussion of the requirements for effective business analysis, which, all too often, is left out by corporate decision-makers.

The authors discuss the importance of strategies, objectives, and planning and highlight the requirements for effective business analysis. They discuss issues raised by the internal business audit, the competitive analysis drill, and the application of what the authors term "key success factors," which reveal business performance strengths and weaknesses.

Next, Keegan and Davidson appropriately address the need for strategic planning and insight to grapple with anticipating the future. Developing a distinctive future outlook enables the offensive marketer to shape corporate strategy and meet future opportunities ahead of competitors. It is here that the authors correctly identify how marketers are losing influence over the strategic planning process; marketers repeatedly fail to grasp the initiative to drive companies into the future by taking control of the long-term planning process.

Continuing to develop the systematic offensive planning approach, the authors aptly address the development of winning strategies and the creation of strong marketing plans. They challenge corporate decision-makers to use offensive strategy to build competitive advantage through the concentration of resources aimed at the areas of best return. Portfolio analysis and the most frequently used tools of the trade are well evaluated. Lastly, the authors adeptly address an issue that is often left out of the analysis, namely, assessing strategic fit with corporate resources, other opportunities, and expected competitor response.

The cultivation of marketing plans and the marketing planning process is then put into its full context. As acknowledged by the authors, many aspects of marketing planning are technical and practical. Accordingly, Keegan and Davidson bring important insight to marketing planning tools and discuss key questions that often arise in marketing planning. As many books on market planning fail to bring a sense of sequencing and timing to the endeavor, Keegan and Davidson's approach is illuminating and informative.

The remaining seven chapters of the book address effective execution—the "E" of POISE. They cover in detail the important topics of offensive segmentation, brand development, new product development, marketing communications, market research, effective pricing strategies and objectives, and channel marketing. Each topic is explored in detail with many relevant issues updated for today's technology and customer-driven marketing environment. For example, after discussing the important principles of segmentation and the factors driving its use, Keegan and Davidson outline the practical applications of segmentation, a number of its more prominent pitfalls, the characteristics distinguishing offensive segmentation, and a five-step process for developing segmentation strategies.

In the same vein, Keegan and Davidson's twelve conclusions about brand development are important reading to set the stage for strategic brand management, a critical marketing skill. Perhaps the most vital conclusion discussed is that brands are not just names but are business systems.

The authors' approach to new product and service development is distinguished by tying success in this arena to rigorous analytical and planning processes as well as to a delineated process of building competencies in innovation and development. The authors demonstrate how conducting a profit gap analysis, utilizing the marketing alignment process, and following a systematic process that integrates input from various stakeholders vastly increases the success rate of new product and service offerings.

In their discussion of offensive communications strategy, Keegan and Davidson confirm that much of communication strategy remains the same despite broad changes in technology and the ability to reach individuals with personalized messages through a myriad of channels. However, some issues have certainly become more complex including creating an integrated marketing communications program.

The authors' introduction to the chapter on offensive market research begins with the line, "All is not well in the world of market research." So true. Between ROI issues and the questionable relevancy of research that seems to confirm past results, offensive market research needs to distinguish itself as a "frontier" for the exploration of consumer understanding with "big picture" relevancy not tactical implications. Out of this conviction, Keegan and Davidson push market research to strongly cultivating customer intelligence. Vital suggestions and an eight-step process for designing and implementing effective market research plans propel companies toward this goal.

Pricing decisions, as pointed out by the authors, are inherently one of the more difficult issues to address. In fact, pricing often becomes a compromise between targeted volume and market share, and profitability and financial goals. To help solve these difficulties, Keegan and Davidson introduce an effective five-step process for offensive pricing, which begins with the "value equation." By doing so, price effectively translates products or services into value propositions that can then be compared to other market offerings and, during the pricing process, synthesized with an overall strategy.

The last topic addressed is the rapidly changing and challenging field of offensive channel marketing. Keegan and Davidson base their discussion on the often-neglected principle that channels exist to serve customers and to add value to the product or service offering. From this vantage point, the authors correctly steer decision-makers to position themselves and their enterprises to exercise influence over channels and to continuously keep an eye toward developing new channels for market strength and success.

With this synopsis of the strengths and breadth of *Offensive Marketing: An Action Guide to Gaining Competitive Advantage*, it is clear that anyone seriously involved in commercial activity, and understanding the challenges of today's competitive marketplace, should read this book cover to cover. Not only are trends and key concepts described, but they are effectively tied into both overall strategic planning and marketing planning at all stages and considerations. This book is for the competitive business leader who is serious about strengthening his or her marketing skills and thinking. Practical tools are offered throughout the discussion that tie methodologically into a strong conceptual whole that will lend competitive strength to any company seriously following the book's recommendations and insights.

Bravo to the authors who have carefully moved marketing into a new, more relevant and strategic arena of practice and thinking.

Hermawan Kartajaya
CEO MarkPlus & Company
President, World Marketing Federation
Jakarta, September 2003

Acknowledgments

The following tables and figures have been either adapted or reprinted with permission from Hugh Davidson, *Even More Offensive Marketing* (New York: Penguin Books, 1997). The page number where they can be found in *Even More Offensive Marketing* is given in parentheses.

Tables

1-1 (p. 29), 1-2 (p. 30), 1-3 (p. 39), 1-5 (p. 41), 1-6 (p. 47), 1-7 (p. 50), 1-8 (p. 55), 2-1 (p. 65), 2-2 (p. 72), 2-3 (p. 46), 2-4 (p. 48), 2-5 (p. 51), 2-6 (p. 53), 2-7 (p. 93), 3-1 (p. 115), 3-2 (p. 124), 3-3 (p. 135), 4-1 (p. 149), 4-2 (p. 150), 4-3 (p. 152), 4-4 (p. 153), 4-5 (p. 154), 4-6 (p. 154), 4-7 (p. 173), 5-1 (p. 183), 5-2 (p. 184), 5-3 (p. 185), 5-4 (p. 187), 5-5 (p. 204), 5-6 (p. 205), 5-7 (p. 210), 5-8 (p. 210), 6-1 (p. 228), 6-2 (p. 229), 7-1 (p. 262), 7-2 (p. 272), 8-1 (p. 294), 8-2 (p. 303), 8-3 (p. 308), 8-4 (p. 309), 8-5 (p. 309), 8-6 (p. 310), 8-7 (p. 311), 8-8 (p. 312), 9-1 (p. 348), 9-2 (p. 355), 9-3 (p. 358), 9-4 (p. 360), 10-1 (p. 374), 10-2 (p. 374), 10-3 (p. 382), 10-4 (p. 386), 10-5 (p. 388), 10-6 (p. 388), 10-7 (p. 393), 10-8 (p. 395), 10-9 (p. 398), 10-10 (p. 401), 10-11 (p. 402), 10-12 (p. 403), 10-13 (p. 409), 11-1 (p. 440), 11-2 (p. 447), 11-3 (p. 448), 11-4 (p. 451), 12-1 (p. 470), 12-2 (p. 471), 12-3 (p. 472), 12-4 (p. 473), 12-5 (p. 484), 13-1 (p. 493), 13-2 (p. 501), 13-3 (p. 504), 13-4 (p. 506), 13-5 (p. 507), 13-6 (p. 508), 13-7 (p. 511), 13-8 (p. 514), 14-1 (p. 527), 14-2 (p. 529), 14-3 (p. 538), 15-1 (p. 379), 15-2 (p. 557), 15-3 (p. 566), 15-4 (p. 571).

Figures

2-2 (p. 88), 3-1 (p. 114), 5-2 (p. 189), 5-3 (p. 190), 5-4 (p. 194), 7-1 (p. 254), 7-2 (p. 260), 8-1 (p. 295), 8-2 (p. 295), 8-3 (p. 295), 9-1 (p. 351), 9-2 (p. 359), 10-1 (p. 375), 10-2 (p. 376), 10-3 (p. 377), 10-4 (p. 404), 11-1 (p. 420), 11-2 (p. 421), 11-3 (p. 427), 12-1 (p. 462), 14-1 (p. 522), 14-2 (p. 522), 14-3 (p. 523), 15-1 (p. 560).

The following figures have been either adapted or reprinted with permission from Malcolm H.B. McDonald and Warren J. Keegan, *Marketing Plans That Work*, 2nd ed. (Boston: Butterworth Heinemann, 2002). The page number where they can be found in *Marketing Plans That Work* is given in parentheses.

Figures

8-4 (p. 210), 8-5 (p. 201).

Table 1-4 has been reprinted with permission from Warren Keegan Associates, and Oxford Strategic Marketing Client Surveys.

1 The Offensive Marketing Approach: POISE

INTRODUCTION

The five key principles of Offensive Marketing—Profitable, Offensive, Integrated, Strategic, and Effectively Executed, as summarized in the mnemonic *POISE*—provide the basis for this book and the roadmap for building an effective and successful marketing program across the organization and its partners. In particular, the element of "Integration" has become more relevant as communication and information technologies, the Internet, data base software, and multimedia have increased possibilities of connectivity and networking. In addition, there is growing recognition of the prime importance of "Effective Execution," reflected in the growing popularity of balanced scorecard approaches to business. Chapter 1 defines Offensive Marketing, covers the need for it in today's increasingly competitive marketplace, and outlines the five key principles of POISE, which the remainder of the book develops.

Today, marketing and marketers have never had a bigger opportunity to realize their full potential as companies seek innovation and profitable growth. Offensive Marketing is designed to help companies exploit this opportunity. It is a set of attitudes, approaches, and processes practiced by only a handful of successful companies.

HARLEY DAVIDSON—AN OFFENSIVE MARKETER?

Harley Davidson has twice been on the brink of bankruptcy since the 1960s. Threatened for years by aggressive Japanese imports, it suffered from a decline in quality and was saddled with large debt after a management leveraged buyout (LBO) from AMF, a now defunct conglomerate. Initially, Harley used the political and legal arena to publicize its threat from Japanese competitors who were allegedly "dumping" their product on the American market at prices below those charged in Japan in their bid to increase U.S. market share.[1]

---

[1] See, Glenn Rifkin. *How Harley-Davidson Revs Its Brand*, Strategy + Business, A publication of Booz Alan & Hamilton, Fourth Quarter, 1997. http://www.strategy-business.com/strategy/97403/

With these efforts, it persuaded the United States Government International Trade Commission (ITC) to impose a stiff tariff on Japanese imports. Simultaneously, Harley Davidson management engaged in one of the first and most comprehensive efforts to copy Japanese manufacturing techniques, including "just in time" inventory controls and initiatives like quality circles. Against Japanese global strength, with its deep pockets for advertising and promotion, its speed to market, and long-term commitment to growth in market share and growth, Harley Davidson formulated a unique strategy that, over the past 40 years, has made it the clear leader in the heavyweight motorcycle market segment.

The Harley Davidson strategy is a combination of operational efficiency and world-class marketing, both of which enabled it to achieve quality and cost parity with the Japanese. Harley has achieved a unique level of intimacy with its customers and it makes sure their unique ownership experience is a top priority for the company.

A blend of tradition, heritage, design, and mystique, Harley Davidson is the preferred motorcycle for both cops and robbers. Harley's marketing positioning has tied the HD to the archetype of freedom, freedom that is embodied in the American idea of the open road; it is *the* American motorcycle.

Harley Davidson motorcycles are evolutionary in design, look, and feel. The "Motor Company," as Harley Davidson refers to itself, has never been the first to adopt new technology like disk brakes, abs, fuel injection, and so on. Harley Davidson riders are not interested in riding 175 miles per hour. If they wanted to do that, they would buy a Suzuki Hayabuka, which is cheaper than the least expensive Harley. The Motor Company knows that its customers are interested in the look, feel, and sound of their motorcycles. There is something different about a Harley and this is no accident. It is the result of a clear and deep understanding of the strategic marketing concept and of Offensive Marketing. Harley sweats the details, and listens to its customers.

Harley has also added a very profitable line of motor clothing and accessories, and has created the largest owners group in the world. The Harley Davidson Owners Group, HOG, gives Harley owners a chance to get together in a company-sponsored organization and enjoy the experience of owning a Harley.

In January of 2001, *Forbes Magazine* named Harley Davidson, Inc. as "Company of the Year" and in February, *Fortune Magazine* selected it as one of the nation's "Most Admired Companies." In its sixteenth consecutive year of record revenues and earnings—their seventeenth straight year of domestic, strong earnings, and retail sales growth—Harley Davidson was ahead of original production targets for two years, with retail sales up 14.4 percent. The company's share price increased 36.6 percent during 2001 and HD has increased its dividend for the ninth consecutive year. In addition, the company has now become the number one seller of heavy-weight motorcycles in Japan.[2]

Why has Harley Davidson been so successful? First, the company has had a clear and easily understood vision… "We fulfill dreams through the experiences of motorcycling…"[3] Its company culture and marketing message are intertwined: "Forged by generations of people with a passion for motorcycling, a commitment to honor built on the past, and the determination to seek out new opportunities for the future."[4]

Harley Davidson has also had a strategy. Unlike most companies who are either drifting or copying the competition, Harley Davidson remains focused on customer needs by incorporating their business philosophy of "People, Passion and Progress" into its business strategy. Harley Davidson gives customers what they want and need: a unique ownership experience, which in turn becomes a unique social experience. Owning a Harley Davidson is fun; it is like buying a Christmas tree. Customized by design, Harley owners decorate their product at great expense to themselves and with great profit to the motor company. Every Harley Davidson ends up a unique machine, unlike any other motorcycle. It has an exhaust note many owners may amplify to their liking by knocking out muffler baffles, a distinctive "cruiser" design with superb paint and chrome trim, and a certain feel that riders love.

Elements of "bad" in the Harley Davidson image also appeal to many riders. It is not lost on the RUBBIES (rich urban bikers) that the machines they are riding are the preferred motorcycle of the Hells Angels and all of the other "outlaw" rider groups. The Harley is "bad," and their customers like it that way.

The Harley Davidson strategy includes targeting cops, robbers, workingmen and women, as well as RUBBIES who, when they are

---

[2] Harley-Davidson, Inc. Annual Report. 2001, at pg. 6.
[3] Id, Back cover.
[4] Id, at pg. 5.

not riding, are successful bankers, doctors, accountants, executives, lawyers, engineers, and so on. These customers create a fabulous marketplace for Harley: customers who are wealthy and happy to pay top dollar for motorcycles, gear, and HOG-sponsored rides.

As part of its business strategy and Offensive Marketing, Harley Davidson hires a very specific type of person. Often with dedicated enthusiasm for the products and services of the company, Harley instills a strong company culture that extends out to its dealerships. Dealer relationships for Harley often grow to include newer generation family members. Harley regards their employees as a valuable asset; they provide the support that becomes the company's sustainable competitive advantage. The company also enjoys strong relationships with suppliers and considers them part of the Harley Davidson family. These long-term "partnering" relationships extend to the company's unionized employees who participate in decision-making. This forms the basis for building trust and mutual respect. Harley Davidson envisions its extended employee family as stakeholders in the business of helping to "fulfill customers' dreams."[5]

In addition, Harley Davidson has a distinct management style. Built around informality, and using a collaborative approach to decision-making, Harley management reaches out to newer management to identify both opportunities for growth and cross-functional initiatives. This offers an obvious advantage to present and would-be customers.

Because of its strong product demand, the company invested more than $1 billion in capital improvements from 1995–2000 to maintain its leadership in motorcycle design and increase production capacity. These investments have been complemented by a growing team of talented product development experts who have brought new products to market to meet differing customer segment demands. Product design includes the use of Harley Davidson technologies, like computer modeling and electronic data transfer, to create virtual prototypes that ensure superior part fit and performance. For example, in 2001, Harley Davidson introduced the V-Rod motorcycle with new technology. This product was named "Bike of the Year" by *Motorcycle News*. In a move toward increasing brand awareness, the related Buell Motorcycle

---

[5] Id, at pg. 19.

Company introduced the next generation sport bike in an effort to broaden product appeal to a wider audience of potential users.[6]

Harley Davidson boasts the largest motorcycle enthusiast club in the world. Begun in 1983, with more than 1,200 chapters and a membership of more than 660,000 worldwide, members reside in 115 different countries and participate in HOG rallies and an array of other sporting events around the globe. Harley Davidson management, dealerships, and staff regularly participate in these events and maintain close ties with "end-users" helping to forge relationships through open houses, cause-related rides, HOG and BRAG chapters, as well as an e-commerce program of integrated web sites. In 1999, the company created "Rider's Edge," The Harley Davidson Academy of Motorcycling, which introduced a new generation of riders to the sport. More than instructing potential customers and end-users to ride, the Academy builds customer confidence as well as camaraderie between the dealer and customer, which has the potential to last far longer than the actual purchase, and which helps build the company's market share.

Lastly, Harley Davidson is finding new customers who don't necessarily want to own a motorcycle at all. The company has expanded its brand name in a variety of directions to include a very successful retail sales division of Motor Clothes (apparel and collectibles), and a Parts and Accessories division that meets owners' demand for customized bikes. Such a strategy creates a stable revenue stream. By stressing quality, Harley Davidson strives and remains focused on satisfied customers who are more likely to remain loyal and generate lifetime revenue.

OFFENSIVE MARKETING

You have just read an example of Offensive Marketing at its best. "As an American icon, Harley Davidson has come to symbolize freedom, rugged individualism, excitement, and a sense of 'bad boy rebellion' ... many things Americans dream about."[7] By combining the virtues of risk-taking with modern approaches to

---

[6] Id, at pg. 35.
[7] Id, Glenn Rifkin. *How Harley Davidson Revs Its Brand.* (Quoting, in part, Benson P. Shapiro, Harvard Business School.)

marketing, Harley Davidson embodies successful Offensive Marketing.

Offensive Marketing describes attitudes and practices that encompass everything the company does in bringing a product to market. It means having a clear strategy, following it through with investment and persistence, anticipating future needs, and following suit by meeting those needs quicker than the competition.

What Offensive Marketing Is *Not*

The following are misconceptions with respect to traditional concepts of marketing.

Marketing is a Sophisticated Form of Selling Done by MBAs

Many consumers and journalists falsely interpret marketing as manipulative, exploiting consumers and pushing prices up. "Added value" means adding more frills and doubling the price, or using deception and exaggerated promises in order to attract business. This, in fact, is not Offensive Marketing; it is simply offensive. Indeed, it is unethical and unprofessional marketing.

Although marketing is not selling, selling is an important marketing task. It is one of the many forms of marketing communications. Marketing communication encompasses all forms of communication including advertising (e.g., purchased media time on radio, television, the Internet, banner and pop-up ads, and billboards) and public relations (e.g., favorable editorial reference about a company, its brands, and/or products), to name only two broad categories.

Marketing is Communications

Communications includes advertising, sales promotion, selling, public relations, direct mail, and any other medium of communications including the Internet, outdoor advertising, cinema, and so on. The above definition is often followed by traditional marketers and advertising agencies. Employers think they are "embracing" marketing by hiring people with a marketing title or by contracting with agencies for specified marketing services. But in either case, what they are doing is merely adapting a series

7

of marketing services to a financial or operations approach to business.

Marketing is What the Marketing Department Does

Marketing is everyone's responsibility, from the CEO to the Operations Staff, including Manufacturing, R&D, Logistics, Finance, Accounting, Customer Service, Technical Support, and so on.

The Four "P"s—Product, Price, Place, and Promotion

The four "P"s, also referred to as the "marketing mix," are the key marketing decisions, with "the mix" being a reference to the need to carefully integrate these decisions to create customer value and competitive advantage. "Products" include the physical product or service, which is the product core, and the product "surround," which includes brand image and after-sales service, both important sources of value for consumers. "Price" is the cost of the product to the consumer, including out-of-pocket expense and "switching" cost to the customer. "Place" is widely viewed as distribution or channels, whereas "Promotion" usually includes selling and advertising as well as promotion via sales.

The "marketing mix" recognizes that true marketing is done outside the Marketing Department. Its limitation is that it describes marketing *activities* rather than marketing *approach* while also failing to include profit, a necessary component of any successful marketing effort.

As traditionally defined, "The goal of marketing is to meet consumer needs at a profit." Based on a sophisticated misconception, the above definition, though often used in textbooks, fails to recognize the potential conflict between meeting consumer needs and making a profit. Every company has to do both in order to survive, but should the aim be to maximize profit, or to make a fair profit? Recently, ignoring profit levels has resulted in a public relations challenge for pharmaceutical companies accused of selling their prescription products at prices deemed excessive by many users. This definition of marketing really begs the question of as to what level of profit is appropriate. The real goal of marketing is to create a mutually beneficial relationship, which is one in which the value of the product or service is recognized by the consumer and where pricing levels ensure the profitability of the company.

Why is marketing so difficult to define? Both an approach to business and the name of a specific function, marketing is often organized as a department leading to some confusion perhaps between *marketing* and *marketers*. Marketing is no more the exclusive role of marketers than profit is the exclusive responsibility of the Finance Department.

Marketing approaches are diverse, often intangible. Along with this, marketers have failed to evangelize the important role every employee plays in driving the marketing approach. Credit for successes is too often appropriated by the Finance or Human Resources Departments.

Offensive Marketing: Defined

Offensive Marketing is defined as *creating superior and recognized customer value and above-average profits*. Key elements in this definition include customer focus and profit orientation by the entire organization.

Strategically, and in practice, Offensive Marketing involves "every employee building superior customer value very efficiently for above-average profits."

Offensive Marketing Involves "Every Employee."

Jobs are evaluated on two axes:

1. Contribution to consistently superior customer value
2. Contribution to above-average profits

Two examples are cited below of employees having a relatively strong marketing orientation. However, notice that the marketing-oriented shift manager and accountant in the following examples do not meet the customer. Meeting the customer, as the employees of Harley Davidson do, is the basis for the strongest Offensive Marketing business strategy.

She is 28, has a degree in electrical engineering, and works shifts of 9 days on, 4 days off. She works at a company that purchases materials cheaper than the competition via worldwide sourcing and that runs 3 shifts,

168 hours per week, compared to its closest rival that has standard 8-hour shifts and clocks a lot of overtime.

Her company is excellent at process engineering while its closest competitor has undifferentiated machinery and processes and does not reap the benefits of leveraged scale buying advantages. This employee's new product development team has buying, sales, and engineering input and has well-informed consumer intelligence capabilities. Its closest competitor has little market knowledge and efficient personnel with somewhat narrowly defined objectives. Further, it has little knowledge of competitive machinery speeds and labor rates, while this employee's company has labor costs per ton one-half that of its closest rival.

This employee's company has no Marketing Department, yet is more profitable and maintains a steady gain in market share. Its closest competitor has a Marketing Department and is losing market share.

Manufacturing, Operations, and Production employees in a service-oriented company are among the most important Offensive Marketers. They control the cost, quality, consistency, and delivery of the customer proposition, whether it is frozen foods, insurance, or consumer durables. Inefficient, high-cost operators cannot be Offensive Marketers because they cannot deliver superior consumer value at competitive profit margins.

The accountant who follows in the example below in the Finance Department of an international airline supports an Offensive Marketing strategy, but again does not meet the customer.

He provides accurate and timely data to all his internal customers keeping their costs down. He sticks his neck out by forecasting future costs to his customers as well as comparing competitors using a wide range of measures. This paragon is also working on a special project with 0Marketing, Sales, and Operations to establish, for the first time, profitability by First Class, Business Class, and Economy, and types of customer (Business and Leisure).

Clearly, these involved employees understand their company's vision and strategies. They employ that knowledge with a certain innate skill in customer service.

"...Building...."

Offensive Marketers are builders; they do not downsize or strip assets. Striving for efficiency and low-cost operations, Offensive Marketers form a platform for superior consumer value. The ability

to identify growing segments and to transform markets by anticipating the future also enables them to *build* revenue growth.

In recent years, many companies have pursued downsizing as
a strategy, and have consequently lost market share and, for those
employees retaining their jobs, have become miserable places to
work. These companies have become locked into a scenario of
reducing cost and investment, and squeezing out a precarious,
nonsustainable profit growth.

"...Superior Customer Value...."

This is achieved when customers recognize that a company is
offering a combination of quality, price, and service superior to its
competitors. Superior value is delivered in numerous ways—
higher quality/same price or same quality/lower price are just two
of many possible combinations.

Superior customer value is difficult both to achieve and to
sustain. It must be real rather than imagined, and based on objective
customer measurement. Many companies say their products or
services are superior, but if they have no hard evidence to prove it,
they may be deceiving themselves and undermining their future in
the process.

Sustaining superior value requires consistently improving performance, since every innovation is eventually successfully copied
and competition is constantly moving on. Superiority should be
developed against direct competitors and then against all newcomers. Customer experiences in other categories can affect your
own by raising expectations. For example, the speed of service at
McDonalds makes customers impatient about queuing at super-
market checkouts. Faster copiers and e-mail make fax machines
seem very slow.

There is a virtuous circle between delivering superior customer
value and profit levels: the reward for consistently superior value
is achieving a high level of loyalty from customers, thereby greater
retention. Based on studies by Bain and Company, "the companies
with the highest retention rates also earn the best profits."[8]

Everyone in business has customers. They may be colleagues
inside your company to whom you are providing a service. They
may be external customers or consumers who buy your products.

---

[8] Frederick F. Reichheld, *The Loyalty Effect*, Harvard Business School Press, 1996.

Whoever they are, one thing is definite: *They* are the judges of whether you are delivering superior value, and their views on this topic are the only ones that matter.

"...Very Efficiently...."

This phrase has a number of very specific meanings within the context of Offensive Marketing. First, it means that companies need to match their strengths to the best opportunities in the marketplace. Companies achieving an efficient match will have happy customers and happy shareholders. Second, it requires companies to be low-cost operators, with high productivity and relentless checking of whether each cost adds to customer value. Japanese companies like Toyota, Canon, and Olympus are very skillful in this area through target costing and value engineering.[9] If a company is a high-cost operator in relation to its competitors, how can it possibly deliver superior value profitably?

"...For Above-Average Profits...."

"Above average" means better than industry norms on a range of profit measures such as return on sales (ROS), return on capital employed (ROCE), and economic value added (EVA), all of which will be reviewed in Chapter 2.

Profit is the reward earned by companies for building superior customer value very efficiently. Offensive Marketing is focused on generating long-term profit growth. If a company consistently invests in relevant new products or services, controls risk by rigorous testing of alternatives, and keeps an iron hand on cost, it is likely to deliver constantly improving customer value and to enjoy both short-term and long-term profit growth.

SHORT-TERM PRESSURES FACING OFFENSIVE MARKETERS

You may have observed that many companies have short-term profit problems although their long-term outlook is good. From this

---

[9] J. Johannson and I. Nonaka, *Relentless—The Japanese Way of Marketing*, Butterworth-Heinemann, 1996.

observation, traditional marketers feel that the definition of Offensive Marketing does not address the constant tension between the short-term demands and long-term goals. A question many marketers ask goes something like this:

> *We hear what you say about Offensive Marketing, and we would love our company to adopt it. But what can we do when they say it's not affordable? Despite our protests, the company under-invests in plant, new products, and new services. It has cut advertising, and our sales attractions badly need refurbishment. Prices have been increased and we are losing customers. Our revenue is flat, but the company has increased profits by cutting more costs. We spend sixty hours a week running to stand still. Short-term profits are grossly over-stated, as they contain no element of future investment.*

Does Offensive Marketing have an answer to this concern? In practice, a company such as the one described, has no future with its current strategies. In time, it will deservedly get a new owner or a new Chief Executive. This will provide an opportunity for a major profits write-down or a big reorganization charge, which will give the company the funds and breathing space to convert to Offensive Marketing ... if it has the good sense to do so.

While Offensive Marketing is a long-term approach, which can take years to develop fully, the reality is that marketers have to hit short-term objectives in order to be around to enjoy the fruits of their long-term efforts.

CEOs are unlikely to be impressed by marketers, who, having missed profit budgets two years running, point to the brilliance of their new five-year plan. If the CEO is polite in these circum-stances, he will stress that his only interest is in next year's budget, because he knows that if it is not hit, neither he nor you will be there in two years, never mind five.

In the short term, Offensive Marketers need to be strong tacti-cally and be very good executors. There are many steps they can take to leverage short-term profits without mortgaging the future. Some of these are covered in Chapter 2. For the long term, they require vision and strategic skills. Marketers have to run the short term and long term concurrently, working with both hands at the same time. This is why both strategy and execution are strongly emphasized in this book.

The lead-times necessary to change internal attitudes and radically improve consumer value are at least two years and

Table 1-1 Example: Quality of Profits Comparison

%	Virtuous Inc. (%)	Dissembler Inc. (%)
Sales revenue	100	100
Cost of goods sold	43	61
Gross profit margin	57	39
Advertising	11	3
R&D	5	0
Capital investment	7	2
Investment ratio	23	5
Operating expenses	20	20
Operating profit	14	14
Key trends	Past 5-year revenue growth 10% Heavy advertising, investment in new, improved products Premium-priced products, new plant, and low cost of goods sold	Flat revenue, declining volume No recent product innovation, little advertising Discounted pricing and high cost of goods sold

often longer. Such change is certainly not feasible to make the change within a fiscal year, and will usually reduce profits during this period since investment will precede revenue benefits. This is why Offensive Marketers need to be skilled in turning up the profit meter in the short term to compensate for longer-term aspirations.

Table 1-1 illustrates, in a simple example, the difference between an Offensive Marketing company and a non-Offensive Marketer within the same industry. Taking a moral tone, we will call them the Virtuous Inc. and the Dissembler Inc. The companies in this example do everything in-house.

On the face of it, both companies are making similar operating profits of 14 percent. However, the *quality* of their profits is very different. Virtuous Inc. has a higher gross profit margin because its superior value proposition enables it to command a premium price in the marketplace. It is *investing* 23 percent of its sales revenue in future development—in advertising, R&D, and capital investment. This is clearly no guarantee of future success unless the money is wisely spent, but Virtuous Inc. has a superior proposition, launches successful new products, and has a good innovation pipeline and sound future prospects.

What about Dissembler Inc, a competitor in the same industry making identical profit margins? As you can see, Dissembler Inc. is spending weakly on the future—its investment as a percentage of sales is only 5 percent of revenue. It has unsustainable profit

Table 1-2   Fourteen Percent Operating Profits

Factor	Virtuous Inc. (%)	Dissembler Inc. (%)
Profit on existing products over 3 years old	21	15
Losses on products recently launched or in development	(7)	(1)
Total operating profits	14	14

margins, which disguise a grisly future: a bare new product cupboard, a weakening consumer franchise, and an inability to finance effective R&D, plant upgrade, or advertising programs.

Table 1-1 illustrates that profit viewed in isolation may be a misleading measure. For the Offensive Marketer, a more relevant measure is profit and investment as a percent of sales. Investment is defined as "anything with a payback longer than one year." This covers advertising, R&D, capital investment, training, strategic market research, and most direct marketing (but not sales promotion, which should pay back quickly). These are often the costs that many companies cut to inflate short-term profits.

Let's take one final look at Virtuous Inc. and Dissembler Inc.'s profit profile before moving on. For Offensive Marketers, current-year profits may include large investments in new products recently launched or still in the pipeline. In other words, profits from established products will exceed total company profits (Table 1-2). This second perspective on Dissembler Inc. confirms that it is severely under-investing in its business, and probably faces big trouble ahead. By contrast, Virtuous Inc.'s investment in tomorrow should enable it to sustain or improve on its 14 percent operating profit.

How can Dissembler convert into a virtuous cycle? The path will be hard and long, and it is certain that Dissembler will have to raise investment and cut profit margins in the short term.

HARLEY DAVIDSON: REVISITED

Over the past decades, Harley Davidson has been an Offensive Marketer, although it has never been a company that participated in high-visibility marketing campaigns highlighted by slogans or catchy one-liners. It has quietly built a strong reputation on the sales of quality products supported by a well integrated marketing effort. Now let's check Harley Davidson against the components of the Offensive Marketing definition:

1. **"...Involves every employee...."** Harley employees are deeply involved in the marketing effort. Many of the employees ride and personally experience the company's bikes. Harley motorcycle rallies, often with appearances of Harley demo bikes, are staffed with employees from every part of the organization, and are a key marketing effort as well as a major point of contact with customers for employees.
2. **"...Superior customer value...."** Harley Davidson strives for superior customer value not only in its products but also in its total offering. Its value proposition is tied very strongly to a network of family-styled company relationships involving suppliers out to dealerships, and everyone has contact with end-users. The superior value of the Harley is in the total ownership experience: from the fun and pleasure in owning and riding a Harley, to the exceptionally high resale value of a used Harley.
3. **"...Above-average profit...."** Measures indicating profitability have increased over the past years. Harley Davidson has grown shareholders' equity each year since its initial public offering (IPO). Its earnings per share have grown, as have its cash dividends and its share price. The total return to shareholders has been exceptional. From the IPO until today, Harley is in the top 1 percent of investment returns for all marketable securities in the world.

Therefore, it is clear that Harley Davidson is indeed an Offensive Marketer. But, will it remain one in the years to come? The answer is very likely "Yes," because Harley understands Offensive Marketing. As a company, they will continue to do what they have done so successfully in a market they helped to define, and they will continue to create unique value for their customers, opportunity for their employees, and superior return for their shareholders.

Like the employees of Harley Davidson, the Offensive Marketer anticipates and confronts issues frankly, then decides, invests, and takes risks. She does not compromise, sidestep, temporize, or shelve issues.

WHY ISN'T EVERYONE AN OFFENSIVE MARKETER?

Since Offensive Marketing is a "best practice" approach to marketing, by definition, few companies will fully achieve it. What is more surprising is that so few companies even attempt to climb to the heights of Offensive Marketing.

Theodore Levitt's comment is still disturbingly relevant:

"When it comes to the marketing concept today, a solid stonewall often seems to separate word and deed. In spite of the best intentions and energetic efforts of many highly able people, the effective implementation of the marketing concept has generally eluded them."[10]

The practice of Offensive Marketing remains the exception rather than the rule. Why?

- **Most companies lack a vision or strategy:** The typical company rushes along from year to year in frenzied activity without a clear vision of the future, lacking distinctive or superior value propositions. It will cut costs, undertake "initiatives," and housekeep efficiently. It will avoid undue risks or major investments and keep a close eye on competitors so that it can remain in step. It will over-reward its top executives and think more about its share price and "street" opinion than it will about its customers. It will focus on financial short-term quarter-to-quarter returns, and ignore the strategic marketing concept of creating a mutually beneficial relationship with its customers.
- **Shortsightedness:** This is a well-known disorder. Companies are run on a fiscal year, rather than a three- to five-year basis for the benefit of shareholders who have no long-term interest or stake in the success of the enterprise. They often pay more attention to security analysts than to customers. In this light, any expenditure with a payback of over one year will be regarded with suspicion, even hostility.
- **Lack of understanding of the Offensive Marketing approach:** Companies either fail to grasp the importance of making customer relationships and satisfaction their central justification, or are often unable to determine how to do this profitably.

---

[10] Theodore Levitt, *The Marketing Mode*, McGraw-Hill, 1969.

- **Lack of character:** Many companies understand the basics of the Offensive Marketing approach, but do not have the qualities of courage, determination, persistence, and risk-taking necessary to apply it. Offensive Marketing is less a matter of intelligence and ability—since most companies have plenty of both—than of attitudes, strategy, and teamwork. It is a set of shared values, grounded in a commitment to operational efficiency and creating unique customer value.
- **Misguided Marketing Departments:** Conventional marketing has often become a victim of its own success. The acceptance of the Marketing Department has multiplied its role as coordinator and created floods of paper. The day-to-day pressure is so great there is no time left to innovate. In many companies the Marketing Department, far from innovative and enterprising, has become a bureaucracy, spewing paper and generally acting as a "passive arranger" of products and their placement.

HAS MARKETING FAILED?

This question hangs over discussions about long-term investments, such as R&D, advertising, new product investment, customer service improvements, and long-term warranties. While few would disagree with the theory of the marketing approach, many would question the cost and efficiency with which this theory has been implemented.

CEOs' arguments might include the following:

- **"Marketing" is not giving us a clear view of the future.** We spend a lot of money on consumer research, but it seems to tell us little about the future. Consumers can't articulate their future needs or priorities, especially if they know less than we do about tomorrow's technology and the vistas it will open.
- **We're constantly being surprised and outflanked by our competitors.** They seem to be getting to market quicker with new products, and we spend our time running to catch up. We have a big new product development program, but the failure rate of new products is still incredibly high.
- **Marketing-oriented companies are not necessarily the most profitable.** Some of the most profitable companies in recent years have been built up via acquisitions and deals focusing on low operating costs and maintaining speed of reaction.

- **We spend a vast amount on advertising, but I question the means used to evaluate it.** Marketers, aided by their advertising agencies, always say we are under-spending, but often can't justify the present level of expenditure on this medium.
- **Fast-moving consumer goods companies that originated marketing seem to have lost initiative.** Many of them appear to be struggling in mature markets with indistinctive brands and some are producing low-margin private label products for retailers just to survive. What on earth can they teach us?

With all of these looming questions, you may wonder whether Marketing Departments are needed. Religions can flower without churches, or even, as the Quakers have shown, without priests. Mercedes, with a distinctive and premium-priced product range and good margins by car industry standards, only started its Marketing Department in the late 1990s.

However, there are many sound reasons for having a Marketing Department:

1. **Double perspective:** The Marketing Department is the only one with a clear view of external customer needs and internal company skills. The ability to understand and match these is critical to business success. Finance and Human Resources Departments have a bird's-eye view of the internal workings of a company, but little knowledge of customers and their needs. Accordingly, their perspective is often one-dimensional.
2. **Strategy and planning input:** Successful company strategies start by defining future market and customer needs. They then target those needs that their particular competencies enable them to meet in a superior way. Marketing people are well placed to set and lead this strategic agenda because of their familiarity with market needs, their ability to forecast future trends, and their objective knowledge of company competencies.
3. **Market and segment prioritization:** Marketers can advise which markets and market segments have the most future attraction, which should be dropped, and how resources should be allocated across markets and brands.
4. **Coordination and long-term project management:** Most major improvements and innovations involve wide cross-departmental cooperation, and frequently include many external agencies.

The Marketing Department can coordinate proactively using business planning processes, especially on multi-country or global projects.

5. **Category and brand management:** Someone needs to develop, plan, and monitor the day-to-day business, with eyes fixed on the customer. Depending on the type of business, this will include tasks like sales forecasting, customer service, support programs, results monitoring, analyzing competitive activity, and so on.

6. **Expertise:** Marketing people should possess specialized competencies, such as:
   - Ability to anticipate future customer needs through knowledge of the market and technology trends.
   - Skill in value analyzing the use of resources—for example, evaluating the customer value of the various elements in a product or service and relating each of these to their cost.
   - Business analysis and strategy development, targeting consumer groups that would bring the highest benefit to future offerings.
   - Management and motivation of people over whom they have no direct authority.
   - Skill in identifying opportunities and allocating resources to areas of best return on investment.

In summary, then, the Marketing Department has a potentially very important and unique role in the business organization. However, marketers spend the vast majority of their time on day-to-day operations and (often unwillingly) neglect longer-term issues such as strategy development and innovation. They are also often enticed to change jobs much too frequently to build these competencies. If Marketing Departments are to meet their potential, these issues must be tackled head-on.

THE FUTURE CALLS FOR EVEN MORE OFFENSIVE MARKETING

Offensive Marketing is a set of attitudes, principles, and processes that release the potential of the marketing approach to transform businesses. Offensive Marketing is not a formula, a fad, or an academic theory. It is a demanding and practical approach to business, which requires courage, persistence, and determination. It is designed to make your competitors followers. This is the reason why it is practiced by only a minority of companies.

FIVE ELEMENTS IN THE OFFENSIVE MARKETING APPROACH

The five elements of Offensive Marketing form the structure of this book. They are encapsulated as follows: Profitable, Offensive, Integrated, Strategic, and Effectively Executed, again summarized by the mnemonic POISE (Table 1-3).

Let us take a look at the individual ingredients of Offensive Marketing in broad terms:

Profitable

The object of marketing is not just to increase market share or to provide good value for consumers, but to increase profit. Offensive Marketers will encounter conflicts between giving consumers what they want and running the company efficiently. One of their skills is to reach the right balance between these sometimes opposing elements.

Offensive

An offensive approach calls for an attitude of mind that decides independently what is best for a company, rather than waiting for competition to make the first move.

Table 1-3 Offensive Marketing: POISE

P:	Profitable	• Proper balance between firm's needs for profit and customer's need for value
O:	Offensive	• Must lead market, take risks and make competitors followers
I:	Integrated	• Marketing approach must permeate whole company
S:	Strategic	• Probing analysis leading to a winning strategy
E:	Effectively executed	• Strong and disciplined execution on a daily basis

Integrated

Where marketing is integrated, it permeates the whole company. It challenges all employees to relate their work to the needs of the marketplace and to balance it against the firm's profit requirements.

Strategic

Winning strategies are rarely developed without intensive analysis and careful consideration of alternatives. A business operated on a day-to-day basis, with no long-term marketing purpose, is more likely to be a follower than a leader.

Effectively Executed

No amount of intelligent approach work is of any use without effective execution. Effective execution is not just a matter of good implementation by marketing people. It is also vitally dependent on the relationship between marketing and other departments as well as external channels and on how strongly common strategies and objectives are communicated and implemented between the key players.

HOW MARKETERS CAN SPEARHEAD OFFENSIVE MARKETING

To be effective and to respond purposefully to justified cynicism, Marketing Departments and marketers will need to change radically in the next few years. Best-practice marketers are already moving forward on five fronts:

1. Structure
2. Relationship marketing
3. Competency development
4. Marketing process management
5. Priorities

Structure

In mature Marketing Departments, line-marketing people frequently spend 80–90 percent of their time on short-term tactical activity (see Table 1-4). In newer departments, they often have a service role, focusing on marketing activities. The result is that marketers often fail to lead the development of corporate strategy, a role they are ideally qualified to spearhead because of their double perspective: a focus on both the organization and its capabilities and on customers and their needs. Finance or HR people often inadequately fill the vacuum because of their narrower perspectives.

To remedy this, marketers need to do two things. First, restructure the Marketing Department so that the most gifted line marketers have time to think about strategy and win the future.

Second, marketers need to transform their relationships with other departments whose efforts are critical to the success of Offensive Marketing. It is remarkable how inward-looking marketers can be. They spend vast amounts of time attending seminars on how to get the best out of their advertising agencies, but give little thought to the much more important issue of how to get the best out of other departments like Finance, Sales, and Operations and align them with the Offensive Marketing strategy. This merits more attention and will be fully addressed in Chapter 4 on the topic of "Integration." Above all, marketers need to spend more time talking to customers and consumers (Table 1-5).

The need within the Marketing Department to separate development from housekeeping has become obvious. One proposed

Table 1-4 Typical Time Allocation in a Mature Marketing Department

Development	Housekeeping	
• Strategy development	• Sales promotion	• Internal communications
• Innovative market research	• Routine advertising • Routine market research	• Distributor marketing
• New product development	• Pricing/discounts strategy	• Routine analysis
• Value improvement	• Sales forecasting	• Budgeting
• Channel strategy	• Product line extension	• Writing memos
• Relationship marketing	• Monitoring results	• Administration
• External communication		
20%	80%	

Table 1-5 Time Allocation by Contact Point

Contact point		% of time
External agencies	Advertising, direct marketing, packaging, research, sales promotion	26%
Others within Marketing Department	Colleagues up, down, across	26%
On own in office	Analysis, planning coordination, administration	25%
Other departments (Sales, Operations, etc.)	Routine 18%, strategic 2%	20%
With customers or consumers		3%

way to achieve this is by having Brand Equity Managers, with overall responsibility for business performance, primarily focusing on managing the six development drivers capable of dramatically improving competitive position:

1. *Deep understanding of consumer needs and habits*, and awareness of likely *future* changes in markets and technology.
2. *Strategy* and *portfolio management* testing *tomorrow's* agenda for the whole *company*.
3. *Product* and service development.
4. *Prioritizing* and *monitoring investment* in plant, *service* improvements, *and* consumer relationships.
5. *Marketing value analysis* looking at every product or service cost and relating it to direct consumer benefit.
6. Actively managing the Offensive Marketing approach across departments, and *identifying key company competencies* to be exploited.

Specialists in a central department can handle important housekeeping tasks like sales forecasting, distributor or trade marketing, sales promotion, direct marketing, and routine communication. In recent years, more routine marketing functions have been downsized or dispensed with altogether. The result has been to overload line-marketing executives so that only the short-term objective gets done. There is a need to increase the number of routine marketing specialists to enable the Brand Equity Managers to develop the future; a task they are best qualified to do.

Relationship Marketing

One of the biggest future opportunities for marketers is leadership in further developing the concept and practices of Relationship Marketing, which focuses on keeping the customers you have as opposed to "conquest marketing," which focuses on acquiring new customers. Profitable companies understand that the key to marketing profitability is keeping the customers you already have because they are, compared to new customers, free. You do not have to spend to acquire existing customers because you already have them.

A number of important factors, discussed next, will continue to drive Relationship Marketing's growth.

Growth of Internet and Global Connectivity

The pervasiveness and increasing networked ability of the World Wide Web permits businesses to have dialogue and interaction with their customers down to a segment of one.

Falling Costs of IT

Over the past few years, the cost of holding and developing consumer databases has plummeted and will continue to do so as infrastructure and transaction costs decrease. Telecommunications costs are also declining, though not nearly so steeply.

Feasibility of Building High-quality Databases

Companies can build their own databases through mailings, questionnaires, and promotions; buy them from specialist operators; or, as usually happens, do both. Some of these databases contain quite detailed information, like type and age of car, size and neighborhood of house, pets owned, frequency and location of holidays, and so on, leading to integrated cross-selling efforts and other creative initiatives limited only by marketers' imagination.

Growing Sophistication of Consumers

As every marketer knows, today's consumers are very much in the driver's seat. They have strong bargaining power, often buying in markets with surplus capacity, and often have an excess of choice. Consumers seek superior value and want to be treated as individuals, not as anonymous numbers or mass-market targets.

Response by Marketers to Consumer Trends

Modern Relationship Marketing views customers as potential long-term income streams as contrasted with "one-shot" selling opportunities. Marketers of fast-moving consumer goods have always instinctively recognized this potential. They know that the cost of generating a single sale is uneconomic, and that the success of any brand depends on its ability to achieve repeat purchases. However, by heavily promoting price-parity products, and investing in large numbers of price-driven brand switchers, marketers have often failed to translate this logic into reality.

A further reason why Relationship Marketing appeals to companies is the opportunity it gives to make direct contact with the customer, and thereby remove reliance on intermediaries. This opportunity is fundamentally changing the competitive face of distribution channel marketing.

Improved Measurement of Customer Economics

Two valuable tools in Relationship Marketing are long-term customer profit and share of customer concepts.

1. **Long-term customer profit.** Long-term customer profit involves calculating how long you are likely to retain a particular customer, estimating the value of purchases less cost of retention over that period, and adding on a bonus for customer referrals. These calculations are sometimes referred to as lifetime customer value (LCV). Knowing LCV can guide you on splitting resources between customer retention and gaining new customers.

    Various studies have demonstrated not only the obvious point that existing customers are more profitable than new ones, but also that companies tend to under-invest in existing customers. One of the best studies shows that, across a number of markets, *a 5 percent increase in annual customer retention can increase total company operating profits by over*

50 percent.[11] It illustrates that existing loyal customers are by far the most valuable because they:

- Involve no business acquisition costs.
- Buy a broader range of products due to familiarity with the company's total product line.
- Cost less to service, through their understanding of the company's business system and using it efficiently.
- Recommend products to other customers.

Most businesses lose 25 percent of their customers annually and yet most companies spend *six times* as much on generating new customers as on retaining existing ones. This is an important insight and is often lost on marketers.[12]

2. **Share of customer.** Assuming you avoid this trap, and achieve a high customer retention rate, "share of customer" is another valuable measure to consider. It should supplement "share of market," not replace it. "Share of customer" indicates the depth of commitment each customer has to you, and charts your opportunity to increase revenue among existing customers.

"Share of customer is the brand's market share of the individual."[13] Clearly for this analysis, it is important to define the competitive framework.

"Share of customer," especially among heavy users, is an important measure in fast-moving consumer goods. Together with loyalty measures, it indicates the level of commitment to your brand as compared with competitors on a trend basis. Brands with low loyalty scores and poor "share of customer" will decline, even though these brands may be supported by a steadily increasing series of price reductions (which may in fact speed up their journey to oblivion).

Ability to Develop Tailored Products and Services Economically

Although the move by manufacturers to mass customization has been greatly exaggerated, techniques to tailor products efficiently on a low-volume basis are certainly improving. This is particularly apparent in the car industry, where each basic model has scores of options. The apparel industry has seen the entrance of

---

[11] Frederick F. Reichheld, *The Loyalty Effect*, Harvard Business School Press, 1996.
[12] Theodore Levitt, *The Marketing Mode*, McGraw-Hill, 1969.
[13] Garth Hallberg, *All Consumers Are Not Created Equal*, John Wiley & Sons, 1995.

custom fitting apparel ordered through the Web and the PC industry has seen its sales and delivery model change with the success of Dell in recent years. Dell's success is based in large part on its outsourcing of component parts and its ability to aggregate those parts based on customer direction.

However, this trend should be viewed with caution. Set against the growing *capability* to customize products is the reality that high-volume manufacture of a limited range of items may continue to be more efficient at least in the near-term. Recognizing the consumer desire for better value and the trade-off between price and choice, many leading manufacturers are deliberately cutting choice in their efforts to set up efficient, low-cost regional manufacturing sites supporting worldwide strategies. They are using this strategy in their quest to improve overall customer value by driving down price in real terms.

Services are usually much easier to tailor economically to the needs of groups or individuals, especially as IT costs decline. The customization of financial services over the recent few years is a case in point.

Fragmentation of Media

The increasing cost of mass media, especially TV, makes this means of advertising affordable and effective only for larger brands with large promotional budgets. How to market secondary brands efficiently has become a big issue for marketers. Relationship Marketing has a part to play in the solution, as relationship-based initiatives make mass marketing less attractive both to the customer and the company. At the same time, because of fragmentation, media is becoming more customized with the growth of specialist TV channels, niche magazines, the Internet, and growth of online advertising including directed e-mail programs. All offer new opportunities for tightly targeted Relationship Marketing efforts.

Competency Development

At present, some marketers, despite having a high level of formal education and MBA degrees, lack the necessary skills to be effective in today's environment. These deficiencies will become cruelly exposed in the future.

Tomorrow's marketer needs to be:

- Knowledgeable about the strategic concept of marketing
- Knowledgeable about the essentials of operations, the supply chain, and channel management
- Able to understand the key technologies of the business
- Literate in finance and IT
- Skillful in project planning and management
- A first-class business analyst, using data creatively to develop succinct action plans
- A skillful manager and motivator of the scores of people, inside and outside of the company, who help implement the integrated marketing approach
- Expert in opportunity identification, market research, advertising strategy and evaluation, direct marketing, and customer service

This inventory of required skills is much broader than today's typical specification of the more limited resource marketer. If marketers are truly to help realize the full potential of the marketing approach, more will have formal marketing qualifications and be drawn from technical, financial, as well as arts backgrounds.

Table 1-6 summarizes today's and tomorrow's required Marketing Department competencies. There will be a move from marketing management to corporate business management, as the table demonstrates.

Table 1-6   Marketers' Competencies

Today:	Tomorrow:
Strategic business analysis and business unit strategy	Overall corporate strategy and business management
Innovation	Continual innovation
Project management	Aligned project management across the organization
Coordination	
IT skills	Technology knowledge
Strategic skills	Database marketing
Cost management	Cross-department leadership
Consumer understanding	Operations know-how
Marketing techniques	Alliances and acquisitions
Marketing management	Corporate business management

Marketing Process Management

For many years, people in Operations and Selling and, to some degree, Finance, have followed process management. Their activities have been divided into a series of processes, which are clearly understood and can be equally accurately evaluated.

For example, Operations people may be assessed on number of transactions or units produced, quality, timeliness, customer service levels, and cost. Sales people may be measured by revenue growth, cost of sales, quality of relationships, and, in the case of a field sales force, interviews, orders per day, distribution, service levels, and so on.

All these activities are evaluated quantitatively, either fully or in part. Performance can be compared with objectives and previous year performance, across other business units or countries, or even benchmarked against external best-practice companies. And most of selling or operations activities are executed in a disciplined way, following prescribed sequences, which have been developed and refined over the years per the company's internal intelligence.

Marketers have managed to avoid many of the rigors of accountability and the disciplines of process management because their activities are diverse, often hard to predict, and difficult to measure. Discipline has sometimes been resisted because it is perceived to stifle marketing "creativity." Marketers tend to be very articulate people, and some would rather operate on the qualitative high ground of intuition and judgment than on the lowlands of quantitative evaluation.

This is all changing, and rapidly. Marketing is becoming more scientific, more accountable, and more process driven. The best marketers are leading the way, and senior management, with financial senior staff at their side, will continue to insist that this change takes place.

Priorities

Changes in marketing structures, competencies required, and a more disciplined process-driven management style will all provide marketers with the opportunity to make a quantum leap in effectiveness. These changes will also lead to new priorities (Table 1-7).

Table 1-7   Future Priorities for Marketing Departments

Priorities	How
Corporate strategy business development	New structures
	New competencies
	Cross-departmental focus
Broaden competencies	Widen personnel selection criteria
	Build technical, IT, financial skills among marketers
	Rotate people across departments
Evangelize Marketing's approach across company	Regular market reports in readable form for all departments
	Invite other managers to sales meetings
	Enhance motivating skills of marketers
Strengthen Marketing's leadership role	Finance and Operations managers to make regular field visits
	Marketers to identify and exploit companies' key skills

Above all, marketers need to encourage everyone in the company to talk to customers.

SUSTAINABILITY OF OFFENSIVE MARKETING

Going back to our distinction earlier in the chapter between Virtuous Inc. and Dissembler Inc., it will be difficult and challenging for Dissembler Inc. to become an Offensive Marketer, while Virtuous Inc. and Harley Davidson may not remain Offensive Marketers forever.

However, it is certainly easier to remain an Offensive Marketer than to become one. Every Offensive Marketer carries forward the momentum of accumulated past investment, successful risk-taking, and purposeful strategies.

The primary traps for Offensive Marketers are misreading future needs and complacency. As an example among many, IBM fell victim to both:

IBM's first major setback was the failure of its PC in the late 1970s. While it continued to generate annual net profits of $5 billion to $6 billion through the 1980s, it lost momentum.

From 1991 to 1993, IBM lost $16 billion. Earlier in 1990, when net profit was $6 billion, the Annual Report sighted no hurricanes on the horizon. Here are some quotations from it:

> *"The future of large computers is one of continued healthy growth."*
> *"Our strategy is straightforward and consistent:*
> > *To provide customers with the best solutions*
> > *To strengthen the competitiveness of our products and services*
> > *To improve our efficiency."*
> *"We are offering the strongest line-up of products and services in our history."*

Few annual reports of any description contain as many references to "customers" as did IBM's in 1990 before the earthquake struck.

Some years later, Louis Gerstner, IBM's then Chairman, observed:

> *"At the heart of the turmoil is one simple fact: IBM failed to keep pace with significant change in the industry."*
>
> *"We have been too bureaucratic and too preoccupied with our view of the world. We have been too slow getting things to market."*

Within a few short years IBM moved from bluest of blue chips to virtual basket case. For years it had hired the cream of the graduate crop. The company had a powerful internal culture, which drove performance but not change. Its R&D Department boasted a number of Nobel prizewinners. The company had virtually invented the computer industry, but became preoccupied with technology rather than superior consumer value. IBM had vast resources, but misread the future and under-invested in software and PCs. Poor marketing exacerbated its problems.

Under Gerstner, IBM again became an Offensive Marketer. IBM began an intense focus on the customer and its targeted markets, creating a strategy driven by customers' need for increased productivity and e-businesses' ability to deliver cost-effective and efficient business solutions. Under Gerstner and his successor, Sam Palmisano, the company has focused on building a sustainable future on services and software, moving away from its roots in the hardware industry. From consulting on systems design to running technology operations for its clients, IBM has refocused it energies toward the client; whatever fires up their customers, they embrace as their own business goal. Palmisano has continued a strong focus on building for long-term profitability, pushing for team and employee involvement in targeted goals at all levels; efficient operations through often expansive, integrated program execution; and strong competency development in those areas most sought by its customers. Palmisano brings strong sales and marketing experience along with a keen sense of market developments to his operational leadership.

Yardsticks to Measure the Sustainability of Offensive Marketing

If Offensive Marketing is as practical a concept as has been claimed, it should be possible to set up criteria by which the Offensive Marketing rating of a firm can be judged. Like any comparison between firms, the result will inevitably be biased and subjective due to differences in definition and market situations. The battery of Offensive Marketing yardsticks (Table 1-8) will not escape these criticisms; however, they contain sufficient objectivity to be useful.

All yardsticks are applicable across industries; however, some yardstick scores may point to initiatives that need to be addressed sooner than others in industries where change is occurring rapidly, although all are instrumental to the company aligned behind an

Table 1-8 Yardsticks for Measuring the Sustainability of Offensive Marketing

Scale: 0 = no position or response 10 = highest possible position or level of response	The goal	Your score
A strong and differentiated customer proposition	10	
An ability to anticipate and act on future trends quickly	10	
Success in launching profitable new products/services, which add incremental sales	10	
New markets successfully entered in past 10 years	10	
Strong customer focus of total company including Operations, Distribution, and Finance	10	
Strong profit focus of whole company including Marketing and Sales	10	
Clear long-term strategy led by Marketing	10	
Commitment to constant improvement in quality and value for money	10	
More efficient lower-cost operator than competitors	10	
Level of investment compared with competitors (facilities, databases, technology, advertising, R&D, people development)	10	
Total	100	

Offensive Marketing strategy. The relative strength of each yardstick will indicate where the company needs to put its resources and focus. Each yardstick should be measured on a score of 10, with the total score indicating the strength of the firm's Offensive Marketing position.

Harley Davidson: A Strong Offensive Marketer

Table 1-9 summarizes the key strategies and style of Harley Davidson, a strong Offensive Marketer. Each company must take the yardsticks set out above in Table 1-8 and incorporate them into their own unique formula for success: the value proposition reflected in the firm's offering.

You may find it instructive to complete a table such as the one below for your own company or prime competitors. It should take no more than fifteen minutes to complete, because answers are usually clear-cut. An Offensive Marketer will have a distinctive or superior approach to most of these topics. Remember, in going

Table 1-9   Harley Davidson: A Strong Offensive Marketer

		Score
Strategy	Harley Davidson is evolutionary and unique	10
	Harley Davidson is a unique value in the motorcycle market	
Positioning	Harley Davidson offers a riding and ownership experience, not just a motorcycle	10
Products and Services	Must be superior as evidenced by consumer tests and ranking	10
	Sustainable advantage and value	
Change	Give customers what they want	10
	Change to create greater value	
Support	Achieve wide distribution and trial for new products	10
	Build long-term consumer relationships	
Pricing	Premium, but must be justified by superior value	10
Operation	High quality, lowest cost	10
	Multi-country scale economies	
R&D	Heavy spend	10
	Focus on constant improvement and evolution	
Customers	High service levels	10
	Partnership for joint efficiency	
Style	Global	10
	Very competitive, very determined	
	Long-term approach	
	Seek leadership in all markets	
Total		100

through this table, the task is to first be clear about your strategy, and then make sure that you implement your strategy. For most companies, copying Harley Davidson would be a disaster: Harley Davidson is unique and that is why the company is successful. You should also strive to be exceptional in creating value for your customers out of your own uniquely crafted value proposition.

CONCLUSION

Marketing and marketers are under attack. Executive Officers are questioning whether marketing is working. They rightfully point to the lack of innovation in their companies, the high failure rate of new products, and their inability to develop sustained competitive advantage.

Marketers, in turn, criticize their own companies for short-sightedness, an unwillingness to take longer-term risks, and for burdening Marketing Departments with day-to-day tactical responsibilities so that they have little time for strategic thinking. Simultaneously, new and more mature industries are hiring marketers and marketing agencies, and business think tanks and boards are impressing Executive Officers to adopt a marketing approach and build long-term customer relationships down to a "segment of one."

Why the paradox? Because even as companies claim to be marketing-oriented, their actions and planning point otherwise. "Me-too" products and services, ill-conceived brand extensions that dilute brand strength, vague visions of the future and what the customers want, and the lack of determination to develop and invest in winning strategies while consistently overstating their real corporate health, are results of this paradox.

Functional structures inhibit company-wide approaches to marketing and Marketing Departments themselves have adopted a narrow and inward-looking role. Failure to spearhead the company's future vision and strategy has contributed to the unworkability of much current marketing practice.

We have seen how Harley Davidson exhibits the "best-practice" approach to marketing. Harley involves every employee deeply in the marketing effort and creates opportunities for employees to participate directly with customers. The company strives for superior customer value not only in its products but also in its total offering experienced by its customers. Out of these efforts, which themselves are made up of hundreds of decisions with a long-term view to build efficiency into its operations and processes, Harley continues to experience above-average profits for its industry and has significantly grown its shareholder wealth over the years.

As shown in the Harley corporate experience, Offensive Marketing, involving "every employee building superior customer value very efficiently for above-average profits," enables marketers and marketing to achieve their full potential. Following the elements of *POISE*—Profitable, Offensive, Integrated, Strategic, and Effectively Executed—creates the opportunity for real marketing leadership in the organization and the foundation for sustainable competitive advantage in markets that are sure to get only more combative.

2 Profitable: The "P" of POISE

INTRODUCTION

This chapter covers the "P" of POISE. P, in this case, stands for Profitable. One of the fundamental goals of Offensive Marketing is the balance between a firm's need for profits and the customer's need for value. Profit is the reward companies earn for delivering superior customer value very efficiently. It cannot be viewed in isolation.

The first section of this chapter describes and challenges the financial view of profit and outlines how the Offensive Marketer can campaign to change the rules. The second section of the chapter explains how the Offensive Marketer can build above-average long-term profits in part by using the Marketing Alignment Process (MAP). The third section outlines how the

Offensive Marketer can leverage short-term profits responsibly to meet the demands of the future.

HOW THE FINANCIAL AND MARKETING VIEWS ON PROFIT CONFLICT

Marketing and Financial people often clash in their views on costs and profits. Finance Directors tend to regard Marketing Departments with suspicion. They see them as havens for big spenders with low accountability. Marketing Departments, in turn, get very frustrated by the short-term approach of many of their companies, especially when cuts are made to spending on such things as advertising, research, new plant and product development, as soon as the profit picture gets weak. Marketers prefer to think longer term but find their plans thwarted by short-term profit demands.

Why does this clash in views happen and what can be done about it? Again, the differences result from Finance's and Marketing's views of profit. Marketers, however, can change the rules of financial reporting and the way they are applied to give longer-term strategies the chance to succeed. This longer-term view is necessary for Offensive Marketing to succeed.

The key principles of financial reporting were established in the first half of the last century, pre-dating the marketing approach to business. Financial reports, however, continue to fail to give a true and fair picture of a company's future potential because there is no requirement to disclose intangible investments like advertising, market research, or R&D. These initiatives can take two to five years to reap any payback, yet they strongly influence future success. Similarly, there is no process for identifying levels of investment on new products, processes, or services.

This outdated model of financial reporting chokes innovation and long-term investment. As Baruch Lev, Professor of Accounting at New York University says, "The generally accepted accounting principles don't allow for some of the prime drivers of corporate success—investments in intangible assets such as know-how, patents, brands and customer loyalty."[1] In Japan and Germany,

---

[1] *Fortune*, December 23, 1996.

the accounting rules do permit building reserves and a degree of smoothing, which enhances a longer-term approach. Companies also take a longer view toward profit in these countries. While financial reporting in the United States needs to change, there is, within existing accounting rules, considerable flexibility to decide whether to take profits this year or next. Unfortunately, many CEOs tend to utilize this flexibility negatively to maximize short-term profits. Indeed, we have recently seen the serious negative consequences of over-reaching in accounting methodology with the downfall of the likes of Worldcom, Enron, Global Crossing, and Qwest.

Marketers should seek to change the rules on profits by pushing for greater disclosure of a company's customer position, intangible investment for the future, and innovation. They should also press CEOs and CFOs to use their creativity to take a cautious view of this year's profits, so that offensive long-term strategies can be consistently pursued and given the time they need to succeed. Financial reporting would then be more supportive of Offensive Marketing initiatives.

The Financial View of Profit

Accounts are drawn up objectively by Finance Departments using well-established accounting principles, confirmed by external auditors. The results look authoritative, precise, and logical. Financial accounts speak to past occurrences, yet they do not disclose why things happened or reveal tomorrow's prospects. They do, however, provide a useful short-term scorecard. The main financial ratios are summarized below in Table 2-1.

Table 2-1   Financial Scorecard

Ratio	Basis	What ratio measures
Sales growth	% revenue growth year to year	Customer response
Return on sales (ROS)	Operating profit as % of revenue	Skill in adding value
Return on capital employed (ROCE)	Operating profit as % of fixed and current assets less current liabilities (see below)	Efficiency of capital utilization

Sales growth is a result of changes in the size of your markets and of your firm's share in them. Your market share is determined by the relative customer value your products or services offer, their level of accessibility, and consumer awareness.

Return on Sales (ROS) reflects the cost per unit of delivering customer value, accessibility, and awareness, compared with its price. You may achieve excellent customer value through under-pricing, but fail to make a profit.

Return on capital employed (ROCE) shows how effectively management is using capital.

As business people know, considerable judgment is neces-sary to arrive at these seemingly authoritative ratios. In the bubble market of the 1990s, many of these measures were manipu-lated by companies to present false and misleading pictures of operations.

As an example, outside the United States, there is much greater opportunity to build reserves on a legal basis. In Germany and Japan, it is acceptable to use good years to build reserves and to "even out the bumps" in bad years. The difference in treatment of reserves is influenced by tax legislation but also reflects the longer-term approach of German and Japanese businesses, compared with U.S. companies. For the Offensive Marketer, the largest reserve—which encompasses investment in customer understanding and relationships, brand and new product development, and compe-tency building—does not appear anywhere in the financial view of profit held in the United States.

What's wrong with the view of profit held by Finance people? We have seen that the financial view gives only a partial, short-term picture of past financial performance and very limited guid-ance on the future. We have also seen how the financial view provides few insights on the *quality* of company earnings. It does not differentiate between Company A, which has mort-gaged its future and struggles to declare $100 million in profits, and Company B, whose $100 million profits includes future investment.

From the standpoint of Offensive Marketing, the financial report often fails to give a true and fair picture of a company's health. With the exception of tangibles—plant, property, and equipment—the financial view fails to take into account the future value of investments with a payback beyond this fiscal year.

Investments generally not covered include:

- **Advertising.** New programs or significantly increased advertising spending takes time to work and rarely pays back in profit terms in less than one year.
- **New brands.** In fast-moving consumer goods, new brand payback is generally considered positive if, in five years, investment costs in R&D, plant, advertising, and launch promotion are recouped by matching profits. For new consumer healthcare brands, payback can be seven years; for pharmaceuticals, even longer. As we have recently witnessed in the dot.com era, many dot.com businesses with strong Internet brands were not able to turn a profit and have not continued as viable businesses. Compare some financial services like Charles Schwab, where a new brand introduction incorporating web-based services may reimburse more rapidly.
- **Basic R&D.** Standard accounting practice now allows R&D spending on specific development projects—such as a new product or process for next year—to be carried forward as an expense into next year. Investment in pure or applied research cannot be carried forward.
- **Basic market research.** This covers fundamental research into consumer attitudes or habits, new products, or services.
- **Competency development, culture change, and training.** These are fundamental to any business, but especially those where people are a major part of the product (e.g., travel, leisure, and hospitality). Development costs can be high and impact time lengthy.
- **Marketing R&D.** This tests and capitalizes on changes in consumer attitudes. It also covers activity to understand technology, services, and communications for both the present and future.
- **New customer acquisition.** Time-scale and cost will vary by market. In consumer goods, new customers can be acquired (but not necessarily retained) quickly and cheaply. Many dot.com ventures were able to build traffic and one-time customers, but were not able to keep them over time. Success was the exception rather than the rule.

Does it really matter that conventional financial reporting fails to recognize important intangible investments, where cost has to be taken this year but benefit will occur some years hence? To the Offensive Marketer, it certainly does, because it actively penalizes many important investments, which are the lifeblood of a company's future.

Kaplan and Norton's comments in *The Balanced Scorecard* are right on target:

"Unfortunately many organizations espouse strategies about customer relationships, core competencies, and organizational capabilities while motivating and measuring performance only with financial measures … in the short term, the financial accounting model reports … spending cutbacks as increases in reported income, even when the reductions have cannibalized a company's stock of assets, and its capabilities for creating future economic value."[2]

The Offensive Marketer's View of Profit

To provide a true and fair picture of a company, investors need to be given better information to answer two key questions: "Why?" and "What are future prospects?" These answers should focus on areas critical to Offensive Marketing.

Table 2-2 lists the elements of three key measurement areas and their ratios, which should, at a minimum, appear in all annual reports.

You can already hear the chorus of objections by those "sound" people opposed to change. "Naïve! Impractical! Manipulable!".

Here are likely objections to Table 2-2 measures:

- **Many companies don't know their market sizes or market shares.** Determining market size and market share is often difficult and sometimes impossible, but every company should make a real effort to determine market size and share because it is one of the most obvious measures of potential revenues or growth and of competitive position in the market.
- **Most large, midsize, and many small companies compete in scores of markets and countries across the world.** Global companies could state their shares by market and major world region. This would certainly make their annual reports more informative. If possible, a "share of customer" measure should also be included.

---

[2] Robert Kaplan and David Norton, *The Balanced Scorecard*, Harvard Business School Press, 1996.

Table 2-2   Specifics of Three Key Measurement Areas for Reporting

Activity	Measurement data
Customer value	• Total market trend (revenue and volume) • Market share (revenue and volume) • Relative price v. market average • Customer loyalty and retention (%)
Investment	• New plant • Advertising • Customer databases • Market research Each as • Training/people development % of revenue • R&D
Innovation	• Products or services launched in past 5 years as % of sales • Profits split by products over and under 5 years old • List of innovations in progress

- **Companies in the same markets might define them in different ways.** The definition of a market is a strategic decision: the market focus of a company is determined by its target market definition. If the company strategy is to be a leader in a niche, the market focus must be narrow. If the strategy is to expand in a market, a narrow market focus will need to be expanded if the company has succeeded in dominating the narrowly defined market.
- **Why is the investment as a percent of sales ratio (I/S) relevant?** It is relevant because investment-spending elements reduce this year's profits, while providing the engine for future growth. Gillette calls them the "growth drivers" and is committed to at least increase them as fast as sales revenue.
- **Advertising levels will vary by year, depending on the company's strategy and competitor activity.** True. Advertising is part of the marketing mix and needs to be adjusted regularly.
- **Companies may inflate their innovation ratios by including only marginally improved products as innovations.** Yes. As we indicated earlier, existing financial accounts can be manipulated to reflect current targets.
- **What are innovations in progress (IIP)?** IIPs include test markets or test countries. If Disney is making a big drive with theme

parks in Asia Pacific, and has opened two in Hong Kong and South Korea, investors need to know the progress of these initiatives. IIP also includes new customer service initiatives, new products, competency development programs, or customer relationship initiatives. In disclosing IIP activity, companies have discretion, and investors should look for sensible, original and relevant activity.

How Offensive Marketers Should Change the Financial View

From the Offensive Marketing perspective, the outdated model of financial reporting is limiting innovation, enterprise, and intangible investment.

However, there are signs of change, such as the discussion on valuation of brands and databases, which are a small part of the much bigger issue described above. Through public scrutiny and pressure, annual reports are becoming clearer and more informative, often providing selective figures on market trends, shares and new products. After the Enron bankruptcy filing, and the legal mandate for CEOs to certify accounting reporting, those responsible for reporting veracity have even more pressures to do so with clarity and transparency. In addition, short-term downsizing now scores fewer points on Wall Street than profitable growth. And some leading companies now focus on building shareholder value.[3] Shareholder value is the present value of estimated future cash flows, which includes the benefits of new product investment. These trends favor the Offensive Marketing approach to profit. However, they do not go nearly far enough.

Clearly, certain constraints have to be recognized. The effect of today's intangible investment in advertising or R&D cannot be quantified in sales tomorrow, but that does not prevent it from

---

[3] Another recent measure is EVA—Economic Value Added—popularized by Stern Stewart, the U.S. consultants. It deducts percent cost of capital from net percent profit after tax. From a marketing perspective, this offers little improvement compared with more conventional methods, since, as pointed out by the Lex Column in the *Financial Times* (23 December, 1996), "A business can boost EVA in any one year by running down the value of its assets—for example, by failing to invest in training, brand development, and so forth."

being reported. Investors can form their own judgment. Companies reducing today's profits with intangible investments for tomorrow are more likely to get a future payoff than those who do not invest at all.

Confidentiality is another constraint. No company wants to publish its new product development program, future launch timetables or process engineering or customer service secrets. Yet, the impact of these disclosures may have been exaggerated. Many company reports contain detailed outlines of future strategy. In their briefings to security analysts, companies provide vast amounts of information valuable to competitors. Indeed, most Chief Executives understand and address the needs of analysts and investors much more readily than those of customers.

So what is the Offensive Marketing agenda for company reporting, and the treatment of investment, profit and competitive position? Although most of the existing information in financial reporting is useful and should be retained, the following subsection outlines the Offensive Marketing approach to expanding the view on profits.

The Offensive Marketer's Annual Report Summary

Here, in Table 2-3, is a simplified Annual Report Summary of a hypothetical leisure company from the perspective of an Offensive Marketer.

What does this report summary tell you? It gives a reasonably clear picture of the company's competitive position, and its future prospects if compared with the previous year's report containing the same information breakdown. Trend comparison is critical in judging the following:

- **Market growth by business type and country.** This gives a picture of market and business potential.
- **Market share and relative pricing trends.** If the company is discounting prices in the entertainment business, have prices deteriorated in the past two years, or are there signs of an upturn?
- **Trends in customer retention, and comparisons with industry averages.** For instance, 35 percent repeat business may be good for a leisure entertainment complex, while 70 percent may be poor for a chain of business hotels.

Table 2-3   Universal Leisure Company

Description of business: Competes in casinos, hotels, entertainment complexes in U.K., U.S., Japan

Customer value	Casinos	Hotels	Entertainment	Total
Market size ($)	140	300	60	500
Market share (%)	10	2	5	4.6
Net revenue ($)	14	6	3	23
Relative price indexed to market average	105	125	80	107
Customer retention				
% of last year's customers buying this year	65	70	35	65
Profitability				
Operating profit ($)	3.5	0.9	0.3	4.7
ROS (%)	25	15	10	20
ROCE (%)	20	15	10	17
Investment (% of Sales)				
New assets, refurbishment, equipment	5	5	15.0	6.3
Innovation				
Investment to sales ratio (% of Sales)	8.8	9.3	26.0	11.2
Trend Comparison				

Note: Innovations in progress would be listed inside the annual report, not in the Summary. Summary would also contain breakdown by U.K., U.S., and Japan.

- **Trends in investment spending and innovation.** This is important information for anyone with an interest in the future of the company.

This sample summary report tells you many useful things omitted by today's financially driven reports and enables the reader to draw additional conclusions. For example, it is clear that the relatively poor profits in this leisure entertainment division are influenced by heavy investment as a percent of sales (I/S ratio of 26 percent, double the company average), and a high level of innovation. A look at the "Innovations in Progress" report—a separate report—should indicate how effective these investments have been.

HOW OFFENSIVE MARKETERS BUILD ABOVE-AVERAGE, LONG-TERM PROFITS

Changes in the economic landscape have dramatically altered the balance between consumers' need for benefits against a company's need for profits. The classical model of marketing, developed in the 1960s, concentrated on meeting consumer needs profitably but paid little attention to the efficient exploitation of a company's strengths in the form of assets and competencies. Assets are defined as things: property, brands, factories, and cash. Competencies are skills created by people often by exploiting assets. Technology (information and communications) integration, new product development and speed to market are some examples of corporate competencies.

The modern model of marketing tightly matches a company's assets and competencies to the best opportunities in the market place. This involves very precise selection of markets, segments, channels, and customers. The aim of Offensive Marketers is to focus effort on areas where assets and competencies can be fully exploited. This enables them to concentrate resources on attractive markets where they have real skills, thereby delivering superior customer value and above average profits—the essence of Offensive Marketing.

The typical classical definition of marketing, deriving from the 1960s, has already been referred to: "The role of marketing is to satisfy consumer needs profitably." The approach was market-led, demanding: "What do customers want, and how can we satisfy their needs profitably?" It did not strive to maximize profitability by matching superior skills to the best opportunities, or recognize the frequent conflict between the company's need for profits and the consumer's need for benefits. Marketing's role in balancing and aligning corporate competencies was not appreciated.

The New Model: Asset- and Competency-Based Marketing

A more workable model was put forward in the late 1970s,[4] summarized as "asset-based marketing." Alan Wolfe later described this approach as follows:

> "Asset-based marketing is a supplement to, not a substitute for, customer-orientation. Alongside the search to identify customers and understand their needs should run an examination of the assets of the company and ways to use them more effectively in the market-place."[5]

---

[4] J.H. Davidson, series of articles in *Marketing Week*, 1979.
[5] Alan Wolfe, *Profit from Strategic Marketing*, Pitman, 1993.

Table 2-4   The Evolution of Marketing

Market-based		Market- and asset-based	Market-, asset- and competency-based	
1960	1970	1980	1990	2000

Based on the work of Gary Hamel and P.K. Prahalad in the 1990s on "core competencies,"[6] this asset-led approach can now be extended to asset- and competency-based marketing to establish a new working model.

Table 2-4 shows how the approach to marketing has evolved over the last forty years.

In the 1960s, too little attention was paid to cost, and there was over-investment in marketing, often in sectors where the company had limited competence. In the 1980s and 1990s, the pendulum had swung too far in the opposite direction, with too much emphasis on squeezing assets, an unwillingness to take risks, and a corrupting short-term focus. The new model of asset- and competency-based marketing seeks to achieve the best balance between market needs and business assets and competencies. This is the key to maximizing profitability and delighting customers:

Offensive Marketing builds above-average profits by relating a company's exploitable assets and competencies to future customer opportunities.

Figure 2-1 illustrates the role of marketing. On the left side are the assets and competencies of the firm; these generate costs. On the right side is the marketplace; this generates revenue.

The job of marketing is to achieve the best mix by converting company assets and competencies into consumer value. In this process, two things happen at once. The marketplace is probed for opportunities and the company's assets and competencies are refined and exploited. Marketing is there to achieve an ideal fusion between assets, competencies and markets. The Offensive Marketer will be constantly asking, "How can we use our assets and competencies to successfully enter new markets?" The answers come in the application of this new model.

---

[6] Gary Hamel and P.K. Prahalad, *Competing for the Future*, Harvard Business School Press, 1994.

Figure 2-1
*Offensive
Marketing Model:
Asset- and
Competency-
Based*

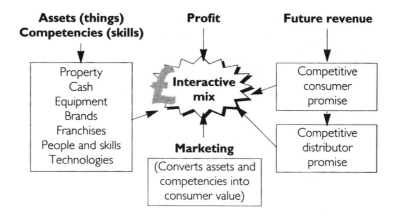

Exploitable Assets and Competencies: Defined

What is an exploitable asset or competency? How do they differ? Does it matter? Are some unexploitable? And what is a "core" competency? This section will discuss these and other questions as a basis for building the Marketing Alignment Process (MAP) described next. As you will see, the MAP approach is critical to achieving above-average profits.

First, with regard to a definition, *assets* are things: property, brands, factories, and cash. This is the marketing definition of assets. It differs fundamentally from the financial definition, which generally only includes tangible assets like property, inventory, money due, and cash on hand. Occasionally, a company's financial balance sheet of assets will also include brands.

Second, as previously discussed, competencies are skills, created by people, often by exploiting assets. While a brand is an existing asset, and a successful brand extension program will involve the application of competencies, how well assets are exploited depends on the level of competency applied to them. Two companies may have identical customer databases, but one may be much more skillful than the other in exploiting this asset to build customer relationships. The same goes for property or any other kind of asset. For instance, an energy company might close down a high-cost, outdated power station and have no use for it. But a leisure company could transform that same asset into a highly profitable entertainment complex. Competencies add value to assets, as every asset is potentially exploitable.

Is it important to differentiate between assets and competencies? Yes, because competencies represent the means to obtain the best return from assets. Assets have a value today. They can often be satisfactorily quantified, even in the case of intangible assets like brands or databases. In the future, they may rise or fall in value, depending on the effectiveness of the competencies applied to them.

In fact, today's assets reflect yesterday's competencies. Tomorrow's assets will be determined by today's competencies. What assets and competencies have in common is that both are potential company strengths and both can be exploited well or badly.

A core competency is a bundle of related skills, leading to a key consumer benefit, and competitively unique.[7]

As an example, on-time delivery is a key consumer benefit of Federal Express. The core competency that drives this benefit is logistics management for package tracking, itself comprising a bundle of related skills such as the effective and efficient use of bar code technology and wireless communications. Other examples include Wal-Mart's efficient and cost containing supplier program, hub-based distribution facilities and logistics management; Dell's direct to consumer sales program and customer support to configure a hardware and software package that meets the individualized needs of the purchaser; and Amazon's personalization technology that creates growing opportunities for online interaction and brand loyalty.

Marketing Alignment Achieves the Right Balance

Marketing alignment is the process that matches markets, channels, and customers with assets and competencies to build above-average profits. It is the task of the Offensive Marketer to recommend the right fit. No one in the company is better placed to do this, since only marketers have the knowledge both of external customer needs and internal competencies. The process directs the company to market areas, products, and programs that create a unique, aligned fit for the company.

---

[7] Id.

The Five-Step Marketing Alignment Process (MAP)

MAP implements the Offensive Marketing approach by matching markets, channels, and customers with the firm's assets and competencies to help achieve above-average profits. The phrase "help achieve" has been used deliberately because MAP will only deliver above-average profits if the other elements of the definition of Offensive Marketing are met; namely, involvement of every employee, building superior consumer value, and a high level of efficiency.

There is a linkage between all of these elements. MAP drives consumer value and efficiencies as well as profits, by linking a company's strengths to areas of best fit. There are five MAP steps, which are summarized below in Table 2-5. They will be covered individually on a top-line basis.

Step 1: Identify Exploitable Assets

To build up a list of company assets, marketing people need to review the assets, some already identified, others perhaps not, of other departments thoroughly and objectively, through mutual discussion and analysis.

The process of involving other departments in building an inventory of assets and competencies not only makes everyone in the company more understanding of the customer-orientated approach, but also gives marketers a leadership role in developing corporate strategies.

Identified and exploitable assets are areas where a company can create a unique competency to become stronger than the competition. Some examples of exploitable assets include landing slots at major airport hubs for American Airlines, a database of millions

Table 2-5   The Marketing Alignment Process

Rank	MAP steps
1	Identify exploitable assets
2	Identify exploitable competencies
3	Rank attractiveness of priority business areas
4	Match assets and competencies to future market, channel, customer opportunities
5	Identify assets and competencies to be strengthened

of households for Kraft or Procter & Gamble, a partnership with Disney for McDonald's, a strong brand image and franchise for BMW, joint technology incubator agreements for Motorola, or strong retail outlet presence for Gap, Inc.

Coca-Cola and McDonald's have built competencies around certain strategic assets. They both have well-placed assets involving worldwide distribution. Disney has a whole stable of famous cartoon personalities, Sony has a global brand name that stands for quality and Mars has superb modern production equipment backed by unique processes. These assets would be a valuable source of competitive advantage even to companies without skills or competencies to exploit them.

Step 2: Identify Exploitable Competencies

Exploitable competencies are those where your company has or can build an edge over competitors. The Offensive Marketer should meet with other department heads to list the competencies that matter in building superior customer experiences, and rank your company on each one. This will both identify a list of exploitable competencies and point to important skill areas that need to be improved to match or beat competition in the future. Lists will differ by company department and market.

Exploitable competencies may include customer service such as that exhibited by Land's End, one of the original outdoor clothing catalogue companies. They might include brand positioning like Nike, Tiffany's, Jaguar, or Old Navy (the discount clothing franchise owned by Gap, Inc.). Exploitable competencies may include global brand development similar to Procter & Gamble or Heinz, process engineering as exhibited by Toyota, or supplier management and cost containment shown by Wal-Mart, Lowe's, or Home Depot.

Step 3: Rank Attractiveness of Priority Business Areas

This step involves reviewing the magnetism of markets, channels, and customer groups, both current and future. This ranking will subsequently enable your company—in Step 4—to match attractiveness with the firm's exploitable assets and competencies. Clearly, the ideal is to identify attractive markets that fit your company's exploitable strengths. However, the fact that a market is

Table 2-6   Criteria for Assessing a Market

Rank	Criteria
1	Market size
2	Market growth
3	Market profitability
4	Real pricing trends[8]
5	Competitive intensity
6	Future risk exposure
7	Opportunity to differentiate
8	Segmentation
9	Industry, distributor, or retail structure

attractive does not mean that you are qualified to compete in it. The ultimate object of this exercise is to focus effort in markets and channels, which are best suited to your company's identified competencies.

The finest way to rank market attractiveness is by quantified portfolio analysis. Prior to explaining portfolio analysis in detail, let's take a top-line look at this analysis. For the purpose of illustration, market, rather than channel or customer attractiveness, will be discussed. The same technique, however, can be applied to all three.

Quantified portfolio analysis of markets involves developing a list of assessment criteria, weighting them by importance, and scoring markets and segments against them. The advantage of this system is that it enables all markets to be compared on common criteria. The need to develop quantified scores enhances objectivity. The system also allows markets to be scored across business units within countries and across countries.

Selection criteria and their weights will vary by market. However, the following list of criteria, shown in Table 2-6, is usually critical to assessing any market's attractiveness.

For particular markets, it may be appropriate to add other criteria. For example, in sectors where property is important, such as retailing, site availability can be critical.

In doing this analysis, it may be worthwhile to construct a written guide concerning how to quantify and score each criterion.

---

[8] Real pricing is defined as price change, excluding effect of inflation.

Having determined the maximum weighting of key criteria, you can then score individual markets against them. For example, in frozen foods there are dozens of product segments, such as frozen vegetables, pizza, and prepared meals. If you were a frozen foods marketer, you would need to decide in which of these segments to compete. No one, not even the market leaders, competes in every product segment. Most frozen food companies are involved in a minority of segments; so how do you rank each segment against the maximum score?

Again, it would be useful to construct a scoring guide sheet. This would help you decide whether to give a particular segment the maximum score for market growth or a much lower one. For example, would an annual volume growth rate of 5 percent qualify for the maximum, or is that too low? A scoring guide sheet would help to show that it all depends which market you are in. Five percent annual volume growth is stimulating in a mature sector like processed food but would be depressing in computer software.

What is the practical application of this quantified approach? For a company already in frozen foods, it would provide guidance on which of the many product segments to prioritize for future investment and dominance. For a company considering entry into a particular market, it would highlight the more and less attractive segments.

Step 4: Match Assets and Competencies to Future Market, Channel, Customer Opportunities

This step involves matching and aligning Steps 1 to 3 to identify where it will be most effective for your firm to compete in the future. This prioritization will maximize your opportunity to deliver superior value and make above-average profits.

The three sets of data you have already developed consist of exploitable assets, exploitable competencies, and the relative attractiveness of various areas of the marketplace to which these can be applied. You are therefore ready to implement the Marketing Alignment Process (MAP).

The MAP analysis below has two axes:

1. Strength of assets and competencies, derived from Steps 1 and 2.
2. Relative market attractiveness, covered in Step 3. It provides guidance on investment priorities, and will help to focus activity on market segments where the company can deliver

superior value and above-average profits. It will direct you away from markets that are either intrinsically unattractive, or attractive but wrong for the company.

Figure 2-2 outlines the investment action underlying a MAP analysis.

If a market is intrinsically unattractive, yet one in which your company has strong assets and competencies (as in the bottom left box in the figure), the first question is whether the company can transform it into an attractive market. Yamaha did this with the home piano and organ, developing a convenient and easy-to-use product, appealing to people who were not trained instrumentalists. If you do not think that the application of the company's competencies can achieve this kind of transformation, your firm should cut costs and maximize profitability (see bottom middle box).

The other side of the coin is that a market may be highly attractive objectively, but fail to match the company's assets and competencies. In this case, you have to judge whether it is practical to radically improve these assets and competencies, either by internal development or by acquisition (see top right box). For example, the "soon-to-be-hot" wireless local area network (WLAN) in the United States presents an opportunity for service providers to improve their offerings and their competencies to meet the demands of the mobile data connectivity of predominantly professional portable PC users.

Through incubation partnerships or acquisition, service providers will need to address better location information and

Figure 2-2
MAP Analysis

Strength of assets and competencies

	High	Medium	Low
High	Invest heavily	Invest, strengthen competencies	Exit or acquire competencies
Medium	Invest	Redefine strategy	Exit or acquire
Low	Maximize profits or transform market	Maximize profits or exit	Exit

Market attractiveness

network detection software as part of a well-positioned service proposition. Security features as well as pricing are key ingredients to success in meeting the demands of this market. Clearly with WLAN, they must transform their company to meet the demands of the market.

Here are some examples of failures and successes in matching assets and competencies to market opportunities.

McDonald's. Over the past decade, McDonald's has attempted a number of new category entries in the U.S. market, including pizzas, low-calorie foods, and children's leisure complexes. However, "McPizzas" were in test-mode for years, the leisure complexes were sold to Discovery Zone, owned by Viacom, and low-fat "McLean," a beef and seaweed burger, also failed.

McDonald's proceeded to try and widen its customer franchise from children and their families to adults. The "Arch-Deluxe" burger took two years to develop, and fifty-two different types of mustard were tested.[9] Eventually, this burger was dropped from the menu.

While the adult fast-food market is certainly attractive, it fails to align with McDonald's assets and competencies—their products, purchasing, and noisy family environment just don't fit. As this example shows, marketing alignment can be applied to total markets or to sub-segments, to divisions or brands, to existing markets or potential ones. The reward for doing so effectively will be above-average profit growth.

Sony. In late 1989, Sony entered the American movie and TV film business by acquiring Columbia Pictures Entertainment Inc. for $3.4 billion.[10] The initiative appears to have been driven more by Sony's vision of the future than by a tight alignment of strengths and opportunities. The reason given for buying Columbia was "that to develop our hardware business in the future, it is necessary to augment our music software with image-based software."[11]

Sony lacked two of the key competencies to enter the American movies category: English-language and entertainment skills. It aimed

---

[9] *Fortune*, November 11, 1996.
[10] *Fortune*, December 23, 1996.
[11] Sony Annual Report, 1990.

to acquire them via acquisition. After five years, results were disappointing. In 1995, Sony wrote off $3 billion in goodwill in its Pictures Division as well as recording $562 million in losses. In 1996, Sony's picture revenue was no higher than it had been in 1992.

Vivendi Universal. Many companies continue to be in flux with respect to marketing alignment. A prime example of a marketing misalignment may be Vivendi Universal, the French conglomerate that moved away from its roots in water and waste management to embrace the entertainment and telecommunications industry with a fast-paced set of purchases. Despite the fact that it borrowed heavily to finance its buying spree, its strong vision (shared by other large multi-media firms including AOL Time Warner), of bringing forth the digital broadband revolution of delivering all content, including image, sound and data, across all platforms, was the basis for its broad foray. Although timing played its fateful part, whether it ever had or could acquire the competencies to manage and grow the disparate businesses, remains an outstanding question, even in light of a heavy debt burden and missteps by former Chairman Jean-Marie Messier.[12]

Nokia. Nokia, the Finnish company that has been beating out Motorola and Ericsson in the wireless communications market in the past decade, moved beyond its heritage as a maker of everything from rubber boots and toilet paper, to become the number one producer of wireless phones and equipment in the world.[13] This success was based in large part on marketing savvy and customer-driven technology, growing both assets and competencies to meet this new identified challenge and creating company-market alignment.

Bic. A classic example of successful marketing alignment was Bic's entry into the razor market with a disposable product.

Bic had a strong worldwide position in low-price ballpoint pens, under the leadership of Baron Bich. One of its major

---

[12] See, for example, "Vivendi Will Move Quickly to Sell Many Assets," *The New York Times*, September 26, 2002, Business Day, at pg C1; and "Impending Breakup of Vivendi Reflects Change in Attitude in Media Universe," *The New York Times*, July 3, 2002, at pg. A1 and C5.
[13] "Nokia's Next Act," *Business Week*, July 1, 2002, at pg. 56.

assets was the ability to manufacture small plastic items in very high volume, at low cost per-unit while maintaining high-quality standards.

Bic was keen to diversify into new consumer markets where it could innovate by exploiting its competencies in plastics technology. Investigation of a number of consumer categories led Bic to the wet-shaver market dominated by Gillette, which, at the time, was trading up customers to increasingly elaborate and expensive products. Suddenly, Bic introduced to those same customers a low-priced disposable razor sold in multi-packs, mainly in supermarkets.

Gillette was predictably slow to react since it faced a painful choice. Successful Gillette entry with plastic disposables would trade down the value of the whole market. Inaction would result in market share loss. Gillette did eventually introduce a successful plastic disposable product, but too late to prevent the establishment of Bic as a strong competitor in many countries.

Step 5: Identify Assets and Competencies to be Strengthened

The final step in MAP analysis is to review your company's assets and competencies for the future.

While conducting Steps 1 through 4, you may have identified attractive markets, channels, customer groups, or other opportunities that could not be exploited because the company lacked the competencies to do so. A decision would therefore need to be made whether to develop or acquire the necessary competencies. Simultaneously, your review of assets and competencies may have revealed critical weaknesses that need to be strengthened. These may require changes in structure, personnel, or training and development programs.

While Step 5 is the final one in the MAP analysis, the process should be continuous, as the internal and external business environment changes to reveal new opportunities and the balance in marketing alignment shifts.

However, the Marketing Alignment Process only gives you the *opportunity* to build above-average profitability. In order to attain it, the company needs to exploit that opportunity by developing winning strategies—("S") and by executing effectively—("E") with the right attitudes—two of the remaining elements of POISE.

LEVERAGING SHORT-TERM PROFITS RESPONSIBLY

The Marketing Alignment Process is primarily designed to maximize medium- and long-term profitability. It is less relevant to short-term marketing pressures.

How do Offensive Marketers respond if they find themselves in a position where they have to gear up profits sharply in the next six to twelve months? The first question to ask is how your firm got into this situation. Is it because you have just joined a company with a few short-term problems but ambitious future investment plans? Is it a one-time situation that occurs infrequently in the company? Or is it an annual event, due to a lack of clear strategy and future commitment on the part of leadership? To solve the one-time problem, the Offensive Marketer will find a solution that does not mortgage the longer-term future of the business.

Here is an example of a short-term profitability gap and what responses are most appropriate for the Offensive Marketer to achieve profitability goals.

Sales and market share of a particular shampoo brand are declining. Consequently, advertising has been cut and the brand is being heavily outspent by major competitors, who have just launched better-quality products. The new-product development cupboard at your company is bare. The brand has been spending heavily on sales promotion, especially couponing. Neither its advertising nor its promotion seem particularly effective. It therefore faces further cuts in its spending budget, and is under pressure to increase price in order to make budget. Some major accounts are threatening to de-list the brand. Senior management has just decided that you are the ideal person to sort things out quickly and make budget.

What do you do in this pressure situation? Your task as an Offensive Marketer is to increase profit in the short term without damaging your brand's long-term prospects. With your right hand, you fix the short term, and with your left you build for the future. Both hands will work in unison.

Table 2-7 is a checklist of responsible short-term profit improvement opportunities for you to consider. These are actions that will pay back immediately or in a period of months.

In the very short term, the most fruitful areas to leverage for fast profit improvement are usually sales promotion, product quality,

Table 2-7   Checklist

Opportunity areas	Issues
Product and packaging quality	• Is it currently meeting specifications? • Can costs be cut without affecting performance? • Can quality be significantly improved without adding much to cost?
Sales promotion	• Have past results been deeply analyzed? • What type of promotion works best or worst in your market? • Is promotion clearly targeted by consumer group, trial, loyalty, trade channel, and account?
Advertising	• Is it working? Has it been pre-tested? • Is strategy clear and is strategy being effectively executed? • Can buying efficiency be improved? • What is the right spending level for the short or long term? • How imaginative is your use of communications and media? (How integrated are your media efforts?)
Product development	• Has R&D got any potential line extensions that would add incremental business? • Can any be developed quickly? • What is happening in shampoo in other countries?
Pricing	• Develop a price elasticity model using regression analysis and modeling techniques.
Distribution channels	• Develop a medium-term recovery plan. Present retailers with your short-term action to hold listings and space for the next year.
Customer service	• Can quality be improved? • Can service areas be extended?
Product range	• Are there too many marginal small sizes, which may prove unprofitable on an activity-costing basis? If so, trim the range.
Other company departments	• How do you motivate them to give your brand a new chance? • How quickly do you tell them about your new plans?

and consumer value, including pricing. Changes in advertising, customer service, and direct marketing normally take longer to develop and to impact the bottom line.

Let's look at what the Offensive Marketer in the shampoo example did. Here's what she had to say:

> The brand had been under-invested in the past, and was in serious decline. Its big plus was its distinctiveness, but this had not been fully exploited. Fortunately I had worked on this brand in other smaller countries, so I came to this new job with some clear ideas.
>
> The first problem was quality, which was rather variable. This was fixed in a few weeks and we merchandized the improvement strongly to the trade. I then looked at areas where we were spending large amounts of money, frankly,

rather ineffectively. The advertising was off-strategy, so I quickly switched to the strategy and execution that had proved most successful in smaller countries. The change was achieved in three months and once implemented, started to work right away.

On the promotion side, the strategy had rightly been to build customer loyalty, but it was not being executed because most of the spending was on smaller sizes. We changed to focus on larger sizes, and ran fewer, but more exciting promotions. We also cut out the couponing program, which builds trial but not loyalty. Unlike other countries, there were not many tailor-made promotions for individual retail accounts in this country, so we developed a menu of eight or so tailor-made propositions, which did not disrupt manufacturing. We offered each account a choice of promotions as long as they placed firm orders twelve weeks ahead. This wasn't rocket science, but it built profitable promotion volume and pleased retailers.

Our major medium-term initiative was a distinctive premium-priced line extension, which was linked to our core brand strategy and positioned to generate incremental business. We advertised it and it has proved very profitable.

Two years after beginning to address the profitability gap, I am glad to see brand share rising again and profits 45 percent up.[14]

This Offensive Marketer skillfully avoided falling into some of the common traps that beset marketers under profitability pressure. Some of these are:

- Despite internal encouragement, she did not raise prices. For a declining brand with a quality problem, this would have been a bad move in the medium term, even if it looked like an option in the very near term.
- While she improved quality to parity with competition, she did not use this as the basis for a pseudo "re-launch": all sound and fury but no substance.
- She was able to resist pressure to cut advertising further by adopting a sharper strategy and proven new execution. In fact, she increased advertising spending and financed this by eliminating couponing and promotions on smaller sizes.
- She spent less on sales promotion, but radically improved effectiveness.
- Most importantly of all, she worked with both hands, on the short- and medium-term problems. In Year 1, her new approach

[14] This is a real life example based on a 1996 interview. Category and country have been disguised to protect confidentiality.

to sales promotion was the main lever to hit budget. But she also spent time in Year 1 on product and advertising quality and on the winning line extension. All of these efforts gave the brand momentum in Year 2.

- She did not, in any area, reduce consumer value, even though she was searching intently for cost savings. On the contrary, her strategy was to build consumer value effectively.

There are three improvement areas for leveraging short-term profits. Their short-term appeal is that they can have a rapid effect on revenue at limited additional cost, and create a profit surplus the first fiscal year out.

Following are three illustrations of short-term leverage areas, with some tools and examples.

Value Engineering (VE)

This is also sometimes called Marketing Value Analysis. The Japanese are the experts on VE. The key questions VE addresses are:

"What is the customer value of each part of every product or service and how does this relate to its cost?"
"How can we translate cost into greater customer value?"

VE is at the heart of Offensive Marketing, constantly balancing the changing ratios of cost and value for the benefit of both customers and producers. It is most effective when applied at the product or service design stage because as much as 90 percent of a product's costs are designed in at this stage. These costs can't be avoided without redesigning the product; once a product is designed, the majority of its costs are fixed.[15]

However, VE is also relevant to existing products or services, as a means to leverage short-term profits. Critical to effective VE is an intimate understanding of the key elements of consumer value in a product or service. Marketers need to map out the total customer experience, break it down into value elements and judge the relative importance of each one.

---

[15] Robin Cooper, *When Lean Enterprises Collide*, Harvard Business School Press, 1995.

The whole value engineering process needs to be done on a cross-departmental basis involving people from Finance, Operations, Engineering, and led by Marketing.

Once a value breakdown has been completed, the cost of each element needs to be established. Using activity based costing may be most appropriate. You then relate the two and search for areas of high cost/low value—where the response would be to cut cost, or areas of low cost/high value—where you would invest to create more revenue.

Product or Service Range

Most companies offer consumers too wide a product range. This can create confusion, add unnecessary cost, generate service or inventory problems, and reduce value delivered. Very often companies proliferate line extensions because their core products fail to offer superior consumer value. They desperately broaden the range in an attempt to shore up revenue. However, the fact that customers have individual needs should not obscure the reality that almost everyone wants superior value.

Simple recognition of this can generate significant short-term profit savings, and Offensive Marketers should lead the search for opportunities to trim ranges. In early 1996 in the United States, IBM offered customers 3.4 thousand unique PC configurations. The goal in 1997 was to cut this to 200.[16] Although this seems like an extreme paring down of product offerings, there are companies that are successful with many less offerings. Mabuchi Motor, the world's largest producer of small electric motors for CD players, serves 70 percent of its customers with just twenty different models.

Asset Utilization

What is the present level of utilization? Has the company got its price/utilization sums right? Can higher-value products be developed for use of existing plant capacity? Can new services be launched using existing people? Are there any modified products or services that could be launched using existing facilities?

---

[16] *Fortune*, November 11, 1996.

> Kellogg's had a problem. The percentage brand share of Kellogg's Corn Flakes was declining over the long term. The company had spare manufacturing capacity for corn flakes but a firm policy of not producing for stores' private labels.
>
> Kellogg's solved this problem by launching Kellogg's Crunchy Nut Corn Flakes, priced at a heavy premium to the customer. It gained a 2–3% market share, mainly incremental to other Kellogg's brands.
>
> Kellogg's exploited existing assets of its brand name, flake technology, sales force, and plant facilities, but with a separate advertising positioning that attracted new consumers at high margins.

Similar questions can be asked about other assets, such as brands or customers. How can we incrementally extend our brands? (See Chapter 10 on Offensive Brand Development.) Are there any new usages for our products or services? How effectively are we using our customer databases, and how can we raise our level of customer retention? What other products or services do our customers need?

Amazon.com provides a pertinent example. To more effectively use their expansive database and extend the brand and online market share, Amazon has been aggressively adding products to its total offerings including CDs, apparel, toys, and consumer electronics, to name a few. With its push to enlist other e-merchants like Living.com and Drugstore.com to host stores on its site, Amazon aims to build on its brand recognition and identity to bring customers back to its site and to build overall profitability.

CONCLUSION

Every marketer should have the skills to leverage short-term profits without mortgaging the future. Admittedly, this may be difficult with short-term profitability gaps and a conventional emphasis on the financial model of accounting.

Yet, the Offensive Marketing approach can build above-average long-term profits by matching company and brand strengths to the best opportunities in the marketplace. In this way, assets are invested in areas giving the best return by meeting customers' needs. The Marketing Alignment Process (MAP) provides a systematic process for identifying and prioritizing these opportunities.

Strategies include value engineering, optimum product and service range, as well as efficient asset utilization.

An Offensive Attitude, the "O" of POISE—which is the subject of the next chapter—along with the other elements of Offensive Marketing, is instrumental to the effective execution of building long-term profitability. Profitability cannot stand in isolation from the other elements of POISE.

3 Offensive Vision and Attitudes: The "O" of Poise

INTRODUCTION

Offensive Marketing begins with vision and attitudes. The vision of the Offensive Marketer is analogous to the vision needed by the classic Jaguar owner: to drive a classic Jaguar you need to keep one eye on the road, one eye on the oil gage, and a case of oil in the trunk (in case you develop a sudden oil leak). An Offensive Marketer needs to keep one eye on the market and competition, one on the organization and its ability to deliver unique value, and reserves that can be called on quickly to maintain the company's competitive edge.

Offensive Marketing is a marketing mindset: it is an approach to marketing that recognizes the importance of initiative and a proactive competitive stand in the marketplace.

WHY OFFENSIVE ATTITUDES ARE IMPORTANT

How do your competitors regard your company? Is it seen as formidable—offensive, to the extent that existing competitors are apprehensive and would-be competitors carefully avoid any direct attacks? Or is it viewed as an easy win, a source of future revenue gains by competitors in predatory mode? Does it set the agenda for the industry, or follow the leader?

And how do your colleagues enjoy working there? Do they arrive expectant every Monday morning and depart tired but fulfilled on Friday evening? Is there direction, progress, teamwork, and fun, or is life an endless treadmill of lengthy meetings, deferred decisions, and unpleasant internal politics? Are you trudging wearily behind competitors, vainly trying to catch up, or are you setting the pace from the front?

The survivor attitude de-motivates people and impairs performance. It is evident that superior results may be drawn from average material, or that very able people can produce poor results. One of the keys to performance is attitude, which, in turn is molded by the leadership, motivation, and working environment provided by senior management. Attitudes are therefore, one of the keystones of the Offensive Marketing approach: the "O" of POISE.

VISION AND ATTITUDES: START AT THE TOP

Some of the topics covered in this chapter are outside the normal scope of a book on marketing. But this book is not about Marketing Departments or marketing activities; it is about the *marketing approach*. Whether or not a company adopts an Offensive Marketing strategy is decided by top management and the board of directors, not by marketing people. Boards following the offensive approach have to make hard decisions about attitude with respect to quality, investment, costs, ethics, and the consumer. In difficult times, and with the familiar pressures to cut back on advertising, R&D, product quality, service levels, and capital investment, what is needed is direction, steadfastness, and courage. Marketing people should always aim to influence the board and energetically lead the execution of the Offensive Marketing approach.

Offensive attitudes are a set of shared values and approaches, grounded in a daily commitment to customers and to low-cost, efficient operation. They give companies cohesion and momentum, and employees pride and a sense of mission. They are the fuel that powers the machine.

These attitudes, which underpin the Offensive Marketing approach, are not to be confused with "aggressive" marketing. One sometimes sees headlines in the marketing press announcing that Company X is launching an "aggressive" marketing campaign. It will describe how money is being thrown at a problem by launching a huge promotion or advertising campaign. The informed reader can often recognize the desperate attempt of an ill-prepared marketer following a competitor/leader too late, or attempting to disguise a product's lack of competitive edge by making a lot of noise. Offensive Marketers will certainly be competitive, but they are also thoughtful, imaginative, and forward thinking.

THE SEVEN SPOKES OF THE OFFENSIVE APPROACH

While a bicycle wheel with seven spokes would be of offensive use to a cyclist, the analogy is useful for communicating the seven attitudes that comprise the offensive approach. The bicycle wheel (see Figure 3-1) illustrates the links between all seven elements:

Figure 3-1
The Seven Spokes

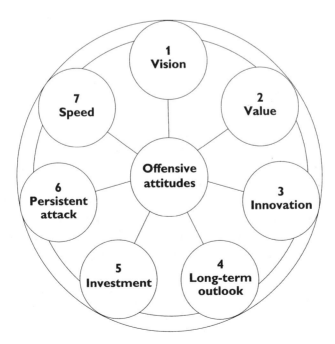

69

Vision moves the wheel;
value is driven by *innovation*;
innovation depends on *long-term outlook* and *investment*;
and each of the elements, along with *persistent attack* and *speed*,
connects with the center, to build a core of *offensive attitudes*.

Spoke #1: Vision and Purpose

To succeed in the long term, businesses need a vision of how they will change and improve in the future. This vision gives the business vitality and motivates those who work in it. According to Jack Welch, former CEO of General Electric Company (GE), "Good business leaders create a vision, articulate the vision, passionately own the vision, and relentlessly drive it to completion."[1]

A successful vision will usually meet six requirements. These requirements are set out in Table 3-1.

Table 3-1 Six Requirements for Success

Requirement	Comment
1. Provides future direction	• Anticipating the future
2. Expresses a consumer benefit	• Successful vision looks outward
3. Realistic	• Believable to customers and employees
4. Motivating	• Vision must motivate and inspire employees
5. Fully communicated	• All levels and functions both inside company and outside
6. Consistently followed and measured	• Avoid temptation to compromise when the going gets tough

Bill Gates' vision or corporate mission for Microsoft was, "A computer on every desk and in every home."[2] Through the years, this has been updated and revised to "empowering people through great software—any time, any place, and on any device"[3] as demands have grown with advances in computing technology. Both vision statements meet all six key requirements.

Compare the Johnson & Johnson credo, written by R.W. Johnson Jr. in 1943, although it has been subject to some slight revision in

---

[1] N. Tichy and R. Cjharan, "Speed, Simplicity, Self-Confidence: An Interview with Jack Welch", *Harvard Business Review, September-October*, 1989, pg. 113.
[2] Bill Gates, *The Road Ahead*, Viking, 1995.
[3] Microsoft Annual Report, 2001.

wording, it has remained virtually constant over the years:

"We believe our first responsibility is to the doctors, nurses, patients and to the mothers and all others who use our products and services. In meeting their needs, everything we do must be of high quality. We must constantly strive to reduce our costs in order to maintain reasonable prices."[4]

A clear business vision will look into the future and allows a business to prepare for change ahead of its competitors. Audi's vision makes this explicit: "Never follow." Sony Corporation's Chairman Morita expressed his philosophy for the company in this way:

"The key to success for Sony, and to everything in business, science, and technology for that matter, is never to follow the others...Our basic concept has always been this—to give new convenience, or new methods, or new benefits to the general public with our technology."

Indeed, as innovation, creativity, and technology have taken prominence in recent years, vision and mission statements have followed suit by emphasizing their importance. Take, for example, Intel's mission statement:

"To succeed we must maintain our innovative environment. We strive to embrace change, challenge the status quo, listen to all ideas and viewpoints, encourage and reward informed risk taking, and learn from our successes and mistakes."

Requirements for Success

A vision statement should guide the organization toward success. The requirements for success are listed below.

1. **Provides future direction.** Reflecting on the challenges facing a company like General Electric, CEO Jack Welch stated that the first step is for the company to "define its destiny in broad but clear terms. You need... something big but clear and understandable." Here was General Electric's vision statement until a few years ago:

   "We will become number one or two in every market we serve and revolutionize this company to have the speed and agility of a small enterprise."[5]

---

[4] J. Collins and J. Porras, *Built to Last,* Century Business Books, 1996.
[5] Robert Slater, *The New GE,* R. Irwin, 1996.

After pursuing this vision for over a decade, Welch reversed it. Every business was directed to define its market so that it had no more than 10 percent of the world market share.

Why the turn about? GE's focus on becoming number one or number two had become a limiting straitjacket that was constraining GE's growth. Presumably, the greatest vision statement in the history of business had become obsolete.

There are two lessons here: The first is that to copy strategy is fatal; every company needs its own unique strategy. Second, nothing is forever; it is possible to create a sustainable competitive advantage only if you are willing to change and adapt your strategy. GE retains its growth objective, but it has revised its market position strategy to enable it to continue to grow.

2. **Express consumer benefit.** Corporate visions deal with the future through the eyes of the consumer. Corporate objectives turn these into shareholder value. The BMW Group's statement of purpose is a good example of a consumer-driven future vision. BMW's "ultimate driving machine" combined with its "pure, premium brand strategy"[6] has helped make it one of the most successful premium car producers in the world.

3. **Be realistic.** Future vision should be imaginative yet achievable, stretching but within grasp. This requires more than elegantly crafted statements. AT&T's vision of "Universal Togetherness"[7] is ambitious but as of yet, unrealized. Various opportunities such as developing global wireless service, strengthening their position as a strong cable provider, strengthening their presence in local phone markets, increasing their ability to deliver services to multinational corporations, and making online services more accessible to a wider audience are goals, that, although full of vision, are perhaps unattainable and unrealistic in the present environment.[8]

On the other hand, Maytag Corporation's mission statement is quite realistic:

"To improve the quality of home life by designing, building, marketing and servicing the best appliances in the world."

---

[6] BMW Annual Report, 2000.

[7] The sweeping wording of AT&T's vision is: "We are dedicated to being the world's best at bringing people together—giving them easy access to each other and to the information and services they want and need—anytime, anywhere."

[8] See, "AT&T: The Problems Keep On Coming", *Business Week*, October 19, 1999; and, "Armstrong's Last Stand", *Business Week*, February 5, 2001.

It is important for a company's mission statement to aspire to greatness but it must be realistic and obtainable.

4. **Motivate.** Creating future vision is as much about the creation of meaning for employees as it is about establishing a direction for the company and its future pursuits.

   The future vision of CIBA, which has since become part of Novartis, was neither clear nor motivating, as reflected in its mission statement:

   "We strive to achieve sustainable growth by balancing our economic, social, and environmental responsibilities.... Empowered employees and a flexible organization support our commitment to excellence."

   Compare the mission statement of Merck & Co: "We are dedicated to achieving the highest level of scientific excellence and commit our research to maintaining human health and improving the quality of life."[9]

   General statements about shareholder returns, empowered employees, or economic, social, or environmental responsibilities are unlikely to exact a response from the employees or partners. Merck's mission statement is one in which employees or customers (for public relations and marketing purposes) can recognize themselves and their own aspirations or needs, and are therefore able to align themselves with the company's larger motivations.

5. **Communicate your vision fully.** Is the future of your company stated in terms that are clear and motivating? The easier it is to communicate, the more readily it will be accepted by employees.

   Visions need to be simple and easily understood. Communication has to be constant throughout the organization—up, down, and across the organization's functional silos and departments.

6. **Consistent participation and measurement.** Do people in back offices and plants understand, believe in, and act upon the company's strategic vision? Is it part of their everyday life, followed day in and day out? And, most importantly of all, does senior management conduct the business in good times and bad in ways that are seen to "hold the dream"? If not, the future vision

---

[9] P. Jones and L. Kahaner, *Say It and Live It: The 50 Corporate Mission Statements That Hit the Mark*, Currency Doubleday, 1995.

will rapidly lose credibility and soon be viewed as empty rhetoric. Many Boards and Chief Executives spend vast amounts of time designing corporate visions, selling them heavily to employees, and then promptly make decisions that undermine the vision. For example, a vision centered around world-class technology is unconvincing if the company concerned makes heavy cuts in its R&D budget under the guise of "focus" or "efficiency."

Spoke #2: Value

Value is a changing ratio that relates benefits to price. It can be expressed as the brand value equation.

$$V = B/P$$

whereby V is value, B is benefits, and P is price.

This equation enables you to separate the three elements of brand value and to assess the relative contribution each makes to the whole.

The marketing mix is integral to this equation. Benefits are a combination of product, price, place, and promotion. As a general rule, value is perceived by the customer—the variable to the left of the equal sign and can be increased in two fundamental ways. The numerator, B, can be increased by improving the benefits along any point of the continuum affecting the marketing mix.

Alternatively, value can be increased by reducing the price. If a company can offer both superior benefits and lower prices relative to the competition, it enjoys an extremely advantageous position.

Toyota used the marketing mix in the 1980s, along with Hyundai in the 1990s, to create a successful entry into the U.S. market. Although Hyundai appeared to have an early reputation for poor quality, which reduced the product's perceived value, they had to increase value by decreasing the price to be competitive. The same is true for Samsung in the computer monitor market. Samsung has been forced to sell at a price below Sony even after they raised product quality because its image continues to lag behind the reality of the product.

The bottom line, with respect to the value equation, is that a company can succeed in a market only if it has perceived value *that is equal to or greater than* that of its competitors. The upside of understanding the value equation is that when a company's perceived value is strong, the company can charge a premium for the same product.[10]

Functional Benefit

This is the objective performance of a product or service, shorn of its imagery, the naked product? For example, statistics collected by motoring organizations show that the luxury Lexus is an extremely reliable car.

Functional benefit is feasible to establish for most products, from fast-moving consumer goods to consumer durables, where they can be blind-tested. It is more difficult for service products, but realistic if comparative performance figures are used. For example, punctuality in consumer transport, and speed of service in retailing or fast food, are key performance indicators. In business-to-business markets, functional benefits can often be evaluated through technical testing.

Perceived Benefit

This is based on the consumer's perception of branded products or services or the fully clothed version. For example, most whisky drinkers have difficulty in differentiating between various products in a blind taste test. Yet, they will pay high premiums for certain brands because the presentation and heritage create a strong perceived benefit. As discussed above, all elements of the brand value equation are relative in comparison with competition. The difference between objective performance—the functional benefit—and the perceived benefit is often described as the brand image.

How can perceived benefit be quantified? The best method is to use customer attitude scores based on consumer research. Customer loyalty or retention levels are also useful indicators of relative perceived benefits.

As with most marketing tools, the brand value equation is a judgmental process rather than a formula to be blindly applied. You cannot say, for example, that a 60:40 blind-test win on a consumer product justifies a 50 percent or even a 15 percent

---

[10] Material on the value equation comes from Warren Keegan, *Global Marketing Management*, 6th Ed. Prentice Hall, 1999.

price premium. You can be sure, however, that it will sustain a higher price. The exact level will depend on the market, competition, the brand's starting-point, its capacity situation, and future aspirations.

The brand value equation is a good example of the direction in which marketing is moving. It is an inexact process that adds discipline to decision-making, but requires deep understanding of customers and markets. The quantification is tempered and refined by informed judgment. Determining value needs to be done by knowledgeable marketing people, not by number-crunching accountants.

Most products or services at best offer parity benefits at parity prices, and therefore fail to deliver superior value. Companies or brands in this position are unlikely to survive in the long term, since customers will have no particular reason to seek out their products or services. That is why a powerful commitment to value, by every employee every day, is "Spoke No. 2" of Offensive Attitudes.

What are the main indicators of value? The market regularly provides clues, hints, or even screaming headlines about each company's value offering. Here are some things to look at and questions to ask:

1. What is the sales trend of existing products in existing accounts? Sales figures are the mirror of a product's value.
2. What is the level and trend of market share? Look at existing products in existing accounts: declining product value can be obscured by gains from new distribution, line extensions, or inventory building.
3. How do your products or services perform when objectively assessed by your customers against direct competition?
4. Can your products sustain a price premium? If not, how can you pretend they are better?
5. How loyal are your customers in relation to competitors? What is your level of repeat business? What is your percent annual retention level of customers? What are their future purchase intentions?[11]
6. What proportion of the customer's category purchases are

---

[11] See, in general, on the topic of customer retention, Robert C. Blattberg, Gary Getz, and Jacquelyn S. Thomas, *Customer Equity, Building and Managing Relationships as Valuable Assets*, Harvard Business School Press, 2001.

of your brand? In other words, what is your share of the customer's purchasing, and how is this trending?

The gold standard in value is to provide a superior product or service and be a low-cost operator. This results in both satisfied customers and high profits. Customers' value requirements continually increase as their expectations change. Tomorrow they will expect your company's products and services to improve in quality and reduce in price.

It is important to determine if everyone in the company understands how they contribute to creating superior value in the customer's eyes. Above all else, value is an attitude; an attitude of really individually caring about delivering customer value, at every opportunity, at all customer "touch-points,"[12] day in, day out, whatever the circumstances.

Spoke #3: Innovation

The Offensive Attitude to innovation is the determination to lead rather than follow. "Innovation" is a word often used to describe high-profile breakthroughs like the mini-van sector innovated by Chrysler, or new pharmaceutical drugs or new breakthrough technologies in the appliance and computing world.

In this book, innovation is used more broadly to embrace any improvement in customer value or in cost of operation: the two arms of Offensive Marketing. Therefore, while the Japanese are not always innovative in terms of R&D, they continually innovate in production and engineering techniques. Over the years, this has enabled them to produce better products at lower cost.

Innovation is most effective when viewed as a continuing process, applied to every area of the business. It is much easier to translate a bundle of individually minor developments into a major step forward than to seek and find the breakthrough innovation.

Innovation: Big Bang and Drip Feed

"Big bang" innovations usually involve heavy investment, high risk of failure and long lead times. They have a transforming

---

[12] See, Patricia B. Seybold, *Customers.com*, The Patricia Seybold Group and Times Books, a Division of Random House, Inc. 1998.

impact only when ultimately successful. Often driven by technology or by creative exploitation of distribution channels, examples include Chrysler's mini-van, the Canon Copier, Dell Computing and its direct-to-consumer sales model, the Gillette Sensor, Federal Express's logistics technology, and Intel's Pentium chip.

The cost of "big bang" innovations is high and the ability to predict success low, especially where new technology is the key driver.

While "big bang" innovation typically involves a small number of people in R&D, Marketing, Sales, Distribution, and Finance, "drip-feed" innovation is the province of every employee and affects every business activity large or small. Table 3-2 illustrates this difference.

"Drip feed" innovation is evolutionary, not revolutionary. It gains by small increments on a daily basis. However, these mount up quickly over time and become successful competitive advantages.

Companies good at steady and continuous "drip-feed" innovation include Land's End, with their focus on customer relationships and mass customization production, and 3M, Compaq, BMW and Toyota, who all continue to succeed by creating in their employees an attitude which is always questioning and open to ideas with respect to how to perform better and less expensively.

Let's look at 3M's "drip-feed" innovation strategy.

3M occasionally achieves a big-bang success, as with Post-it Notes, but relies on a continuous drip feed of innovation in every area of the business, especially with respect to new products.

As stated in their 2001 Annual Report, "much of 3M's rich culture comes from the principles that former President and Chairman of the Board, William L. McKnight, set forth." McKnight believed "management that is destructively critical when mistakes

Table 3-2 Key Drivers—Big Bang versus Drip Feed Innovation

Big Bang	Drip Feed	
• Technology • Distribution Channels	• Process engineering • Training and competency • Marketing value analysis • Customer relationships • Product development	• Service development • Information systems • Re-segmentation of markets • Brand development • Brand positioning

are made kills initiative. It's essential that we have many people with initiative if we are to continue to grow." It is this growth that continues to make 3M a leader in the twenty-first century.

Over the years, 3M has aimed to meet two broad innovation objectives—7 percent of annual revenue in new products launched annually, and 30 percent through products introduced in the last four years. It usually achieves these objectives.

In doing this, it has drawn on thirty core technologies, activated by over 8,000 scientists and technologists (who account for about 10 percent of the total workforce). They work with colleagues in Marketing, Manufacturing, and other departments to discover unique solutions to customer needs and to bring new products to market faster. Many of these create new markets and change the basis of competition.

Over the years, the day-to-day drip feed has swollen into a torrent of new initiatives. Many of these new initiatives stem from 3M's culture that stresses both creativity and innovation. As the saying goes "Creativity is thinking up new things. Innovation is doing new things." While innovation is the "practical application of creativity," both are seen as necessary to 3M's continued growth and success.[13]

It pays both to pursue daily drip-feed innovation as well as to invest in the potential big bang, which can radically expand customer franchise if successful.

How does a company create an atmosphere where innovation thrives? As seen in 3M's focus on both creativity and innovation, the daily drip-feed innovation is primarily a question of frame of mind, which depends on senior management's modeling and emphasis. Even though the big bang type is more difficult to sustain because it involves risks both for individual employees and for the business, drip-feed as well requires that employees and partners stick their necks out and champion new ideas. Both large and smaller companies need the right structure and a supportive attitude to facilitate risk-taking. These structures include compensation packages that reward risk-taking and not just successes, public recognition among employees of both successes and failures, and senior management's speaking the talk and walking the walk of nurturing creativity and bold enterprise.

---

[13] 3M Worldwide Annual Report, 2001, at 3M, "Innovation Chronicles and Innovation Stories."

Company senior management usually feels a lot more comfortable with drip-feed than with big-bang innovation, as the classic Xerox computer example demonstrates.

> *The early history of the personal computer revolution was the Altair in 1975, the Apple 2 in 1977, the IBM PC in 1981, and the Apple Mac in 1984. The Apple Mac, designed by a team with an average age of 21, was the first modern computer, with an easy to use screen-graphical interface. Yet, as early as 1973, Xerox, in its now well-known Palo Alto, California lab, had developed the mouse, the printer, networking capabilities, which linked a hundred Alto computers, and a graphical interface.*
>
> *Apparently, Xerox senior management in New York lacked a clear vision of the future. While they had the foresight to invest heavily in computer innovation, they did not know what to do with the Alto when shown it.*
>
> *In 1982, Steve Jobs of Apple asked for and was given a demonstration of the Xerox Alto. According to a Xerox researcher, "The Apple team understood more about the Alto after one and a half hours—its technology and presentations—than senior Xerox decision makers."*
>
> *Steve Jobs quickly hired a hundred engineers to copy and improve upon the Xerox approach. His vision for the Apple Mac was that it should be "insanely great." No design issue was too small, and it was never too late to get it right. The Apple Mac was launched at a premium price in late 1984. In the view of some, Xerox could have owned the computer industry in the 1990s—as they had both the technology and resources to do so a decade earlier.[14]*

Other examples of missed opportunities to innovate abound, such as IBM's inability to disentangle critical competencies out of its PC initiatives. These programmatic initiatives were designated as an "independent business unit," and therefore did not have access to IBM's competencies in operating systems and semiconductors. By forcing the project to seek supplier partners, Microsoft and Intel profited expansively from IBM's initial incursions into the PC market.[15]

The lesson of the Alto and IBM example is that both senior management and marketers need to understand the implications of new technology and have a vision of that innovation for the future.

---

[14] "Triumph of the Nerds," Channel 4, April 1996.
[15] Gary Hamel and C.K. Prahalad, *Competing for the Future*, Harvard Business School Press, 1994.

Fortune Magazine polled a large sample of American business school professors, consultants, and security analysts, and developed a list of "Eight Masters of Innovation."[16] It then interviewed these companies to discover what made them successful innovators. They concluded that:

1. Driving forces behind innovators include a commitment to new technology and the fear of being outpaced by competitors.
2. Effective corporate structure includes lean, decentralized units, where engineers, marketers, and finance experts are thrown together in tight working groups.
3. Top management needs access to raw data rather than reconstituted summaries compiled by middle management.
4. Direction must be clear to channel and prioritize the flood of ideas through the innovation process.
5. To control risk, top management must limit the number of innovations: put their toes into the water, check back with the consumer, and then slide their way in.

The driving forces of technology and the fear of being left behind have to be converted into profitable new developments by individuals or teams of individuals. How well a company does this can often be answered by asking three questions:

1. What major innovations have we achieved in the past ten years?
2. Who was responsible?
3. What happened to those people and where are they now?

If the answers to these questions highlight that the persons responsible for the innovations of the last ten years are retired, have been passed over for promotion, sometimes repeatedly, or have been relegated to strategic insignificance, the company may want to take a second look at its innovative potential and how it structures and supports entrepreneurship, skunk works, or efforts to thrive on "chaos."

Spoke # 4: Long-term Outlook

The importance and value of a long-term outlook was covered in Chapter 2; however, short-term performance pressures have become

---

[16] Stratford Sharman, "Eight Masters of Innovation," *Fortune Magazine*, October 16, 1984.

intense, and a year is now a long time in the life of a company. Many of the most important business initiatives take three to five years to pay back. This is why many companies now structure their management bonus systems on a longer-term basis.

The effect of these short-term pressures is to:

1. Encourage senior staff to silently leach away long-term assets for short-term profits. They cut advertising, R&D, and investment while simultaneously driving prices up.
2. Force a focus on tactics rather than long-term strategy.
3. Shift priority from product-led innovations, using design and technology, to skilful use of short-term marketing tools in order to sustain products lacking long-term competitive edge.[17]
4. Discourage investments that require a long-term view that can be justified only in the longer term.

Faced with this present reality, how can a company foster a long-term outlook? Among the array of less than perfect answers, some of the better ones are the following:

- Remove the revolving door from the offices of senior staff, especially in subsidiary companies belonging to international divisions. This would help stop the operation from being run solely to further the short-term career aspirations of incumbents.
- Fully exploit the possibilities of asset- and competency-led marketing (see Chapter 2).
- Ensure that your firm is a low-cost operator and has brought efficiencies to bear on all operations so as to survive, or win, a price war should one occur.
- Persuade senior management to follow a highly conservative accounting policy. Reserving funds in the good years to keep resources for lean years for future-oriented projects.
- Accumulate a repository of fully tested ideas, so the company can draw on them in a time of crisis.
- Manage the expectations of Wall Street from a conservative base and sell the company's long-term vision clearly.

---

[17] Bennett and Cooper, "The Misuse of Marketing," *McKinsey Quarterly*, Fall 1982.

- Be prepared to continue to make investment essential to the company's long-term health, even though it may result in temporary profit shortfalls.

Spoke # 5: Investment

The concepts of profit and investment (P&I) from an Offensive Marketer's perspective were described in Chapter 2. The level of a company's investment is the best measure of its commitment to a long-term outlook. Investment obviously needs to be directed to the right opportunities, and, as Hamel and Prahalad point out, "resourcefulness in choosing the best opportunities is more important than resources."[18]

For example, Corning, one of the world's largest manufacturers of fiber optics, invested heavily in meeting its evolving market realities. Although it had developed the first fiber optics and supplied telecommunications industry leaders like MCI, customers were demanding lower prices, consistent attributes, and standards for quality, information, loads, and speed. With the market becoming commodity driven, Corning continued to improve quality while simultaneously lowering prices through process enhancement. Customer demands continued to evolve, and Corning responded with a company-wide transformation to mass customization where it gained efficiency and forged build-to-order manufacturing processes that linked to sales operations, distribution lines, quality control, and customer service. As it prepared for the next set of market driven demands, Corning invested in its future and moved from process enhancement to mass customization.[19]

Spoke # 6: Persistent Attack

A great deal has been made of the analogies between marketing and military strategies. They are often described under the heading "Marketing Warfare." Some of these analogies are useful. Von Clausewitz, the nineteenth century Prussian general's book

---

[18] Hamel and Prahalad, Id.

[19] Bart Victor and Andrew C. Boynton, *Invented Here: Maximizing Your Organization's Internal Growth and Profitability*, Harvard Business School Press, 1998.

On War, has become a frequently quoted source of strategic maxims. For example, his observation about strategy is a classic and timeless formulation of a key and fundamental principal of marketing:

"The best strategy is always to be very strong, first generally then at the decisive point … There is no more imperative and no simpler law for strategy than to keep the forces concentrated."

Because no war is ever won through persistent defense, an essential element of the offensive approach is persistent attack. This does not mean that a company should be attacking on all fronts all the time. At any given moment a company is likely to be attacking on some fronts, defending on others, and retreating from non-strategic areas where the prospects for success look dim.

The term "persistent attack" is meant to convey that the over-all focus of a company's activity should be to attack and win. Any defensive effort becomes part of a long-term plan that culminates in a fresh attack. Defense is a temporary situation, part of an over-all plan that results in attack when the time and place are right.

There are several advantages for a company in encouraging an attacking frame of mind:

1. **Increased motivation.** Great satisfaction can be achieved by attacking and winning. Most people are prepared to hold a defensive position for some time, but to do so for years without any offensive sorties is discouraging.
2. **Sustained pressure for competitors.** Planned attack keeps competitors under pressure, forcing them to react and reducing their ability to frame sound, long-term plans.
3. **Sustained internal pressure to remain competitive.** Since no company likes to lose a battle, a tradition of aggression creates internal pressures to remain competitive in product performance and cost. Persistent attack makes most sense when allied with the other six spokes of the wheel, especially value and innovation.

Companies following the offensive approach respond to setbacks by counter-attack and maintain their persistence and will to fight back from disaster.

Procter & Gamble decided to enter the tampon market in the late 1960s and by the mid 1970s successfully test-marketed a unique and superior tampon called Rely. As Rely moved to new areas in the United States in the late 1970s, it was still achieving percentage market shares in the low 20s, even though Playtex and Tampax had by then improved their products.

Disaster struck in the early 1980s, when cases of alleged toxic shock syndrome began to appear, and Rely became the focus of product liability suits. Procter & Gamble withdrew Rely and took a $75-million write-off in 1981.

Having exited from tampons, Procter & Gamble opened a new front in the feminine protection market by launching Always, a thin and more absorbent pad, aiming for a 20 percent market share in the United States. The Always product line achieved 17 percent in year one, equivalent to sales of $125 million. The product was distributed worldwide in the 1990s, and has been highly successful.

Spoke 7: Speed

Speed, either as an innovator or a fast responder, is a test of a company's fitness. Speed is becoming increasingly important as a source of competitive advantage. The Offensive Marketer will respond quickly to changes in customer needs or in the business environment, and will counterattack competitive thrusts. Slow response usually indicates a problem in organizational structure or attitudes.

At one time it was fairly accurate to describe a big, often multinational firm as a "supertanker." A smaller, more agile business was characterized as a "cruiser," maneuvering quickly around the supertankers in the competitive marketplace. This was probably true not too long ago.

However, many of the more effective large companies are seeking and gaining the advantages, simultaneously, of both the scale and resources of bigness and the agility and focus of smallness. For these companies, a more accurate analogy is a fleet of cruisers serviced by a battleship. 3M regards itself not as a multibillion-dollar company but as over a hundred individual profit centers around the world. Johnson & Johnson has a similar approach in viewing itself as operating companies of five hundred people or less. Similarly, GE prides itself on the competitive swiftness of its myriad of smaller businesses.

For international companies, there are two issues with respect to speed. The first is project start to launch in the first targeted country, and the second is speed from this first country launch to global expansion. Leading consumer goods companies like

Procter & Gamble or Unilever expect to get non-food brands from Country 1 to Country 30 in a couple of years at most. The days when you could launch Pampers in the United States in 1961, start rolling out internationally in the late 1970s, and complete in the 1980s are long gone. In the computer industry, new product development lead-time, from start to launch, was 18–24 months in the late 1980s, but is now 9–12 months today. Windows 95 was launched simultaneously worldwide as are many of the newer PC products. The challenge is to move fast and market the right product to as many markets as feasible from Day 1.

It is not enough to be a fast innovator and expander. A business needs to be a fast responder as well, since companies can be ambushed. When this happens, your firm must quickly answer three questions:

1. Is this just a skirmish, or is it a serious threat to our business?
2. Should we respond very fast with a proposition?
3. Or, should we take more time and respond with a superior offer, in terms of product, service, and value?

The response will depend on the seriousness of the threat and the type of business you are in. When Nabisco was ambushed by Procter & Gamble and PepsiCo in the American cookie market, it decided to take the threat very seriously.

For decades Nabisco had ruled the roost in the U.S. cookie and cracker market with a market share of over 40 percent. Two very formidable new competitors entered this market with distinctive ranges of cookies. PepsiCo's Frito-Lay Division, a brand leader in snack foods backed by a 12,000-strong sales force, launched Grandma's Cookies, a high-moisture product well geared to Frito-Lay's skills in selling short-life merchandise. Then, shortly afterwards, Procter & Gamble introduced a similar type of cookie, crisp on the outside and chewy on the inside, with a long life and allegedly patent protected.

It was not clear at this time whether soft cookies would become a small niche sector or whether, despite premium pricing, they would establish a strong position. The question was irrelevant to Nabisco, who knew that if they allowed either Procter & Gamble or PepsiCo to gain even a foothold in the cookie market, there would be big trouble ahead.

So Nabisco regarded the threat as a head-on attack and although taken completely by surprise, responded fast and offensively. Within six months, they launched a soft cookie range, exploited their brand and distribution strength, and challenged Procter & Gamble's patent. After a sustained battle, they saw both Procter & Gamble and PepsiCo fail in their market initiatives.

Several criteria exist for rating a business and its Offensive Attitude toward the marketplace. These criteria are set forth in Table 3-3. These criteria include: a vision for the future of the endeavor, a commitment to a valued proposition and market offering, innovation as the backbone of that value offering, long-term objectives as compared to short time-line initiatives, investment to match that long-term approach, and speed of proactive implementation and response shown in an offensive, attacking competitive stance.

Table 3-3   Criteria for Rating a Business: Offensive Attitudes

1. Clear, realistic, and motivating **Vision** of the future, understood and accepted by most employees.

2. A strong commitment to providing superior **Value** to customers, backed by low-cost operations.

3. Strong emphasis on **Innovation** throughout the business, both daily trickle and big bang, in the right balance for the industry. Stress on technology, support, recognition, and reward for successful innovators. Structure where innovation can flourish.

4. Ability to achieve required short-term results, but strong focus on **Long-term Objectives**.

5. Commitment to continued **Investment** in all assets and competencies, like brands, people, skills, technology, new products, and equipment, even when faced by strong short-term pressures.

6. Overall focus on **Attacking** competition, but at carefully chosen times and places.

7. **Fast** good-quality response to new opportunities or competitive threats.

CONCLUSION

This chapter has provided the analogy of a bicycle wheel with seven spokes representing the seven attitudes, which comprise the offensive approach to marketing and illustrates the linkages between them for success.

If we were to construct a flow chart of building Offensive Attitudes with the aim of leading markets, taking risks, and making competitors followers, it would start with *vision* as the first spoke of an integrated wheel. This vision should be customer-driven (as we saw in the Corning example with its push to mass customization), realistic, simple and easy to communicate, as well as capable of motivating and inspiring employees and partners.

An emphasis on determining what is the company's *value* proposition and communicating its superior combination of benefit and price is integral to an Offensive Attitude and marketplace positioning.

The vision and value proposition must be supported by strong *innovation* and a *long-term outlook* with respect to *investment*. Resourcefulness in selecting the future direction may itself be as important as the scale of the investment itself, although scale must ultimately match the opportunity envisioned. These latter three requirements are coordinated by an overarching frame of mind that prides itself on *persistent attack*, although parts of your firm may temporarily be on the defensive because of competitor moves. Be driven by the need for *speed*: This becomes an overall test of a company's fitness to meet marketplace demands that are constantly changing at ever more rapid rates.

4

Integrated Marketing Approach: The "I" of POISE

INTRODUCTION

Offensive Marketing is an approach to business that affects everyone in the organization and its partners. It is not a specialized discipline practiced by a single department. Everyone should be thinking and directing their efforts to both customers and profits.

Integrated marketing policies should be spearheaded by the Chief Executive Officer and Board, and should rest on a firm foundation of delivering superior customer value and profitable growth that is delivered by all departments, permeated by an Offensive Attitude. The starting point is corporate strategy created in an open dialogue with participation from all departments and led by marketers with their duel perspective on external markets and internal competencies. The result of these dialogues and plans will be a market- and consumer-driven corporate strategy with cross-departmental responsibilities and implementation guidelines.

INTEGRATED MARKETING

Integrated Marketing means that every part of the business combines to deliver superior customer value at minimum cost.[1] This is the driving force of Offensive Marketing. Unfortunately, Integrated Marketing has been used in recent years to describe a much more narrow approach by integrating the increasingly diverse range of marketing communications. This has included advertising, relationship marketing, sponsorship, event promotions, public relations, and web initiatives. For our study and purpose in this text, Integrated Marketing will be used in its original, broader sense.

Howard Morgens, a former Chairman of Procter & Gamble, put the case for integrated marketing succinctly:

"There is no such thing as marketing skill by itself. For a company to be good at marketing, it must be good at everything else from R&D to manufacturing, from quality controls to financial controls."[2]

Marketing is an approach to business rather than a specialist discipline. It is no more the exclusive responsibility of the Marketing Department than profitability is the sole charge of the Finance Department. Unlike the more specialized roles of Production, Purchasing, Sales, and R&D, marketing is everyone's business. The marketing approach challenges everyone in the company to relate his or her work to the needs of the marketplace and to balance it against the firm's own profit needs.

For example, in a marketing-oriented automobile company, the plant manager will ensure that quality tests evaluate those things with respect to the product that matters most to the consumer. She will also strive to develop new techniques of flexible mass production in order to give customers the combination of low-cost and wide-model choice they seek. The Finance Department will clearly identify the needs of their internal and external customers, and will satisfy these cost-effectively and on time. Within the company, the Marketing Department should lead and catalyze the application of the marketing approach.

To be effective, Integrated Marketing requires the full belief and support of top management. Where the marketing approach flows through the bloodstream of a company, the impact of the

---

[1] *Integrated Marketing* has also been referred to as the *Total Marketing Approach*.
[2] *Duns Review*, December 1970.

whole is much greater than the sum of the individual parts. Where marketing is strapped on to the corporate body like a wooden leg as a separate and distinct function with little integration, the reverse is true. Marketing is much too serious a thing to be left to Marketing Departments alone. Both leadership and integration throughout the organization are required for success.

Integrating Company Vision and Attitudes

Integration should be spearheaded and monitored by the Board, using its Marketing Department as integrators and evangelists. This means that the seven spokes of Offensive Attitudes (discussed in Chapter 3) need to be applied by everyone in the company. The "O" and "I" of POISE work closely together demonstrating that POISE is a total marketing system, not something leadership and Offensive Marketers pick and choose from.

Developing a Corporate Strategy for Integrated Marketing

Almost every company these days has a long-term strategy. All too often the strategies are tactical and plans focus on short-term financial numbers that give no indication of how they will be attained.

Corporate strategy will be covered briefly in this chapter as a means to achieving clear Vision, Marketing Alignment (see MAP, Chapter 2), and Integration. It is a process that the Offensive Marketer should be heavily involved in.

Time frames of corporate strategies and plans will differ by industry, influenced by development lead-times. Longer-term plans tend to be broad and companies using them generally also have more detailed three- or five-year plans. Long-term and medium-term plans provide the foundation for one-year budgets. In a marketplace where change is happening quicker because of underlying technologies or uses, some companies, including many of the dot.com's that persist today and technology-based companies, have one-year and three-year planning cycles.

The following ten areas, set forth in Table 4-1, encapsulate the areas of focus that the Offensive Marketer would like to see in a corporate strategic plan. These also provide the foundation for the Integrated Marketing approach.

Table 4-1 Ten Elements of Corporate Strategy

Future Market Vision
Future Priorities
Company Vision
Target Market Position
Target Financial Returns
Future Investment
Key Supporting Strategies
Key Plans and Milestones
Testing Program
Summary of Department Responsibilities

This integrated corporate strategy is very different from the conventional approach that sets a series of revenue, cost, and profit objectives and then splits responsibilities for hitting these by departments. The conventional approach involves a compilation of budgets and plans by Operations, Sales, Marketing, Finance, and other functions that are merged together to form the "big picture."

In contrast, a strategic plan, including these ten elements, is developed *across* departments, *centered on future needs of markets, customers, and consumers.* Only at the last stage, where summaries of departmental responsibilities are created, does corporate strategy split into department responsibilities. This interdepartmental dialogue is led by marketers because of their unique knowledge of markets, costs, and internal competencies.

Table 4-2 demonstrates the difference between a conventional, department-based corporate strategy and an integrated one.

IMPLEMENTING INTEGRATED MARKETING VIA CORPORATE STRATEGY

Integrated Marketing is designed to achieve the twin objectives of Offensive Marketing: superior customer value and higher profits.

It follows logically, therefore, that everyone in a company should be judged on three criteria:

1. **Contribution to superior customer value.** Innovation, customer relationships, and investment are key drivers.

Table 4-2   Departmental vs. Integrated Approaches

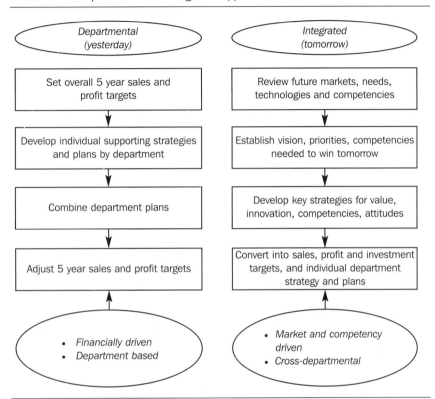

2. **Contribution to superior long-term profit growth.** Cost reduction, productivity, and value engineering are key drivers.
3. **Inter- and cross-departmental teamwork.** Creating unique value for customers requires an integrated effort of every individual and department in the organization.

To illustrate, take two ways of describing the job of an aircraft maintenance worker. One of these is conventional, the other an Integrated Marketing description.

First description: Ensure all aircraft meet full engineering specifications, within agreed budget.
Second description: Ensure that airline has a perfect safety record and the best punctuality record of any airline at minimum cost.

Which is the more motivating description? There is nothing inaccurate about the first description but it is inward looking. In contrast, the second one looks both externally and internally. It considers customers, competition, and cost while also tying the employee to the larger goals of the organization.

Five Key Tools

There are five key tools, contained in the Offensive Marketing approach, for implementing an integrated corporate strategy to ensure that everyone thinks on the same lines:

1. Integrated job objectives
2. Integrated job specifications
3. Integrated competency development
4. Integrated performance appraisal
5. Integrated rewards and bonuses

Each will be discussed separately. We will track some of these tools through the eyes of two imaginary Marketers, Chris Basker and Jill Smith. Neither has a marketing title or belongs to a Marketing Department. Chris is a 32-year-old plant manager for a bathroom products group, Park Lane, and Jill, 30, is an IT manager at a new decorative hardware and lumber company, Utopian Building Society.

Integrated Job Objectives

Chris Basker's responsibility as plant manager is the production of the mid-priced Park Lane line. Primary customers are contractors/homebuilders, and consumers, ages 45 to 65, who are refurbishing their homes. Distribution channels are merchandisers like Home Depot, Lowe's, and bathroom retailers. Chris has a product range of 8,000 items, and has already discovered that one of the industry's principal problems is weak customer service. He became plant manager two months ago, and is about to write his job objectives for next year. He looks at his predecessor's objectives.

You can see what is wrong with these job objectives. (Table 4-3). They are all inward looking. Chris rightly saw his first task as sorting out who are his internal and external customers. Having done that, he asked them what they wanted. He talked to

Table 4-3 Park Lane: Previous Job Objectives (simplified for brevity's sake)

1. Produce budgeted volume of $2.5 million, equivalent to 110K units
2. Control spending within budgeted figure of $1.2 million or 45% of sales
3. Manage capital expenditures of $600,000 with 4-year payback
4. Reduce labor turnover from 20% to 15%
5. Develop, with Marketing and R&D, improved processes for new product development

Sales, Marketing, R&D, IT, and Finance, and visited a number of homebuilders, retailers, and builders' merchants. These conversations enabled him to draft a new set of job objectives, which he circulated to other departments for comment (Table 4-4).

These objectives clearly need to be supported by a detailed action plan, with quarterly milestones. How do Chris's objectives differ from those of his predecessor? You will notice there are fewer numbers. These will be specified in his plans. In any case, Chris sees hitting budgeted cost and output as an *assumption*, not an objective. The main differences are that "Tomorrow's Job Objectives" are both inward and outward looking. They focus on

Table 4-4 Park Lane: Tomorrow's Job Objectives

Customer definition and needs	
External customers	*Needs*
• Customers—distributors or retailers	• Range and service
• Consumers—all end users	• Value
Internal customers	*Needs*
• Sales Dept	• Quality, service, cost
• Marketing Dept	• Innovation, quality, product development
• Finance Dept	• Data, efficiency, output, budgeting

Objectives
1. Meet the quality, timing and service needs of all external customers, on a superior basis to competitors at lowest possible cost.
2. Raise customer service levels from 80% to 92% in next 18 months.
3. Develop innovative processes, work practices, and competencies, designed to enhance (1) above.
4. Contribute to new technology, and launch new products on time, faster than competition.
5. Manage, motivate and develop all employees to industry best practice in planning, operations, inventory control and cost. Cut number of lines from 8K to 5K, working with Marketing Department.

customers, consumers, competitors, and cost to meet needs better than competitors.

In reality, Chris Basker's customer network is quite complex and requires considerable skill to manage and balance. You will also have spotted that he aims to raise customer service levels to 92 percent from 80 percent, the industry average. He feels that anything less than 90 percent is unacceptable in any industry, but that the cost of moving as high as 95 percent would involve carrying uneconomic levels of inventory. His plan to radically reduce the number of lines produced from 8K to 5K will certainly help him improve service levels, an issue he has already discussed with the Marketing Department.

Now let's look at our second example:

Jill Smith is going through a similar process as IT manager at another company, which is also in the middle of a major downsizing program. In Table 4-5, very briefly, are her old job objectives.

Table 4-5   Utopian Building Society: Previous Job Objectives

1. Reduce cost budget from $3.0 million to $2.5 million through automation
2. Maintain current levels of service and reliability
3. Upgrade computer capacity in 20 branches at a capital cost of $400,000
4. Develop software to handle new range of general insurance products for September launch.

Jill has developed a different set of objectives for the future (Table 4-6 on the next page).

Jill's previous job objectives were, like Chris Basker's, internally focused and cost-based, not customer driven. Their purpose was to do broadly the same things, but more efficiently and at less cost. Her new objectives do this too, but also meet customer needs better. The emphasis is concentrated on improving customer experiences, at minimal cost.

Integrated Job Specifications

Job objectives describe desired results over a specified period, usually one to several years.

Job specifications outline responsibilities, levels of authority, skills required, and reporting points. While job specifications

Table 4-6 Utopian Building Society: Tomorrow's Job Objectives

Customer definition and needs	
External customers • All existing Utopian consumers	*Needs* • Clear, accurate and timely information
Internal customers • Branch staff, Telesales, operators, Utopian commercial management	*Needs* • Customer profiles, history, current holdings

Objectives
1. Since Marketing Dept moving to life stage market segmentation, add life stage data to all consumer profiles.
2. Review competitor practice on IT, and improve upon it.
3. Integrate building society and direct marketing customer information bases, so that consumers can be managed consistently across trade channels.
4. Develop system for targeting best prospects for new range of general insurance products.
5. Review future IT needs of Utopian commercial management. Set up training and development plan.

will inevitably be descriptive, responsibilities should center on customers and costs as shown in the two examples described previously. Job specifications should not change often, but need to be regularly reviewed, in line with changes in customer needs and competitor performance.

Integrated Competency Development

Competency development needs to be looked at across departments, and fed into job objectives and specifications. For example, Chris and Jill's companies want to develop a core competency in Relationship Marketing, backed by powerful IT and data-mining capabilities across the organization. This clearly affects Jill Smith and is included in her new job objectives. People in Marketing, Branch Management, Finance, Product Design, and Direct Sales will *also* have objectives relevant to Relationship Marketing.

Having the capability to learn new processes, learn about and use new sources of information, and learn how to incorporate this into new ways that directly impact the consumer in positive ways is the challenge of the knowledge economy. Integrated competency development is at the core of creating a culture that stresses learning across the organization. Georg Von Krogh, Kazuo Ichijo, and Ikujiro Nonada have written a recent book in which they have identified five knowledge enablers—ranging from instilling a knowledge vision and mobilizing knowledge activists, to globalizing local knowledge. These enablers, and others like them, can help companies design practical tools for knowledge management and competency building despite historical organizational barriers.[3]

Integrated Performance Appraisal

Performance appraisal will monitor how well people are meeting their objectives. This means everyone will be evaluated on his or her contribution to superior customer value and profitability, the twin cornerstones of Offensive Marketing.

Integrated performance appraisal aligns everyone behind the "work" of the organization. This so-called "work" is communicated through the mission and vision statements discussed in Chapter 3 on Offensive Attitudes. Designing integrated performance appraisal throughout the organization is the task of the Human Resources Department in conjunction with the functional departments.

Integrated Rewards and Bonuses

These would be paid to all levels based on the achievement of agreed-upon objectives. This would further enhance the move to Integrated Marketing, as this example shows:

When former Boeing executive, Gordon Bethune, became Chief Executive of Continental Airlines, the company had suffered years of losses, downsizing, wage cuts, and reorganizations. He found demoralized employees bickering as planes departed half full and arrived late.

To persuade travelers that Continental would become a different airline, he decided he had first to convince its own employees. So he told all departments that they would be measured together on what mattered to customers most— punctuality.

Every department was required to approve the new timetable. Bethune promised that for each month Continental was in the top half of the federal government's on-time ranking, every employee would equally share half the savings

---

[3] Georg Von Krogh, Kazuo Ichijo, and Ikujiro Nonada, *Enabling Knowledge Creation: How to Unlock the Mystery of Tacit Knowledge and Release the Power of Innovation*, Oxford University Press, 2000.

of $6 million. This was what it had cost Continental each month to book delayed or stranded passengers on to other airlines.

By the second month of the offer, Continental had moved from last to first in the punctuality league table, and business passengers began returning. Share price rose nine-fold in 18 months. As a Continental baggage handler said: "Getting the plane off the gate isn't my job or your job. We act like it's everybody's job."[4]

The Continental example contrasts with conventionally ill-conceived incentive schemes, which handsomely reward senior management but provide little in the way of incentives for the vast majority of employees who, together, provide the core of Offensive Marketing initiatives and programs. The recent wave of accounting scandals has revealed the fallacy of awarding massive pay packages to poorly performing CEOs. This practice has demoralized investors, left dedicated and loyal employees without jobs, and weakened the economy. Providing integrated rewards and bonuses as incentives for performance that benefits the bottom line is not only opportune but also long overdue.

Implementing Integrated Marketing via Corporate Strategy

Integrated Marketing is a key concept for corporate strategic planning. Building superior customer value and above-average profits requires aligned program elements consistent with the five key tools discussed in this section. Creating job descriptions and objectives that contribute to customer value and long-term profit growth is not only logical but aligns employees' actions, responsibilities, and accountability with overall corporate goals. Employees see the daily effect and more long-term integrated results from having their work aligned with co-workers, departments, and across the organization. Less frustration and more "big picture" effort can be interwoven along lines of accountability. Job specifications, including required skills and responsibilities, necessarily focus on the customer and the costs of providing a satisfying purchase or experience. This goes far in turning employees' attention toward the market and the customer experience.

---

[4] Derived from an article in the *Wall Street Journal Europe*: Scott McCartney, "Back on Course," *The Wall Street Journal*, May 21, 1996.

The development of organizational competencies flows directly from corporate strategic planning. Identifying those unique competencies, which must reside in employees' knowledge base and their technical resources, is a prime objective of overall corporate planning. The development of these should be cross-departmental and cross-functional and be relevant to Relationship Marketing in its fullest context.

Integrated performance appraisal itself synchronizes the efforts organizationally on the customer's total experience in dealing with the company and in providing value from the customer's perspective. Lastly, integrated rewards and bonuses throughout all levels of the organization provide meaningful incentives toward an Integrated Marketing approach. A scheme of integrated rewards and bonuses provides the visibility, consistency, and logic to those whose efforts are rewarded and to those who aren't.

BARRIERS TO INTEGRATED MARKETING

Chrysler historically provides a good example of the "disintegration" of market-facing initiatives and also demonstrates the barriers that continue while attempting an Integrated Marketing Approach. When Lee Iacocca joined Chrysler, he soon concluded that, "All Chrysler's problems really boiled down to the same thing. There was no team, only a collection of independent players."

He discovered weaknesses in financial planning and projecting. "Even the most rudimentary questions were impossible for them to answer."

Equally serious, the factories were producing to schedules not related to customer or dealer demand, with the result that there were massive inventories and monthly "fire" sales, to reduce excess stocks.

The system worked like this: "At regular intervals, the Manufacturing Division would tell the Sales Division how many and what types of vehicles they were going to produce. Then it would be up to the Sales Division to sell them…to dealers…. It had nothing to do with a customer ordering what he wanted on the car, or a dealer ordering what the customer was likely to ask for."[5]

There are many reasons why companies do not follow the Integrated Marketing Approach. Here are six of the most common.

---

[5] Lee Iacocca, *Iacocca: An Autobiography*, Sidgwick & Jackson, 1985.

1. **Not putting the customer first.** The first is also the most obvious. Businesses that are not close to the customer have not taken the first step on the road to Offensive Marketing, and are therefore in no position to achieve the Integrated Marketing approach. Many of these industries have suffered historically from a lack of competition and now find themselves in a tougher deregulated environment. Examples include telecommunications, transportation, public utilities, and banks.

   Some businesses that have not been close to the consumer are dot.com companies that have experienced a debilitating lack of fortunes as the dot.com bubble burst, and which, in retrospect, were more interested in IPOs than in developing tangible markets and business plans to sustain their creative business efforts. Many of these companies did not shift their focus from revenue to profits or value capture soon enough and instead followed what was a flawed strategy—business determined by scope or scale.

   Sam Walton, founder of Wal-Mart, the world's largest retailer, summed up the Integrated Marketing approach succinctly:

   "We put the customer ahead of everything else...if you're not serving the customer, or supporting the folks who do, then we don't need you."[6]

   By putting the customer first, Wal-Mart created competitive advantage by reaching an efficient scale in their business model. Lowe's and Home Depot have followed similar business models.

2. **Failure to implement.** A second barrier to Integrated Marketing is top management's failure to implement their verbal commitment to improvements. They say one thing, and then do another as in this example:

   The Board was reasonably committed to the idea of improving product quality and some members, including the Chairman, advocated this strongly to employees. At the same time, it was pushing hard on cost reduction, with impressive success. However, the pressure for short-term profits made it impossible to invest sufficiently in measures to improve quality. Indeed, some cost cuts affected quality negatively. Those responsible for improving quality became discouraged at the gap between top management's statements and actions.

---

[6] Sam Walton and John Huey, *Sam Walton: Made in America*, Doubleday, 1992.

3. **Lack of consensus.** A third barrier is lack of consensus on important matters of strategy at the Board level. This can prove a decisive barrier to integration, since it spawns disruption and division—what Field Marshal Montgomery described as "poor atmosphere." However, it may prove to be only a temporary barrier if the disagreements are resolved prior to implementation.

4. **Undermining.** The fourth barrier exists where a company has a clear marketing-led strategy, but integration is undermined by demarcation disputes or personal rivalries. The following example, from one of the author's experiences, will ring a bell with many marketers:

> The Managing Director of this subsidiary of a global firm reported to the President in New York. His Manufacturing Director reported on paper directly to him but had a strong link with the Vice President, Worldwide Operations, also located in New York. Both American-based executives were of equal status, and pursued a strong but muted rivalry.
>
> The Sales and Marketing team had been strengthened and made some good moves. As a result, volume of orders improved by 35 percent over a 12-month period. Unfortunately, the factories could not meet this sales requirement, partly because sales forecasting was weak, but mainly because manufacturing never seemed to be able to achieve planned production levels —"a sustained record of failure," as the Sales Director acidly observed. Furthermore, management in New York showed a marked reluctance to commit to any large increase in capacity in case business gains proved only temporary.
>
> Short or late delivery to customers had become the norm. Although the Managing Director spent three days a month personally chairing all production planning and sales forecasting meetings, he had little leverage over his Manufacturing Director, who was reporting back to his boss in the U.S. Production blamed Sales and Marketing for poor sales forecasting; Marketing blamed Production for failure to hit promised production schedules and inability to increase capacity.
>
> The situation was exacerbated by the "contribution" of staff groups and task forces from the corporate office in New York. In no time there were, in effect, two companies: Sales/Marketing/Finance on the one hand, Production on the other. What should have been a Marketing-led volume and profit breakthrough by a highly capable team deteriorated into backbiting and, ultimately, customer dissatisfaction.

5. **Tubular bell effect.** The fifth barrier is similar to the "undermining" barrier where it is the customer's experience that ultimately suffers. The "tubular bells" effect exists where each

department reports upward with little contact between them, their communications only meeting at the Chief Executive level. Interdepartmental discord rarely occurs openly, since there is insufficient contact to make it heard. But when it does occur, it clangs up and down the tubes, since no one at a lower level has the authority to create harmony. The net result is that the customer is left on the sidelines.

6. **Technology.** The sixth barrier to Integrated Marketing can be technology itself. In rapidly expanding markets like telecommunications, information technology, or software, technology investment is often pursued for its own sake, rather than as a way to better serve the customer. Take customer relationship management (CRM) as an example. Because a technology breakthrough can have a transforming effect on a business, there is a temptation, especially in high-tech sectors, to neglect the study of consumer needs and invest in the technology with little understanding of its actual ROI or synergy with existing business practices or future needs.

   This is what happened in the CRM market in the late 1990s. CRM applications were purchased to "remain competitive" but with little understanding of an integrated one-to-one marketing approach. With customers' expectations quickly rising, companies were quick to respond with technology, ubiquitous tools, and services. However, new technology—such as call centers, the Internet, and automated voice systems—have been used to cut cost for the most part rather than to improve CRM and service. Until these CRM facilities get integrated with overall company strategy and its particular ways of doing business, customers often find the results frustrating and disappointing. Simultaneously, companies often find the ROI of these initiatives unpredictable at best.

THE MARKETING DEPARTMENT'S ROLE IN ACHIEVING INTEGRATION

There is no perfect analogy to illuminate the workings of the Marketing Department. Opponents of the Offensive Marketing approach might suggest that the octopus—with its eight suckered arms around a mouth—provides a close likeness. But probably the best analogy is the one that relates the Marketing Department to the orchestral conductor. Although this is flattering to Marketing because of the conductor's leadership position on the rostrum, the image may give a glamour and status out of proportion to a marketer's true authority or actual contribution in conjunction with an integrated effort.

What the marketing person and the conductor have in common is a program whose execution depends on the combined efforts of a number of specialists. In the case of the conductor, these are instrumentalists; for marketers, they are design engineers, production managers, operations people, accountants, sales people, copywriters, and researchers.

Neither the symphony orchestra nor the marketing plan will succeed unless specialists clearly understand their roles and how these roles relate to the roles of others. Equally, the failure of specialists to perform effectively can sabotage the whole program. It follows that, like the conductor, marketers must know their overall objectives, and inform, motivate, and coordinate the myriad of specialists in order to achieve integrated results.

Marketers therefore depend heavily on colleagues in other departments, over whom they have no direct authority. To be a successful marketing executive, one really needs to know how to motivate people. The Offensive Marketer occupies many roles, as decision-maker, recommender, coordinator, motivator, adviser, evaluator, liaison, and leader. In each situation, the marketer has to know what role to play and the nuances of how to play it most effectively. In light of the many faceted roles of a marketer, it is no wonder that typical marketing executives have too little time for their strategic and important role as leader. With this in mind, management skills are equally important as marketing skills to the successful Offensive Marketer.

To be more effective as integrators in future, Offensive Marketing executives will have to raise their personal skills and involvement dramatically in six areas:

1. **Strong involvement in developing corporate strategy and planning.** Marketers are best placed to lead the process. Their frequent failure to do so is more often due to lack of time and priority than to any Machiavellian plotting by the Finance Department or others.

2. **Upgrading people skills.** Many high-level people-management skills are required by marketing executives. These include, to name a few, the ability to motivate, persuade, and describe, or to be a team member, visionary, and creative agent. Unfortunately, the relatively arcane skill of managing and motivating people across departments is given little emphasis in either marketing training or personnel appraisals. The result is a strategic weakness in both cross-departmental integration and project management.

3. **Broadening knowledge base.** Tomorrow's successful marketing executives will need to develop much deeper knowledge of Technology, Finance, Engineering, and Operations, in order to work most effectively across departments. The knowledge itself need not be overly deep, but should be sufficient for a meaningful dialogue and understanding among colleagues.

4. **Resuming the role of innovators and entrepreneurs.** This is the most important task of the Marketing Department, but is increasingly neglected as the volume of routine tasks multiplies in our current business environment.

5. **Developing a cross-departmental style.** Marketers have a responsibility to keep everyone in the company fully informed about the marketplace, by word of mouth, e-mail, web-enabled communication tools, newsletters, presentations, and even informally, giving recognition to others for successes in the process. Company-wide intranets, e-mail, and video-conferencing make these tasks more efficient and widespread.

6. **Staying in marketing jobs longer.** Fast rotation of marketers through marketing jobs is a long-standing and perennial problem in corporate America. Few marketing people hold the same job within a company for more than two years. This brevity of tenure, which does not apply in any other department, is damaging both to Marketing Departments and to their contribution to the Integrated Marketing approach.

PRACTICAL TOOLS FOR ACHIEVING INTEGRATED MARKETING

Reaching a state of Integrated Marketing is mainly a matter of vision, structure, strategy, and attitude, initially led by the

Board and supported by its mandates. However, on a tactical level, certain practical tools can be helpful:

1. **Move people across departments.** This is common in Japan but uncommon in Europe and the United States, where people change companies more often. Lateral departmental moves can be short or long term. Some successful marketers have a production background and engineering qualifications. The roles of Sales and Marketing Departments are converging as channels become more complex and customers more powerful. Lateral moves across departments have the beneficial effects of broadening individual experience as well as breaking down barriers between functional silos as more people get to know and dialogue with each other.

2. **Meet customers and consumers in person.** There are many ways to do this time efficiently. A day with a field sales person, or a couple of hours listening in to telemarketing calls, is always highly educational, whether you are a plant manager, a warehouse supervisor, or a credit clerk. Historically, the assumption has been that meeting customers is something that only management does (or fails to do). If you believe that everyone is a marketer, it follows that everyone should spend some allotted time with customers to facilitate an understanding of the customer experience.

3. **Communicate openly and honestly.** This is a sound everyday principle, and modern technology has made it cost effective and feasible. Many larger companies are setting up their own TV channels or web capabilities, where executives can report progress or outline future plans at given times to either a section of employees or to the whole company, either simultaneously or in an employee's own time. Intercompany e-mail, e-newsletters, and video conferencing are all relatively recent new tools. It should be noted that open communication is not dependent on modern technology, but arises out of a commitment to integrated communication throughout the organization.

4. **Spread bonuses fairly and widely.** Widespread recent events arising out of the dot.com bubble have shown that payments of disproportionately high bonuses to senior executives have replaced the old style executive dining room as a divisive factor in companies. Such policies assume that a few strategic decisions and deals, made by senior management, are the decisive factors in business success. Not so. While strategies are important,

attitudes across the company, teamwork, and effective implementation by all employees are most critical in ensuring long-term success. Integrated performance appraisals and integrated rewards and bonuses are the tools for spreading incentives fairly and widely.

5. **Locate all departments on the same site**. Integration across departments works best on single sites, preferably centered in Operations. Although this is not always possible, the breakdown of companies into dedicated business units is making it more feasible. Proximity to Operations enables the Marketing Department to understand and integrate internal competencies better. However, new communications and information technologies are making this requirement less important as voice data, including full motion video, and transportation technologies continue to shrink the barrier that distance imposes on communications and integration.

6. **Organize large companies into smaller business units.** Wherever possible, break down big companies into business units, with their own divisions of Operations, Sales, Finance, and Marketing Departments. A minimum size of perhaps $50–60 million is often needed in order to achieve the necessary economies of Operations and Manufacturing, and to justify the overheads of separate Sales and Finance Departments. This minimum will differ widely by industry, and would obviously be much higher for vehicle manufacturers or durable goods companies. Business units work best with their own dedicated operations, where they control all their costs, very much like autonomous companies.

Although the company that Jack Welch built is an old-fashioned conglomerate, which significantly increased in size after its acquisition of Honeywell (and with it AlliedSignal), Jeffrey Immelt, the new CEO of GE, speaks about GE global business:

"We're a $130 billion growth business because we don't run it as a $130 billion blob. We run it as a $10 billion medical business, a $1 billion ultrasound business. We know how to get double-digit growth in this environment."[7]

The big advantages of business units are speed of decision-making, teamwork, commitment, and integration. Managers that tend to understand the business well communicate with

---

[7] "A Talk with Jeff Immelt," *Business Week*, January 28, 2002.

each other often. This effectively removes barriers between depart-ments and cuts bureaucratic decision-making time. Synergies between units can be built upon and successes at one unit can be melded into another. Take, for example, GE's present synergies existing in its aerospace units after its purchase of Honeywell, which enables it to cross-sell and market other products and services to its large customers such as Boeing. In addition, GE's past successes with Six Sigma, the manufacturing-efficiency pro-gram, which have been brought into Honeywell's operations, can increase productivity by curtailing operational inefficiencies and add to GE's bottom line. The most positive results from these operational synergies will arise only with effective and inte-grating communications, both at a personal and at an organiza-tional level.

A TEST FOR TOTAL MARKETING INTEGRATION

Table 4-7 provides a total Marketing Integration score sheet for a company to test its ability to implement a total Marketing Integration program. You will notice that slightly different weights are given to different elements of the scoring sheet.

Table 4-7   Total Marketing Integration Score Sheet

Topic	Maximum score
Does the Board understand and stress the total Marketing approach?	15
Is there a corporate strategy with convincing vision, priorities, and strategies?	10
Was this developed on a genuine cross-departmental basis?	10
Are there agreed strategies for quality, value, innovation, competencies, and attitudes?	10
Are these understood and acted upon by every department?	10
Is the Marketing Department active as an integrator and evangelist?	8
Has every employee identified his/her customers and really understood their needs?	10
Are job objectives and specifications customer driven, consumer focused, and competitive?	10
Are job objectives, appraisals, and rewards fully aligned?	10
Are key integration tools being used?	7
Total	100

CONCLUSION

This chapter has been about how to make Integrated Marketing an everyday reality instead of something that companies talk about but actually do little with. Unfortunately, *integration* has become a "buzz" word with little substance. As this chapter has shown, there is much substance to an Integrated Marketing approach where all employees and partners recognize the needs of their internal and external customers and align their actions with customer-driven job objectives that mesh with overall company goals.

It is through an Integrated Marketing approach with identifiable strategies and tactics that superior customer value is created at minimum cost. Once the principles of integrated marketing are understood and communicated, formulating a corporate strategy that integrates department and job objectives, builds on competency development, and provides tactics for achieving an Integrated Marketing approach across the organization, can be designed and implemented. Barriers to achieving Integrated Marketing can be identified and addressed. Throughout this process, Offensive Marketers have a leadership and facilitating role in setting key plans and milestones.

To take a strategic approach, you have to first set the groundwork. The next chapter, Conducting Offensive Business Analysis, is the first chapter of four addressing the "S" of POISE: the strategic element whereby a company conducts the analysis that leads to winning strategies.

5 Strategic Offensive Business Analysis: The "S" in POISE

INTRODUCTION

Offensive business analysis is the foundation on which to build future strategies and plans. This is the first chapter of four that address the "S" of POISE—Strategic. Winning strategies are a necessity for any business that plans to succeed. Rarely do winning strategies develop in a flash of inspiration; more often, they evolve over time, as a result of trial and error and rigorous business analysis. That business analysis—where a company is presently and where it intends to go in the future—is the focal point of this chapter by addressing customer needs, competitive positioning, and the overall business environment.

Business analysis is a prerequisite to identifying objectives, which, in turn, describe the desired destination. Strategies and plans describe the route and vehicles necessary for attaining those objectives.

THE THREE STAGES OF BUSINESS STRATEGY

Effective action is usually preceded by logical steps, which may be elaborately documented or followed intuitively. These steps are outlined as the objectives, the strategy, and the plan:

1. **Objectives describe destinations ("Where are we going?").** They are usually stated in terms of revenue and profit, and should be quantifiable and measurable.
2. **Strategies set out the route or the means for achieving the objective ("How do we get there?").** Often a number of alternative strategies are evaluated before a final one is chosen.
3. **Plans constitute the vehicle for getting to the destination ("What's the plan for getting there?").** Plans form the detailed execution of the strategy.

These three simple steps, followed in order, provide the framework for decision-making. Simple and yet all too often we find executives who have lapsed into detailed discussions of plans and ideas before they have first agreed on objectives or strategies.

Xerox's recent turnaround efforts provide an example of a well thought out and sequential strategic approach.

In the 1970s Xerox had dot.com like valuations. Over the last three decades however, the company failed to capitalize on its technologies, lagged behind its Japanese competitors, and made acquisitions in the financial services sector that cost it time and money. In its heyday, it was another Cisco Systems, at full strength with strong technology and dominant in its market.

Xerox soon became a victim of its own success in the copier market, failing to spur new growth as the copier business matured and new competitors emerged. Disruptive technology was not the problem: copier business thinking dominated resource allocation and growth strategies. The company boggled its digital future by underestimating the market power of the inkjet printer. Hewlett-Packard created a profitable division around the inkjet printer, which is now larger than Xerox itself.

Under then CEO Paul A. Allaire, Xerox staged a grand comeback capturing back its copier franchise and heading into the digital marketplace. In 1998, it had record operating profits of $2.7 billion, up 18 percent from 1997. By 1999, however, success had blinded it to the threat of desktop printers, which enabled Microsoft and Electronic Data Systems Corporation to make huge inroads in the office technology market.

Prior CEO Richard Thoman's strategy, in the late 1990s, was to create industry-based solutions, similar to the IBM model that addressed the digitized office challenge. His objective was to take Xerox to the next level and to help it become a stable and healthy company.[1] "We're positioning ourselves around knowledge and the document is the DNA of knowledge." They implemented plans that included reorganizing the sales force into teams targeted to the needs of specific industries, cost cutting initiatives, and acquiring XLConnect, adding skill and knowledge resources to integrate copiers and printers with other office technology.

Despite set backs, including culture issues and an imperiled liquidity crisis in the latter part of 2000, this strategy continues with new CEO Anne Mulcahy's early tenure. Despite the strategic error of spending heavily to challenge HP after the fact, and with Ricoh Company and Canon continuing to nibble away at Xerox's market for super-fast commercial printers, Xerox continues to implement its strategies and plans for a sustained upturn in growth, cutting its losses and refocusing on its people, customers, and new products.

Xerox must now change the way it accounts for equipment leasing revenue and restate its earnings from 1997–2000. It continues to clean house by cutting jobs and divesting itself of businesses that are draining cash. It has farmed out functions that can be better done by others, including much of its manufacturing. A new joint venture with GE Capital will handle customer administration and provide financing.

GE Capital has also brought Six Sigma to Xerox with fifteen quality projects being worked on as of mid-2002. Most importantly, though, it has repaired some organizational glitches. For example, although sales representatives continue to be responsible for specific industries, sales representatives for less expensive office machines are back to their customary routes and relationships.

---

[1] See, "Xerox, Can New CEO Rick Thoman Turn its Digital Dreams into Reality?," *Business Week*, April 12, 1999.

These current efforts support CEO Mulcahy's objective of strengthening customer relationships and the Xerox brand name. Indicative of what might be Xerox's future strategy, it has quietly reduced the size of the words "The Document Company" in its logo, with the aim of perhaps shifting the image away from copying and printing toward the storage and management of data. In fact, Xerox Global Services, formed in the fall of 2001, has as its business goal to create and sell packages of document processing and storage services that used to be free to equipment customers.[2]

Both Xerox's failure and success provide examples of how instrumental strategy, objectives, and planning are to timely responsiveness and growth-oriented initiatives. They also prove that no matter how brilliant or lifeless a strategy is, its ongoing *execution* (the "E" of POISE) is pivotal to many elements of success. Xerox's failures in the past have been, in many ways, a result of the inability to execute, and its successes in the future will arise out of both strong execution and well-chosen strategic direction.

STRATEGIES—AREN'T THEY RATHER ACADEMIC?

Strategies are sometimes viewed as too academic and further, that any discussion that does not relate to immediate action is theoretical and therefore of no value. Xerox's failure to take decisive strategic action at times over the past three decades has led to some close calls with only bankruptcy protection as a safety net.

Strategies are academic in the sense that their development arises from a close analysis of all relevant facts and the conclusions drawn from them. There was nothing academic about the results achieved by Johnson & Johnson, Merck, IBM, Microsoft, Federal Express, Visa, Sony, and Amazon.com. These companies' every success was enhanced by strategies that accompanied every major initiative, from new products, markets, and delivery systems to their entry into new countries.

A good strategy will give a clear indication of direction but allows variety in its execution. For example, a company's product strategy may be to achieve and maintain performance and styling

---

[2] "At Xerox, the Chief Earns (Grudging) Respect," *The New York Times*, June 2, 2002.

superiority over all brands in the same price bracket. The detailed ways in which this can be executed are infinite and offer great flexibility. But there would be no flexibility to market a parity performance product. In this sense, strategy does limit freedom to maneuver but that is its objective: to limit choice and direct decision-making.

The criticism that strategies are too time-consuming is based on the need for discussion with a large number of people in many departments. But such criticism is misplaced.

Strategies are fundamental to Integrated Marketing. Wide-ranging discussion across departments is essential to achieve an integrated approach. The very fact that strategies create controversy is a sound reason for giving them visibility and voice. It is much better to resolve disagreements early than to ignore them and risk slowing down action initiatives.

A strategy serves as a basis of agreement for all parties with respect to the goals toward which effort is to be directed, and helps ensure coordinated action. If there is no agreed strategy, the action taken may reflect varying assumptions as to how the objective is to be achieved. This zigzag course may result in a loss of time, resources, and money.

A cohesive well-conceived strategy forces management to ruthlessly prune the less vital goals of the business. If a strategy has been painful to determine, it is more than likely a good one.

REQUIREMENTS FOR EFFECTIVE ANALYSIS

A well-known text for young lawyers points out that native grit is even more important than native wit. In other words, thorough preparation matters more than the occasional brilliant insight. In any case, the two usually go together.

The same applies to the development of strategy. Strategy development is hard work and most successful when proceeded by rigorous business analysis, where every relevant fact and number is cross-examined in a disciplined sequence.

Table 5-1 summarizes the benefits of disciplined business analysis.

Effective analysis is comparable to a manufacturing process. It selects relevant data, converts it into knowledge, and finally into understanding, the end product of analysis. As with manufacturing, the quality of raw materials and care in processing are

Table 5-1 The Benefits of Disciplined Business Analysis

Benefits of doing	Penalties for not doing
• Understanding of business • Control of business • Quick/correct tactical decisions • Basis for clear strategy • Put pressure on competition • Spot opportunities early	• Lots of undigested data • Always firefighting • Inconsistent tactical decisions • Reaction strategy • Always taking pressure • Late with innovations
↓ ‹Leader›	↓ ‹Follower›

essential for a good result. Business analysis is a continuous sequential process (Figure 5-1).

We are living in the days of a data glut. Marketers and all others in the corporate environment often flounder beneath a torrent of information. For a company to turn the tide of this information blitz in its favor, it would need to ensure that the routine paperwork from sales, profit by product and account, market analysis, service levels, and so on arrives on employees' desks in usable form.

Producers of routine reports like Finance, Sales, Administration, and the Marketing Departments tend to be production orientated and therefore the recipients of these routine reports need to make it known exactly what they want and in what form.

Effective analysis has only one purpose—and that is action. Sometimes analysis becomes an end in itself leading to stagnation.

Figure 5-1
The Wheel of Analysis

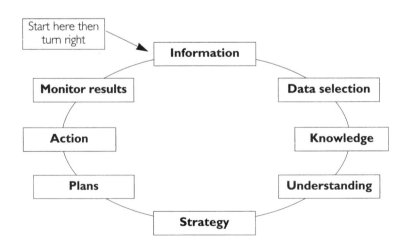

There are six requirements for effective analysis, as shown in Table 5-2.

Table 5-2 Six Requirements for Effective Analysis

1. Right data
2. Systematic approach
3. Focused approach
4. Thorough and probing
5. Must lead to action
6. Continuous improvement

Right Data

Data needs to be organized in a user-friendly way. Modern IT systems have the potential to achieve this but often fail to do so. In most companies, IT systems are set up by the Finance or Accounting Department and are designed for control purposes rather than enlightenment. Providing actionable management information tends to be a secondary consideration.

Offensive Marketers need to take a strong line on this, and insist that they are provided with quality sales and profit data by distribution channel, category, brand, and major account. They also need to think very carefully about whom to target in data-based customer relationship programs, what type of information they need by customer, and how the data is used. These are important building blocks for decisions on resource allocation in many areas.

Quality information is not easy to develop, but should be made available if serious planning is to result.

Systematic Approach

Quality data consists of "must have" external data as well as certain selected internal data. Categories of "must have" data are summarized in Table 5-3.

Focused Approach

A common error is to analyze every piece of available data, build up a massive business review, and then ask the question,

Table 5-3   "Must-Have" Data Check List

Market data	Internal data
• Market size and trend	• Overall sales, costs, profits
• Key segments	• Sales, profit breakdowns by market segment,
• Key channels, size, and trend	channel, brand, account, and customer
• Key account analyses	type
• Brand shares by market, channel,	• Marketing spend overall and by activity
customer	• Summary of direct marketing data
• Customer demographics and loyalty	• Volume sensitivity analyses, e.g. effect of
• Customer usage, attitudes, retention	*+20 percent* and *–20 percent* in sales,
• Competitor shares	on profits
• Brand shares by region	• Brand histories
• Marketing spend by brand	• Price movements and elasticity
• Channel and account margins	• Customer relationship monitors
• Size of product ranges	
• New product success/failure	

"What action can we take based on this review?" Unfortunately, the answer often is, "Not much." This approach has two drawbacks. First, so much energy is put into the analysis that little is left for strategy and action. Second, and most frustrating of all, the analysis may uncover few opportunities for action.

In sharp contrast stands the focused approach to data analysis. Before starting any analysis, write down a list of possible hypotheses for an action. Then work out the data needed to prove or disprove these hypotheses. To begin with, your list of hypotheses will be quite long, perhaps ten or fifteen ideas. You will find that some of these can be quickly screened out as the process continues.

In addition, as the analysis proceeds, you are likely to develop new hypotheses to add to the original list. Your aim will be to finish the analysis with three or five hypotheses for new initiatives still intact. These will form the basis for a revised set of strategies and plans.

Table 5-4 gives a list of possible hypotheses you might draw up if you were Marketing Director of a leading airline. For the sake of brevity, only four will be listed, though in practice, you would aim to start with a lot more.

This example demonstrates the "focused approach," which enables you to concentrate on data that may be dynamic, highly relevant and help you to avoid wasting time on dead-end analysis.

Table 5-4 Possible "Starting" List of Hypotheses for a Major Airline Carrier

Hypotheses	Data needed to prove/disprove
1. We need a European partner	• Estimated additional revenue through code sharing with Euro partner • Review of possible partners
2. We should upgrade our economy-class product	• Review sales and profits of own economy class • Compare proposition with competitors • Analyze differences by route length, purpose of travel
3. We may need to start or buy a discount airline	• Range of likely sales and economics • Review research on competitor discount airlines • Analyze comparative prices, occupancy levels
4. We should increase our customer relationship activity	• Analyze past results by frequency of travel and class • Review competitor activity—database size, quality; segmentation method; club and loyalty propositions; strategy, spend

Thorough and Probing

By limiting the total amount of data reviewed, you will be able to consider the material you do review in greater depth. The real answer to many issues may be buried two or three levels down in the inquiry, and may not be visible to the inexperienced eye. Like peeling an onion, you need to patiently peel off each layer until you get to the core, asking questions like:

- How good is the quality of this data?
- Is it consistent with my own experience or with common sense?
- Is it consistent with other information from different sources? If not, what are the reasons for the differences?
- Does external market, consumer panel, or customer data conform to internal sales data? If not, why not?

Lead Toward Action

This is fully covered in the previous sections. There are people who are very good at analysis, but have great difficulty in making decisions or taking action. Analysis without action is an ineffective half of the equation.

Continuous Improvement

Good online IT systems enable effective analysis to be treated as a continuous process rather than something done once or twice a year. Continuous updating makes analysis more actionable and reduces the workload peak during the strategic planning process as well as the yearly budgeting season.

THE FIVE-STEP PROCESS FOR STRATEGIC ANALYSIS

While there are many ways of approaching this, Offensive Marketers usually adopt a five-step sequence, as set out in Figure 5-2.

1. The analysis of the business environment involves looking at the direct, indirect, and macro factors affecting the business now and in the future.
2. The internal examination is a medical check of the business, involving a great deal more probing than the often informally conducted typical executive check-up.
3. The competitive analysis defines the company's competitors, evaluates what they are doing both well and poorly, and postulates what actions they are likely to undertake in the future.
4. Key factors for success lists the things that really matter in the company's markets and identifies the priority areas for building competitive advantages.
5. The SWOT analysis pulls together the whole exercise, and involves a listing of the company's Strengths and Weaknesses, plus the Opportunities and Threats facing the firm.

Figure 5-2

Five-Step Process for Strategic Analysis

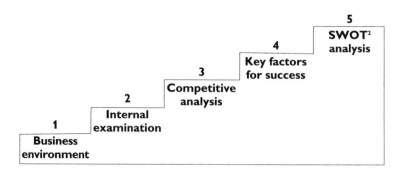

Figure 5-3

The Three Wheels of the Business Environment

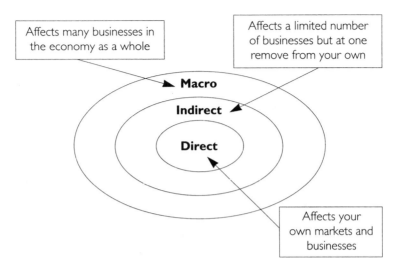

Step 1: The Three Wheels of the Business Environment

Figure 5-3 divides the business environment into three wheels that represent the macro, indirect, and direct factors that affect business. Macro is symbolized by the outside ring, with the main effects of macro factors usually less immediate than direct effects like price changes or product improvements made by major competitors.

The elements covered by the macro and direct circles are straightforward. The indirect circle requires further explanation. It includes businesses that intrude on the edge of your company's territory, although they are not direct competitors. It also covers related markets that are noncompetitive, but whose success greatly affects your own. For example, sales of agricultural equipment are heavily affected by the profitability of farming. Equally, changing fashions in outerwear influence the styles of lingerie women require.

Use the three circles as a stimulus for thinking about the shape of your company's markets in three to five years time. What are the key drivers for change? What effect will they have? Asking questions like these will lead your business toward its vision of the future, and a view with respect to differing scenarios is likely to emerge. It is to be noted that the solid lines surrounding each

121

circle are misleading in their air of certainty. Indirect factors often leak into or even crash through the direct circle, and the placement of factors within circles often changes. For instance, in Figure 5-3, the falling cost of IT and "declining customer loyalty," which would both fit within the macro circle, represent an opportunity for enhanced Relationship Marketing within the direct circle.

There are also linkages between circles and action time frames. Direct factors are more likely to have a short-term impact on sales and profits than macro factors, which tend to have longer-term impact. However, these linkages can change rapidly or morph over time with respect to their influence.

Step 2: The Internal Examination

Like a health check, the internal examination should be formally carried out once a year. The best time to do it is a couple of months before the annual update of the strategic plan, which itself should precede formulation of the budget for the following year.

The crux of this internal examination is a factual analysis of the business. Managers are then able to ask a number of candid questions about past performance, attitudes, strategy, and quality of execution. The answers to these questions provide new insights into the strengths and weaknesses of your company's internal competencies and their contribution to the firm's products or services.

The factual analysis of the business also enables you to look at the past year's events and put them into perspective. Simultaneously, it is one of the strongest tools you have for ensuring that the marketing approach permeates the whole business, since, as part of the internal examination, you will also be reviewing selling, operations, and financial factors that affect your firm's overall competitive position.

Figure 5-4 illustrates the sequence of this combination of analysis and the ensuing questions and answers. The internal examination is divided into five audit areas: knowledge, performance, attitudes, strategy, and execution.

Let's take a quick look at each of the stages of the internal examination set forth in Figure 5-4.

1. **Knowledge.** Number crunching, thinking, and discussion with colleagues, partners, and customers will be involved, and will probably absorb two-thirds to three-quarters of the total time

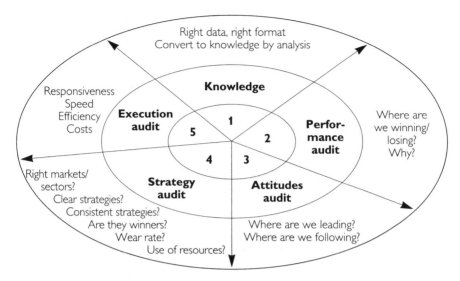

Figure 5-4 *Model of Internal Examination*

spent on internal examination. The objective of this stage is to convert facts and knowledge into understanding through analysis. The six requirements for effective analysis, summarized in Table 5-2, should provide a useful guide in collecting the right information. The information is likely to be a bundle of facts, opinions, and hypotheses. The challenge is to use them in the most appropriate way.

This first stage in the process is very important, since it provides the basis of knowledge for making analyses and judgments in the next four stages. It certainly makes sense to look ahead to the questions you and others will be asking during Stages 2 to 5, to ensure that the basis of knowledge and understanding accumulated in Stage 1 can provide the framework for future judgments.

2. **Performance audit.** Where are we winning? Where are we losing and why? During this stage, as in most of the others, you will probably be focusing on markets, channels, consumers, customers, products, innovation, and profits. For example, you may find that you are winning with a stream of successful new products, but not making the most of them because you are losing on distribution and customer service. Alternatively, your

short-term profit performance may look like a winning hand, but you know you are losing long term with few innovation initiatives and declining customer loyalty.

3. **Attitudes audit.** This will provide some important pointers as to how far you are pursuing the Offensive Marketing approach. The overriding question is whether you are leading the market or following your competitors. Consider some of the following questions:

   How do some of the more recent hires to your company feel about working in the company? Is it a fun place to work?

   Is the company making progress and moving forward with new initiatives in the marketplace? Does it seem to know where it is going?

   If you overheard a conversation, would your staff be caught bragging about perks like daycare, partner benefits, and the comfort and joy of non-working weekends? Or would the conversation be more discouraging, perhaps even referring a friend elsewhere for work opportunities?

   On the other end of the spectrum, is the company going beyond meeting the needs of customers by delighting them with new offerings and service?

4. **Strategy audit.** Building on the previous three stages, you will now want to consider some fundamental questions:

   Are main strategies working or not?

   Which are working best and which is a disaster?

   Are the company's strategies gaining momentum or wearing out? Have they been consistent or are they being changed needlessly? Have these strategies been properly considered in a way that aligns company competencies with marketplace opportunities?

5. **Execution audit.** Companies should aim to win on quality of strategy as well as quality of execution. Although this may not always be possible, excellent execution can often transform an average strategy into a winning formula for success. Poor execution may be the reason that a great strategy ultimately fails.

   This fifth stage concentrates on a few key execution elements such as responsiveness both to customer needs and to competitor initiative, speed, efficiency, and relative cost position. The areas to focus on will obviously depend on the company's type of business and the key factors for success in it.

Clearly, speed to market with new products is much more important in the software and financial industries than in the home furnishings or wine industries.

Five Examples of Internal Examination

Internal examination has many facets to it. Here are five examples:

1. **Sales trend audit.** An analysis has been done identifying sources of growth, by type of account and products, comparing overall sales with brand share.

   The analysis shows that all growth has come from new accounts and a recently launched line extension. However, trade stocks of the brand are heavy because of a year-end deal promotion, in light of the fact that the line extension was not selling out. Sales grew but brand share grew less in a static market.

   The difference represents inventory build-up by the trade. Next year, retailers are likely to cut back on inventory. Budgeted growth from the analysis for next year looks ambitious. Indeed, next year's budget as planned may be quite unrealistic; here, you would do well to hold volume, never mind increase it. The obvious lesson: never take total sales figures at face value. They should be broken down and further analyzed. Different causal factors point to different strategies.

2. **Industry capacity analysis.** This analysis is equally relevant to both a manufacturing and service business as an indicator of future price trends.

   A typical market historically grows fast, attracts new competitors who build extra capacity, and then matures to zero growth. The future in such a market is one of intense price competition since future industry production is much greater than the market requires. Only a competitor whose brand is very distinctive may be set to do well.

3. **Competitive position audit.** This is one of the most useful audits. The technique is to list the main consumer or customer needs in your market, score them in order of importance, and then rank your brand or company performance on each need. The basis for building this hierarchy of customer needs is a combination of research, knowledge, and judgment and is very

informative about future possible courses of action, both as to your firm's strategy and your competitors.

4. **Innovation audit.** There are two aspects to consider with respect to innovation. The first is output, or the number of your company's innovations that reach the market. The second is success rate. Your firm may have a high percentage success rate, but if the company's total output is low, innovation performance is not satisfactory.

However, be cautious of cannibalization of existing products by new ones. For example, a company with 25 percent of current sales in products launched in the past five years would appear to be innovating well. However, if half of the new product sales have been taken from existing ones, a much smaller percentage of sales may be incremental and therefore sales innovation may be weaker and payback on new products may have actually worsened.

A key action to take to address possible cannibalization is to improve understanding of market segmentation and to target new products at segments where the company is relatively weak in order to boost incremental new revenue.

5. **Customer relationship audit.** The issue is to identify the kind of information your company needs in order to build a customer-relationship marketing strategy.

Consider this example:

A company's business is reasonably successful. Its core business is the sale and servicing of new executive cars.

The service department is run efficiently, but very impersonally, and the VP of finance is a retired bank manager. Main promotion events are new car launches, to which all customers are invited, and sponsorship of a local Little League club. There is no information on number of customers, lifetime customer value, customer retention levels, or customer profitability.

The company wants to commence a Relationship Marketing program, and expects to build growth and profitability by applying it. It is prepared to spend on IT including investing in customer databases.

Following the Offensive Marketing approach, you start with two simple questions. First, what are the key areas of actionable knowledge to acquire? Second, what information has to be accessed in order to build this knowledge? With respect to actionable knowledge, recognizing that the company can't learn everything immediately, you prioritize six key groups of questions as a basis for building a customer Relationship Marketing program:

1. How many customers do we have? Who are they and what do they think of the experience of being a customer of the company?
2. Can customers be segmented into types by level of potential and profitability?
3. What is the firm's retention level of existing customers? Is this good or bad? What is the retention level of the firm's major competitors?
4. What is the customer lifetime value (CLV)? This estimates how many cars the average customer would buy from the company based on current retention levels, level of service income, and extra revenue generated by word-of-mouth referrals. On this basis, customer lifetime revenue and profit could be estimated. This is a useful measure to guide you with respect to how much to invest in retaining existing customers and acquiring new ones.
5. What is the basis for targeting new customers, and how successful is it?
6. What proportion of total advertising and promotion funds are being spent on existing versus new customers?

Having defined the questions to ask, you now have to decide what information is needed to answer them, and how to acquire it. For reasons of space constraints, this discussion will be limited to one of the six question groups: customer lifetime value.

Again, Customer Lifetime Value (CLV) is information gleaned from a customer survey and compiled through questions asked at the time of purchase, showing average customer age. It also shows that the majority of customers are male with a life expectancy of 75 years, a buying interval of five years, at an average cost of $45,000 per purchase. The average trade-in cost per car has also been calculated. This has to be deducted from CLV calculations.

To determine the CLV for an average customer, one would calculate longevity and annual expenditure, the average gross margin on that revenue, minus the average cost of customer acquisition and maintenance (discounted for the opportunity cost of money).[3] You may also want to factor a percentage increase on net new car prices for service income.

None of this allows for the positive effect of referrals by satisfied customers (or the devastating effect of negative word of mouth by unhappy customers).

Conclusion

The company decides to target the most profitable customers by focusing its communications on this audience to build stronger customer relationships. It also decides to redesign its service department to make it more personalized and convenient for these customers. In the process, it has also identified IT requirements necessary to create an ongoing customer relationship program. The company recognizes that through targeted data collection it can add to the total customer experience, build customer loyalty, and, over time, increase profitability.

Step 3: Competitive Analysis

Why bother to analyze competitors? Some companies think it best to get on with their own plans and ignore competition. Others follow competitive moves in obsessive detail, and end up copying or reacting to competition. Offensive Marketers strive to lead and to make their competitors followers. In order to lead your company's competitors, you must know who they are and what they are doing, as the competition represents one of the standards your firm has to beat. The others are standards that customers set through increasing expectations.

For clarity, the issue of competition has been divided into two sections: "Step 3, Competitive Analysis" identifies what you need

---

[3] Philip Kotler, *Marketing Management*, *The Millennium Edition*, Prentice-Hall, 2000.

to know about competitors and how to acquire that knowledge; "Step 4, Competitive Analysis Drill" (to come) deals with how to use that knowledge. In this section, Step 3, we will stick to three questions:

1. What does your firm want/need to know about its competitors?
2. What are the main sources of information about competitors?
3. How can your company develop a good-quality system for analyzing competitors?

Now, let's answer each individually.

What Your Firm Wants/Needs to Know About Your Competitors

Table 5-5 summarizes the main things the Offensive Marketer would like to know about her firm's competitors. The items on the left of the table will be known to most companies that conduct market research and remain alert.

A few companies know most or all of the items in both columns, even though information on competitive cost position and profit by market or brand may be fragmentary and based on enlightened estimation. None of this requires industrial espionage or unethical conduct. It can be generated by hard, persistent, and well-organized effort on a company-wide basis, led by the Marketing Department.

Table 5-5 What You Need and Want to Know About Competitors

What most companies know about competitors	What most companies do not know about competitors
Overall sales and profits	Size, quality of databases
Sales and profits by market	Relative-cost position
Sales revenue by brand	Customer service levels
Market shares by brand	Future strategies
Organization structure	New product or service plans
Distribution system	Profit by brand
Identity of key executives	Profit by distribution channel
Advertising spending	Database marketing results
Consumer attitudes	Sales efficiency
Past marketing strategies	Marketing efficiency
Customer retention levels	Future investment plans

Your Main Sources of Competitor Information

There are three main data sources: recorded, observable, and opportunistic.

1. Recorded data is easily available in published form either internally or externally. Competitor annual reports are an example. In addition, a competitor's website may contain a wealth of information.
2. Observable data has to be actively sought and often assembled from a number of sources. Competitor pricing falls within this category. While doing store checks, look at the competition too.
3. Opportunistic data requires planning and organization, because information often seeps through different departments and needs to be coordinated to be understandable. Much of this type of data is anecdotal, such as conversations with equipment suppliers or competitors at trade fairs.

Table 5-6 illustrates data types by major source.

Competitive data is like a jigsaw puzzle. Individual pieces do not usually have much value. Collecting the pieces and assembling them into an overall picture is the goal. This process enables easy identification of missing pieces, assuming that the team will take every necessary step to collect all of them.

Using determination and skill, you can normally find out anything you want to about a competitor without breaking the law. Unfortunately, this rarely happens since few companies seek, organize, and evaluate competitive data. Recorded data is not evaluated

Table 5-6   The Three Main Sources of Competitor Information

Recorded	Observable	Opportunistic
• Annual reports	• Pricing	• Suppliers
• Published data	• Distribution levels	• Trade shows
• Credit reports	• Promotions	• Sales people
• Trade press	• Advertising	• Seminars
• Brokers' reports	• Planning applications	• Social contacts
• Presentations to security analysts	• Results of tenders	• Ex-employees
• Market research	• Patent applications	• Distributors
• Government reports		• Relationships
• Websites		

over time; observable data is most often not recorded or coordinated and opportunistic data is not actively sought or disseminated.

Results of poor competitive data handling include, among others, the failure to preempt competitive threats, regular surprises in the marketplace, and an unrelenting reactionary role that can negatively impact attitudes and employee morale.

Developing a System of Competitor Analysis

Superior competitive analysis is a source of competitive advantage. The problem in most companies is that responsibility for evaluating competitors is widely dispersed within and across departments. The jigsaw puzzle never gets assembled and no one knows which pieces are missing. Competitor analysis can only be effective when the total Integrated Marketing approach, examined in Chapter 4, is applied.

Competitive Analysis Drill

With a sound base of competitive knowledge, the next step is to put it to use. One of the best systems for doing this, which fits the Offensive Marketing approach, is the competitive analysis drill. Used by General Electric,[4] the following drill targets seven key issues regarding your competitors.

1. **Who is the formative competition now? Three years from now?**
   Major competition consists of products or services that the consumer regards as a viable alternative. It follows that the product may have different competitors in different segments of a market. The identity of a company's or a brand's major competition should be reviewed regularly because the situation may change.

   Beware! Don't just keep tabs on the usual competition, but also watch out for newcomers that lurk in unsuspected corners and are using new technologies or distribution systems.

   Factors that can cause changes in competitor identity include:
   - **Rapid growth:** Acquisitions, mergers, joint ventures, or strategic alliances that increase the strength of competitors
   - **Imported strength:** Pressure on domestic industries that can cause them to respond in ways they otherwise would not

---

[4] Michael G. Allen, *Competitive Business Strategies*, McKinsey & Co., 1978.

- **Distribution channel changes:** Changes in the relative importance of distribution channels especially where new distribution channels are introduced
- **New technology:** The application of new technology and the redefining impact of "killer-apps"
- **Changes in raw materials:** Major changes in base raw materials used in the basic product or in the delivery of the product
- **Changes in legislation:** Changes in the law, including privatization and deregulation that reshapes industries as a whole and changes the competitive landscape.

All of these factors need to be watched closely in order to determine who up and coming competitors will be.

2. **What are the investment priorities, objectives, and goals of the firm's major competitors?** Knowing what your competitors have done in the past can provide many clues as to what they are likely to do in the future. The attitudes and philosophies of your competition deserve careful close study. With successful competitors, these attitudes tend to be deeply ingrained in the culture and change little. For many years, General Electric's objective was market leadership: to become number one or number two in every "market" it had entered. If you could accurately determine GE's market scope, you knew what their objective was. Any company with a strategy is "readable" and any company without a strategy is also readable in the sense that you know they will not pursue a charted course.

Another indication of competitive priorities and goals is previous successes or failures. It is quite normal to continue with a successful formula or to change a strategy that is not working. For example, if a competitor has been psychologically scarred by a particular product category or market, this information will become part of its own historical perspective and will influence future decision-making.

Another indication of future competitive goals is a competitor's advertising expenditure direction and capital investment. Rational competitors advertise most heavily on products, services, or markets that they believe have the most future potential. Knowledge of competitive capital investment, which can often be picked up from equipment suppliers or planning applications, is an invaluable guide to future competitive intentions.

A final indication is relative cost position. We are assuming that your company has mapped out its relative cost position by major markets and by competitor. Since your firm's competitors may well have conducted a similar exercise, it is logical to expect them to try hard to reduce costs in markets where they are high-cost operators. The message: never be complacent about a lower-cost position as it may be further eroded by others' strategic efforts.

3. **How important is your firm's specific market to each competitor and what is the level of its commitment?** Each competitor is likely to defend or improve its position in markets targeted by your company. The factors influencing level of competitive commitment to a product or category are:
   - Percentage of company profits in this category in the United States and worldwide
   - Whether the category is perceived as a growth area
   - Management attitude toward growth and Offensive Attitudes
   - Profit margins

   For example, any firm attacking Microsoft in any of its core markets can expect aggressive and sustained effort to achieve leadership in the market.

   As Microsoft pursues its strategies into the home networking arena, building links into every piece of software in order to make PCs, set-top boxes, stereos, and handheld devices work in concert, other top players, including Sony and AOL Time Warner, Inc., will have their work cut out to meet Microsoft's competitive commitment to this market.[5]

4. **What are the competitors' strengths and limitations?** When measuring your competitors, it is important to use your own business as a yardstick. In what respect is each competitor better or worse than your firm? Which of its strategies are working and which are not? Is it safe to assume that the former will be continued and the latter changed?

   Some of the more important areas for evaluating competitors are listed in Table 5-7.

5. **What weaknesses make the competitors vulnerable?** Knowing what the weak spots are gives your company a trump card.

---

[5] "On to the Living Room! Can Microsoft Control the Digital Home?," *Business Week*, January 21, 2002, pg. 68.

Table 5-7   Key Areas in which to Evaluate Competitors

• Customer franchise	• Persistence and determination
• Cost of operations	• Innovation
• Product quality and value	• Financial position and attitudes
• Service quality and value	• Attitude to risk
• Speed of response	• Willingness to make long-term investments

You can then attack competitors with your strongest forces at their weakest points. A list of possible weaknesses that make competitors vulnerable is given in Table 5-8.

Low market share is a conspicuous weakness. But a competitor with a high market share can also be in peril, despite apparent dominance. It may have become complacent. It can also become victim to a price war. A company with a high market share may have a limited interest in launching new products in light of the risk of cannibalizing existing ones.

Every company likes to hit its estimated budget. A good time to attack a competitor with a major initiative, like a new brand launch, is the last quarter of its fiscal year. The competitor has the choice of doing nothing and giving your company's initiative a free ride for three months, or it can respond with heavy defensive spending, missing its annual budget, which may cause adverse effects for both company morale and careers.

6. **What changes are competitors likely to make in their future strategies?** This question will usually answer itself if the first five questions have been thoroughly analyzed. However, it is

Table 5-8   Weaknesses That Make Competitors Vulnerable

• Lack of cash	• Unclear priorities
• Low margins	• Low customer retention
• Poor growth	• Predictability
• High-cost operations or distribution	• Product or service obsolescence/weakness
• Over-dependence on one market	• High market share
• Over-dependence on one account	• Low market share
• Strength in falling sectors	• Premium-price positioning
• Short-term orientation	• Slow moving/bureaucratic
• People problems	• Fiscal-year fixation
• Inconsistency	• Liable to be acquired

worthwhile at this stage to estimate where competitive divisions or brands stand in the portfolio analysis of the group to which they belong. Are they seen as strong investment candidates or "cash cows" to finance new programs and products?

It is always more comfortable competing against a cash cow on which profits are being maximized, than against a "star," on which heavy investment is richly lavished.

7. **What effects will all your competitors' strategies have on the industry, on the market and on your strategy?** Understanding competitive positioning from a comprehensive perspective of the future direction of the industry gives your company the big-picture analysis against which to formulate its own strategy to create competitive advantage.

Step 4: Key Factors for Success

Having completed the first three steps of the three wheels of the business environment, we are now ready to discuss Step 4, the Key Factor(s) for Success (KFS).

Plotting the KFS in your markets enables your company to identify how well equipped you are to enter or compete in them. You should not attempt to look at all factors for success, only the handful of most important ones—perhaps between four and five. An inability to meet these usually constitutes a barrier to entry into new markets, or points to poor future prospects in existing markets.

The main value that KFS brings to the equation is that they enable you to judge your company's fitness for entering existing or new markets, and help to identify priority areas for building competitive advantage. An edge over competitors in any of the KFS is likely to be important and exploitable.

The nature of KFS will vary widely by market. Useful questions to ask in determining KFS include:

- What are the largest areas of cost in this business? What can be done to reduce these costs? Not only should cost inefficiencies to addressed, but a look at critical elements of the business, could reveal new ways of doing business, particularly when customers are looked to for input.
- Looking at other companies in this business, what have been the main reasons for their success or failure? Has customer service

suffered while product innovation moved forward? Has technology driven the offering instead of customers' needs, whether articulated or not?

- In which areas of your business is it possible to build a competitive advantage? There may be opportunities that have been overlooked by competitors. It is these "white" spaces that creativity must address. Exploratory forays into the market provide feedback and experience and are an important tool for exploring the building of competitive advantage.

As markets continue to prove, Key Factors for Success change, and companies themselves are often the impetus for changing KFS. Canon did so in copiers for small offices and home use. Canon's PC machines were largely self-maintaining due to the use of cartridges and replaceable parts, reducing the need for a well-organized sales-service force and creating the opportunity for Canon to sell its personal copiers through new distribution channels of office product retailers and mail order.

McDonald's gained a strategic advantage through the use of mass production as a KFS. McDonald's has revolutionized dining worldwide with its strong articulation and rigorous implementation of the best way to make and sell a hamburger. Its competitive advantage stems from making the most consistent, standard meal package in the fast food industry. This KFS has provided a threat to existing dining experiences and has provided, over the years, new opportunities for new entrants in the fast food industry.[6]

Step 5: SWOT Analysis

This familiar technique is the final step in the strategic groundwork. It translates the four previous steps into a format that provides the basis for developing winning strategies.

The SWOT analysis is a summary of your company's *S*trengths and *W*eaknesses, and of the *O*pportunities and *T*hreats facing your firm. It can be applied to brands, markets, channels,

---

[6] Bart, Victor and Andrew C. Boynton, *Invented Here: Maximizing Your Organization's Internal Growth and Profitability*, Harvard Business School Press, 1998.

divisions, or companies, and has three main functions: planning, offense, and defense. In planning, SWOT creates links between business analysis and strategy development. With respect to offensive maneuvering, SWOT identifies strengths on which to formulate attack strategies, targeted to competitors' weaknesses and to exploit the best opportunities. With respect to defensive maneuvering, SWOT highlights threats in the business environment, gives a "heads-up" to these threats and provides the insight for preparing a counter-attack.

The quality of a SWOT analysis will obviously depend on the thoroughness of the four steps preceding it. Its practical usefulness can be enhanced by following a few simple rules:

1. Keep the analysis brief.
2. Relate the statement of strengths and weaknesses primarily to the KFS identified in Step 4. This will ensure that you concentrate on the important strengths.
3. Strengths and weaknesses should, wherever possible, be stated in competitive terms. You are looking for *exploitable* strengths, areas in which you are stronger than the competition. It is reassuring to be "good" at something, but it is more effective to be "better."
4. Statements should be specific, without limiting opportunities. The right statement opens up possibilities. For example, by defining its strength as "the best manufacturer of high-quality small plastic objects at low cost," Bic decided to use this strength as a means to challenge Gillette by creating the market for disposable plastic razors.
5. The SWOT analysis should not just be confined to marketing issues, but should cover the whole company's operations. For example, relevant topics could include technological opportunities and risks, the company's relative cost position versus competitors, comparative service levels, attitudes to investment and risk, degree of marketing orientation, and core competencies.
6. Be objective, both about your own company and about competitors. The SWOT analysis is an important strategic tool, not a device for confirming past successes. Objective analysis of competitors is also difficult. In general, companies tend to overrate the strengths of large competitors and underrate those of smaller ones.

CONCLUSION

The groundwork for strategy is prepared in five steps—an analysis of the business environment, an internal examination involving a candid analysis about the company and its brand(s), a competitor analysis that takes a broad view of both present and would-be competitors, an identification of Key Factors for Success (KFS), and a SWOT analysis to put the big picture together.

The internal examination is a model that lets you focus on the company's past performance, its attitudes toward, among other things, an Offensive Attitude in the marketplace, the results of its strategies and the quality of their execution. Was the firm a leader in the marketplace, or was it a follower? Where is the firm winning and where is it losing? Is the company in the right market and customer sectors? Is the firm's current performance indicative of strategies that are showing signs of lessening strength?

The competitive analysis discloses what your firm needs to understand about competitors and their strategies and how to acquire that knowledge. The competitive analysis drill involves answering several questions that put competitive knowledge into context.

Identifying Key Factors for Success reveals the performance areas in which your company must at least match, or beat, the competition. KFS helps you judge the fitness of your firm in existing markets, its chances for success in future market scenarios, as well as to identify strategic areas for building competitive advantage. Lastly, a SWOT analysis is the unifying conceptual link between business analysis and strategy development.

Strong strategy development is based on the conceptual understanding of consumers, customers, competitors, and costs. Intensive business analysis gets you there. Having completed the strategic business analysis, we now need to turn our attention to developing a clear vision of the future.

6 Anticipating the Future: Strategy Revisited

INTRODUCTION

This chapter is a continuation of our discussion on *Strategic*, or the "S" of POISE. As the factual framework for strategy development has already been established, it is important now to fit this framework into tomorrow's challenges. Developing a distinctive view of upcoming prospects enables the Offensive Marketer to shape corporate strategies and exploit opportunities ahead of competitors.

Successful anticipation of future marketplace changes—which include technology, distribution channels, and shifting customer needs, to name a few—is a critical marketing skill. Anticipation, used in this context, differs from forecasting. Its purpose is to confront tomorrow's issues today. Unfortunately, and to their ultimate detriment, many companies rush into strategies without first establishing a vision and future direction that is suited to the firm's competencies, history, and culture.

This chapter will discuss the six key factors driving future change as well as outline a number of offensive principles for thinking about the future.

ANTICIPATING THE FUTURE

The purpose of anticipating the future is not to forecast, since nearly all forecasts will inevitably be wrong. The purpose is to understand the possibilities so that you can build strategies that will last and exploit opportunities ahead of your competitors.

This involves analysis, reflection, and insight, which lead to perceived opportunities, creative scenarios, and an understanding of issues. In this way your company will become a leader rather than a follower.

Anticipating the future is both exciting and difficult. Key variables include the possibility of specific technical successes or failures, the speed of change in the marketplace, cost levels and marketplace adjustments, competitor initiatives and response, and convergences between and among markets and industries. Not even Microsoft's Bill Gates or Oracle's Larry Ellison knows how the future unification between software, entertainment, computing, and telecommunications is going to play itself out. With clear vision, however, they can make an educated guess as to what capabilities will be necessary to be a player in the race, and how the race itself may unfold.

Those companies that fail to address future technology and consumer issues at a deep strategic level will certainly find this to be a main cause of their lack of future competitiveness.

Strategic Anticipation: Rarely a Strong Competency

Anticipating the future and planning to exploit it now is one of the fundamental tasks of the Offensive Marketer. All too often, companies leap straight from analysis to strategy, omitting the vital steps that accompany future vision. Companies that fall into this trap usually write strategies to meet yesterday's market conditions rather than tomorrow's. Such strategies are unlikely to last long and are likely to be changed frequently. By changing strategies frequently, the whole competitive element that strategy brings to corporate action and response loses its effectiveness.

Bringing a view of the future that is not distinctive, exciting in its vision, and actionable (triggering innovative thinking) is not to do justice to the visioning process. Highlighting the existence of future pricing pressures or greater segmentation in the marketplace, or only reducing cost bases and increasing industry capacity by itself, does not lend to a distinctive view of the future. There are painful contrasts between the few Offensive Marketers who surge into the future with powerful headlights at full beam, and the majority of marketers who creep forward peering in the rear-view mirror.

Yet, having a distinctive view of the future does not guarantee business success. The view may prove to be misguided or competitors, with the same vision, may get there first, as happened when Matsushita beat Sony to the post on VCRs. The cost of the vision may be too high, like the Iridium satellite project, or the price may be too low, like the difficulties that discount airlines encountered prior to the successes of Virgin, Southwest Airlines, or JetBlue.

Indeed, the company may develop the technology to support the vision, but lack the marketing skills to exploit it. For example, Xerox's Palo Alto computer project failed to bring a marketable product to the consumer, leaving the technology to others.

However, a deeply considered view of the future makes business success much more likely. Motorola's success in the pager, two-way radio, and cellular phone markets grew out of Paul Galvin's carefully tested vision of the future, based on business analysis, knowledge of customers, costs, and technology.[1] Similarly, Dell Computer's success in its "direct to consumer" sales model grew out of Michael Dell's understanding of customers' growing need for personalization and control over the product, aligning it with a made-to-order manufacturing process.

---

[1] *Motorola: A Journey Through Time and Technology*, Motorola Museum of Electronics, 1994.

Offensive Marketers Lead Future Thinking

Developing a distinctive view of the future is the responsibility of the Board, but it cannot be built by a few people sitting behind closed doors in a boardroom. It requires the best thinking of the whole organization from technologists to process engineers, from sales people to IT managers.

Marketing Departments are best placed to manage the process and gain commitment to the results. Offensive Marketers can do this by postulating a vision and organizing data analysis across the organization's data collection capabilities.

One of the reasons why many Marketing Departments are losing influence over the strategic planning process is that they repeatedly fail to grasp the opportunity to lead companies into the future by taking ownership of the long-term planning process.

There are six major factors driving future change. These need to be closely studied and understood as part of the long-term planning process. Table 6-1 lists them.

Table 6-1 Six Key Factors Driving Future Change

1. Customer needs
2. Channels
3. Technology
4. Regulation
5. Costs
6. Competition

The need to anticipate the future is more obvious in industries that are experiencing rapid changes in technology, such as electronics, or changes in regulation as in the financial and telecommunications sectors. It is less obvious, but equally important, in low-technology industries, although this is rapidly disappearing as computing, the Internet, and information and communication technologies impact nearly all ways of doing business.

THE SIX KEY DRIVERS DRIVING FUTURE CHANGE

Future vision examines today's business rules and practices and figures out how to change them to your firm's competitive favor, in light of tomorrow's demanding marketplace. Understanding the "customer" requires an analysis of his or her basic needs, the demographics most aptly describing your firm's customer base, the life stages that your customers experience, and how these impact the use of your product or service. Understanding the habits and usage patterns surrounding your offering as well as the attitudes of end-users toward your product and company, are integral to bringing the customer's experience "inside" your firm's decision-making process.

Other elements of comprehending tomorrow's marketplace include the impact of fast-changing distribution channels on your business model; how technology will change your offering and business processes; what regulation changes will impact your industry; how cost, pricing, and therefore profit may change; and lastly, how the impact of all of these may change the competition your company will face. We will look at each one of these areas individually.

Customers

Table 6-2 gives a brief checklist of consumer opportunity areas that are further developed in this chapter as well as in Chapter 9 on Offensive Segmentation.

Basic Needs

These always exist and change slowly most of the time. Consumers are often unaware of undefined future needs usually because the products that will meet these needs do not yet exist or the technology required to meet these needs has not been created. As an Offensive Marketer, you should concentrate on defining basic and expanded needs, based on your customer's experience with your products and services. This is done, most often, through a continuing dialogue with customers, whether through e-mail, direct contact, or at point of purchase or service.

Understanding your product's areas of weakness may point to radical or incremental improvements. For example, although today's customer may be generally satisfied with the automobile on the basis of performance, reliability, styling, safety, and image, many elements of the driving experience remain less than optimal. Traffic congestion, parking limitations, unpredictable journey

Table 6-2   Customer Future Opportunity Checklist

Area of opportunity	Questions to ask
Basic needs: Anticipating the Future	• How could these needs change in the future? • If prices were halved, what would happen? • What could upgrade expectations? • How well are our basic needs being met? • What added value features are being sought? • What are the special needs? • What are main areas of dissatisfaction and with whom? • What are the trade-offs between those needs?
Demographics	• How well is each demographic or industry group served? • What new demographic groupings can be developed, e.g. single parents, extended families? • What is the future trend?
Life stages	• What are they? How are they changing? • How well is each life stage served by the industry?
Habits and usage	• Where and when is the product used and not used? • Why isn't it used all the time? • What is in-home versus out-of-home usage? • Which usages are growing or declining? Why? • How does usage differ by demographic group?
Attitudes	• What is the customer attitude toward the industry and specific products or brands? • How will attitudes to environmental and safety issues develop? • How is this likely to change in future? • What industry changes are necessary to improve attitudes?

times, costly purchase outlays, and loss of value as well as the inconvenience of refueling, may propel growing consumer preference for a permanently powered, low-cost method of personal transportation.

Basic needs develop over time. As each is successfully met, another emerges. For example, in the hair shampoo product category, basic needs have evolved to include not only cleaning but also meeting the needs of differing hair types and treating color, permed, or damaged hair. In addition, products have grown to meet the needs of the frequent user and consumers who demand natural ingredients. Overall health and shine of hair has become an important product benefit. Specific product categories have also emerged to address, for example, anti-dandruff treatment. In the shampoo market, therefore, basic needs have become quite complex. Pioneering new brands have used technology and skillful marketing to create new benefits and added value for the end-user. Accordingly, a new shampoo brand launched today on a platform of just *superior cleaning* would likely fail, because the consumer has moved beyond this basic defined need.

Demographics

Demographics should be categorized on both a commonsense and creative basis. While conventional demographic categories are useful, applying more imagination than pure numbers, for example, can lead to greater insight. Instead of simply identifying the segment of older Americans in the target community, understanding that they are more actively involved with grandchildren, parents, and other grandparents in their daily routines, leisure activities, and entertainment can lead to identifying new segments, new patterns of behavior, and perhaps new uses for a product or service category.

In the 1980s, the automotive industry missed the opportunity to develop mid-price sports cars targeted at affluent males over 50, nostalgic for the days of their youth when they couldn't afford a sports car. The booming market in vintage sports cars should have alerted manufacturers to this opportunity. Equally, car manufacturers have consistently under-marketed to women in relation to both their demographic importance and wallet potential.

Life Stages

Life stages can be defined as a set of occupational and family circumstances that affects attitudes and habits. Life Stage revolves around work, marital status, children, parents, income level, and the balance between work and leisure, to name a few life-defining circumstances that are often considered.

Identifying the life stage model most relevant to your firm's market, and projecting it forward, will help you identify future changes in consumer needs. Two often discussed future trends are the growth in the elderly population, and the reduced ability of the government to finance health care. Consequently, the move to self-medication, over-the-counter medicines, and retirement homes for younger, more active people, all continue to have strong growth prospects.

Habits and Usage

The Sony Walkman is often exemplified as an intuitive invention that could not have been identified by research. Twenty years ago a direct question to a consumer such as, "Would you be interested in buying a product that enables you to listen to high-quality taped music in private as you sit or walk?" would have produced a mystified response. Having lived without the product, it would be difficult for the consumer to visualize its benefits.

A more circumstantial approach to habits and usage would have revealed a future need for the Sony Walkman.

Consider these facts:

The fixed location of taped music centers meant that they could only be listened to at home, and therefore, at limited times.

People had become used to listening to radios outside the home, in cars and, to the frequent annoyance of others, outdoors.

People have private preferences in music and often like to listen independently.

They often have periods in their day when they can't read or talk, but could listen to music, news, or call-in shows.

The most popular music is listened to by young people who are considered more flexible in terms of changing their habits as new kinds of music appear.

In fact, the Walkman was developed by Sony engineers who were told to develop a personal, portable sound device by Mr. Morita, the company's founder. He had a golf partner who carried a large tape player and headphones on the golf course. Mr. Morita believed that there was a market for portable personal sound, and that Sony engineers could create such a product. When told to develop the product, the engineers first said that it could not be done. Morita is said to have told them, "Do it or you're fired." They went to work and the rest is history. Sony is a leader in portable personal sound to this day.

While envisioning the future, a set of logical presumptions, circumstantially woven together, can produce new and different answers. One of the most useful questions to ask about future habits and usage is, "Why doesn't the user use our product all the time?" For example, when this question was applied to cleaning teeth, it led to the successful development and introduction of dental gum.

Attitudes

Attitudes such as confusion or cynicism can play a pivotal role in product success.

To take an example, in detergents, the number of product variants has quadrupled in the past decade. Consumers are confused by the plethora of powders, concentrates, liquids, bios, non-bios, color cleaners, and refills, all in an overwhelming range of sizes. It appears that consumers want a sophisticated solution rather than an all-in-one brand. The first manufacturer or retailer to design a product range that really meets consumer needs simply and intelligently will have a successful product.

Some industries—such as energy, utilities, including cable, telephone and wireless, financial services, or pharmaceuticals—are scarred by consumer cynicism. This cynicism provides an opportunity for trusted branders from other industries to enter the market in the future.

Channels

In many industries, distribution channels have and will change faster than consumer needs. A company with competencies only in yesterday's channels will gradually lose access to the consumer. Equally, development of new channels can be integral to entering new markets as Dell has demonstrated through the direct-to-consumer marketing channel with computers; Canon, through office retailers, with personal copiers; Amazon, through its online innovative personalized services; and UPS, with its expertise in overnight mail logistics.

There are two key questions to ask about the future of distribution channels. First, what will future consumer needs be and how well are existing channels likely to serve these needs?

A simple grid where channels are ranked with respect to things that matter to the customer—including convenience, product range, accessibility, quality, customer services, after-sales service, competitive pricing, and stock availability—is useful. For instance, in the apparel industry, it may be productive to rank department stores, specialty and outlet, direct mail, and online sources.

Complete the grid by applying numerical rankings to each need and scoring each channel against that need. The result will gauge future channel strength. Together with historical trends, this score can be used to evaluate the prospects of each channel.

As an example, the inconvenience of shopping and home preparation has led to the premium pricing of food in restaurants. Grocery retailers are losing share of the total food sector to restaurants and to fast food establishments and are fighting back with increasingly sophisticated prepared food sections.

The second question to ask about the future of your firm's channels is, looking at trends in other industries, what alternative channels might emerge in the future?

In light of recent experience, it is also important to ask questions such as, "Can groceries be delivered door-to-door after an online order has been placed?" Peapod has created its business model around this alternative channel. Alternately, can oil deliveries be made from a digitally coordinated grid of trucks that are closest to the end-user? Several companies have done this successfully with significant impact on the bottom-line and on customer satisfaction.

Some markets, like soft drinks, have a wide range of channels that serve the consumer well. Their channels will change slowly. Other channels serve their consumers poorly and are liable to change rapidly in future or are currently in the midst of changing. You can now order via the Internet and receive delivery of customer fitting jeans or chinos without ever visiting a store or tailor. You can visit houses for sale across the globe and view virtual layouts and rooms. You can create a digital image of yourself and try on various hairstyles before visiting a hair salon, or download personally selected music with a subscription.

Technology

The importance of technology to shaping the future is obvious. That is why the Offensive Marketer must have a grasp of major technologies and a view of future scenarios based on interaction with experts in fields such as computer and chip miniaturization, genetic engineering, and digital technologies and interfaces.

The most important future technologies are those with the potential to meet basic consumer needs better, as this statement by David Packard, joint founder of Hewlett-Packard, indicates:

"To warrant serious pursuit, an idea must be both practical and useful. Out of those ideas that are practical, a smaller number are useful. To be useful, an invention must not only fill a need, it must be an economical and efficient solution to that need."[2]

It is not enough to be familiar with the implications of technology in your own market. Technology in related or converging markets is also relevant; telecommunications companies need to understand the technologies of computing, broadcasting, electronics, and entertainment, as well as telephone and cellular communications.

And technology in unrelated markets—such as home-shopping, interactive media, virtual reality training, robotics, and personal communications—is likely to affect the future of most businesses because it will fundamentally influence consumer habits.

The decline and fall of *Encyclopedia Britannica*, between 1990 and 1995, marketed as the world's most prestigious and comprehensive encyclopedia—and its brand extensions of atlases and yearbooks, to CD-ROM encyclopedias including Grolier, Encarta, and Compton—is a prime example of leadership failure in understanding the impact of changing technology. The CD-ROM was not the threatening technology; instead, it was the PC itself that enabled a new medium of learning and information dissemination.[3]

Regulation

New legislation, deregulation, privatization, regional and global voluntary codes, and newer more stringent security regulations can all shape your future business environment and competitive position.

Possible future change can be evaluated by talking to industry experts, civil servants, those in the academic community, and regulators; by identifying the probable, the possible, and the unlikely; and by setting up lobbying objectives and plans to achieve change that would accrue to your company's favor.

---

[2] David Packard, *The HP Way: How Bill Hewlett and I Built Our Company*, Harper Business, 1995.
[3] Philip Evans and Thomas S. Wurster, *Blown to Bits: How the New Economics of Information Transforms Strategy*, Harvard Business School Press, 2000.

Cost, Pricing, and Profit

What drives cost, pricing, and profit in your firm's industry? How likely are they to change in one to three years or even in the shorter term? What are your main cost elements and how will they be different both in the short and long term? How are they affected by volume? What degree of cost reduction is necessary to radically increase demand? At what point is most profit made in your company's industry and how is this likely to change?

An example of the shift in profits occurred in the PC industry in the early 1990s. From 1990 to 1995, sales doubled from $44 billion to $90 billion, but net profit plummeted from $3.5 billion to $1.3 billion. Where did these profits go? In 1990 to 1995, there was a massive transfer of profit from PC manufacturers, such as IBM, Compaq, and Apple, to microprocessors, notably Intel, and operating system providers like Microsoft. By 1995, microprocessors accounted for only 13 percent of PC industry revenue but 61 percent of industry profits.

Clearly, sources of industry profits shift dramatically as new technology moves into the mainstream and becomes the foundation of new products and services, which, like the PC, expand in their uses and their possible connectivity to other merging and emerging technologies.

In another example, not industry specific and over a longer period, there has been a fundamental change in the way industry profits are divided between manufacturers and retailers. Manufacturers used to be more profitable than retailers, while today the reverse is true, as retailers increase their relative bargaining power and move closer to consumers.

Competition

By their activities, competitors shape the future of your company's industry and the expectations of consumers. They, like your firm, will be developing plans to improve products, reduce cost, increase productivity, and enter new market sectors. If they are good competitors, they represent a constantly improving standard. This means that to improve your firm's long-term market position significantly, you have to beat your competitors' customer offer.

FUTURE STANDARDS ALWAYS RISE

"Today's competitive differentiators become tomorrow's price of market entry."[4]

The hair care example, earlier, illustrates how consumer need develops over time, stimulated by competition, innovation, and customer expectations. Product or service elements that differentiated specific competitors yesterday are rapidly copied today. They become the norm, or minimum requirement to compete in a market, and no longer provide a source of competitive advantage.

In win-tomorrow scenarios, firms must do the basics well but also offer superimposed added value products or services. Today's "compete and win" propositions merely add up to a "compete" position tomorrow. They quickly fall behind unless innovation and responsiveness are corporate competencies.

In the airline industry, the best competitors, British Airways and Singapore Airlines included, all offer competent staff, punctuality, safety, roomy seats, quality meals, relationship marketing, global alliances, frequent flyer miles, and other bonuses. These are the foundation building blocks necessary to compete in that sector of air traveler.

When airlines redefine the rules of a marketplace, they need to be sure that the value proposition they are offering meets some underlying demand that has not been previously addressed, like low-cost air fare without the frills, plus convenience and reliability. Hence, the success of Southwest Airlines, JetBlue, and Virgin. Yet, even in this market, share builders rapidly again becomes tomorrow's competitive norm.

OFFENSIVE APPROACH: DEVELOPING A POWERFUL VIEW OF THE FUTURE

Several marketing principles exist for effectively applying the six key drivers of future vision.

---

[4] Hamel and Prahalad, *Competing for the Future*, Harvard Business School Press, 1996.

Develop a Deep Understanding of the Past

The first is, begin with a real perspective and deep understanding of the past. Do not, however, project this past understanding and knowledge into the future without additional insight.

With markets changing so rapidly in light of technology, increasing customer expectations, regulation and deregulation changes, industry mergers, and channel evolution, projecting past experience onto future opportunities can be both limiting and dangerous. However, certain knowledge about competitors' response in the past to market changes or demands, for example, can bring insight into future competitive moves and responses. The bottom line: past experience must be used selectively and appropriately.

Determine Impact of Key Drivers

The second marketing principle is to determine how the impact of each of the six key drivers will change in the future.

One of the worst ways to anticipate the future is to extrapolate past trends mathematically, either with or without computer generated regression analysis. Instead, try to carefully extract the factors driving past change and forecast their likely impact in the future. For example, was consumer spending in the past due to an increase in the number of people buying or trading up to higher value products or service, or was it higher frequency of use? Has it been influenced by new product innovation, total market pricing, or levels of advertising? How will these change in the next 12 months? The next three years?

Assess the Impact of Change

The third marketing principle in assessing the impact of change with respect to the six drivers is the assignment of probabilities over time.

This approach is particularly useful in markets where regulation or technology is changing rapidly. Often it is reasonably straightforward to decide whether something is likely to happen, and much more difficult to determine when.

A good process is to list key change factors, and to label them *definite*, *probable*, *possible*, or *unlikely*, over one-year, eighteen-month, and three-year spans.

Simple scenario options like these can stimulate discussion across departments and among experts.

Use Your Imagination

The fourth marketing principle is to use imagination to change the rules of the competitive game.

Swatch is a good example of this.

ETA was a leading Swiss group making mechanical watches. It was operating at the top end of the market, but this market was shrinking. The company badly needed to build volume by also competing in lower-price sectors dominated by quartz watches, which ETA did not make.

The company decided to avoid the Japanese middle ground and to target the low-price sector. It set a target retail price of $25 per watch. In view of high trade mark-ups and other costs, the real production cost worked out to about $5 per unit. Quality was to be high, with maximum standardization. Variation was allowed in case appearance, the dial, hands, and strap.

These specifications were achieved by using innovations involving seven patents. The watch was marketed as a fashion accessory to young women and men between the age of 18 and 30. Fun, excitement, fashion, and design were the core of the proposition, which was heavily supported by high-impact advertising and promotion. Distribution included fashion stores, sports outlets, gift boutiques, and shops within department stores.

With its success, Swatch transformed and greatly expanded both the world and the Swiss watch industry by developing a differentiated view of the future.[5]

Swatch used the six key drivers to envision this differentiated view. To Swatch, customers aged below 30 wanted low-cost fashion items that were exciting. The company selected unconventional channels consistent with the consumer image. The company applied new technology, such as welding the face cover to the case, to achieve targeted consumer value.

---

[5] *Strategic Innovation,* edited by Charles Baden-Fuller and Martyn Pitt, Routledge, 1996.

> It sought to drive down cost through technology, standardiza-
> tion, high volume, and low labor content. Swatch had to
> change the rules of competition to compete successfully with
> low-priced competitors in a high-labor cost country.

Know the Latest Selling Formats

The fifth marketing principle is to become familiar with the latest
selling formats and technology tests.

If you market through retailers or distributors, visit the most
recently opened stores or any public test events. Familiarize yourself with the parameters of new technology even if they are not
mainstreamed as of yet, but could affect your firm's consumers or
channels tomorrow. This may include: robotics, video on demand,
videophones, expanded use of smart cards, virtual reality shopping including kiosks, Web-based access to the end-user, interactive TV, wireless technologies, telecom partnerships offering new
services, as well as relevant overseas innovations that because of
more maturing or differing consumer tastes, have become popular.

Challenge Price/Performance Assumptions

Lastly, the sixth marketing principle is to challenge price/
performance assumptions.

Success stories here include Canon and its production of the
$1,000 copier, which challenged Xerox's higher-priced product,
although the company was only 10 percent of the size of Xerox
at the time.[6] Another is CNN, which managed to provide 24/7
news coverage with a budget estimated at one-fifth of what was
required by CBS to broadcast a single hour of evening news.[7]

Canon and CNN are proof that even a significantly smaller
resource base will not impede successful price/performance
challenges. In addition, Honda's success, compared with GM or
Ford, demonstrates that there is little, if any, relationship between
accumulated volume of product experience (Ford and GM having

---

[6] Hamel and Prahalad, Id.
[7] Id.

years of introducing a plethora of new models), and the ability to create drastic productivity improvements. Honda has proven that it is the relative efficiency with which a firm learns from each foray into the market that determines the rate of improvement.[8]

Successful companies create a distinctive view of the future to confront tomorrow's issues today. Everyone agrees that doing so is critical to competitiveness, yet few firms devote the time to it.

CONCLUSION

Anticipating the future is a realistic endeavor. It envisions scenarios and opportunities whose purpose is to confront tomorrow's competitive issues today in order to create competitive advantage. Most business people agree that it is important and yet few firms spend the time required on it.

The Offensive Marketer should lead the organization in thinking about the future. He or she is in the best position to organize the process across the organization: to interview, analyze, interact, and dialogue with customers, suppliers and partners, fellow employees, and thought leaders in disciplines impacting the competitive environment.

The ideal internal tool to integrate both the process and end product is the long-term plan. The failure of marketers to control and direct long-term planning is one reason for their declining influence in determining corporate strategy and implementation. From this dual perspective, able to look both out into the marketplace while understanding the complexities of internal competencies unique to the firm, the Offensive Marketer has much to bring to the process.

The six key factors driving future change give structure and content to both the inquiry and process. Understanding that future competitive standards always rise, the Offensive Principles outlined in this chapter should be integrated into processes that create an understanding of the past and move strategically into the future.

---

[8] Id.

7 Developing Winning Strategies

INTRODUCTION

"Supreme excellence consists in breaking the enemy's resistance without fighting. Thus the highest form of generalship is to baulk the enemy's plans. The next best is to prevent the junction of the enemy's forces. The next in order is to attack the enemy in the field. The worst policy of all is to besiege walled cities." *Sun Tsu*

This chapter is the third on strategy, or the "S" of POISE. It translates the findings from the two previous chapters, on business analysis and anticipating the future, into winning strategies that are robust and forward looking.

Offensive strategy involves the development of competitive advantages and the application of these to build winning strategies. Key strategic decisions involve concentrating resources into areas of best return and selecting the most effective points to attack. The ideal strategy concentrates your company's strongest resources and strategic vision against your competitors' most weakly defended areas.

Five main ways to develop winning strategies are covered:

1. Portfolio analysis to build strategic priorities through resource allocation.
2. Developing a competitive advantage by doing something better or different than the competition.
3. Turning competitive advantages into winning strategies.
4. Selecting the right strategies for your company.
5. Recognizing and avoiding strategic burn-out. Winning strategies are as vulnerable to life cycles as are products. Here, it must be recognized that strategies will wear out unless they are nurtured, updated and modified in response to changing market demands.

DEFINING VISION: CORPORATE OBJECTIVES AND VALUES

Various terms are used by writers and business people to describe future strategic direction: *vision*, *values*, *mission* and *objectives*, to name a few. Although vision has already been described in Chapter 3, we need to clarify how these expressions differ and how they are related.

Vision has a similar meaning to *mission*. Both terms imply a strong measure of foresight, imagination, and vocation. Their role is to provide clear signposts to the future and a motivating horizon for employees. If your company has clear signposts, developing winning strategies to get there becomes easier and more relevant. And, if you can point to inspiring horizons, people will work harder to reach them.

Corporate objectives are usually more specific and mundane than visions. They translate visions into quantitative goals, such as revenue, profits, or earnings per share.

Values describe the beliefs, personality, and style a company aims to cultivate in pursuing its vision and corporate objectives. For example, some articulated values of The Body Shop include "being a different kind of company," one that addresses human rights campaigning, fair trade and affirmatively declines to test their products on animals. The Body Shop is "sensitive and supportive" to community projects around the world; "alternative," by doing business alternatively like sourcing indigenous products to support local culture and way of life; "standing for good value" by having a refill service for products and minimal packaging; and, "being responsible and a good global citizen" by doing business in an energy efficient manner and minimizing waste. The Body Shop's values are communicated to customers as an important part of the company's brand image and way of doing business.

STRETCHING CORPORATE OBJECTIVES

Corporate objectives convert vision into measurable goals. These are usually financial in nature, and are expressed as a certain targeted percentage increase in earnings per share, return on stockholders' equity, or a return on capital. Many of these targeted percentage increases are lofty challenges to "business as usual" sometimes in the range of 10–20 percentage points.

In addition to these financial goals, 3M, for example, adds "Sustainability Strategies"[1] to its long-held objective of having "at least 30% of sales in any one year derived from products introduced within the four previous years."[2] These strategies "encompass the pursuit of customer satisfaction and commercial success within a framework of environmental, social and economic values."[3]

---

[1] 3M WorldWide Annual Report, 2002.
[2] 3M generated $5.6 billion in sales in 2000—fully one-third of its revenues from goods that didn't exist four years prior. See, "3M: A Lab for Growth?" *Business Week*, January 21, 2002.
[3] 3M WorldWide Annual Report, 2002.

This framework includes an environmental health and safety management system, "life cycle management" to improve the environmental, health and safety of products, processes, and a program to "make pollution prevention pay," through the development of new technologies and products.[4] These have the effect of challenging the workplace toward a more community-oriented and holistic sense of corporate success. These programs often speak to individual employees and their personal aspirations, which can be met in the workplace context.

OFFENSIVE STRATEGY

The purpose of Offensive Marketing is to win. Everyone would like to find a fast-growing market with high margins and little competition. Few are so fortunate. The most important question for marketing people is "Why should a customer choose to buy our products or services rather than the competition's, now and in the future?" Unless the answer is clear, convincing, and backed by unambiguous evidence, your firm does not have a winning strategy.

Offensive strategy is all about setting priorities. It involves:

1. **Selecting the most effective point at which to attack.** The classic military offensive concentrates the attacker's strongest weapons on the enemy's weakest lines of defense. Marketing follows similar principles and the most successful attacks are pinpointed on targeted segments, against selected competitors, who have lacked the vision to push the envelope of the industry or business practices prevalent in the industry.
2. **Directing business resources to the areas of best return.** This usually calls for the movement of resources including operations, talent, advertising, or R&D from areas of low return into areas of high return. Offensive Marketing follows similar principles and the most successful attacks are pinpointed on targeted segments, against selected competitors.
3. **Developing competitive advantages.** In order for your company's planned attack at a selected point to be effective, it is essential to develop competitive advantage.

---

[4] Id.

BUILDING STRATEGIC PRIORITIES: PORTFOLIO ANALYSIS

Portfolio analysis is a graphic device useful for examining the competitive position of products, services, or businesses and for conducting a similar exercise on competitors. It is too crude to use in isolation but is helpful in focusing the more extensive analysis described in Chapter 5, or in triggering detailed strategic discussion. The structure of the portfolio also forces company decision makers to set priorities and make choices. Portfolio analysis is most often used to determine resource allocation.

Portfolio analysis has developed from the original Boston Consulting Group matrix of "Stars, Cows, Question Marks, and Dogs," through to the second-generation McKinsey/GE market attractiveness and competitive pluses model to the third generation of quantified portfolio analysis. All three are valuable tools in building strategic priorities. They will be examined in turn—their advantages, disadvantages, and applications summarized.

The Boston Consulting Group (BCG) Matrix

BCG invented portfolio analysis and its original model is still useful.

The BCG matrix relates relative market share (RMS) to market growth. For example, if your firm has a 40 percent market share and your nearest competitor has a 20 percent market share, your firm's RMS is 2.0. Likewise, your competitor's RMS is 0.5.

A product with a high RMS in a growing market is a Star and a minor product in a falling market is a Dog. In between, there are Cash Cows with high market shares in mature markets, whose cash can be used for investment, and Question Marks with low shares in fast-growing markets and whose futures remain undetermined.

Figure 7-1 summarizes the BCG Portfolio Matrix.

In allocating development resources like advertising, R&D, and technology spending, the theory is that the vast majority are funneled into Stars, allocating some into Question Marks in the hope that they can be turned into Stars. You starve the Cows and Dogs, the principle being that Cows finance the investment costs of Stars. The Question Mark is a temporary box; sooner or later the company will have to decide whether to promote this market offering to a Star or relegate it to the Dog category.

Figure 7-1
*BCG Portfolio
Matrix*

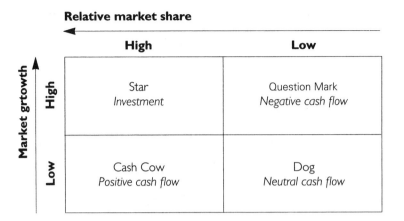

Relative market share

	High	Low
High	Star *Investment*	Question Mark *Negative cash flow*
Low	Cash Cow *Positive cash flow*	Dog *Neutral cash flow*

Market grtowth

Evaluation:

Pros. The BCG matrix is simple and elegant. As a graphic device, it propels decision-making. It remains a useful, quick guide to resource allocation by country, market, or brand, to be used for your own firm or the competition.

Cons. For most companies, an overabundance of markets and brands fall into the Dogs category. This is not surprising when you consider that many markets are mature or are maturing, and only a small minority of companies or brands are market leaders within these matured or maturing markets. This restricts the value of the BCG matrix since most brands and markets tend to sit around the mid-point to bottom right of the total square.

A fast-growing market is not necessarily an attractive one. Growth markets attract new entrants, and if capacity exceeds demand, the market may become low-margin and therefore unattractive. Furthermore, growth markets often run into long-term problems. No market keeps on growing forever. There is always the risk that companies will gear up capacity a year or 18 months ahead for growth that shudders to a halt.

Witness the telecom industry after the dot.com bubble burst in March of 2001. Ramifications from the current shakeout continue to impact the industry even after many accounting methodologies that propped up baseless gains have been curtailed. From the largest players: AT&T, Global Crossing, WorldCom, and Qwest—and their equipment providers including Lucent, Nortel and

Cisco—to the smaller players, they are all feeling the dramatic effect of a growth market being rationalized.

With so many companies flocking to the long-distance sector during the latter part of the 1990s, deploying so much available capital building networks and systems, there were just too many similar networks and business models to survive when consumer and business demand ultimately failed to materialize.

High relative market share is only one measure of the strength of a brand or company. For instance, General Motors had for decades been market leader in the U.S. automobile market with a high RMS. However, in recent years, many company initiatives have been aimed at addressing its steadily declining market share because of structural weaknesses and growing competition.

For instance, a relatively large market share disguised troubling weaknesses at GM. Although it has had 34 percent of the production capacity in the United States, GM has had only 28 percent of the sales. With such overcapacity and higher cost structure, even with cost containment and reduction, GM has been on a campaign to increase profits with strong sales.

To increase sales, GM has had to get to market quickly with strong products in growing segments including luxury cars and SUVs, where it goes head to head with Ford, DaimlerChrysler, and newer Japanese imports. In 2001, although GM had stabilized its market share at 28 percent and stole the truck market lead from Ford, its use of incentives cut into its profit margins. In addition, GM has failed to manage its brands well, with fragmentation and overlap of well-known and historically strong brands leading to sustained losses of sales revenue. Pulling the plug on its Oldsmobile division in December of 2000 was an initial step to cutting its losses because of steeply declining sales. Oldsmobile had 1 million vehicle sales of the 103-year old Marquee in the 1980s compared to just 300,000 in 2000.[5]

In addition, GM has the largest pension fund and healthcare costs of any U.S. company, each with the potential of gobbling up huge amounts of much-needed cash.[6]

---

[5] "GM: 'Out With the Olds' Is Just the Start," *Business Week*, December 25, 2000; "GM Warms Up Its Branding Iron," *Business Week*, April 16, 2001; and, "Finally, Skid Control at GM," *Business Week*, March 25, 2002.

[6] "GM's Cash Guzzlers: Profits Are Up but Pension and Health-Care Liabilities Are Staggering," *Business Week*, June 17, 2002.

The McKinsey/General Electric Matrix

This matrix overcomes a number of the disadvantages of the BCG model.

Market attractiveness replaces *market growth* and includes a broad range of measures. *Competitive pluses* replaces *relative market share*, which is only one of the measures used. A table similar to the BCG matrix can be created using two axes; one of market attractiveness and the other, competitive pluses.

Market attractiveness includes the consideration of market size, market growth, competitive structure, real pricing trends,[7] historic profit levels, current market profitability, competitive intensity, opportunity to differentiate, retail structure, segmentation possibilities, market cyclicality, and regulation. Other elements may be added that are relevant to your firm's industry. *Competitive pluses* include market share, size of the company relative to competitors, quality of product offering, technology relevancy both of offering and processes, cost structure, and profitability measures.

Each competitive offering is measured on a high, medium, or low scale with respect to each axis. The objective is to identify which offering to develop, which to maintain, and which offering to milk.

Evaluation:

Pros. The McKinsey/GE Matrix is a valuable development of the BCG portfolio analysis. Its broader range of measures generates more insights and the user is encouraged to think in more complex terms.

Cons. It gives too little emphasis to competencies in the competitive pluses category. The allocation within boxes may be subjective and unquantifiable.

Quantified Portfolio Analysis (QPA)

QPA works on similar principles to the McKinsey/GE matrix but on a more quantified basis. It has two axes, market attractiveness and

---

[7] Real pricing is defined as price change, excluding effect of inflation.

relative strength, and consists of a quantified process outlined briefly below. Both axes consist of a number of criteria that are given a maximum weighted score based on relative importance. A scoring guide helps quantify scores for companies or brands that are being assessed. The resulting output is a percentage score for each company or brand on both axes of the portfolio. This increases objectivity and accuracy, and allows for comparability across markets, brands, or countries.

This section will describe how QPA can be used to prioritize brands. Here, the company selected, Unilever's Bird's Eye, in the U.K. frozen foods market, is used to illustrate brand rather than market sector prioritization. Obviously, this will change the key criteria used to measure attractiveness. Those weighing relative brand strength include measures such as brand profitability, relative customer value, differentiation, innovation record, relative brand share and trend, market sector position, awareness and loyalty measures, and investment support. The approach to creating a matrix on market attractiveness for brands will use relative brand strength on one axis and market attractiveness on the other. In doing so, brand prioritization is based on a combination of the two. Obviously, the ideal is a strong brand in an attractive market.

Once all Bird's Eye markets and brands are scored on both axes' criteria, a brand-range portfolio could be constructed, and might look something like Figure 7-2.

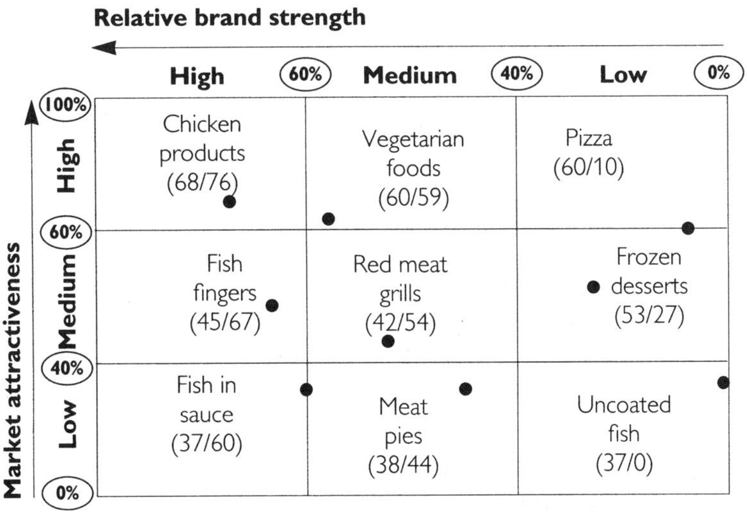

Figure 7-2
Bird's Eye Brand Range: Quantified Portfolio Analysis

165

This is what the portfolio analysis reveals:

Chicken products are an attractive sector (scored at 68 percent) and the Bird's Eye brand within it is very strong (scoring 76 percent). The combination of strength in market sector and brand, adds up to a powerful position for Bird's Eye which justifies placement in the prime top left box.

At the other extreme, the bottom right is the category of uncoated fish. This is an unattractive commodity market (score 37 percent), with low margins for suppliers, dominated by private labels. Bird's Eye has chosen not to compete in this market segment (score 0 percent).

This portfolio analysis can be used as a guide to resource allocation and strategic priority. For U.K. Bird's Eye, chicken products clearly merit high priority. Vegetarian foods and fish fingers also deserve investment, while meat pies and frozen desserts do not.

Portfolio analysis facilitates decision-making and helps pinpoint issues. For example, with respect to red meat grills, the brand is reasonably strong but the market unattractive. The strategic question becomes: Is it practical to make the market more attractive in the future and therefore justify investment?

Evaluation:

Pros. The requirement to quantify adds additional objectivity, but many elements remain subjective.

Because it is process driven, and clearly defined, QPA can be used for cross-country and cross-market comparisons.

Cons. It is more time-consuming than BCG and McKinsey/General Electric matrices.

QPA requires judgment by experienced line managers in order to be fully effective, and, unlike BCG, cannot be constructed by analysts.

Overall Evaluation

Portfolio analysis is a useful tool to guide strategic investment priorities by market, business unit, channel, or brand. A considerable amount of offensive analysis is necessary to get good results and simplistic application is dangerous. Some of the choices are subjective, yet objectivity can be greatly increased by setting up a quantified process and using a common scoring system across markets and countries.

DEVELOPING COMPETITIVE ADVANTAGES

Competitive advantage is achieved whenever your company does something better than competitors. If that something is important to consumers or if a number of small advantages can be combined, your firm has an *exploitable* competitive advantage. One or more competitive advantages are usually necessary in order to develop a *winning strategy*. This, in turn, should enable your company to achieve above-average growth and profits in its industry. Competitive advantages are the concrete expression of exploitable assets and competencies.

Competitive advantages are worth having. They enable your company to develop winning strategies and put you in the driver's seat placing pressure on your competition.

To reiterate: There are six key elements in developing competitive advantage. These include: possessing an offensive vision and attitude; having an integrated marketing approach; conducting offensive analysis; anticipating the future by offensive business analysis; conducting portfolio analysis; and finally, cultivating a familiarity with types of competitive advantage. This last element will be reviewed next.

Types of Competitive Advantage

There are many types of competitive advantage. Table 7-1 shows the main ones, which are:

Table 7-1   Main Types of Competitive Advantage

1. Superior product or service	6. Superior assets
2. Perceived advantage	7. Scale advantages
3. Global skills	8. Attitude advantages
4. Low-cost operator	9. Legal advantages
5. Superior competencies	10. Superior relationships

1. **Superior product or service.** A superior product or service benefit is based on reality not perception. Such benefits are real, provable in fact, and recognized by consumers. Proof can be established by consumer and technical testing for products, and by performance levels and consumer attitudes for services.

Routes to superior benefits with respect to a product include but are not limited to superior design, ease of use, reliability, better end-result or longer lasting, customization, or personalization. With respect to services, superiority often includes speed, quality of performance, flexibility, reliability, personalization or customization, and early responsiveness.

Having a better product or service is one of the most powerful competitive advantages. Self-deception in this area is, however, rife. Many companies assume their products or services are better, even though they have no supporting evidence. Others succeed in establishing proven technical advantages, which are either not apparent or not important to their customers or consumers.

Federal Express offers real service superiority to their customers. They have responded to the challenge of electronic commerce with the understanding that information is key to their creation of competitive advantage. In addition, they understood that information technology would circulate around the needs of individuals/homes to a great extent. By maintaining control of information and processes, they created a bundle of skills and technologies—namely, logistics management—which the consumer experiences as a superior service and on-time delivery. This bundle of skills grows out of the integration of technologies as well as the learning of individuals and organizational groups. These are not just constituent skills, but have been "aggregated" into an organizational competency and capability.[8]

Other examples of well-known product or service benefits include Honda engines for their reliability, Apple products for their user-friendliness, Disneyland for its quality of family service, Polaroid for its speed of results, Wal-Mart for its efficient warehousing operations leading to low-cost structure, Amazon.com for its personalization, and Mercedes for their high resale value.

2. **Perceived advantage.** The superior benefits just covered can be physically proven by demonstration, by objective evaluation, or by blind product tests among consumers. Perceived advantage,

---

[8] This paragraph is based on material in Chapter 9, "Building Gateways to the Future," Hamel and Prahalad, *Competing for the Future*, Harvard Business School Press, 1994.

by contrast, is in the mind of the consumer and is a result of a product's imagery and personality. The auction of Jackie Kennedy's or Elvis' possessions are examples of perceived value. The buyer does not purchase a rocking chair, for example, or a guitar, but an image—a perceived association with a famous individual. Perceived advantage is also at the basis of Ralph Lauren's Home Furnishing successes and Tommy Hilfiger's clothing line.

Perceived advantages are usually built through advertising and presentation. With the Internet and the ability to grow online support for user communities, branding built around perceived advantages has grown in importance.

Some products have a sufficiently strong brand image to overcome apparent product weaknesses. Coke came out ahead even as its launch of New Coke failed. Perceived advantage can also be developed through design, heritage, or styling. Porsche Carrera is an example of a product that other manufacturers have come to model their newer designs off, both to attract purchasers with lesser incomes, as well as attempt to take market share from the leader in the field.

While it could be argued that the Porsche is better engineered, more reliable, and has outstanding resale value, the main reason why customers pay high prices is perceived image advantage over new-comer offerings such as the Audi TT, the BMW Z8 sports car, and the Mercedes coupe.

Other types of perceived advantage may stem from design, such as in fashion wear, an image generated by advertising such as the classic "Marlboro Man," an association with certain personalities, early adopters or authority figures such as those sporting Nike or, exclusivity fostered by limited availability through exclusive outlets or high price, such as Cartier, Tiffany, or Rolex. Recently, the health genre itself has become a perceived advantage. Bottled water, vitamins, and herbal and homeopathic remedies have used this category well to establish advantage vis-à-vis substitute products.

This discussion of perceived value is more relevant to products than to services. It is difficult to achieve a perceived service advantage. If the advantage is not real, the service reputation will rapidly dissipate, even through a single incident. The global financial services industry is suffering because of this. Their alleged misuse of the brokerage relationship to recommend securities that did not meet client investment needs but which were recommended because of financial interests on the part of the firm, has negatively impacted the public's trust and the profession's image. Charles Schwab is capitalizing on this to grow market share at the expense of firms such as Merrill Lynch who find themselves in the hot seat of public scrutiny.

3. **Global skills.** This competitive advantage includes: global distribution; ability to produce and market effectively on a multi-country basis; skills at entering new countries; and structures that achieve global efficiencies in R&D, manufacturing, sales, distribution, and marketing, while simultaneously meeting local needs and providing a motivating work environment for those dispersed around the globe.

   Coca-Cola, with a leading share of the worldwide soft drinks market, is widely distributed in most countries of the world. Together with companies such as McDonald's, Caterpillar, Glaxo SmithKline (the pharmaceutical giant), Nestle, Yamaha of Japan (the world's largest supplier of pianos), and Nokia (the world leader in mobile telephones), they are also skillful at successfully entering new countries and new markets. They have learned to leverage knowledge around the globe from local subsidiaries; to prospect and access pockets of emerging customer trends; and have learned to mobilize knowledge and technology throughout their supply chain and partners to generate revenue, innovate, and create shareholder value.

4. **Low-cost operator.** This is not a matter of simply working cheaply, and it goes beyond low-cost production. A low-cost operator (LCO) strives to achieve lower costs than its competitors for similar products or services, on all elements built into the final delivered offering. This requires low costs not only in operations but also in selling, distribution, administration, IT, and even marketing. A LCO is striving for a cost advantage to provide a winning strategy of superior value at less cost.

   Marketers can play an important part in achieving LCO, by cutting out unnecessary products, forecasting sales accurately, and relating cost to actual customer value.

   There are many ways to develop competitive advantage through low-cost operation. A company can look to high productivity through increasing sales per square foot; increasing capacity utilization in plants, hotels, and planes; or focusing on the concentration of synchronized factories, suppliers, and distribution networks and partnerships. It can look to lowering overheads acting on the philosophy that "small is beautiful," use effective capital investment, or eliminate costs that do not benefit the customer. The firm can also look to low-cost selling with a focus on smaller numbers of larger customers, high productivity, and the effective use of IT and communications technology including the Web and Web-based initiatives.

5. **Superior competencies.** Discussed in Chapter 2, superior competencies usually take a long time to build and are important competitive advantages since they are difficult and time-consuming to copy.

One might argue, with some justification, that all the competitive advantages listed here are examples of effective exploitation of assets and competencies. For instance, IKEA, the home furnishing retailer, has a competitive advantage in purchasing, enabling it to offer consumers high quality at low prices. This advantage is based on superior competencies in "product design and engineering, in warehousing, and in purchasing raw materials and packaging at the most favorable prices."[9] Discounters have continued to press their rivals by offering fashion labels, brands, and expansive merchandizing. IKEA now will customize maple kitchen cabinets, Kmart offers Martha Stewart house wares, and Target sells Courant fashion jeans.

Similarly, Wal-Mart has used better competition, better management, and technological innovations to make goods cheap and available. For example, the big box format enables Wal-Mart and its rivals—including Kohl's, Kmart, and Target—to encourage customers to buy more goods, often on impulse, and to spread fixed labor costs like cleaning crews and management across more sales. Its efficient logistics management is well known and rivals have begun incorporating their best practices, including building stores around hub distribution centers. Indeed, as the 1990s came to a close, Wal-Mart increased its efficiency by not only maximizing efficiency at their warehouses, but it also began to analyze costs over the entire shipping process. It discovered, for example, that not completely filling a pallet with goods can save so much time in stocking that what appears to be inefficient at first glance, becomes most efficient when looking at the whole business model.

---

[9] Charles Baden-Fuller and Martyn Pitts, eds. In *Strategic Innovation*, Routledge, 1996.

Building superior competencies is not a matter of saying, "Let's do more training." The process needs a firm foundation of consumer understanding, skills in IT and technology, clear strategic direction, and offensive attitudes.

6. **Superior assets.** These may consist of property, hard assets, manufacturing capabilities or flexibility, cash, distribution warehouses, or contractual rights such as retail agreements. Superior assets may also include soft assets such as intellectual capital in the way of talent, intellectual property like patents or trademarks, or brands, all of which can be leveraged into the future.

7. **Scale advantages.** Size can be a source of competitive advantage (or the reverse if size produces complacency or bureaucracy). In almost any business, size and therefore influence and capital can generate a financial advantage particularly with the use of advertising dollars. Several million dollars worth of advertising will result in a given impact whether your company is large or small, particularly if these dollars are used well in the present-day, fragmented media market.

The principle of scale also applies to selling. If a company has a sales force twice as big as its nearest competitor, but a market share three times greater, its sales force cost ratio will be lower. It, therefore, has a larger resource at less relative cost. Of course, other ways of selling, as in the effective and efficient use of the Internet and Web technology, often make issues of scale less important.

Scale advantages also continue to operate strongly in manufacturing and service operations. If your firm is a large retailer, property developers or investment groups are much more likely to contact you about prime development prospects. Often, capital markets relate positively to scale and make it easier to obtain the financial support for making large-scale, technology upgrades.

The competitive advantages of scale largely explain why market leaders usually achieve much higher profit margins than the second or third contenders, and why market leadership is often an important objective for the Offensive Marketer.[10]

---

[10] R. Buzzell and B. Gale, *The PIMS Principles*. The Free Press, 1987. Buzzell and Gale, using four-year averages of 2,611 business units, show that businesses with market shares over 30% achieve around three times the percent return on investment, versus those with a share of under 10%. They attribute this difference to scale economies and higher relative quality.

8. **Attitude advantages.** Any of the attitudes described in Chapter 3 can constitute an important competitive advantage.

9. **Legal advantages.** Patents, copyrights, sole distributorships, exclusive retail agreements, or protected positions can provide competitive advantages. Patents are particularly important in the pharmaceutical and electronics industries and can provide both offensive and defensive protection as competitive advantages.

10. **Superior relationships.** Superior relationships may be with customers, influencers, or decision makers. These range from relationships with distributors, partners, or government leadership, to civil servants, suppliers, or institutional investors. For a company in the international fine art business, Christie's or Sotheby's, for example, strong relationships with a number of major collectors are an essential requirement in order to gain the larger, more exclusive sales. Strong relationships with major museums and dealers are also necessary to realize solid prices. Of course, the two are connected, as a company will not gain access to fine collections unless it has a good reputation for successful and prestigious sales.

    On a more localized level, your local Kinko's or print shop may have established many strong customer relationships merely by remembering people's names, and giving them superior and timely service and fair pricing.

    Increasingly, relationships are being managed on a remote but individual level through digital relationship databases, and between organizations, such as supplier and retailer, or companies working together on joint brand or product development. There are a growing number of joint efforts across industries from the automobile industry to pharmaceuticals and entertainment. The goal of these initiatives is often to establish relationships with the end-user and provide the easiest purchasing experience for the product category. In other situations, the objective is to utilize digital technology or other customized technology to do business more efficiently and faster, with more information.

Which Types of Competitive Advantage Matter Most?

Are all types of competitive advantage equally important? Can they be ranked? Are some hotter than others? And how do they relate? The answers to these questions are not straightforward.

The relative importance of each type of competitive advantage will vary by market. For instance, superior performance is very important both in services and in product markets where end users can objectively evaluate real performance. By contrast, in markets where imagery is critical, and social elements are key purchase motivations, perceived advantage is often what matters most. Offensive Marketers in fragrances, soft drinks, spirits, cigarettes, and luxury goods know this well.

Competitive advantages that are growing in importance include:

- Low-cost operation to satisfy increasingly value conscious consumers
- Superior competencies, which can create many types of competitive advantage that are difficult to copy in the short term as the market continues to become more competitive
- Superior relationships, which is benefiting from increases both in the understanding of the economic value generated by customer loyalty over time, and in cooperative partnerships between companies

By contrast, competitive advantage based on superior actual product performance appears to be lessening in importance, as the capability of others to copy that superior performance quickly improves. In a world of growing deregulation, where regions and individual countries take a different view of patent protection, legal advantages may also continue to decline in significance.

Many types of competitive advantage are related. Asset or competency exploitation underlies most of them. Actual or perceived product superiority builds brand share, and drives scale, attitudes, and relationships in a favorable direction.

If a single type of competitive advantage had to be chosen as most important from an Offensive Marketer's perspective, it would be superior product or service quality in the eyes of target customers with respect to aspects of the offering most important to them. This is supported by analysis done by Buzzell and Gale based on their PIMS (Profit Impact of Marketing Strategies) findings.[11]

---

[11] R. Buzzell and B. Gale, Id.

Analysis among thousands of businesses of relative product quality, relative cost, market share levels, trends, and return on investment yielded these conclusions:

- In the long run, the most important single factor affecting a business unit's performance is the quality of its products and services relative to competitors.
- In the short term, quality yields increased profits via premium prices.
- In the longer term, superior and/or improving relative quality is the most effective way for a business to grow. Quality leads to both market expansion and gains in market share.
- On average, businesses with superior quality products have costs about equal to those of their leading competitors.

FIVE LEVELS OF COMPETITIVE STATUS

There are five levels of competitive advantage. The highest and best is the use of one or more large advantages. The second highest is the use of a number of smaller advantages adding up to a large advantage. The third tier of competitive advantage is where advantages are available to the company but are not fully exploited. The next tier is that advantages are just not present or available to the company. And, the bottom rung of competitiveness, is that competitive disadvantages actually exist.

The objective of any company should be to move up to one of the top two levels. Those in the two bottom levels will struggle to survive. Many companies are at the bottom tiers of competitive advantage. They have failed to exploit competitive advantages that do exist or have begun to lose advantages through changes in customer needs, new technology, or competitor initiatives. Perhaps they have failed to pull together smaller advantages that can add up to a market-significant position vis-à-vis rivals.

One or More Large Advantages

Coca-Cola, Disney, Toyota, Procter & Gamble, Wal-Mart, Hewlett-Packard, Amazon, and Honda are among companies in this enviable position.

Honda's large advantages lie in core competencies in engine design and manufacture, which are leveraged into competitive advantage across the focused range of products that Honda manufactures and sells: motorcycles, cars, and power products like lawnmowers and small boat engines.[12]

Amazon's competitive advantage lies in its use of digital technology that personalizes the customer experience. This advantage continues to expand as new tools become available and as understanding of how end users interact with the medium of the Web is deepened.

A Number of Smaller Advantages Add Up to a Large One

Many companies claim this status and may indeed have a number of smaller competitive advantages. But, if their effect is dispersed, they will not add up to the sustained competitive effects of a large one. Take the case of McDonald's internationally. The company's advantages in site selection, staff training, advertising, store design, lighting, supplier management, and globalization generate consistently strong consumer experiences. This has been achieved despite a relatively pedestrian product offer, and a modest record of recent innovation.

Advantages Present, But Not Fully Exploited

Priceline.com may be a company that has competitive advantages, but, has not to date, fully exploited them in the context of their patented "name your own price" online system. In markets that have oversupply—such as airline seats, hotel rooms, and rental cars—in which customers are looking for deals but not necessarily brand or convenience, Priceline.com's business model is a good match. It has remained the dominant player in its niche market because of its successful technology and the fact that its market of bargain conscious travelers exists in both good and bad economic times. After perhaps broadening its line-up of consumer products too rapidly, getting back to its core of providing discount airfares may enable it to

---

[12] Charles Baden-Fuller and Martyn Pitt, eds. In *Strategic Innovation*, Routledge, 1996. See "Case Study on Honda Motors" by Andrew Mair.

deepen its strategy's distinctiveness and continue to explore and expand on new relationships between seller and buyer.[13]

No Significant Competitive Advantages

Most companies fall into this category. They often lack either distinctiveness or competitive edge. Often their business proposition is not sustainable over time.

Competitive Disadvantages

Companies in this category usually only survive in the long term if they enjoy monopoly positions, protection from competition, or compensating competitive advantages.

TURNING COMPETITIVE ADVANTAGES INTO WINNING STRATEGIES

A company that has developed its competitive advantages is now in a position to carve out a winning strategy. A firm has at its disposal a wide range of possible offensive strategies. The eight main ones are summarized in Table 7-2.

Table 7-2   Strategies for Exploiting Competitive Advantages

1. Head on	5. Regional concentration
2. Flanking	6. Product range
3. Encirclement	7. Guerrilla
4. Niche	8. Diplomacy

1. **Head on.** This strategy involves a direct frontal attack to drive back or overwhelm a competitor. To apply a head-on strategy successfully, a company needs strong products and heavy marketing support, since existing competitors are likely to counterattack in order to maintain their position.

---

[13] Allen R. Myerson, "Behind 'Name Your own Price' Lies a Mesh of Partners," *The New York Times*, March 29, 2000, at pg. C24.

A head-on strategy is most appropriate for a large, well-financed company prepared to fight a long battle of attrition. Head-on attacks in business rarely produce quick break-throughs. Companies like Procter & Gamble, Coca-Cola, Glaxo SmithKline, and Microsoft have successfully used the head-on approach. To succeed with a head-on strategy, your firm needs a strong proposition and lots of staying power.

Retailers frequently pursue a head-on strategy when launching their own label brands. A typical approach is to meet or beat the quality of the brand leader at a lower price. Head-on attacks are also frequent in markets where technology or product models change frequently, as in cars, computer hardware, software, or over-the-counter medicines. An example of a head-on attack playing itself out over the past few years involves Microsoft's competing handheld operating software set against Palm's dominant technology in handheld computing.

2. **Flanking.** This strategy involves attacking a competitor on a flank that is weakly defended. The competitor may lack skills in this sector, regard it as a low priority, or be committed to a "milking" strategy. In any event, a flanking attack is likely to draw a much weaker response than a head-on offensive, because the defender may not feel directly threatened, at least in the short term.

Flanking strategy follows the classic approach of attacking the competitor's weakest point with your firm's strongest weapon. It needs to be followed through succinctly, because the threat posed by the flanker becomes clearer over time and can eventually lead to a strong competitive response.

In general, more companies use flanking than a head-on strategy, as flanking tends to be lower risk, and often has a higher probability of success. The classic flanking moves in business tend to involve pricing (high or low), neglected segments, or product innovation. Bic flanked Gillette in razors by innovating the low-priced disposable sector. Here, the longstanding market leader was slow to react, aware that strong reaction would accelerate the growth of a new, lower-margin sector.

Another flanking approach is to change the rules of competition through product, technology, or distribution channel innovation. Dell is an example of a company that gained leadership in the market for personal computing by changing the distribution channels to use direct contact with the end user: offering customization, personal contact to build a sense of relationship and continuing dialogue. Prior to Dell's success, network computing changed the rules on IBM and its mainframe computer success. Canon changed the pricing rules on Xerox and the industry method of doing business with its introduction of the changeable ink cartridge. It made Xerox's sales force dispensable and changed the rules of competition. Amazon changed the rules on Barnes and Noble and other booksellers by using the new, unproven online channel.

The Internet also changed the rules on Encyclopedia Britannica early in the game, and has brought new competitors into the market in many industries, creating not only new ways of doing business that older, more established bricks and mortar firms have had to respond to, but also creating new industries. In many of these and other examples, the flanking strategy turned into a frontal attack as the newer product or newer model of delivery took hold.

Accordingly, a flanking attack by a competitor should not be ignored just because it increases the total market and leaves your firm's sales unaffected in the short term. It is more likely to reduce your share of the market and may turn into a head-on attack in the longer term.

3. **Encirclement.** Encirclement occurs when a brand or company is surrounded by a hostile competitor, attacking it from a number of points. This is a difficult strategy to mount in competitive markets, and easiest to sustain in mature, low-technology sectors, where new technology provides little basis for a breakout by the encircled company or brand.

4. **Niche.** Niche markets are too small or specialized to attract large competitors. Factors that can make niche markets uninteresting to large competitors include the need to acquire specialized skills or the lack of volume against which to amortize high overheads. Successful niche players include Ferrari at the high end of the automobile industry; Harley Davidson motorcycles in the heavy duty motorcycle market; Samantha's fresh, natural drinks in the health-food industry; VitaminWater in the bottled water market; and Ben and Jerry's in the high-end, natural ice cream market.

Almost without exception, niche products are premium-priced to compensate the marketer for lack of scale in production and distribution. In addition, they usually command above-average profit margins.

A niche strategy can lead in a number of directions. The niche may be an end in itself, as in the case of the examples cited above. In the alternative, it may be a means to establish a toehold in a larger market as the recent history of Snapple or Toyota has shown. The Japanese often use a niche strategy as an entry point and subsequently expand across the larger market, usually very successfully. Snapple, originally marketed as a health drink, quickly moved into the mainstream of the soft drink market.

When does a niche become a mass market? Some niches grow steadily over time and convert into mass markets when they attract competition attacking the original niche product or company.

Premium beers used to be niche and are gradually becoming mass market. The same may be happening to premium, natural brewed pre-packaged tea sold in single servings. Volvo started off as a niche product, appealing to the minority of customers who wanted a safe, functional, long-lasting car, and who were not particularly interested in styling or performance. It has since broadened its appeal, with improvements in performance and styling to become a mainstream product that other manufacturers emulate in safety and performance.

A niche can rapidly convert into a mass market, where prices fall as volume grows and the early niche marketers are confronted by mass marketers with large resources. Three of the main circumstances driving conversion are:

1. **Market growth.** A niche market may grow in size to the point where it becomes attractive to mass marketers.
2. **Acquisition of a niche company by a larger business, with brand development skills and a commitment to build volume.** This was the early intent of Quaker with its purchase of Snapple.
3. **Entry to a niche market by a major industry player.** This tends to attract other mass-market competitors.

Niches are discovered by deep understanding of how markets segment. The secret is to ensure that a niche is the right size—large enough to be profitable, but not sufficiently large to attract the super firms, at least not in the early days when the company is establishing a position.

A genuine niche product or service will be clearly differentiated from mass-market competitors, deliberately targeted at a specific minority group of consumers at a premium price.

5. **Regional concentration.** The principle behind this strategy is that it is better to be a large fish in a small pond than the reverse. In addition to local market knowledge, regional concentration can give the Offensive Marketer the advantages of brand leadership in miniature, allied with speed of reaction and market responsiveness unavailable to a national or international operator. Local beer breweries or wineries are good examples of successful regional concentration by local producers.

   Like a niche strategy, regional concentration can be used as an entry point to a market. Regional concentration can also be used as a permanent strategy, and many companies have decided to focus only on larger home markets. Regional concentration remains a viable strategy, especially in large countries (or groups of countries), for companies with genuine local strengths, and in markets where speed or service levels are important. There are many successful local companies in beer, wines and spirits, chilled foods, utilities, retailing, and banking, but few in industries like pharmaceuticals, paper, entertainment, computing, software, or consumer durables, where global reach, R&D, and economies of scale are important.

   As consumer tastes and markets converge, and global and meta-national companies continue to strengthen their positions, regional concentration may become a less attractive strategy. A counterbalance to this, and what may protect regional and local players, is the preference that consumers express for locally crafted goods and services.

6. **Product range.** Product proliferation through offering a very wide product range is sometimes described as a "saturation" strategy. The principle is that you offer retailers or distributors every conceivable product type and option, absorb a high proportion of stock and display space, and thereby limit opportunities for competitors. The privately owned Seiko Corporation of Tokyo is one of the most skillful practitioners of this strategy, with its worldwide range of over 2,000 watches under the Lorus, Pulsar, and Seiko brands. Olympus is another practitioner of a wide-product line strategy.

   There are obvious dangers in a strategy of product proliferation. It may create major manufacturing dis-economies, and is vulnerable to a focused attack by a supplier with a narrower range and targeted specialization.

The Mars Group's strategy is the opposite of Seiko. Mars believes in a very limited range of "power brands," strongly advertised and very efficiently produced in high volume. Establishing the right product-range strategy, which achieves the best balance between meeting the needs of target customers and achieving efficient low-cost operation, is often a complex question and is frequently given too little priority in overall corporate strategy discussions. In practice, it should be a prime area for leadership by the Offensive Marketer.

Some of the issues identified as relevant to developing a product range strategy include:[14]

- **Market segmentation**. In constructing a range strategy, it is essential to have a clear understanding of how the total market is segmented, and what the product or service needs of each segment are. This enables a company to cover all segments in which it wishes to compete with a comprehensive range involving minimum overlap. The fifteen-plus automobile divisions and marques of GM are a fundamental source of GM's competitive decline since the mid-1970s compared to BMW's single marque, Toyota with the Toyota and Lexus marques, and Honda following suit with its two marques, Honda and Acura.

- **Blocking Competition.** By designing a full product line, a firm gives its customers minimum reasons to look at competitive offerings and virtually eliminates niche competition.[15]

- **Trading up customers**. Many companies prefer to compete in a number of price segments, so that they can trade up customers over time and retain long-term relationships with them as their expectations increase.

- **Building competencies.** One of the reasons why Olympus follows a full-line strategy is its desire to filter down the high-end technology developed for more expensive products into higher-quality products at the lower end of the market.

7. **Guerrilla strategy.** Che Guevara,[16] defines the main elements of guerrilla strategy as:
   - Defeat of the enemy is the final objective.

---

[14] Robin Cooper, *When Lean Enterprises Collide*, Harvard Business School Press, 1995.
[15] Robin Cooper, Id.
[16] Che Guevara, *Guerrilla Warfare*, Penguin, 1969.

- Use of surprise.
- Tactical flexibility.
- Concentration of attacks on ground favorable to the attacker.

The analogy with business is inexact, since the business attacker does not aim to defeat its large competitors overall and is quite satisfied to win skirmishes that give it longer-term advantages. However, the three other elements mentioned by Guevara have application to the small business competing with larger operators.

Typical guerrilla tactics involve attacking a competitor's weak product, its status with a specific retailer or distributor, or attacking a small geographical area. Whereas small companies usually employ guerrilla tactics because they require speed of reaction and flexibility, they are sometimes used by larger operators in the form of "fighting brands." These are a means either to use up spare capacity, or to put pressure on competitors in market sectors important to them, but where the attacker has a low market share. Fighting brands are usually floor priced, and can be used tactically in the short term as well as strategically in the longer term.

Smaller companies, following Che Guevara's advice, often use surprise and tactical flexibility as weapons against large competitors. Virgin is a good example. Virgin has consistently competed against large international businesses, whether in music, airlines, or financial services. Among the unconventional weapons Virgin uses are:

- **Legal action, or the threat of it.** Virgin rarely goes to court, but when it does, it usually wins. Legal initiatives serve both as a deterrent to competitors and as a source of favorable editorial and consumer awareness, on grounds favorable to Virgin. Big companies tend to be ill at ease when defending themselves against allegedly illegal tactics directed at a smaller competitor.
- **Event marketing.** Activities like the transatlantic speed record for ships, and round-the-world ballooning, not only generate millions of dollars worth of low-cost publicity, but also foster Virgin's image as adventurous and fun.
- **Issue advertising in the national press.** On topics affecting Virgin, like airline competition policy, this advertising

spawns wide media publicity and become news stories in their own right.[17]

It is difficult for small companies to successfully sustain a guerrilla strategy over the long term. They are likely to either become much larger or, after some tactical successes, sell out to a bigger competitor.

8. **Diplomacy.** A strategy of diplomacy covers many forms of external development, such as acquisitions, joint ventures, licensing, partnerships, or other cooperative ventures with third parties. Strategic arrangements that fall short of acquisition or mergers are gaining in popularity especially as companies move into overseas markets. Their value is to fill gaps in knowledge or skills of each of the parties or to pool compatible resources toward a mutually desired objective.

Diplomacy is a way of winning a war without firing a shot. It is probably the fastest-growing type of strategy, driven by convergence between markets, external industry benchmarking, globalization, and the high cost of developing new technology and distribution networks. The result is that companies are cooperating with other businesses in some countries and markets, while simultaneously competing in others.

An increasing number of companies are establishing local or global alliances, especially in high-tech industries, communications, entertainment, and pharmaceuticals. Such alliances have as their goals obtaining access to proprietary technology or manufacturing capabilities, to gain access and knowledge of foreign markets, to reduce financial or political risks, or to achieve competitive advantage. Some of the better known include: GM and Toyota created Nummi Corporation as a joint venture to provide Toyota a manufacturing facility in the United States and to gain access for GM to Toyota's low-cost, high-quality manufacturing expertise; Matsushita successfully overcame Sony's Beta system by sharing its VHS technology with other companies; and, in the early computing and data networking environment, IBM and AT&T created competing global networks with multiple partners to gain both expertise and additional resources.[18] Another large-scale strategic alliance involved Motorola as a leader in wireless communications.

---

[17] Article by Edmund O. Lawler, *Advertising Age*, November 13, 1995.
[18] Richard D'Aveni, *Hyper-competition*, The Free Press, 1994.

The Iridium satellite communications program involved upwards of a dozen companies from around the world, including Lockheed, Raytheon, Martin Marietta, and Siemens A.G. The alliance was based on skills, know-how, and technology instead of a specific market or product.[19]

PICKING THE RIGHT STRATEGY TO WIN

In selecting the right strategy, it is important to be aware of the repertoire available, to consider alternatives, and to make clear choices. All of the strategies outlined above are possibilities for any size of company, except the head-on strategy that is recommended only for large and very seasoned companies.

The main factors affecting your company's choice of strategy will be size and resources, strengths, competitive weaknesses, and market opportunities. A careful consideration of these will enable you to select a winning strategy.

In most markets, there is room for a brand leader, a differentiated No. 2, a low-price product, and niche brands. If your company or brand is a "me too," or No. 3 or No. 4 in the industry, you do not have a strategy and will not survive for long unless you develop one.

SPOTTING STRATEGIC FATIGUE

Winning strategies need to be nurtured, updated, and modified to meet changing consumer needs and competitive challenges; otherwise, they will soon wear out and become losers. Companies with previously winning strategies, such as Polaroid, Eastman Kodak, Avon, Encyclopedia Britannica, Sears Roebuck, and General Motors lost their competitive edge. In the case of Polaroid, slow growth in amateur photography and improved product performance from non-instant competitors blunted the competitive advantage it had enjoyed. Kodak was slow to respond to Japanese innovation and changing technologies, Avon lagged in reacting to the challenge to its distribution system posed by the growing number of part- and full-time jobs available to women and the economic necessity that caused women to return to the work force. Sears was

---

[19] Warren J. Keegan, *Global Marketing Management*, 6th ed., Prentice Hall, 1999.

slow to respond to changing customer needs and in purchasing preferences as well as threats to its longstanding catalogue business model. Encyclopedia Britannica failed to see the challenge that online information and computing was to its sales-force-based business model. General Motors failed to capture the purchasing power and imagination of its strong customer base.

Factors that contribute to strategic fatigue include changing customer requirements and growing expectations. These can be based upon shifts in technology that cause changes in distribution efficiencies, innovations by competitors in ways of doing business, poor use of company resources and rising costs, lack of consistent investment in strategic areas, and ill-advised changes to a successful strategy out of "the next new thing" mentality.

1. **Changes in customer requirements.** While these have speeded up, they still tend to occur gradually over a number of years. A company keeping close to its customers should therefore be able to update and refine the execution of its strategies to match changing circumstances. Reasons for not doing so include complacency created by past success, and an unwillingness to tinker with a successful strategy.

2. **Changes in distribution systems.** These usually evolve slowly, however, they are often more difficult for companies to respond to than changes in consumer needs. Companies tend to be loyal to existing customers, are loath to upset them by participating in new channels for fear of cannibalizing their older relationships, and may in fact lack the organizational competency to do so.

3. **Innovation by competitors.** This is always a significant threat, both from existing and from new competitors, as the competitive marketplace continues to evolve.

4. **Poor use of resources and control of company costs.** These can smother a strong strategy through weak execution.

5. **Lack of consistent investment.** Even strong strategies wither over time if they are not well supported by product, IT, or service or plant investment, and by spending on customer communication and support.

6. **Ill-advised change to a successful strategy.** This can happen for a variety of reasons. The company may be acquired and its new owners, almost as a reflex action, may decide to strike out in new directions. New management may be hired from

outside, and react similarly. Strange as it may seem, some companies just get tired of long-standing strategies, successful though they may have been, and seek change for its own sake. Sometimes the strategy becomes poorly executed, and successive groups of managers may forget or never relearn its original intent, or not surprisingly, misapply it. If a long-standing strategy is up for change, it is essential first to understand its history correctly, then evaluate whether the strategy or the recent execution of it is at fault; and finally, to thoroughly test the replacement strategy against the original one before dropping it—particularly if it shows continuing vitality.

In summary, the following questions should be reviewed to determine the strength of your company's strategy or the strength of its brand strategy.

1. Does your firm's strategy call for superiority in at least one area of high importance to customers…reflecting your firm's competitive advantage?
2. Is this superiority consistently achieved?
3. Is your company's strategy underpinned by at least one significant competitive advantage or a robust and integrated collection of smaller ones, or neither?
4. Is your firm's strategy viewed by customers as differentiated from that of your competitors and has it been consistently followed through?
5. Are the basics of the strategy well understood by your firm's management team and has it been well communicated across the organization?
6. Is the strategy strengthening, weakening, or standing still and what does this say about changes in the marketplace?
7. Is the company investing enough and in the right places to ensure the strategy is sustainable? Are alternatives being explored?
8. Is the strategy regularly updated in execution in line with changing market demands and changing customer needs?

CONCLUSION

Although this chapter is lengthy, it covers many important concepts in developing winning strategies. Winning strategies are built out of an offensive strategy and the development of competitive advantages.

By using portfolio analysis, your company can make determinations as to strategic resource allocation by market, channel, business unit, or brand. Your firm can make a determination as to how to develop competitive advantage over your competitors by cultivating and leveraging assets and competencies that are unique to the firm and best suited to the competitive marketplace in which your firm finds itself. This competitive advantage may involve a superior product or service, a perceived advantage from the perspective of the consumer, global skills including global distribution, global production and marketing, and skills at new market identification and entry. In the alternative or, in tandem, these advantages may involve being a low-cost operator, having superior assets or competencies, or having scale advantages or alliance-building talents.

Once a competitive advantage has been identified and cultivated, your company will have a wide repertoire of strategies to pursue depending on what is most appropriate from a strategic perspective. Some of these strategies include a head-on attack, flanking, a niche position, guerrilla tactics, product range possibilities, regional concentration, diplomacy, and encirclement. The right strategic fit will be influenced by your firm's size, its resources, its assets and competencies, by the opportunities available, and competitor weaknesses or expected responses.

Winning strategies are as vulnerable to life cycles as are products. Strategies must be nurtured, updated, and modified in response to changing market needs and new competitive moves.

8

Offensive Marketing Planning

INTRODUCTION

This is the last chapter in the section on Strategic, or the "S" of POISE. With material that has been pulled together from previous chapters, especially those on offensive business analysis and offensive strategies, marketing planning is placed in its full context.

Marketing Planning is a complex topic. A certain amount of detail is essential to communicate it effectively. Marketing planning is also highly practical, which is why tools for marketing planning are discussed in this chapter.

The objectives of marketing planning are to learn from the past, anticipate the future, identify opportunities, develop winning strategies, and to turn them into excellent, executable plans. Common setbacks in marketing planning include the lack of integration with other company plans, such as those for Sales, Manufacturing, R&D, and Operations; a corporate-wide overemphasis on analysis, often resulting in decision makers complaining about being deluged with meaningless or irrelevant raw data; and, the lack of effective action either coordinated between and among departments or as a single, quantifiable program. Effective Offensive Marketing planning is designed to achieve balance between analysis and creativity and between thoughtfulness and practicality. As marketing becomes more global, so too the integration of country, region, or brand marketing plans grows in complexity.

Other key issues decided in marketing plans include time frame, the level of detail of directives, people involved, responsibilities and roles of different management levels, and the process used to come to an integrated effort.

MARKETING PLANS: GOOD AND BAD

Much time and effort is often spent on business analysis not directly related to marketing planning and less time is spent on cultivating and creating possible actions. Issues to be targeted need to be identified early in the process and then addressed specifically.

For example, in a market where opportunity is seen to exist, should a major investment in developing a special range of products tailored to the particular needs of the identified market be made—or, are there changes that need to be made in distribution capabilities? In marketing planning, effort is needed to get the right balance between rigorous analysis and creativity. Too often, completion of the formats required by the plan is so time-consuming that marketers get quickly submerged by the weight of paper and have little energy left to devote to strategy and innovation. At the other extreme, creative plans built on superficial analysis may prove misdirected.

Offensive Marketing planning is designed to achieve balance and competitive advantage using a process that is time-efficient and practical. Avoiding falling into common traps of endless analysis, overly simplified business review and general discussion takes strong facilitation and focus. Similarly, planning processes that become highly tactical and short term lose much of, if not all, their strategic clout.

Table 8-1 outlines some of the characteristics of a good and bad marketing plan.

Table 8-1   Good and Bad Marketing Plans (*read across*)

Good marketing plans	Bad marketing plans
• Brief and concise	→ Lengthy and overly general
• Relevant analysis	→ Endless analysis
• Majority of effort in opportunity identification, strategy development, action	→ 90% of effort in business review, general discussion
• Focus on competitive advantage	→ Focus on completing complex formats
• Cross-departmental involvement	→ Planning in marketing silo
• Plans in constant use	→ Plans lie undisturbed for a year
• Strategic and actionable	→ Highly tactical, short term
• Updated regularly	→ Ignored until next plan
• Monitored constantly	→ Not monitored
• Motivating	→ Demotivating

Marketing planning and the resulting plan should be concise, based on relevant analysis and study, with a majority of the effort going toward opportunity identification, strategy development, and action. The focus should be on generating unique value and competitive advantage through cross-departmental and cross-functional involvement and commitment. When execution is underway, plans must be coordinated to be successfully implemented.

Plans should constantly be in use, updated regularly with relevant changing market insight and experience gleaned out of creative market incursions.

WHERE DO MARKETING PLANS FIT?

Marketing plans cover different levels, depending on the structure of the company. For a global or multinational company competing in a range of market categories, marketing plans will need to derive from the corporate marketing plan, and link into total country plans as well as worldwide plans for the product category. Figure 8-1 shows how a marketing plan for a multi-category, global company fits into the larger corporate strategic planning scheme.

Figure 8-1
Marketing Plans for a Multi-Category Global Company

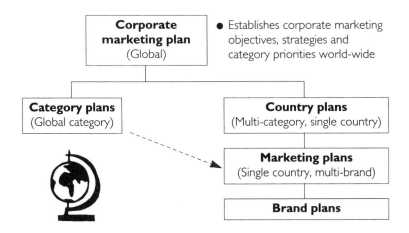

For a single-country company with a number of separate business units, the situation is less complex. Business unit marketing plans should link into the total business unit plan and the corporate marketing plan. Figure 8-2 shows marketing plans for a single-country company.

Figure 8-2
Marketing Plans for Single-Country Company

Every marketing plan, whatever the level, must be aligned to a total strategic business plan and Operations, R&D, Manufacturing, IT, HR, and Finance's plans (see Figure 8-3). In any business, alignment of the marketing plan to other related internal plans throughout the organization is essential to avoid duplication of effort and to ensure consistency of those efforts and goals. The internal dialogue establishing this consistency and goal setting provides an opportunity for the Offensive Marketer to lead with marketing vision, making the whole company market-focused and customer driven.

Figure 8-3
Link of Marketing Plans Above and Across

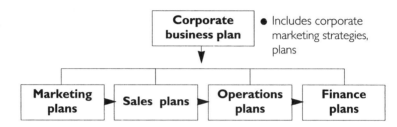

Unfortunately, marketing plans are often developed in isolation from other organization plans and then thrown "over the wall" at a stage too late to be effective. This leads to narrow strategies and weak execution.

The following are some likely outcomes of this isolated approach:

- Account plans are never completed or if they are, remain weak links to brand planning and execution. In this scenario, total revenue for all brands (Marketing) often differs from total revenue for all channels and major accounts (Sales), clouding transparency and true understanding of what is happening.
- Unnecessary cost will be added to plans because there has been no discussion between Marketing and Operations about alternatives or choices. Frequently, two different marketing plans may be equally effective but one will enable Operations to use its capacity much more efficiently than the other. In addition, the more aware Operations is about new products or services or about peaks and troughs in volume, the more effectively and efficiently it will be able to manage change.

- Interaction between brands and trade channels is not properly thought through. Increasingly, brand offerings need to be tailored to the specific requirements of different channels while also communicating a consistent proposition across all channels. For instance, a mortgage product may be sold through retail branches, directly by phone, online, or offered by independent financial consultants. The way the product is positioned may differ by channel, but needs to be credible and consistent in the eyes and understanding of the consumer who visits a branch one day, gets a direct telesales contact two days later, investigates the product online and sees a financial consultant the following week.
- The quality of the marketing plans will be sub-optimal, since the views of R&D, Finance, Operations, Manufacturing, and IT people will be heard too late in the process, if at all.

Walls or impediments to dialogue of any kind must be removed and replaced by a lively and ongoing interaction between Marketing and Operations, both informally and formally. Additionally, as the role of technology and talent becomes increasingly important, IT and HR managers need to be brought into the loop early in the process.

The integrated approach to marketing planning does not take any longer than the "over the wall" method. The integrated approach results not only in stronger, aligned strategies, integrated throughout the organization, but also in dramatically superior implementation. After all, the vast majority of marketing implementation is handled by Marketing and Operations staff, backed by IT capabilities and HR talent. If they understand the purpose of the plans and have actively contributed to their development, they will naturally feel more committed to their success, clued into their monitoring and evaluation and ready to make changes and communicate these as may be needed. The end result is a team approach, consumer-driven and aligned behind a strategic marketing vision.

MORE KEY ISSUES IN MARKETING PLANNING

Marketing planning is a challenging process and many companies have difficulty with it. In addition to the crucial question of integration covered above, there are a number of other key issues that need to be resolved before embarking on the marketing planning process.

What Time Frames Should Be Used?

Most companies have one-, three-, or five-year plans. Some industries, like pharmaceuticals where product development lead times are very long, have a ten-year plan or longer.

Each planning scenario and accompanying process is different. People at the center of the company will probably drive the ten-year or very long-term plan and cover issues such as future market priorities, technology, brand and product development, and possible mergers and acquisitions. This very long-term plan, once completed, provides the context for the medium-term (three-to-five year) plan, which is much more specific, focusing primarily on strategies, targets, and plans including key objectives, major strategies, the allocation of resources over the period of time, and test and development plans. The one-year plan, or budget, stems from these and deals with detailed implementation. It applies the strategies previously agreed as part of the medium-term plan to short-term tactics and objectives.

Every company will have a one-year plan. However, there are advantages in having a longer-term, mid-term, and short-term planning system, even if your firm is not in a long lead-time industry, because:

- The ability to look forward five to ten years is liberating, encourages future vision creation, and stimulates long-term thinking.
- Although the choice for the medium-term plan is usually between three and five years, three is appropriate for most companies. It is far enough into the future to allow for ambitious development, but close enough to provide urgency. For many, the speed of change is such that five years is too long a period for medium-term planning, and 18 months to two years may be more appropriate. Long-, mid-, and short-term plans should be updated annually, and each aligned with the cycle for calendar-year planning.

How Much Detail Is Needed?

Be concise and focused. Avoid too much detail in commentary and relegate it to exhibits. If a plan is too long and complicated no one will read it or understand it except the writer. More importantly, it will end up stuffed away in a file, and not be a working document.

Resources available will also influence the level of detail. By far the most time-consuming part of any marketing plan is the business analysis section. (Refer to Chapter 5, which outlines the requirements for effective analysis.) Productivity can be maximized by building up analyses continuously over the year, rather than trying to handle the whole analysis process within a single month; and, by focusing analysis on particular hypotheses for action, and using it as a basis for proving or disproving them. The worst error is to try to analyze every available piece of data. Accordingly, the analysis itself must have a strategic focus.

Who Should Be Involved in Marketing Planning?

The marketing plan is the primary responsibility of the Marketing Department, especially Marketing Managers and Brand Managers. They must, however, work closely with selected people across the organization, providing brief and clear summaries at various stages of the process and involving others in planning discussion and workshops.

Establishment of an extended brand group on a continuous basis can also provide a valuable framework for cross-departmental communication. The extended brand group consists of anyone who has significant effect on the success of a brand, whether in Marketing, Operations, Finance, R&D, Human Resources, IT, or external partners and strategically aligned companies. The group should not be too large, with members selected on the basis of skills and competencies.

The extended brand group should work together in workshops and formal and informal groups. However, to make workshops and larger gatherings most effective, Marketing people need to prepare carefully and to pre-circulate high-quality summaries of key data.

Should the Marketing Process Be Up or Down?

The answer is both up and down, as well as across. In practice, certain issues like corporate financial objectives and overall strategies have to be decided at a high level and fed down. Input should be given by those closest to the end user, the consumer, and the defined market. Equally, in a global company, various strategic guidelines may need to be established centrally or regionally. For example, it may be uneconomic to develop different automobile bodies for each country, or tailor advertising in every country for a global hair-care brand. Within such top-down strategic requirements, there should be considerable scope for adaptation and innovation by market, brand, channel, and country on a bottom to middle-management basis.

Figure 8-4 shows the strategic and operation planning sequencing throughout an organization from higher tiered corporate objectives and strategies down to unit objectives and strategies.[1]

Figure 8-4
Strategic and Operational Planning

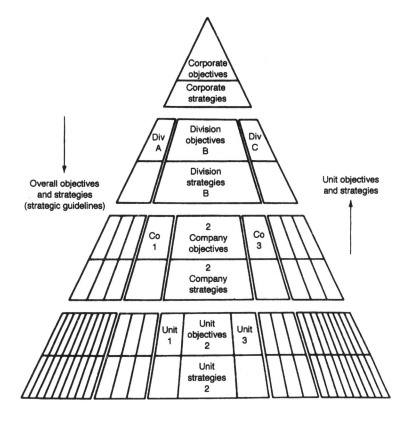

[1] Malcolm H.B. McDonald and Warren J. Keegan, *Marketing Plans That Work*, 2nd ed., Butterworth Heinemann, 2002. pg. 210.

Clearly, in a large, diversified company, operating in global markets, a synthesis of product, market, and functional plans may be required, although the total corporate plan must be aligned with and grow out of the individual building blocks. As size and product diversity grow, the degree of planning and process formalization necessarily increases. Figure 8-5 shows how the degree of formalization of the marketing planning process increases with both size and diversity.[2]

Figure 8-5
Degree of Formalization of the Marketing Planning Process: Size and Diversity

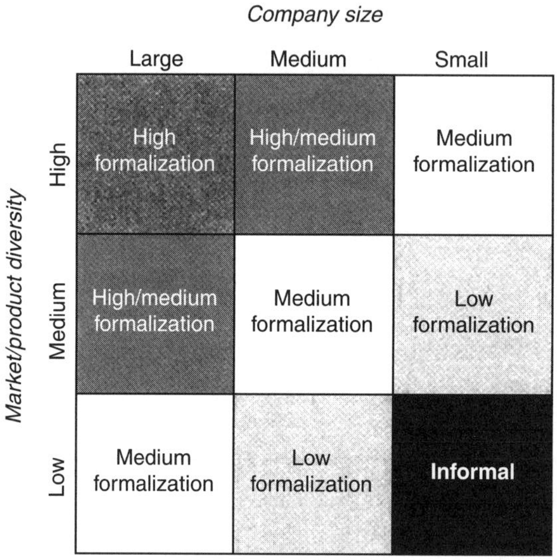

Despite formalization of the planning process to integrate the size and diversity of operations and units, the need for a complete marketing planning process and framework does not change. Businesses that have a framework for marketing planning have systems in place through a hierarchy of top-to-bottom and bottom-to-top processes that balance the need for centralized control and synthesis and local control and input.

OBJECTIVES OF MARKETING PLANNING

Marketing planning is a demanding and time-consuming process. Some may ask why do it at all, and is it even worth the time?

---

[2] Id. at pg. 201. Portions of this section were inspired by the thinking described in Chapter 13.

These questions can be tested by considering how a company would operate without marketing plans. This must certainly be feasible since, until a few decades ago, marketing planning did not exist. The likely style of a company not using marketing planning is top down, where leadership determines strategies often out of a personal vision. However, often in entrepreneurially led companies, tactics can overwhelm attempts at strategic discourse. Accordingly, "seat of the pants" decision-making may be the predominant thinking. Intuitive outlining of strategy and tactics, however, can be a strong beginning to new thinking and creative visioning. Marketing planning enables managers at least once a year to think deeply about their business—both to consider the past and to look into the future. The process also demands answers to difficult questions, which might otherwise be ignored as the demands of the daily marketplace take precedence.

Marketing planning has *six major objectives* against which the total process should be carefully evaluated. These are:

1. To learn from the past
2. To articulate the future
3. To spot and prioritize relevant opportunities
4. To develop winning strategies
5. To allocate resources to best advantage
6. To blueprint excellent implementation

OFFENSIVE MARKETING PLANNING: A SEVEN-STEP PROCESS

This seven-step process is outlined in Table 8-2.

These seven steps are intrinsic to the Offensive Marketing approach. Relevant to any business plan, the seven steps are for any level, whether global or local, corporate or business unit, and for any function such as Marketing, Sales, or Operations. It is difficult to see how any of the seven steps could be omitted without affecting a plan's quality.

The next three sections will review these seven steps. Much of the groundwork that comprises the seven steps has been covered in previous chapters. Step One, Business Analysis, was covered in Chapters 2 and 5 and will be discussed further in Chapter 9. Step Two, Future Thinking, was discussed at length in Chapter 6.

Table 8-2 Seven Key Planning Steps

Step	Topics covered:	Key tools to use:
1. Business analysis	• Business environment • Markets • Channels • Own business • Competition • Technology • Competencies	• 3 wheels of business environment • Internal examination • Competitive analysis • Key factors for success (KFS) • SWOT analysis • Segmentation • Portfolio analysis
2. Future thinking	• Anticipating the future • Reviewing scenarios • Establishing strategic direction • Developing future thinking	• 6 key drivers of future thinking • Probability analysis • 7 spokes of offensive attitudes
3. Opportunity identification	• Identify main opportunity areas • Generate opportunity long-list • Screen and test opportunities • Prioritized opportunity list	• Outcome of Steps 1 and 2 • Extended brand groups • Idea-generation techniques • Concept testing
4. Set objectives	• Market development • Market share • Revenue • Investment • Innovation • Profits	• Corporate strategy and plan • Outcome of Steps 1 to 3

5. Build strategies	• Overall marketing substrategies
	  ➤ Product/service
	  ➤ Pricing/value
	  ➤ Communication
	  ➤ Distribution
	  ➤ Brand development
	  ➤ Sales promotion
	  ➤ Internal marketing
	  ➤ Profitability
		• Brand portfolio analysis
		• Types of competitive advantage
		• Types of offensive strategy
		• Strategic wear-out monitor
		• Extended brand groups

6. Develop plans	• Plans to support strategies • Development projects • Quarterly milestones • Method of evaluation	• Extended brand groups • Monthly activity summary
7. Monitor results	• Monitoring methods • Monitoring timetable	• Quarterly review formats

Setting Objectives and Building Strategies was discussed in Chapter 7 and Integrated Plan Development was discussed in Chapter 4.

APPLICATION OF THE SEVEN KEY STEPS TO MARKETING PLANNING

The application of the seven key steps is at the heart of marketing planning. They comprise the implementation phase to creating a viable business plan.

Step 1: Business Analysis

This analyzes the past and draws lessons for future application using the approaches covered in Chapter 5. Other key tools are segmentation (Chapter 9), which can be used to subdivide markets and channels to achieve an understanding of a more targeted business environment, as well as portfolio analysis, discussed in Chapter 7.

There should be a separate list of conclusions for each of the seven main topics to be covered within business analysis. These topics include the business environment, markets, channels, the firm's business, competition, technology, and competencies.

Key tools to be used include the "Three Wheels of the Business Environment" including the direct, indirect, and macro spheres, and the "Internal Examination," which involves an analysis of data known and used by the firm and its effectiveness. An audit of performance, attitudes, strategy, and execution is also vitally important as is a Competitive Analysis and aligned Key Factors for Success. Helpful tools include the SWOT analysis, segmentation, and portfolio analysis, mentioned above. These topics are covered in detail in Chapter 5.

Step 2: Future Thinking

This step looks into the future and is based on the assumption that the future will be very different from the past.

Step 2 is most relevant at a corporate level since a company's chosen vision and values will guide its approach in all countries, markets, and channels. However, Step 2 also deserves consideration at the market, country, and brand level, since future vision for individual markets should be consistent with the corporate vision and individual brands should play into this vision. Here, Offensive Marketers look at reviewing scenarios, establishing strategic direction, and developing future thinking.

The Six Key Drivers of future thinking—changing customer needs, changing channel effectiveness, technology, regulation, cost structures, and competition—are all major factors in envisioning and understanding the future competitive environment. Using portfolio analysis (discussed in detail in Chapter 7) is integral to establishing strategic direction for the marketing plan. In addition, the Seven Spokes of Offensive Attitudes (see Chapter 3) provides the customer-driven focus that is at the foundation of a strong marketing plan.

Step 3: Opportunity Identification

The main output from this step will be a prioritized list of the most relevant and salient opportunities.

Opportunity identification is covered in more detail in Chapter 11. Here idea generation and concept testing are most relevant as tools.

The overall topics to be addressed during this step are:

- **Identifying main opportunity areas.** There is no point in developing great ideas that prove irrelevant because the company lacks the competencies to exploit them. Therefore, the target areas for idea generation need to be staked out early. These will include key competencies, market or channel segments already prioritized in Step 1, and target consumer groups.
- **Generation of ideas relevant to opportunity areas.** Ideas will flow through via the previous steps, use of idea generation techniques such as brainstorming, and meetings of the extended brand group. The largest cache of ideas may well come from the business analysis in Step 1, since the very nature of this step is to develop a long list of hypotheses, and to prioritize or refine them through analysis.
- **Screening and concept testing.** An opportunity screening method needs to be established. Based on this, a short list of relevant opportunities can be drawn up for consumer or customer concept testing.
- **Prioritized opportunity list.** This will comprise those ideas that have survived screening, and come through the concept testing with flying colors. These are the opportunities to develop further.

Step 4: Setting Objectives

Objectives need to be established for each of six topics including market development, market share, revenue, investment, innovation and profits, on a basis consistent with corporate, country, and business unit objectives.

Step 5: Building Strategies

These will consist of a statement of overall marketing strategies, designed to meet the objectives, and a set of supporting sub-strategies, each covering topics such as product/service, pricing/value, brand development, internal marketing, IT, and communications and distribution. Relevant tools to this strategy building are quantified portfolio analysis for establishing brand investment priorities, and strategic wear-out monitoring for market effectiveness, both discussed in Chapter 7. In addition, many of the types of competitive advantage and offensive strategies also described in Chapter 7 are highly relevant.

The varied perspective of the extended brand or planning group will also be useful at this point.

Step 6: Developing Plans

This step converts the strategies into offensive action plans, which can be monitored and measured. These plans should comprise short-term activity spanning the fiscal year, and longer-term development projects, which may take years to come to fruition. It can be worthwhile to look ahead 18 months by quarter, and to set quarterly milestones for evaluating progress on development projects.

Another key element in plans is a testing program, which involves trying out new approaches to products, services, pricing, or communications, on a limited basis and at modest cost and low risk. This is marketing R&D, the lifeblood of future endeavor. In this competitive environment where speed to market is a main element for competitive success, more and more companies are conducting marketing R&D to gain insight into future product success factors.

Every Marketing Department needs a full cupboard of successfully tested approaches, which can be expanded with confidence in the years ahead as the strategy demands.

Step 7: Monitoring Results

This is a simple step to execute, but often neglected, due to time pressures. The marketing plan should specify the proposed method of evaluation, when it will be applied, and by whom.

APPLICATION OF THE SEVEN KEY STEPS TO BRAND PLANNING

The process of the seven key steps applies equally to brand planning as to market or channel planning. However, there are a number of extra tools to use at the business analysis step, which applies specifically to brands.

These tools include understanding brand history; understanding the brand conversion model; understanding the importance of IDQV, which stands for impact, differentiation, quality, and value—the four key factors affecting brand success; using the brand positioning statement effectively; understanding and implementing the brand scorecard; and lastly, providing for a loyalty check.

Brand History

This encapsulates the key learning, which is preserved through generations of managers. It briefly covers the main brand events over the past relevant years—things like major changes in product, service, packaging, proposition, sizing, range—together with results of major tests, and share history for all major brands. Exceptional factors like product recalls, short-term supply, or quality problems would also be included in the brand history. Major external events such as competitor brand launches or re-launches, exceptional seasonality, or major market events such as deregulation or mergers and acquisitions that redefine the playing field, would also be noted and dated. A pricing history should be completed as well.

A brand history provides an accurate record of past events affecting that brand, so that historical sales and profit changes can be better understood by those currently running the particular brand. As marketers change jobs frequently within and across companies, valuable information can be lost without brand histories. Brand histories should without exception be regularly updated.

Brand Conversion Model

This is a simple and quick way to check a brand's health, its top-line strengths and weaknesses. Three measures among your target customers are used to assess priority areas for developing the brand's business. Recent data on all three measures should be available from your firm's own consumer research.

You have a number of choices in defining each of these measures. The only rule is to use the same definition consistently.

Awareness

Spontaneous awareness—where customers are asked by researchers to, for example, "name any brand of household paint" they can think of without any prompting—is the most demanding measure, and the one used here.

An alternative to spontaneous awareness is "prompted" awareness, where customers are shown a list of household paint brands, and asked which ones they have heard of. Obviously, prompted awareness scores are always much higher than spontaneous scores. This test measures ad quality and the effectiveness of advertising expenditures.

Trial

The most relevant question here is how far back you go. Does a single trial three years ago count? Should you take "ever used" as your measure, or a shorter time-scale, such as "past year," for which the customer's memory may be reasonably intact. Much will depend on your company's product category and frequency of purchase. This type of test measures brand proposition.

Regular Purchase and Loyalty

Again, regular purchase can be defined in a variety of ways. The definition used here is "at least 50 percent of category purchases in your brand." For example, if a customer purchased your product three out of five times she purchased any product in the same product category, she would qualify as a "regular" customer. This test measures actual, perceived value delivered.

Table 8-3 gives an example of the brand conversion model. What do you conclude from it?

Table 8-3   Example of Brand Conversion Model: Soft Drink—Brand A

The 3 measures	% target customers	Conversion ratio (%)	Measures strength of:
(a) Spontaneous awareness	15	–	Ad quality and spend
(b) Tried in past year	10	67	Brand proposition
(c) Regular purchase (b)÷(c)	2	20	Value delivery

Table 8-3 shows that:

- Spontaneous awareness for your company's brand is 15 percent of your target customers.
- Ten percent have tried the brand in the past year, so your conversion rate from awareness to trial is 67 percent (10/15).
- Two percent are regularly using your brand, so conversion rate from trial to regular usage is only 20 percent (10/2).

In this example, your conversion from brand awareness to trial is very high at 67 percent, indicating that your firm has a strong brand proposition—in other words, the brand advertising, availability, and appearance are all working well. However, your conversion from trial to regular purchase is terrible at 20 percent, pointing to weak product performance. The recommended action would be to stop all spending until your company has radically improved the product.

The brand conversion model is most relevant to consumer goods bought at least three times a year. Individual brands can be compared with other company brands or competitors as seen in Table 8-4. Brand A is the same brand as in Table 8-3.

Table 8-4   Examples of Actionable Brand Conversion Models

The 3 measures	Brand A	Brand B	Brand C
Spontaneous awareness	15%	4%	10%
% Awareness to trial	67%	75%	33%
% Trial to regular usage	20%	66%	50%
Action suggested:	• Stop advertising • Improve product quality	• Increase advertising spend	• Improve advertising quality

Here, Brand B has enormous appeal to those aware of it, but its potential is stunted by low awareness because it is being starved of advertising dollars.

IDQV

IDQV stands for *impact*, *differentiation*, *quality*, and *value*. IDQV is a valuable brand-planning tool, developed by Novaction SA, an innovative research company best known for market modeling and simulations. Novaction established IDQV as the four key factors affecting brand success, based on the evaluation of 5,000 case studies involving 30,000 brands. Table 8-5 and the subsequent explanation are derived from Novaction's pioneering work.

Table 8-5 Summary of IDQV

Measure	Elements	Measurement data
Impact	Spontaneous brand awareness × brand availability	• Brand distribution level • Advertising research
Differentiation	Actual or perceived difference v. competitors as viewed by consumers	• Product, service testing • Market research
Quality	Product or service performance v. competitors	• Product, service comparisons among customers
Value	Relative product or service quality related to price	• Conversion from trial to regular usage • Brand loyalty levels

IDQV can be applied to products or services, and consumers or customers. It is also relevant to business-to-business markets. Like the brand conversion model, IDQV can be used to check brand strengths and weaknesses. This may be based on broad judgment and informed guesswork, or on extensive market research. IDQV is a quick-check method and not a substitute for the more detailed brand strength scorecard outlined later in this section.

- **Impact.** Impact covers the questions, "Have I heard of this brand and can I get it easily?"
- **Differentiation.** "Do consumers or customers view this brand as different or distinctive from competitors in performance, design, characteristics, image, or service levels? Or is it another "Me Too" product? The differentiation may be in the consumer's mind, rather than an objective fact, and may be therefore perceived and not actual.
- **Quality.** The question here is whether the brand is viewed by consumers as better than the competition. A brand may be

Figure 8-6
Value Formula

differentiated but not better, or vice versa. These are two different measures.

- **Value.** Value is an equation relating quality to price (Figure 8-6). If a product has parity in quality, but is 10 percent lower priced than competitors, it offers superior value. If it is 10 percent better in quality, but 50 percent more expensive, its value is inferior.

IDQV can be quickly quantified, using judgment, and available facts. What would you conclude from Table 8-6 below?

Table 8-6   Example of IDQV Scoring—Computer Software Brand

	Maximum score	Your brand	Competitor brand
Impact	35	15	25
Differentiation	20	20	5
Quality	25	15	20
Value	20	10	10
Brand strength	100	60	60

In this example, your firm's brand is highly differentiated, but little known and only of average quality. Action is needed to improve quality, then strengthen awareness and availability. Your competitor brand is a much bigger seller, of good quality, premium priced, well known, and widely available. But the lack of differentiation makes it vulnerable to attack, however, only if it is done effectively.

Brand Positioning Statement (BPS)

This is a one-page summary of the key elements that make up your company's brand proposition and personality. It is another way of testing your brand strength. The BPS should be reviewed at least annually at the beginning of the business analysis step in brand planning, and modified if necessary as part of Step 6, Developing Brand Plans, to address deficiencies or build on strengths.

The BPS has a number of components. These are set forth in Table 8-7.

Table 8-7   Elements of Brand Positioning Statement (BPS)

Elements	Issues
1. Brand name	What name do customers or consumers use?
2. Market description	How would customers describe this?
3. Target audience	Who are we selling to?
4. Brand discriminator	What benefits (rational or emotional) does the brand deliver best?
5. Core consumer proposition	Emotional and functional
6. Brand differentiators	How is the brand different?
7. Brand personality	Image and associations

The BPS should never exceed one page in length and should succinctly answer the question: Why should customers buy this brand in preference to competitors' brands?

Brand Strength Scorecard

This is a more elaborate way of evaluating a brand's strengths and weaknesses than the quick-check in IDQV involving the use of the quantified portfolio analysis. An example of how to construct a brand scorecard for Bird's Eye was given in Chapter 7.

Customer Loyalty Check

This is the final tool to use in brand planning at an early stage in the process. The importance of customer loyalty as a basis for profitable growth has been increasingly recognized.[3]

As part of your brand business analysis, you need to evaluate your company's brand's level of consumer or customer loyalty, overall and relative to competition; who your firm's loyal customers are (i.e., what they are worth to you in profits on an annual and lifetime basis); how much you have been spending on them; and where the best opportunities for attracting more loyal

---

[3] Robert C. Blattberg, Gary Getz, and Jacquelyn S. Thomas, *Customer Equity, Building and Managing Relationships as Valuable Assets*, Harvard Business School Press, 2001.

customers lie. The loyalty check of key questions to ask, shown in Table 8-8, provides a beginning tool to do this.

Table 8-8   Brand Loyalty Check: Key Questions to Ask

- What is your brand's level of repeat purchase?
- How does this compare with the industry average?
- What is the annual and lifetime value of a loyal customer, in revenue and profits?
- How are you allocating marketing spending between loyal, and new or transitory customers?
- What is the profile of your loyal customers? How do you recruit more?
- How well are you rewarding loyal customers?
- What opportunities can you give loyal customers to buy more, or to recommend you to others?

Let's look at some industry examples where customer retention has, at least in part, driven marketing planning.

In the United States, average customer repurchase rates in the car industry are a miserable 30 to 40 percent. Yet, Lexus achieves 63 percent, partly because it deliberately targeted Mercedes and Cadillac buyers, who were more difficult to switch, but are easier to hold than younger, more fashion-conscious buyers of Jaguars and BMWs.

After decades of price promoting to get new consumers, similar to the rest of the domestic grocery industry, Procter & Gamble decided to cut down promotions and use the savings to reduce prices. This was a way to reward loyal customers and avoid wasting resources on temporarily attracting new users with a low loyalty attitude. Despite strong initial resistance from retailers, who were addicted to price promotion, the new P&G strategy proved successful with consumers and generated large manufacturing savings by removing the peaks and troughs of promotions.

Amazon.com acquired 11 million new customers in 1999, nearly tripling its number of total customers. Despite this incredible success, Amazon's even greater success was not customer acquisition, but customer retention. Repeat customers accounted for 71 percent of Amazon's sales, up from 63 percent the previous year. How did Amazon achieve these staggering retention rates and high levels of sales to retained customers? It learned about its customers and their needs; it used this knowledge to offer value-added features; and these features, when used by its customers, only added to Amazon's continuing growing knowledge base and increased connections between the customer and company offerings. Amazon's 1-click ordering, Wish List, and personalized recommendations create a customized experience and drive repeat visits and purchases.[4]

To guide you on the economics of direct marketing, you need to know the average and lifetime value of your loyal customers. This requires a clear understanding of the brand conversion cycle-cost per trial-consumer, percent conversion from trial to regular purchase, annual profit value per regular purchaser, and likely loyalty period. Some consumers may only be loyal to a brand for weeks, but other products and services have loyal users for many years, even decades. Examples of firms with consumer loyalty spanning decades and generations include National Public Radio, Mercedes, Harley Davidson, and Maine-based cataloger L.L. Bean.

Why are these statistics important? Because they can guide your firm on the economics of how much to invest to retain a loyal customer, and how to allocate resources between existing customers and potential new ones. Although the profit value of a brand heavy user in detergents is modest, sophisticated marketers like Procter & Gamble and Lever Brothers still justify heavy investment in direct marketing. Early Internet companies failed to recognize that "first-in always wins" may not be the best customer acquisition strategy. Rather than design customer acquisition programs that matched the prospective customer's longer-term equity potential, they raced to acquire "eyeballs" with exorbitant up-front costs and an ultimate business model that did not speak to long-term profitability.[5]

A clear perspective and strategy on loyal versus new customer acquisition is an important issue to resolve in both brand planning, and overall corporate marketing planning.

MARKETING PLANNING: A SUMMARY

Key points to note about the practicalities of a brand-marketing plan are:

- The initial list of hypotheses, regularly updated, helps you focus on action at an early stage, and makes the business analysis quicker and more effective.
- By the time you have completed the business and SWOT analyses, you should have a reasonably clear idea as to how you will

---

[4] Id. at pg. 75–77.
[5] Id. at pg. 31.

develop winning strategies. If not, your business analysis has been too superficial.

- Output of the SWOT analysis should highlight at least 50 percent of future opportunities. Aim to double these during the opportunity identification process.
- Your level of ambition with respect to objectives will be influenced both by future vision, and quality of the list of prioritized opportunities.
- If you have winning strategies, strong plans should emerge.

CONCLUSION

Marketing and brand plans are important blueprint documents for a company and deserve close scrutiny across departments. Having input and ratification across functions, and out toward the consumer, will not only align efforts, but will create motivation toward consistent and viable objectives throughout the organization and its partners.

For marketing and brand plans to have their fullest effectiveness, a seven-step process should be followed beginning with a business analysis both internal and external to the company. Out of this business analysis, future thinking focuses on the competitive environment as it may unfold this will show how the company can both help define that future environment, and participate in it based on its unique set of competencies. The best opportunities need to be identified and objectives and strategies built to address them.

The Offensive Marketing plan sits atop of these objectives and strategies, and directs the implementation of brand planning and action plans as well as all other corporate activities aimed at revenue generation, including cash flow, resource allocation, business model, partnerships, and selected pool of talent.

Once your company has moved through its Offensive Marketing planning process and created a strategic blueprint of where it wants to go and how it is going to get there, it is time to move on to the "E" of POISE, namely "Effective Execution." The remaining chapters of this book will address issues surrounding the successful execution of the marketing planning process. These sections are vitally important as a potentially winning strategy can be made to look mediocre by weak execution, and a parity strategy can become very competitive through outstanding implementation.

9

Effective Execution: The "E" of POISE
Offensive Market Segmentation

INTRODUCTION

Segmentation involves subdividing markets, channels, or customers into groups with different needs, and meeting these needs more precisely.

Markets continue to evolve into increasingly more segmented target groups, as techniques of mass customization and flexible manufacturing make it possible to meet a range of needs economically. However, the driving force behind segmentation is the growing desire of consumers for individualized products and services at reasonable prices.

Companies have to balance the benefits of segmentation against its pitfalls where consumers are offered too wide a range of similar propositions. This can result in consumer confusion and unproductive extra costs, both for the consumer and producer.

Segmentation as an Offensive Marketing technique is forward looking and uses future visioning and creativity. It aims to develop a distinctive, insightful, and practical approach to targeting meaningful consumer segments. Segmentation consists of a five-step process that includes identifying what to segment; establishing a master matrix; developing alternative types of segments; evaluating segment attractiveness; and finalizing segment strategies and priorities.

PRINCIPLES OF MARKET SEGMENTATION

Segmentation is vitally important to the efforts of the Offensive Marketer and to an Integrated Marketing approach. It involves subdividing markets, channels, or customers into groups with different needs to deliver tailored propositions, which meet these needs more precisely. Segmentation is most often applied to markets but it is equally relevant to distribution channels or customers. Because similar principles apply to segmenting all three, this chapter will concentrate on markets.

The word *market* is used to describe total revenue spent on broadly similar products or services. Having a total market figure is useful to manufacturers and retailers and enables them to gauge their market share. However, every market can be divided into segments. Easy to identify and frequently used, some of the segments include:

- Product types
- Product varieties
- Packaging and dispensing types
- Demographic characteristics of the user

- High-value user
- Attitudes of users that affect use of the product

It is evident that possible segments are almost endless depending on the description chosen. In one study, Clancy and Shulman broke down a market 8,515 ways.[1] The frustrating element in the vast majority of these breakdowns is that most so called sub-markets have similar needs. A sub-market only becomes a segment if its members have significantly different needs from the average user. That is why very few sub-markets turn out to be segments in actual practice. Genuine segments are of high interest to marketers especially if they are newly discovered, since products or services tailored to their particular needs will deliver superior customer experiences.

There is usually a trade-off between the opportunities provided by segmentation and the economics of mass production. Companies targeting a number of segments will usually have higher costs per product or brand than those with mass-market products. To justify this, they need to achieve higher prices for their segmented offers.

Ford pioneered mass production in 1908 based on the concept of a car model at the lowest price. General Motors' Alfred Sloan invented systematic market segmentation.

In the early 1920s, Ford's volume share of the American car market was a massive 60 percent, with the low-priced Model T and the high-priced Lincoln. General Motors, with only 12 percent, had nine models and seven brands, but did not compete in the low-price sector dominated by Ford.

By the mid 1920s, GM had divided the total market into a number of price segments and established five price/quality sectors, each covered by a distinctive brand.

GM's cars were usually positioned toward the top of each price segment to compete on quality with lower-priced cars and on price with cars in the segment above. GM's objective was to compete both in a targeted way across the whole market and to trade consumers up the GM brand range in stages that would span a lifetime. By the 1930s, GM's market share had grown to over 40 percent and

---

[1] Kevin Clancy and Robert S. Shulman, *Marketing Myths That Are Killing the Business*, McGraw-Hill, 1994.

its price/quality approach to market segmentation continued for many decades,[2] leading its market-share growth strategy. By the 1960s, GM's share of the U.S. market was over 55 percent and it was the undisputed leader in the United States and in the emerging global auto industry.

Unfortunately, GM failed to respond to market changes and the value of its early segmentation model went into a steady decline. Chevrolet lost its clear identity, while Buick, Oldsmobile, and Pontiac were pushed into the center of the market with similar price bands. Cadillac failed to capture younger entrants to the luxury segment of the market, and the launch of the low-price Saturn range was a misguided attempt to deal with the fundamental problem of competitiveness. If GM had been in touch with the market it would have reduced rather than increased the number of brands in its product line instead of increasing its brand offering. With the exception of Saturn and Cadillac, all GM automobile products were in the middle, trying to be everything to everyone.[3]

Together with pressures to manage brand development in a rational and market relevant manner, over the past century there has been a strong trend from customization based on personal and direct interface in the corner neighborhood grocery store context to mass production and now to mass customization. Because of technology and channel evolution, marketing has made its way back to direct and personalized communications. Mass media, which used to support mass production techniques and benefits of scale, has been supplemented with personalized, targeted communications that support micro-segmentation and flexible production. Mass customization comes full circle. To be most effective, such customization should be highly interactive and supported by individualized production.

There are three important factors driving markets towards greater segmentation:

1. Production characteristics
2. Consumer power
3. Media development

---

[2] Alfred P. Sloan Jr., *My Years with General Motors*, Penguin, 1969.
[3] Id.

In some industries, flexible manufacturing techniques can produce diverse product lines very economically. Consumers have increased their bargaining power in a world full of spare capacity and tend to insist on more individualized products and services, communicating wishes often directly with the manufacturer. Media is now very targeted and particular interest groups can be reached easily through specialist TV channels, the Internet community chat spaces, e-messaging, or special interest magazines.

Segmentation: Two Other Factors

Two additional factors have a role in segmentation:

1. **The trend toward global marketing and multi-country production.** A segment may be small in a single country but if it can be added to demand in a half a dozen countries supplied from a single, often regional production site, demand can be met economically on a scale equaling local mass production.
2. **The desire of companies to trade up average unit price paid by consumers or customers.** Many markets today are static in volume, but revenue can be built by identifying and exploiting higher-priced product segments as customers' expectations are increased.

Practical Applications of Market Segmentation

There are three distinct applications for market segmentation:

1. Segment prioritization
2. Discovering new segments to exploit
3. Gaining incremental business through understanding of market segments.

Successfully applied, segmentation can build both sales and profits and is a potential source of major competitive advantage.

Segment Prioritization

This follows similar principles to market prioritization, covered in Chapter 2. Just as companies select markets on which to focus,

217

they need to decide in which segments within each market to compete. They may wish to compete in every conceivable sector, as Honda does in the Japanese motorcycle market. However, they are more likely to be selective and to only compete strongly in attractive segments, which fit their competitive skills and competencies. For example, Harley Davidson concentrates single-mindedly on large, expensive, high-performance, heavy-duty motorcycles.

If you don't carefully segment a market, decide which to be in and which not to be in and tailor exact propositions to each segment, your company will probably end up "in the middle," offering a generalized product or service that fails to meet the needs of any segment. Such untargeted products are usually forced to compete on price to counter their limited appeal.

Identifying New Market Segments

The opportunity to discover new market segments is always exciting to marketers. Success can open the door to new products, often at premium prices, and incremental sales. Starbucks coffee tapped this potential when it targeted the sophisticated consumer and created a new market for high-end coffee products.

Starbucks Corporation is a chain of coffee shops, which opened in Seattle in 1971. It has grown to 5,689 outlets in 28 countries worldwide. Sales have climbed an average of 20 percent annually since the company went public ten years ago, with annual sales of $2.6 billion in 2001. Profits have increased an average of 30 percent per year, reaching $181.2 million in 2001. Starbucks has no U.S. nationwide competitor.[4]

Starbucks has transformed a commodity into an up-scale consumer accessory.[5] Per capita consumption of coffee in the United States has been falling since the mid 1960s, but in just over ten years, gourmet coffee sales have grown from 10 percent to over 20 percent of total sales, influenced by the success of Starbucks.

Starbucks saw potential in the sophisticated consumer. This segment was defined as people who are health conscious, like to travel, and identify with gourmets. It accounted for 18 percent of all consumers.[6]

---

[4] "Planet Starbucks," *Business Week*, September 9, 2002.
[5] Id.
[6] Starbucks Annual Report, 1992.

> *This sophisticated consumer was targeted with a differentiated proposition, through company-owned coffee shops, which provided:*
>
> - *Superior coffee at a premium price*
> - *Stylish and elegant cafes—"a cultured refuge from everyday hassles"*
> - *Excellent and consistent customer service*
>
> *The reward for identifying and developing the gourmet coffee segment is a cult brand with a loyal following: the average Starbucks customer visits eighteen times a month, and 10 percent do so twice a day.[7] With new attractions including high-speed wireless Internet service to about 1,200 locations in the U.S. and Europe, the company hopes to win over the next generation of customers who tend to be put off by Starbucks' image of latte-sipping sophisticates.[8] Starbucks' recent moves into local grocery store chains with its pre-packaged coffee products is another broad strategy to position itself as a less sophisticated offering.*

Another company to identify a new segment was Fuji, the photo film company. "Quicksnap" was the first single use disposable camera that addressed the segment of consumers who were concerned about dropping or losing expensive cameras in outdoor locations.

In practice, the new camera addressed a much wider segment than that originally envisaged. It could be taken anywhere without risk, and expanded the opportunity to take pictures on impulse. Ease of use also appealed to inexperienced photographers, especially teenagers, children, and older people.

Although Fuji had strong success in Japan, Kodak, using a crash new product program, beat it to the punch in the United States, with a single-use camera called "Funsaver." Kodak's strong entry into the market had the effect of expanding the total film market.[9]

Understanding Segments to Build Incremental Revenue and Profits

Many new products cannibalize sales of existing products. They not only fail to build incremental business, but also weaken current products. A primary reason for this is weak understanding of market segments and how they interact.

---

[7] Jack Trout with Steve Rivkin, *The New Positioning*, McGraw-Hill, 1995.
[8] "Planet Starbucks," Id.
[9] *Advertising Age*, December 9, 1996.

Starbucks' concentrated clustering of stores in neighborhoods and their "predatory real estate strategy"[10] are both tactics to increase market dominance even though such a large number of outlets in close geographical proximity cannibalize stores at a rate of 30 percent annually.[11] The company recognizes the cannibalizing effect of these stores, but weighs market share gains against losses in individual store sales.

New products should capitalize on brand strengths but, as much as possible, target different segments than those benefiting from existing products. Gillette is a good example.

Gillette's primary interest is in the higher price "systems" segment of the razor market, rather than disposables. This is partly because the profit on a systems cartridge refill is around three times higher than on disposables, and partly because Gillette is more skillful at competing on quality and positioning rather than on price and convenience. It is represented in both market segments, with Gillette Sensor on systems razors and Gillette Good News on disposables. Following the launch of Sensor in the United States, total market volume share accounted for by disposables fell from 52 percent to 40 percent and market value accelerated.[12]

Gillette therefore used Sensor not only to build brand share, but also to develop this most attractive segment. Following the success of Sensor, Gillette then extended the brand into a new segment with Sensor for Women. Incremental sales exceeded $40 million in the first six months, way above expectation.[13]

SEGMENTATION: PITFALLS TO AVOID

There are a number of pitfalls to be aware of with regard to segmentation, specifically the concepts of fragmentation and the "majority fallacy."

Fragmentation

The distance between successful segmentation and wasteful fragmentation is short. Fragmentation consists of breaking a market

---

[10] "Planet Starbucks," Id.

[11] Id.

[12] Robert Thomas, *New Product Success Stories*, John Wiley & Sons, 1995.

[13] Id.

into so many sub-segments that consumers become confused, retail distribution is difficult to maintain, and large dis-economies of marketing and production occur.

Fragmentation often occurs when companies focus on very fine differences, which are frequently of little importance to any group of consumers. In-depth customer dialogue, data-mining, and analysis tools become high competitive differentiators in companies that can identify meaningful attitudinal or behavioral differences.

The "Majority Fallacy"

The fact that a prospective new product or service, while being researched, loses out to the market leader does not mean that it will ultimately be unsuccessful. If it has distinctive appeal to a worthwhile segment of consumers, it may have a niche of users.

For example, in a head-to-head preference test among sports car enthusiasts, the Jaguar might lose out heavily to an equivalent priced BMW. Nevertheless, among those preferring the Jaguar, strength of preference would probably be high, giving the car a viable following.

OFFENSIVE SEGMENTATION

The offensive approach to segmentation has a number of characteristics.

Forward-Looking

Segmentation will affect tomorrow's allocation of resources and development priorities. In line with Chapter 6, any segmentation model should anticipate the most likely marketplace situation 18 months to three years from the present.

Actionable

Segmentation must be actionable. The segment target should be clearly identifiable, capable of measurement and of being reached efficiently by a variety of media or sales people.

Distinctive

Developing distinctive segmentations requires both realism and creativity. There are no "correct" answers, and the secret of effective segmentation is to keep an open mind as to the possibilities. Most markets or channels can be segmented in a wide variety of ways, and new ways to segment will always be discovered over time. A combination of deep knowledge of consumer or customer behavior plus a good measure of creativity is most likely to uncover distinctive approaches to segmentation.

Manageable

It is quite easy to construct a segmentation model so complex that it confuses rather than enlightens. To avoid this, a master matrix should be established at an early stage. This aims to identify three or four important segments, where needs vary widely between consumers or customers. For example, in airline travel, key segments are journey length, cabin class, and purpose of travel.

Within each key segment there may be many sub-segments. For example, in airline travel, meal, seating, and entertainment requirements may vary widely by journey length.

Interlinked

Understanding the linkages between segments can generate new insights and reveal new sub-segments. By linking purpose of travel to cabin class in the airline or rail industries, Offensive Marketers may be able to develop specialized marketing packages for premium-class leisure travelers, including first-class ground transportation, travel amenities such as premium bookings for events, or specialized guide packages. Alternately, the company may identify the need for the creation of a new cabin class of full-fare economy business travelers to more specifically address their needs that differ from leisure travelers. Mixes of food services, quality, and service levels may be increased or decreased depending on the segments' expectations.

Quantifiable

For each segment, it should be possible to estimate size, future trend, profitability, and competitive structure in order to prioritize relative importance of future investment.

OFFENSIVE SEGMENTATION FIVE-STEP PROCESS

The offensive segmentation approach can be translated into a five-step process, which should result in a distinctive and creative approach to segmentation and the identification of priority segments. These can then be exploited by brand extensions; new brand introductions; and acquisitions, partnering, or alliances. The totality of the process can be used as a basis for reviewing and improving product and service-range strategy.

The five-step process is summarized in Table 9-1, and reviewed step by step through the remainder of this chapter.

Table 9-1 Five-Step Process for Offensive Segmentation

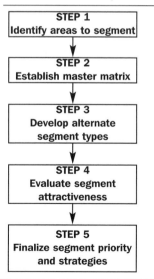

STEP 1 Identify areas to segment	• What market or customer definitions are to be used? • What's the rationale for this?
STEP 2 Establish master matrix	• Develop master matrix based on prior research and market knowledge • Specify any new research needed to fill knowledge gaps • Refine matrix later as knowledge increases
STEP 3 Develop alternate segment types	• Apply types of segmentation • Cross-relate • Conduct any additional research needed
STEP 4 Evaluate segment attractiveness	• Establish criteria for assessing market, channels, consumers, and customers • Apply criteria using quantified portfolio analysis
STEP 5 Finalize segment priority and strategies	• Determine overall segment strategies and final priorities, and develop action plan

Who should be involved in the segmentation process? It is important to execute this process on an interdepartmental basis, both to tap expertise and to gain broad commitment to the results within the company.

How a company decides to segment its markets encompasses a number of very important choices and decisions, including where to compete and where not to compete, a product's range, the allocation of resources, and R&D priorities along with the investment in IT and database management. Therefore, segmentation affects everyone in the company.

Any team is likely to include people from Marketing, Market Research, Sales, Customer Service, IT, and Finance. The reason for the presence of the first four is obvious: They are all customer-facing, and will have a contribution to make to any segmentation study whether it is directed at markets, channels, or customers. A knowledgeable representative from Finance, experienced in activity costing is also essential to help size the segments and establish their current and future profitability. IT leadership will be instrumental in analyzing and implementing any segmenting endeavor.

The critical input areas in developing segmentation strategies are knowledge of consumers, customers, distributors, competitors, and costs. It is important to involve Operations leadership. Team members with customer service responsibilities really must have firsthand knowledge and experience of customers. For instance, it is preferable to involve a sales supervisor rather than her administrative boss, and a field sales person rather than an office bound sales coordinator.

This process is likely to take longer than you may have anticipated. If it is to be conducted rigorously with high standards, at least six months including time for additional market research if necessary, and three to four months if no additional research is needed.

Like every other aspect of Offensive Marketing, segmentation strategy and implementation should be continuously improved. The fact that your company has just completed a massive segmentation exercise is not a reason for shelving the issue for three years until it needs updating. Segmentation methods should be reviewed at least once a year, during the annual marketing planning process and whenever there are any significant changes in market circumstances.

To create effective segmentation strategies, a company must have an information system that provides current data as well as marketing intelligence concerning the external environment. Advanced computer-based internal reports create comprehensive information out of data. A well-trained sales force and customer relationship call-center can provide the backbone for a strong customer relationship program, which, in turn, provides the medium for continuing dialogue and insight. These both need to be complemented by a strong marketing research capability characterized by scientific methodology, multiple approaches, modeling, and cost-benefit measures of the value of information.

To top it off, marketing information requires an analytical marketing capability that consists of advanced statistical procedures and models that develop findings out of the data. Descriptive or decision modeling are important tools here. Many companies have marketing decision support systems that coordinate the collection of data, systems, tools, and techniques through the use of supporting hardware and software that gathers and interprets relevant information to be used in marketing decision-making.[14]

Step 1: Identify Areas to Segment

What definition or experience does your company use in its segmentation process? This is important to determine, because otherwise, as an Offensive Marketer, you may spend time segmenting the wrong market or customer group. For example, in the airline or rail industry, it is much too narrow a focus to look at the customer from the moment he enters the terminal to when he exits. Viewing the total journey experience is more relevant to identifying and satisfying both known and new needs, and expectations including security clearance, amenities for arrival and departure lounges, travel planning and logistics assistance. Determining how widely or narrowly to define markets requires skilled judgment.

Focus on markets and products that are direct or indirect substitutes for your businesses and which ones are also serviced by similar distribution channels.

---

[14] Philip Kotler, *Marketing Management*, The Millennium Ed., Prentice-Hall, 2000. See Chapter 4 for full discussion.

Imagine yourself as Marketing Director of Coca-Cola about to undertake a segmentation study of a major country. How would you define the market to segment and where would you draw the line among categories in Figure 9-1?

Figure 9-1
Coca-Cola:
Definition of
Market to
Segment—Where
to Draw the Line

All of these categories compete with Coca-Cola, although some more directly than others. For manageability it would be practical to draw the line under either level 3 or level 4. These markets would be segmented in detail. Levels 5 and 6 would be covered briefly. Snack foods and confectionery would probably not be segmented although Coca-Cola would bear in mind their importance both as accompaniments to soft drinks and as indirect competitors for the consumer's money. It is feasible to take a more radical approach by including tap water as a competitor (which Coca-Cola, in fact, does).

Step 2: Establish Master Matrix

In the complex jungle of segmentation, the master matrix helps you see the forest through the trees.

Your master matrix should be relatively simple, though not simplistic. It should consist of the top three or four segments within which consumer needs differ widely. A segment may be very important to consumers, but if it is equally important to everyone, it provides no basis for segmentation and is therefore of little interest. For example, in chilled foods, freshness is very important as a customer benefit, but is strongly desired by everyone, whether you divide them by age, income level, frequency of shopping, ethnic group, region, or other classification. Accordingly, it is not a meaningful basis for segmentation.

Working out a master matrix is important, not only to provide clarity but also to guide your firm on the information needed about customers. It will also enable you to decide whether you already have enough internal and external data to carry out a convincing segmentation process, or whether more data is needed to fill gaps.

The master matrix can usually be constructed using existing market research and knowledge, even if your company has not conducted a specific segmentation study previously. As your knowledge base builds, the master matrix can be refined and developed.

Step 3: Develop Alternate Segment Types

While you should know how your firm's competitors segment, it is wise to avoid adopting industry norms.

Companies using similar approaches to market segmentation often move into previously attractive segments and, by doing so, rapidly make them unattractive.

In undertaking a segmentation exercise, it is useful to have a checklist of types of segmentation.

This can never be exhaustive, since skillful marketers will always think of new ones. The remainder of this section provides a comprehensive checklist covering consumers, buyers or customers, and channels.[15]

Types of Consumer Segmentation (within Step 3)

There are eight main types of customer segmentation: physical characteristics, geographical area, demographics, usage

---

[15] We have defined consumers as people who use a product or service and customers (buyers) as people with specialist knowledge who purchase for an organization.

characteristics, benefit areas, financial factors including pricing bands, consumer (buyer) behavior, and characteristics of related products. Each of these will be reviewed separately.

1. **Physical characteristics.** Physical characteristics cover anything the purchaser can see, feel, or smell about a product or service. They include product packaging, size, and variety and, in the case of services, even accompanying literature.

   It is not too difficult to see, for almost any product or service category, how size and color variants, product strength, other product specifications, or service outputs will help to define who are the product's best users. It is also not difficult to project how changes in the physical product or tangible service elements will affect the segment of best-suited users.

2. **Geographical area.** This segmentation method is used to cover straight-forward issues like where does the user live—what region, is it urban or rural, and what is the town size. The development of geodemographics has widened segmentation modes. Geodemographics is "the analysis of people by where they live," or "locality marketing."[16]

   Another term for this type of analysis is *geoclustering*, where several variables are combined to identify ever smaller, yet meaningful segments. Its goal is to yield richer descriptions of consumers and neighborhoods based on categories such as education and affluence, family life cycle, race and ethnicity, mobility and urbanization.[17]

   The main source of geodemographic data is the government census tract and block information, but this may be supplemented by credit information, electoral rolls, or specific market research. The importance of this tool is increasing as it captures the diversity of communities and as the costs of managing databases decline.[18]

3. **Demographics.** We have defined demographics very broadly to include personal characteristics and lifestyle of consumers

---

[16] Peter Sleight, *Targeting Customers*, NTC Press, 1993.
[17] Philip Kotler, Id. See Chapter 9 for full discussion.
[18] Id.

as well as the more conventional breakdowns. Examples of relevant demographic data are given in Table 9-2.

Table 9-2 Examples of Demographics, Personal Characteristics, Lifestyle

Demographics	Personal characteristics	Lifestyle
Age	Height	Make of car
Social class	Weight	Annual mileage
Income level	Clothing size	Age of car
Sex	Skin type	Leisure activities
Family status	Hair color	Credit cards used
Working status	Hair type	Health/slimming
Education	Bust size	Ownership of durables
Ethnic origin	Foot size	TV programs watched
Household size	Medical conditions	Holidays and travel
With/without children	Oral health	Money and investments
Type of home	Fitness level	Pets
Education	Hearing/eyesight	Home details

The vast majority of this data is factual and can be collected from a variety of sources. There are many useful government publications from which to obtain this information, including the Annual Statistical Abstract of the United States; and many periodicals and books, including the *Business Periodicals Index*, *Standard and Poor's Industry*, and *Moody's Manuals*. Commercial data is also available. Nielsen Company provides data on products and brands sold through retail outlets, and MRCA Information Services includes figures on weekly family purchases of consumer goods. Extensive commercial data and information are available online including competitors' websites, government publications, marketing journals, and trade magazines.

Lifestyle data is collected by a number of specialist companies. They regularly mail out lifestyle questionnaires in large volumes. This data is used primarily for direct marketing to identify market segments and can usually be purchased.

Relevance of this type of data varies widely by industry. Demographics provide key segments for most businesses: quite small age differences among children are critical to toy and snack food marketers, for instance. Personal characteristics matter most in industries like hair care, clothing, medicines, and footwear. And lifestyle can be important—although it is difficult to define, measure, and target—in industries such as recreational products, home furnishings, certain types of clothing, and leisure or travel-related services.

Another form of segmentation related to demographics is *psychographics*. Psychographics is concerned with people's attitudes and beliefs. Examples of psychographic groupings that impact segmentation include people that are, for example, categorized as "need-driven," "outer-directed," and "inner-directed." By segmenting possible end users by psychographic categories, it may be possible to identify those individuals who may be most likely to try a product first and therefore, be most influential in convincing others to try or use the product or service.

4. **Usage characteristics.** The main usage categories are place, purpose, time, and occasion of use. Packaging of products in bulk or in smaller packages for lunch or snacking is an example of segmenting based upon occasion of use. Segmenting based on usage characteristics has become a prime method in the food, entertainment, and recreational industries in recent years. Also, markets can be segmented by light, medium, and heavy users. Heavy users may be a small percentage of the market, but may account for a high percentage of total sales. Therefore, marketers may prefer to attract one heavy user rather than several light users of the product or service. Miller's Lite's advertisement "taste great, less filling" was targeted to heavy users with just this strategy in mind.

5. **Benefit areas.** This provides one of the most promising opportunities for distinctive segmentation. Benefit areas change over time and new ones can emerge or be discovered. For example, aspirins used to be taken mainly to combat headache pain, but are now used regularly by many people as a counter to heart disease.

Benefit segmentation has been used successfully in the toothpaste market, to launch new products and to create distinctions among brands. For example, purchasers with larger families at a certain life-cycle stage may be more interested in decay prevention then in whitening. Younger adults, alternatively, may be more interested in both economy as well as whitening as a product benefit. Younger children may be most interested in taste and a marketing tie-in to entertainment characters.

6. **Financial factors, including pricing bands.** "Who pays," the company or the individual, is an important segmentation method in the airline business, since it fundamentally affects price elasticity. "Who pays" classification has also affected successful marketing strategies in the car market. Because car manufacturers and dealers were slow to grasp the growing influence of working women who bought their own cars, or affluent young people who are influencers of purchase decisions, marketing efforts failed to address these constituencies and sales have been impacted negatively.

"How to pay" can be a segmentation issue in retailing or high-ticket consumer products and services. Extended credit and installment payment can be useful marketing tools.

In most markets, "how much" or price-band segmentation is especially important. The most important question in this area is: what are the main price bands in your firm's market, and what is your company's competitive position in each?

Table 9-3 shows a fictional example of price segmentation in the mail-order clothing market. The selling prices have been broken down into seven price categories, based on market research. How many bands to use, and how to bracket them, is a matter of judgment. The figures for Catalog A and Catalog B reflect actual sales by price category. What do you conclude from this price segmentation table?

Table 9-3   Mail-Order Clothing: Price-Band Segmentation

Price band ($)	Revenue by price band (%)	
	Catalog A	Catalog B
Over $120	6	2
$90–$120	9	6
$75–$90	12	9
$60–$75	13	16
$45–$60	15	33
$30–$45	25	19
Under $30	20	15
TOTAL	100%	100%

You will notice that Catalog A's performance is eccentric. It is overachieving in the two bottom and three top price bands, but doing relatively badly in two large price bands between

$45 and $75. There are four possible reasons for this under-performance: too few items offered between $30 and $50, poor value of the products offered, supply problems, or weak on-page presentation. By learning from price-band segmentation, Catalog A has the choice and information to strengthen its future product offer.

7. **Consumer (buyer) behavior.** This method of segmentation centers around what buyers actually do rather than who they are or what they think. It is very relevant to customer relationship management and marketing initiatives.

There are four main questions to ask:

1. What is the consumer's usage status—current user, non-user, ex-user, first-time user, heavy user, or potential user?
2. How are heavy users defined and where are they located?
3. What priority should be given to existing loyal consumers versus potential new users?
4. Who are the loyal users?

Figure 9-2 is an illustrative brand usage map.

Figure 9-2
Brand Segmentation— Usage Map

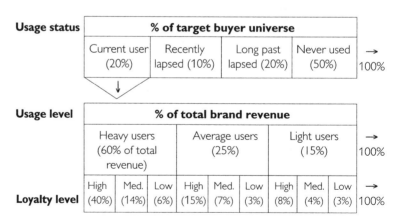

Usage status	% of target buyer universe				
	Current user (20%)	Recently lapsed (10%)	Long past lapsed (20%)	Never used (50%)	→ 100%

Usage level	% of total brand revenue								
	Heavy users (60% of total revenue)			Average users (25%)			Light users (15%)		→ 100%
Loyalty level	High (40%)	Med. (14%)	Low (6%)	High (15%)	Med. (7%)	Low (3%)	High (8%)	Med. (4%)	Low (3%) → 100%

This chart should be read across. It shows that 20 percent of the target buyer universe is currently using your company's brand—current users are the base for evaluating usage level and loyalty level.

The usage level section of the chart indicates that heavy users of the category account for 60 percent of brand volume. Heavy usage needs to be defined for your firm's product category. Does one, four, or eight quarts a week constitute heavy consumption of milk?

The bottom level of the brand usage map covers consumer loyalty levels. The currency here is your firm's brand's share of total category purchases made by each consumer. For example, if s/he buys 15 packs of toothpaste in a year, and chooses your brand ten times, your "share of customer" is high at 67 percent, and this consumer would be classified as high in loyalty to your brand.

Share of customer levels have to be defined by market. For instance, if your brand is a children's breakfast cereal, a 25 percent share of customer might rank as "high" loyalty because cereals are bought on a portfolio basis from a repertoire of brands. People might have five or six different brands in their kitchen cupboards.

You will already have absorbed the major learning about this brand from the chart, namely:

- Current user base is strong at 20 percent.
- Heavy users account for 60 percent of brand volume. This looks quite good, but is it higher or lower than for other brands?
- Sixty-three percent of revenue is accounted for by highly loyal users, most of them (40 percent) in the heavy category.[19]

So, what action would you, as an Offensive Marketer, take, based on the brand usage map?

Here are some possible action steps:

- Focus on high-loyalty heavy users (40 percent of your total revenue), and aim to convert medium-loyalty heavy users (14 percent of revenue) to high-loyalty users.
- Target recent former heavy users and try to bring them back into the fold. Your company's main problem will be to identify who they are and how to reach them as well as to address why they no longer use your product.

---

[19] This 63% comprises 40% + 15% + 8% (i.e. all the high-level customers, where you have a high share of customers, total category purchases).

- Identify why 50 percent of consumers have never used the brand. Is the reason awareness, availability, lethargy, or attitude? What are the likely costs of converting this group, and what, in particular, is the rationale of heavy users for not using your brand?

An important usage segmentation issue for marketers is how best to allocate resources between existing customers and new ones. Every marketer knows that $1 spent on an existing customer is likely to produce a better return than $1 spent on new customer prospecting. This is obvious since to gain a new consumer, your company will have to invest in awareness, access, and sales resources and, in the end, may ultimately fail to make a sale.

Any business, however efficient, is always losing consumers, and needs to at least replace them. Table 9-4 summarizes issues that have to be resolved in determining relative investment priority between the two big usage segments of existing and new consumers.

Table 9-4 Segment Priority Issues: Existing vs. New Consumers

Existing consumer	New consumer
• What is relative profitability of each type of existing consumer?	• Which are the most profitable types of new consumer?
• How does it compare with profit on new consumers, in the short-term and long-term?	• What are the key reasons for non-purchase and how strong are they?
• What are opportunities for increasing share of existing consumer's purchases in the company's category?	• What is the likely cost of gaining a new consumer, what is the payback period, and what is the lifetime value?
• What is the scope for increasing total category purchases among your consumers?	• What are the company or brand growth targets?
• What new categories or products can the company sell to existing consumers?	• How far will existing consumers take your company toward its goals?

And, along with allocating resources between attracting new customers and investing in existing customers, the market position of your company will dictate its focus. Market leaders will focus on attracting potential users and smaller companies will seek to lure customers from the market leader.

EFFECTIVE EXECUTION: THE "E" OF POISE

8. **Characteristics of related products.** This has already been covered in Chapter 5. Changes in household fashion or paint fundamentally affect color and design of household products. Outerwear fashions strongly influence the underwear women wish to buy. And innovations in washing-machine technology or performance will impact the kind of detergents needed. A company, through its partners and their market intelligence and customer relationships, needs to keep abreast of related products that impact use of the firm's offering.

Step 4: Evaluate Segment Attractiveness

You now have the raw material of a long list of possible segments to consider. As an Offensive Marketer, your next decision is to prioritize them—to decide which ones your firm should plan to invest in and develop, which to compete strongly in, and which to exit or ignore. This is where the Marketing Alignment Process (MAP) and the Quantified Portfolio Analysis (QPA) again come in useful.

Using the QPA, you will be able to construct a list of segment attractiveness criteria, develop a quantified scoring system, and score each segment. The same quantified approach can be used to evaluate the fit of the company's assets and competencies to each segment.

The main criteria for prioritizing segment attractiveness will always include:

- Ability to quantify the size of the segment
- Ability to identify and reach the people in the segment
- Segment size and future trends
- Likely future profitability of the segment
- Competitive structure of the market
- Segment fit with the company's assets and competencies

The ideal focus and investment is in highly attractive segments closely aligned to your firm's assets and competencies. These take time and effort to find, and in practice, company leadership may have to settle for less in the short term, until corporate strategy and planning bring the firm into a stronger resource and competency base.

Step 5: Establish Final Segment Priorities and Strategies

You now have a short list of segments that are attractive and fit with the company's assets and competencies. These segments will be candidates for possible future investment. In practice, you may not have the resources to exploit all of them at once, so a further selection process may be necessary. Equally, you will have discovered or confirmed that a number of segments you currently compete in either look unattractive in the future or fail to fit well with the competencies your firm plans to develop in the years ahead. Decisions will have to be taken on whether to milk, exit, or sell out of such segments.

The final prioritization stage is a good time to consider the main types of segment strategy available to the company, and how well each fits with the firm's competencies and future vision. Two of the main strategic issues in segmentation are degree of specialization and level of differentiation.

Companies have the option of competing broadly or narrowly by market, channel, or country. Five of the more widely used segment strategies are; single market, single channel, multi-market, product segmentation across markets, and full market coverage. For instance, Ford competes in all market segments, whereas Porsche competes in a single market segment, namely high-priced sports cars. Mercedes competes in multi-market segments, focusing on mid-to-top priced vehicles. Honda competes across many markets including automobiles, motorcycles and scooters, lawnmowers, and boats.

Creating a segment specialization portfolio analysis may be helpful at this point. One axis of the matrix should be entitled "Channel Coverage" and the other "Market Coverage." It will be interesting to see whether your firm competes in one, some, or multiple channels or markets, and to compare this with your company's competitors.

A NEW LOOK AT LEVELS OF DIFFERENTIATION

Market segment theory distinguishes between a mass strategy, where one product covers a very large market, and differentiated strategy, where a number of products are targeted at specific segments.

The model T Ford is usually given as the first example of "mass strategy."

"Mass strategy" usually involves high volume, low prices, and "me too" products or service design. The basis of competition will probably be price, and to succeed, the firm needs to be a low-cost operator. This type of strategy is falling out of favor due to low margins, vulnerability to price attack, consumer desire for variety, and the development of flexible mass production. Relationship Marketing itself is pushing quickly toward production for a single consumer, based on his or her described needs and wants.

Bottled water is a good example of a differentiated product. The product category and brands have been skillfully marketed: the brands are differentiated, have distinctive image and packaging, and command a price many times that of tap water.

FINAL SEGMENTATION STEPS

Lastly, there are a few final steps that need to be taken in the segmentation process.

Prioritization

Once you have determined your company's strategies with respect to degree of segment prioritization and level of differentiation, you are ready to prioritize the short list of segments you have developed. Segmentation needs to be done in a descending hierarchy. The Marketing function would be responsible for recommending the company's overall segmentation approach and the priority to be given to alternative markets. Cascading levels of coordinated responsibility would flow from communicated segmentation strategy.

Feed Segments into Marketing Planning Process

Once segments have been prioritized, detailed strategies and plans have to be developed. High-priority segments can be exploited through extension of existing brands, development of new brands, acquisitions, alliances, and new country entry. Decisions need to be taken on how to allocate development resources—R&D, advertising, and promotion—between high-priority segments, where the company plans to increase market share, and mid-priority segments where the objective is to hold market share. Plans to maximize profits, exit, or sell brands in low-priority sectors have to be worked out and executed.

CONCLUSION

This chapter has presented five steps for developing segmentation strategies. After reviewing the principles of segmentation, and the tactical steps, you should be able to answer the question whether your firm has a clear definition of its total market, to understand how segments differ from sub-markets and comprehend the strengths of segmentation as an approach. Segmentation is a useful means for building incremental revenue and profits by aligning the firm's competencies with the differing needs of various consumer groups.

The offensive segmentation approach is forward-looking, practical in its implementation, creative in its approach, quantifiable, manageable as a strategy, and uses interlinking between segments to generate new insights and reveal new sub-segments in an ongoing process. By using the various bases for segmenting consumer markets, for instance, your company can begin to understand the size, trends, and profitability of segments and assess their attractiveness for the firm. After identifying relevant and meaningful segments, your firm can then implement a clear investment strategy for each priority segment and dovetail strategies and plans into the marketing planning process.

We are now ready to move on to the second chapter under the "E" of POISE for "Effective Execution." This next chapter on Offensive Brand Development is closely related to the earlier chapter on Offensive Marketing Planning, Chapter 8, which outlined a seven-step marketing planning process and described a number of brand planning tools.

10 Offensive Brand Development: Effective Execution Revisited

INTRODUCTION

This chapter is related closely to the proceeding chapter on Offensive Marketing Planning, which outlined a seven-step marketing process and described a number of brand planning tools. Brand development is covered in more detail here, and how companies fully utilize their existing new and brand resources to achieve growth objectives and sustained profitability is also examined. Questions include:

What is your company's branding strategy and is it a single master brand or a series of self-standing brands?

Why are many traditional brands declining and newer brands having difficulty?

How far can brands be extended and what is the rationale for doing so?

Provided in this chapter are some effective brand development tools and requirements for success in brand planning as well as some answers to these questions.

TWELVE CONCLUSIONS: BRAND DEVELOPMENT AND OFFENSIVE PRINCIPLES

An analysis of twelve conclusions about building brands helps us set the context for a detailed discussion about brand development and brand building tools.

1. **A brand's value lies inside the consumer's mind.** A "brand" is shorthand for a collection of attributes that strongly influence purchase. Brands enable consumers to identify products or services that promise specific benefits. They arouse expectations about quality, price, purpose, and performance.

   A perfume in an expensive-looking bottle branded "Chanel No. 5" will command a high price. If it is cheaply packaged a consumer would be confused. The reality behind this latter purchase would fail to meet their expectations about the brand; rather than thinking "What a bargain," they would probably decide not to buy the product. Chanel No. 5 is a strong brand name for an expensive perfume and it would be suspect as an inexpensive consumer-care product.

   Brands enable marketers to build extra value into products or services and to differentiate them from competitors. Well-known brand names are among a company's most valuable assets. The continuing success of new and older brand name companies, after the fall of many of the once high-flying pure Internet endeavors, was based in great measure on the strength of their brand recognition and public acceptance. Brands represent the accumulation of years of favorable consumer experiences and heavy investment in advertising, presentation, and quality. However, many so-called brands are no more than labels attached to "me too" products. To qualify as a brand rather than a label, a product or service must own a place

Table 10-1 Criteria for Brands Rather Than Labels

- Significant brand-name awareness
- Reasonable availability to target group
- Consistently delivered consumer benefit
- Clear consumer understanding of benefits associated with the brand

in the consumer's mind. Table 10-1 shows how this can be acquired.

How do strong brands differ from ordinary brands? Additional criteria have to be met. How does your company's brand rate? Table 10-2 lists the additional criteria to qualify as a strong brand.

Table 10-2   Additional Criteria to Qualify as Strong Brand

- High brand awareness
- Wide availability to target group
- Superior and distinctive product or service proposition
- Continuously improving proposition

Strong brands such as Coca-Cola, Canon, BMW, Disney, Nike, Barnes & Noble, IBM, and The Financial Times offer superior propositions that deliver strong profit-growth over time. A brand name's value lies inside the customer's mind. Its mechanism can be compared to a continuous production line. The company feeds in raw materials of product or service performance, pricing, advertising, and so on. The customer reacts to and processes these into attitudes and image. The final result is a mental inventory. Then the process begins again, as illustrated in the brand continuum in Figure 10-1. A brand image is

Figure 10-1
The Mechanism of Branding— A Continuous Process

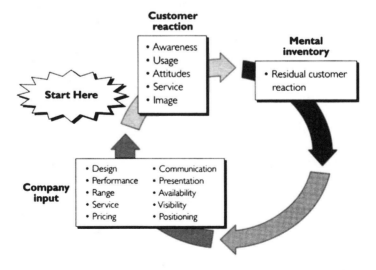

dynamic, strengthening or weakening depending on company inputs. The mechanism of successful branding is a continuous process.

2. **Brands are not just names, but rather business systems.** A company's brand is not just a name; it is shorthand for a distinctive business proposition. Branding goes well beyond names and symbols—they are just the tip of the "Branding Iceberg" or the visible one-sixth. What really matters is the five-sixths that lie below the waterline. Strong branding is the result of successful business strategy. It is not a matter of manipulating advertising, name, and presentation.

The early successes of Amazon and Yahoo, for example, ultimately proved ephemeral with the burst of the dot.com bubble. Despite spending as much as 90 percent of their capital on marketing and advertising, it was difficult for a pure-play Internet company to reinforce its brand in everyday personal experience. Branding on the Internet is reinforced through the online experience with the site and the benefit it provides. Online retailing has suffered its ups and downs in great part because of early failures at completing transactions, addressing security and privacy concerns, and delivering purchased goods on time. Competencies around systems involving the logistics of distribution, delivery, and returns had to be built. In the crowded online brokerage market, for example, E-Trade had to distinguish itself as a cyber-brand by defining itself as a financial portal. The package of bundled benefits was designed to differentiate its offerings from its online competitors. These offerings, backed by consistently applied business systems have made their online experience beneficial. Figure 10-2, the Branding Iceberg, shows marketing tools like brand names, symbols, presentation, and advertising above the waterline. What is not seen is below the waterline: things like, low-cost operations, high-quality controls, strong R&D, and integrated marketing.

You will notice that elements below the waterline are company-related competencies or assets, while those above the waterline refer to what is visible with respect to a specific brand. What drives the brand, whether it is an online or traditional brand, is a business system below the waterline that is company wide and may often cover a number of brands. Figure 10-3 illustrates the Branding Iceberg for a strong financial services

Figure 10-2
The Branding Iceberg©[1]

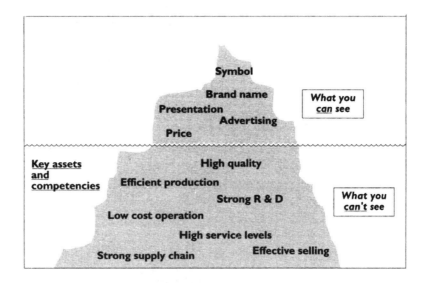

brand driven by a superior business system. Again, what you can see is above the waterline—things like brand names, symbols, presentation, and advertising. What you can't see are the assets and competencies that will drive the brand. Things like integrity, financial strength, low selling costs, personalized

Figure 10-3
Branding Iceberg for a Strong Financial Brand

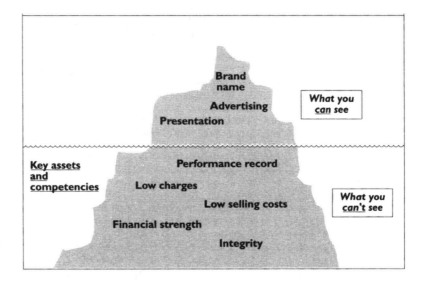

---

[1] Keynote speech to Annual Conference of Marketing Society, November 1989 by JHD.

customer service, and integrated IT. Building a successful brand often takes years of effort that involves creating an identity for the product or service at all touch points with the customer or end user.

The exact elements of the Branding Iceberg will differ by product although most elements found in Figure 10-3 would be included. "Presentation" would be referred to as packaging for consumer goods companies; store interiors are "presentation" with respect to retailing and branch offices; online information and hard-copy literature comprises "presentation" for financial services. Figure 10-2, the Branding Iceberg, highlights that the strength of brands derives more from powerful underlying business systems than from advertising, promotion, or online presence. Of course, talent and people-driven know-how provide the "glue" that holds the superior business system together and moves it forward to address new market opportunities.

3. **There are four main types of brand business systems.** When branding started, both as a concept and practice, it was a means to distinguish the goods of one producer from another. Branding and production were inextricably linked. Increasingly today, branding and production are separating, effecting a number of alternative business systems and choices. Manufacturing, distribution, selling, or even R&D may all be contracted out, with branders concentrating on selected core competencies.

Franchisers or branding companies such as Nike, McDonald's, Nokia, Coca-Cola, IBM, and Intel all engage in product and brand development. They may, however, contract out their actual production, distribution, or retailing. Own-brand retailers like Old-Navy, or its parent company The Gap, may engage in retailing and finance as well as brand development, but out-source production, distribution, and product development. A third group, branded manufacturers like Hewlett-Packard, produce solely for the brands they own, occasionally contracting distribution and retailing. Private label manufacturers often specialize in production for retailer owned brands like Kmart or Wal-Mart, controlling neither branding nor retailing. Other private label manufacturers produce only brands they own, like The Body Shop or Tommy Hilfiger.

To reiterate, there are four main types of brand business systems:

- **Franchisers and branding companies.** A branding company like Nike defines its competencies as design, R&D, brand development, and supplier management. It therefore contracts out production and distribution. Franchisers like McDonald's or Benetton have similar business systems, although they retain at least partial control over retailing that may be franchised or company controlled.

- **Own-brand retailers.** Some retailers, like A&P Supermarkets, market products under their own brand, Anne Page, in addition to offering leading national brands. Production, and sometimes distribution, is contracted out to manufacturers or third parties, while product development is often shared.

- **Branded manufacturers.** Kellogg's and Hewlett-Packard, who produce solely for the brands they own, occasionally contract out distribution.

- **Private-label manufacturers.** Usually not in control of branding or retailing, their bargaining power and margin are primarily dependent on product development skills, low-cost operation, and customer service. Other private-label manufacturers produce for the brands they own and retail, such as Polo/Ralph Lauren and Martha Stewart, where the brander handles finance and product and brand development. Martha Stewart does retain branding control in its retail and distribution arrangement with Kmart, which provides a strong retailing presence and distribution capability for the brand.

Most profit in business systems accrues to the company that controls brand development since this provides the opportunity for differentiation. Franchisers are usually more profitable than franchisees, branding companies generate higher margins than their suppliers, and manufacturer branders are generally more profitable than those supplying private label. Companies vary their branding systems by type of business and by country depending on the local environment and their own competitive position. Determining which branding system or systems to use is an important strategic decision. The separation between branding and production is also spreading rapidly into service industries.

4. **There are many different approaches to brand naming.** There are two major types of branding, namely master brands and individual brands. Ford is a master brand as is Nestlé along with American Express (synonymous with worldwide credit). Twix candy is an individual brand as is 7-Up cola.

- **Master brands.** A single name and proposition used to cover many different product areas. The Japanese and South Koreans favor master brands with names like Sony, Canon, Honda, Samsung, and Hitachi. They may be used on their own, backed by a description of category as in Hitachi TV. They may be accompanied by an individual brand, such as Ford's (master brand) Mustang (individual brand), or by a number, like BMW 320. In the alternative, master brands may be used at a secondary level to endorse an individual brand, as with Nestlé's Kit Kat bar or Microsoft's X-Box.

- **Individual brands.** Usually comprise one product type in one market, and include different models, sizes, product/service options, and packaging formats. The dividing line between master brands and individual brands is not always easy to define. Increasingly, individual brands are being extended into a wider range of categories, and emerging as master brands.

- **The brand name continuum.** Brands may vary from 100 percent master brand to 100 percent individual brand, with many gradations in between.[2] For example, with McDonald's Big Mac, the master brand McDonald's is the most important element influencing consumer purchase, whereas with Nestlé's Kit Kat, the individual brand name, Kit Kat, matters most to consumers as does the individual brand names Pampers, Crest, or Tide, all from Procter and Gamble.

5. **Master branding as a strategy is gaining ground.** The arguments for and against master brands and individual brands are well known. The 100 percent master brand (also referred to as an "umbrella" brand) can generate high volume and critical mass by spanning a wide range of markets. It uses advertising support efficiently because of its size, can be extended into new categories at limited risk, and it is both a flag and a motivator

---

[2] Format for diagram on which this paragraph is based originated by Saatchi & Saatchi.

for employees. Johnson and Johnson, Unilever, Kellogg's, MTV, BP, and Hilton have used this strategy. Most recently, Boeing, the aerospace behemoth, has used a strong branding effort and a headquarters shift to create a broader image for its operations. The main potential drawback of master brands is overextension. If they try to be all things to all people, they end up meaning nothing to anyone. A second theoretical drawback to master branding is that it can spread the effects of adverse publicity from any product within the umbrella of products. This potential adverse effect increasingly applies to individual brands today, where the press and media quickly move to embroil the company behind them, when negative PR points to its involvement. Witness the rapid decline of Ford in the first half of 2001 after its public relations fiasco with Firestone tires and quality problems that reduced earnings from operations by 91 percent from the prior year. Negative brand perception significantly impacted Ford's ability to attract customers and command top pricing resulting in a $6.3 billion reduction in the value of carmaker's name.[3]

Proponents of individual branding include Procter and Gamble, Pepsi, Coca-Cola, R.J. Reynolds, Phillip Morris, and Colgate-Palmolive. They justify their strategy by saying that it creates clear and distinctive identities. These brands are seen as leaders in their chosen areas of expertise and as a result they command premium prices.

Table 10-3 summarizes the advantages and disadvantages of 100 percent master branding. It also describes the position of

Table 10-3   Master Brands: Advantages and Disadvantages

Advantages	Disadvantages
• Offer scale across many categories • Use scale to finance large advertising expenditure • Scale and product range increase efficiency of customer relationship marketing • Strong basis for employee commitment • Platform for alliances with other master brands • New products can be launched with limited spending	• More difficult to achieve distinct brand identity • Quality of products and services within master brand may vary • Tempting, and easy, to overextend marketing • Impact of bad publicity on any item affects total master brand

100 percent individual brands when looked at from the reverse perspective.

Some companies favor master brands and others individual brands. The practice varies by industry and by country. Within the car industry, General Motors has always favored individual brands; BMW, Mercedes, and Jaguar follow the master brand approach; Volkswagen and Ford use both. Within confectionery, Nestlé and Mars are mainly individual branders, while Cadbury employs both Cadbury master branding and individual branding.

What about country practice? The Japanese generally favor master branding. They have many—such as Toyota, Canon, Sharp, NEC, Nintendo, Toshiba, Fuji, Honda, and Casio—to name a few. Admittedly, in some cases, sub-brand names support or even supplant the master brand as with Walkman. Matsushita has a stable of strong individual brands such as Panasonic, but the predominant benefit arises from the master brand name. Johansson and Nonaka in their book, *Relentless: The Japanese Way of Marketing*, identified a number of reasons for this[4]:

- Japanese companies use corporate branding to demonstrate that they guarantee and stand behind all their products. "Most Japanese communications conspicuously display the corporate name and logo."[5]
- Umbrella [master] branding reflects Japanese emphasis on the group and the company rather than the individual. "The corporation's identity and the identity of the individual employee merge, a positive motivational effect."[6]

In addition, the Japanese are presumably aware of the advantages of umbrella branding in generating efficiencies in advertising spending and customer-relationship programs. Furthermore, few Japanese companies use brand management, a system that tends to favor and sustain individual branding over master brand.

Companies that pursue individual branding often have good reasons for doing so.

---

[4] Johansson and Nonaka, *Relentless: The Japanese Way of Marketing*, Butterworth-Heinemann, 1996.
[5] Id.
[6] Id.

First, if they already own strong individual brands, it makes sense to develop and expand them. As discussed earlier, some individual brands are even graduating to master brand status, spearheading a range of products. Priceline.com started with airline tickets and has expanded into other product categories as has Amazon.com among others, seeking to diversify their affiliation and reach, and differentiate their offerings. The jury is still out as to whether these extensions will be successful over the long term.

Second, individual brands may be a long-established part of the company culture bringing with it strong competencies in managing them successfully.

When expanded globally, the scale of individual brands can be greater than many master brands; for instance, Philip Morris' Marlboro, Coca-Cola, and Procter and Gamble's Pampers. Pharmaceutical companies have been spending millions of dollars on creating individual brands such as Viagra or Claritin.

So what does the future hold? While many individual brands will remain strong, and companies will continue to combine master and individual branding, the umbrella system is likely to gain most in the future. Here are some reasons for this view:

- **Continued growth in service industries will benefit umbrella branding.** In most developed countries, service industries—retailing, finance, hospitality, telecom, computers, and entertainment—increase their share of gross national product, whereas the manufacturing sector is expected to decline. Most service companies use master branding, partly because they came later to marketing and partly because the consumer benefits they offer are more transferable across categories. Companies with strong reputations around personalized services, like Amazon.com, Nordstrom's, or Charles Schwab, that establish credentials among consumers for quality, value, and integrity, may be able to stretch their capabilities into new product categories. It is more difficult for manufacturer brands to spread into new categories, even with heavy advertising investment, as they tend to get more typecast by consumers.
- **The future structure and economics of advertising favor master branders.** The cost of mass advertising has grown to

a point where only larger individual brands can afford it. Couple this with the fact that, in the future, communication will become more diffuse as specialized media channels develop. This favors master branders who have the ability to spend heavily on advertising while limiting it to a fairly low percent of sales. Master branders may also find it more economic to launch new products than individual branders. In addition, as corporations continue to engage in the growing global marketplace and reach customers far from their home market, a strong brand can act as an ambassador for the company upon entering new markets or introducing new products.

- **Master branding is in tune with the move to integrated marketing.** As the message that "everyone in the organization is a marketer" spreads, the master brand will become increasingly valuable as a motivating force, to be marketed both to external customers and to employees alike. A strong master brand acts to define strategy in that it helps to clarify what initiatives fit within the corporate brand and which do not.

- **Customer relationship marketing is growing, and benefits most from master branding.** Master brands can run data-based marketing programs and customer clubs across their whole product range. This is cost-effective both because overhead costs are spread across a broad volume base and opportunities are created to cross-sell.

- **Distributor or retailer brands are gaining share in most markets in most countries.** Most are master brands. They are well developed in the West in categories like grocery, clothing, and consumer durables. In the future, these distributor or retailer brands appear likely to grow in all countries, especially developing ones, where retailer concentration is lower.

- **There is likely to be a major culling of smaller brands in the next few years, and individual brands will suffer most from this process.** At present, there are too many brands in relation to consumer needs, retailer space, and companies ability to promote. They become more vulnerable to elimination as retailers strive to improve return on space, companies seek greater operational efficiency and advertising costs escalate. Most of these smaller brands tend to be individual brands rather than master brands.

6. **Brands have different stakeholders with different needs to be met.** Brand names are vehicles for communicating distinctive propositions to a company's stakeholders. Who are the stakeholders?

Most companies have five main types of stakeholder—shareholders, customers or buyers, consumers or users, employees, and suppliers/partners. All stakeholders have an economic influence on the company. Clear and distinctive brand propositions help shape stakeholders' attitudes in the company's favor. Brand names and stakeholders need to be closely aligned in order to achieve effective communication and deliver on the customer experience.

Each brand stakeholder has different needs, and these are likely to be managed by a variety of departments within a company, which can cause inconsistent brand communication. Table 10-4 illustrates this issue for an automobile company.

Table 10-4   Stakeholder Needs and Internal Contact Points

	Shareholders	*Dealers*	*Consumers*	*Employees*	*Suppliers*
Needs	• Security • Performance	Meets Specification • Margin • Superior value	• Superior value • Good service	• Security • Motivation • Reward	• Fair dealing • Confidence
Internal contact point	• Finance Dept • Board	Sales Dept	• Consumer Relations Department • Dealers	• Managers	All Depts. especially Operations

The challenge for companies is to develop core brand propositions, tailor them to meet different stakeholder needs, and manage the process consistently across a range of different departments. If they do not, they risk both the failure to meet stakeholders' needs and the delivery of a confusing and inconsistent message across stakeholders. Therefore, Brand Stakeholder Alignment (BSA) is a critical capability. The Offensive Marketer's job of coordinating company value-adding activities, to align them for the best customer experience, is pivotal here along with brand alignment implementation.

7. **Requirements for success are easy to state, difficult to achieve.** To succeed, a new brand needs to achieve awareness among the target audience and trial purchase. It must also

deliver superior value in order to generate repeat purchases and a long-term profit stream. The requirements set out in Table 10-5 for success in launching a new brand are equally applicable to business-to-business markets, consumer services, or fast-moving consumer goods.

Table 10-5   Requirements for Success in a New Brand

Requirement	Means to achieve
1. Superior consumer or user value	Strong proposition at competitive price
2. Relevant distinctiveness	Product service design and development
3. Low-cost operation	Every department consumer and cost driven
4. Marketing and sales support	Sufficient quality and amount to achieve awareness and trial
5. Superior buyer value	Convincing and profitable sales proposition
6. Acceptable economics	Reasonable return and good level on-going profit margin

The success factors all sound straightforward and easy, yet everyone knows that new brands involve high risk and most often fail. Why is this? Each of the six requirements is in practice quite challenging in competitive markets. There are, indeed, many pitfalls littering the path to new-brand success, even for experienced and wary marketers. Some of these pitfalls are outlined in Table 10-6.

Table 10-6   Pitfalls to New Brand Success

- New brand is distinctive or better, but in performance areas unimportant to the consumer or user.
- Level and quality of marketing support is insufficient to gain consumer awareness or stimulate trial.
- Superior new brand value is not sustained. Competition quickly improves products or services and/or cuts prices heavily.
- New brand beats revenue targets, but heavily cannibalizes sales of other company brands—incremental revenue low.
- Low-cost operation is not achieved in practice, and margins therefore insufficient or price too high.

Failure rate of new products under a new brand is much higher than for new products using an existing brand name. This is because the cost of gaining consumer awareness and trial, and therefore, the revenue necessary to achieve acceptable profits, is much greater for new brands.

8. **Brands survive and retain value if they are creatively managed, and if they continue to deliver their promise.** If not, they disappear.

Chapter 11 covers the product life cycle and the main reasons for a new product's failure. Many of the reasons also apply to new brand failures. However, there is no brand life cycle to correspond with the product life cycle. In most markets, and especially in high-tech ones, products have to be continuously improved. No one today would buy a Model T Ford to drive to work or a 1970 IBM computer on which to conduct their business—but they may consider purchasing a Ford Taurus or an IBM laptop. Their brand name has sustained over the years, over many products and service offerings. In theory, there is no reason why brands should not last forever. In practice, though, most brands have not spanned a normal lifetime. Alcoholic drinks are the most venerable, with some European brands like Chartreuse and Haig tracing a history of hundreds of years. Most, but not all high-tech brands, are from post World War II. Fast-moving consumer goods are somewhere in the middle. An analysis of the Top 100 grocery brands in the UK showed that 38 percent were launched before 1950. The 38 percent accounts for 42 percent of the Top 100 brand values (Oxford Corporate Consultants. A.C. Nielsen).

Today's strong brands could theoretically last for decades. However, most companies have too many brands and too few differentiated, strong ones. It remains to be seen whether today's leading brands will last for centuries, but it is certainly true that many well-established brands have died in recent decades. Why?

- **Growing competition.** Existing brands are extending, new brands are entering our market, especially from overseas, and retailer private-label brands are growing in most categories. These forces exert great pressure on weaker, more undifferentiated, brands.

- **Deliberate execution.** There have been many deliberate brand executions, especially in the car industry as recently demonstrated by GM and its nixing of its category brand Oldsmobile. The main reason for deliberate brand executions is that companies have too large a range of brands in relation to their available advertising or selling resources, and therefore have to discontinue smaller brands in order to concentrate on those with the most potential. Secondly, global rationalization drives branding change—that is why the best-selling Ford Cortina brand was withdrawn, and why Mars changed the name of Marathon to Snickers.

- **Acquisitions.** With the purchasing of other companies and their brands, brand-name duplication is often created. When Burroughs and Sperry were acquired, both names were dropped and replaced by Unisys. The Rowntree name has largely been replaced by Nestlé. Even in the absence of an acquisition, a company may feel compelled to re-brand itself as in the case of Andersen Consulting, which re-branded itself as Accenture to build trust, to rekindle a sense of mission to complement their technical expertise, and to aid the firm in winning multimillion dollar contracts.

- **Weak marketing.** If a product is marketed poorly, it can also kill brands. So can inferior quality or high-cost production. But the main reason for the death of brands is lack of a distinctive business proposition as in the case of GM and Oldsmobile. Weak brands may once have had a distinctive business proposition, but lost it along the way through brand mismanagement. Or they may have never had it and always have been "me too" products.

9. **In many markets, leading brands fail to achieve real sales growth.** It is becoming more difficult to increase real volumes even on major brands as many markets in the United States and Western Europe are flat or declining in overall volume. These markets are simultaneously being penetrated by retailer private labels and new entrants. Even allowing for the increase in retailer brand share, the size of the market for branded manufacturer goods is falling steadily. As a result, in mature markets, the natural momentum for leading brands is real decline. The moral for brand developers is that brand size and power alone do not guarantee growth. For those that have seen growth, large doses of sustained innovation, investment, and effective brand management have been needed.

10. **Brand extensions add new products and services to their ranges, often ill advisedly.** Caught in a dilemma between the high cost of launching its new brands and the need for growth, many branders have indulged in unproductive line extensions

or "brand churn."[7] They add a host of marginal new product varieties to existing brands, and in the process, cannibalize the sales of the parent brand, ultimately failing to achieve significant incremental volume. The result is lower sales per product, added operational costs, and consumer confusion arising from too much choice.

Where many branders struggle to hold real volume with marginal new product varieties, volume per individual variant, a key measure of operational efficiency, often falls.

11. **Effective brand extension has become a critical marketing skill.** Brand extension is the process of strengthening and broadening a brand's franchise through repositioning, performance improvements, or the launch of new products and services.

Marketers often ask questions like, "How far can this brand be stretched?" or, "When will the elastic snap?" Such questions reveal a wrong approach. They imply that brands are things to be exploited, for short-term advantage, rather than developed imaginatively over the longer term. Is your company a brand exploiter or a brand developer? Table 10-7 will help you to assess this.

Table 10-7 Attitudes of Brand Exploiters vs. Brand Developers (*read across*)

Brand exploiters' attitudes	Brand developers' attitudes
• Avoid any spending with payback longer than one year	• Balance short-term profit needs with investment for long-term development
• Do not be "pedantic" about the purity of the brand's core proposition	• Really understand and nurture the core of your brand proposition • Strengthen and develop this core over time
• Be "entrepreneurial" and extend the brand as widely as possible	• Launch new products that both build and extend this core
• Raid the core advertising budget to support new line extensions	• Give new products or services additional support—don't raid the core budget
• Introduce sub-brands, with support in Year 1 only	• Always gain incremental volume
• Create continual "brand news," through new launches and cut back on communication of core proposition	• Build operational efficiency with brand extensions

---

[7] Brand churn: proliferation in the number of brands sold without significantly adding to the volume.

Why is brand exploitation so favored? Because it appears to offer shortcuts, quick boosts to profitability and lots of activity. This is attractive to marketers who do not expect to work on a brand for more than a few years, and to companies striving for short-term profit gains. The Gucci brand was exploited when it was extended across hundreds of categories, often with products such as plastic and canvas handbags, which did not meet the core proposition of top-end luxury assimilation. The situation was decisively corrected by Gucci's present owners. The Cadillac brand was exploited when used on the "Cadillac Cimarron," actually a Chevrolet Cavalier with leather seats and some luxury appointments. It failed but not before hurting the Cadillac image.[8] The new Cadillac SUV as a brand extension may not have the same negative effect, as luxury has been designed into the product.

12. **There is a strong trend towards global brand development, tailored to local conditions.** One could contend that the current level of global branding appears to be overestimated. There are many large local brands, especially in the United States, Japan, and Germany. However, only 48 out of the top 100 advertised mega-brands in the United States in 1994 were true international brands. Further evidence that the trend to global branding could be exaggerated comes from a study of six key globalizers (Colgate, Kraft, Nestlé, P & G, Quaker, and Unilever) by Boze & Patton. Of 1,792 brands studied, only 4 percent were "global." "Global" was defined for the study, as a product being sold in 34 or more countries. As many as 65 percent were marketed in three countries or less, and only five brands— Colgate, Lipton, Maggi, Nescafé, and Palmolive—were sold in all 67 countries studied.[9]

However, despite these statistics, there is no doubt that the trend toward global branding is increasing, driven by pressures on costs, the demonstrable success of the true international brands, and convergence in desired consumer benefits across countries.

---

[8] Kevin Clancy and Robert S. Shulman, *Marketing Myths That Are Killing the Business*, Mc Graw-Hill, 1994.
[9] Betsy Boze and Charles Patton.

While global branding is often explained in consumer terms as a way of meeting benefits that can transcend national boundaries, its main driver is business economics. In industries where origination costs like R&D and advertising development are high and can be handled centrally or regionally, the international brander will gain advantage by spreading these costs against revenue from many countries. Equally, many global operators can achieve lower operating costs through large plants serving many countries, and economies through the bulk purchasing of raw materials, packaging, IT systems, and advertising. However, these advantages can only be gained if a reasonable level of homogeneity in product or service content is appropriate across countries and markets.

To look at the global scenario from a different angle, the term *metanational* has been coined by Yves Doz, Jose Santos, and Peter Williamson in their book *From Global to Metanational: How Companies Win in the Knowledge Economy*.[10] In this important work, the authors describe how metanationals' key advantages will not result from global homogeneity, which deploys homegrown products, technologies, and processes to customers around the globe. Instead, these firms will leverage and thrive on cultivating and exploiting uniqueness—the valuing of cultural and geographic differences. These metanationals will build new types of advantage by connecting and leveraging dispersed pockets of knowledge, thereby potentially creating new and better competencies, including successful global brands.

Where "global spread" is no longer by itself a distinctive competitive advantage and a single national market no longer leads in most industries, valuable knowledge is increasingly scattered and is often quite sophisticated and "sticky"—meaning that it is often deeply embedded in distant and unfamiliar environments.[11] Searching out these "new sources of differentiation" and creating opportunities to "unlock global consumers' latent needs" is just the stuff that the Offensive Marketer excels at in the global economy.

---

[10] Yves Doz, Jose Santos, Peter Williamson, *From Global to Metanational: How Companies Win in the Knowledge Economy*, Harvard Business School Press, 2001.
[11] Id.

Table 10-8 lists some of the characteristics that determine whether an industry is likely to be more global in nature or local. An industry with global potential will exhibit many but not all of these.

Table 10-8 Characteristics Favoring International Branding

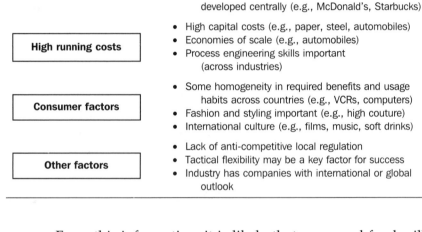

High origination costs	• High R&D as percentage of sales (e.g., pharmaceuticals) • High advertising as percentage of sales (e.g., cosmetics, fashion) • Processes and systems training important and developed centrally (e.g., McDonald's, Starbucks)
High running costs	• High capital costs (e.g., paper, steel, automobiles) • Economies of scale (e.g., automobiles) • Process engineering skills important (across industries)
Consumer factors	• Some homogeneity in required benefits and usage habits across countries (e.g., VCRs, computers) • Fashion and styling important (e.g., high couture) • International culture (e.g., films, music, soft drinks)
Other factors	• Lack of anti-competitive local regulation • Tactical flexibility may be a key factor for success • Industry has companies with international or global outlook

From this information, it is likely that processed food will remain a mainly local industry because R&D and advertising costs are a modest percentage of sales, only limited economies of scale are available, and local tastes vary widely. This is despite the fact that the processed food industry has a number of skillful international marketers such as Unilever, Nestlé, H. J. Heinz, and Kraft. To prove the point, most of their business consists of local brands or products.

International branders do not hold all the cards. Their structures tend to be complex and their costs higher. They are often unable to match the lean local competitor in either speed of reaction, distribution or supply chains and strategic partners, or employee motivation. While they have been quite successful in accelerating speed of new product development and in involving local management more in international strategy, many of their processes continue to remain cumbersome and de-motivating to employees on the front line of the local market.

Many of the issues cited in international branding involve tradeoffs between additional revenue available from meeting local needs more exactly, and additional cost of doing so: between the economies of scale, on the one hand, and local speed, flexibility, and motivation on the other.

THE GROWTH OF INTERNET BRANDS—ARE THEY A DIFFERENT ANIMAL?

Internet branding and the growth of Internet brands are not significantly different animals apart from branding in its more traditional context. Expanding branding through the Internet, with both its individualized and mass appeal, has brought branding to the forefront of marketing management in the last few years. Internet brands have some selective challenges owing to the medium of the Web and how customers and users interface, rely on, and find benefit in online experiences and relationships.

Companies—whether local, regional, national or global, brick and mortar, brick and click, or pure-play Internet companies—certainly have become stronger stewards of brand management out of the dot.com era. We have seen a migration of executives who are marketing and brand czars moving from consumer product companies where the concept and application of branding got its start, to companies having nothing to do with consumer household or food products, including American Express, GM, and IBM. Technology savvy companies including SAP, the German software giant, have based their successful brand management on the thinking that technology marketing not only must address technology but also must be founded in a clear message—for SAP that meant moving from a product-driven culture to a brand-driven culture.[12]

The Internet offers a route to customization and intimacy and the ability to have conversations and listen to customers. It allows a firm to move away from "shouting" its branding message through mass marketing, and integrate one-to-one dialogues with customers and potential end users. By moving to a brand-driven culture, the Internet becomes one more very useful tool for "touching" customers and providing an aligned branded experience. Moving

---

[12] "The Best Global Brands," *Business Week*, August 6, 2001.

beyond the dot.com era—where the Web was going to lead to exponential growth rates, where "free" was looking like the right opening price for products marketed on the Web, and the predominant thinking that market share was everything—the Internet and Web-based technologies are important tools for reaching, and sustaining customer relationships and creating branding opportunities.

GUIDELINES FOR EXTENDING EXISTING BRANDS

This next section addresses six important guidelines for effective brand extension.[13]

1. **Really understand how your markets and channels segment.** A real understanding of your company's markets and how your channels segment will enable you, as an Offensive Marketer, to target brand extensions to build incremental volume rather than cannibalizing existing business. In general, any new product should add more than your company's fair share of the market through clear targeting. (Chapter 9 tells you how to achieve this result.)

2. **Clearly identify the core of your brand proposition.** The core of a brand consists of the elements consumers most associate with it and constitutes the primary reason for purchase. A brand core can be ascertained through consumer and customer research, backed by experienced judgment.

    Among the possible core elements, it is usually most effective to focus on one or two. As an exercise, here are some choices. Which of the attributes in Table 10-9 represent the most important core element of each brand?

    In each case, the most important core element is under (3). The core of Mercedes is superior engineering, and this, together with very limited design changes in new models, builds the other core element of high resale value. High performance, in terms of acceleration, is not core to Mercedes, since many less expensive cars outperform it.

---

[13] This section owes a particular acknowledgement to the SmithKline Beecham Consumer Health, "Marketing Leadership Programme"—a set of best practice approaches and processes developed internally with contribution from Oxford Corporate Consultants.

Table 10-9 Alternative Brand Core Elements

	Possible core elements		
Brand	1	2	3
Mercedes	High performance	High resale value	Superior engineering
Gucci	Fashionable	Leather	Exclusive
Amazon.com	Reliability	Convenience	Personalization

Exclusivity backed by high quality is core to Gucci. That is why the brand languished when it was applied to mediocre products and sold through mass marketers. Since reestablishment of its core proposition, which involved cutting product range from 20,000 to 5,000, raising quality, and tightly selecting outlets, the brand has regained momentum.

Personalization is the core element to Amazon's market positioning. The technology that backs its visitor recognition does provide convenience of shopping online, although this, in itself, is not a distinctive competency over other online sellers. Similarly, technology backing Amazon's product availability provides for reliability in the sense that it can confirm almost immediately if the product is in stock, yet this alone, is not the most advantageous core strategic element.

3. **Strengthen and develop the brand core over time.** Brand development needs to be planned over a least at three- to five-year time frame. Companies readily accept the necessity to plan their capital expenditure three to five years ahead, but are strangely reluctant to apply the same thinking to brands. How many five-year brand development plans have you seen?

Capital equipment has only a five- to twenty-year life-span, while most major brands span decades. Companies not producing three- to five-year brand development plans fail to accept the logic of the often-quoted phrase, "Brands are our most important asset." The centerpiece of a strategic brand plan is future objectives targeting brand positioning three to five years hence. From this, plans to broaden or narrow positioning, to enhance brand distinctiveness, to improve products or services, to enter new markets or channel segments, to capitalize on new usage occasions, or to enter new countries can be developed.

It is less common for brands to narrow down their positioning rather than expand it, but this is sensible if there has been over-extension in the past. Gucci is an illustration of this. So is Xerox. Xerox moved its brand into brokerage, investment banking, and insurance (e.g., Xerox Life). It has now withdrawn from these ill-conceived brand extensions and sold the businesses, returning to its core strategy.

Brand development needs to be planned over time on a graduated basis, which is why three to five years is the minimum planning time scale needed.

4. **Brand line extensions must add significant incremental sales.** One of the most common mistakes in brand development is to add lots of new variations, usually called "line extensions," which draw their sales mainly from your existing products. Ways to avoid this and generate largely incremental sales have already been covered and are summarized in Table 10-10.

Some companies have guidelines on the minimum level of incremental brand sales a new item must generate. As a rule of thumb, if the new item does not add at least 10 percent

Table 10-10   How to Build Incremental Sales With New Items

- Target segments, either market, channel, demographic or usage, where your existing share is below average.
- Ensure the new item meets a new need.
- Give the new items incremental marketing support, to maximize incremental sales.
- Continue to support existing brand items strongly when you launch new ones, to focus pressure on competitors.
- Plan now for additional initiatives on existing and new items over the next twelve months.

incremental sales revenue, it is probably not worth the effort or cost.

5. **Build operational efficiencies into line extensions.** Wherever possible, use existing capital equipment, facilities, raw materials, and assets in developing new items, so as to maximize gross profit margins. This is commonsense asset-based marketing.

OFFENSIVE BRAND DEVELOPMENT TOOLS

This section will briefly outline tools useful in both brand planning, studied in Chapter 8, and Offensive Brand Development. Many of these tools have already been described in both this Chapter and Chapter 9. Table 10-11 can be used as a reference, highlighting the five tools further outlined in this section:

Table 10-11 Seven Offensive Brand Development Tools

Tools	Covered	Reference Chap.		Pages
Branding Iceberg	✓	10	Fig 10-2	p. 243
Market segmentation	✓	9		
Brand conversion model	✓	8		p. 204
IDQV	✓	8		p. 207
Brand positioning statement	✓	8		p. 208
Quantified portfolio analysis	✓	7		p. 164
Brand scorecard	✓	7		p. 259

1. Power brands
2. Brand staircase
3. One-minute test
4. Brand circle
5. Brand development work sheet

1. **Power brands.** These are important brands with growth potential that merit significant future investment. How do you identify them?

   In a quantified portfolio analysis, expect them to be in or near the top left box with high brand strength in reasonably attractive markets. Such brands will also score well on impact differentiation or quality-value (IDQV)[14] tests as well as the brand conversion model. To qualify for the "power" label,

---

[14] IDQV is a system developed by Novaction SA, Paris, France. It derives from research on thousands of brands.

a brand should meet most of the characteristics in Table 10-12 although these will differ by market and company.

Table 10-12 Ideal Characteristics of Power Brands

- Significant volume
- Compete in segment(s) strategically important to company
- Distinctive or superior proposition
- Sustainable proposition
- Responsive to marketing support
- At least average operating profit
- Requirements for success match company competencies
- Demonstrated growth potential
- Identified opportunities for extension
- Multi-country position, or potential to achieve it
- Delivers good value

The same brand may be classified as "power" in one company, but not in another. For a large healthcare company, a mature brand with sales of only $4 million could be unexciting, but for a small company with total sales of only $10 million, it would almost certainly be treated as a power brand and a large amount of resources would be directed to it.

Classifying brands into "power," "secondary," and "other" is a useful shorthand means of allocating brand development resources—R&D, advertising, promotion, IT, and capital expenditures. Power brands should always receive a much higher share of company development spending than their share of company sales or profits.

2. **Brand staircase.** The "brand staircase" is an illustration to indicate where your brand originated and where its headed. The graph can be very simple or complex, covering various aspects of performance such as product, service, and value. It is best to focus simply on propositions and segments and not let the illustration become hindered by too much data. Once the initial staircase is constructed, further detailed staircases can be used to build sub-propositions. The example in Figure 10-4 uses a fictitious insurance company which insures home contents (over $250K) through independent financial advisors (IFAs). To its 45- to 65-year-old high-income customers its proposition includes a lower price with better service due to specialization. The brand staircase indicates how this core proposition can be developed over the next five years.

Figure 10-4

Insurance:

Brand Extension

Staircase

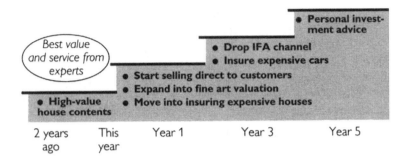

This insurance company's brand development direction is to retain the proposition "Best value and service from experts," to extend its product range into other services for high net worth individuals, and to move gradually away from the independent financial advisor channel into direct selling, including a presence on the Web with personal-service, market research, and transaction capabilities. The Brand Staircase provides a useful summary of future direction and options in a single chart.

3. **One-minute test.** The one-minute test[15] is a simple method for making an early check of a brand's position and potential. The technique is to get people to list anything that comes to mind about a brand, "Starting now … and you've got 60 seconds exactly." It can be used with colleagues in the office—in Sales, in Operations, or with customers and buyers—either individually or in groups. The urgency provided by the 60-second time limit ensures a spontaneous response. When you have got a couple of dozen responses, organize the output under headings including physical product, presentation, target customer, usage occasion, image, and development opportunities, to name a few that are possible. This is clearly not a consumer research technique, but a quick and rough guide.

4. **Brand circle.** This tool visually represents the properties of a brand, and consists of four circles. In the middle circle is the inner core. This comprises the brand's intrinsic qualities such as great taste, premium pricing, and health benefits. The outer core consists of optional attributes, which can be used to stretch the associations of the brand name but which are not essential to its future. The second ring out from the inner core, represents

---

[15] Derived from Andrew Roberts, Director of Taylor Nelson HGB.

the brand as it is today—for example, for a fruit beverage, no artificial flavorings, concentrated drink, glass bottles, family orientation. The third ring out is possible extension areas highlighting directions for moving forward in the future consistent with the inner core descriptions. These might include carbonated beverages, the ready to drink market, out of the home or single-use packaging, enhanced health benefits, the athletic market, additional flavors, or sugar free product. "No-go" areas should be identified as part of the brand circle exercise, since any move into them would erode the inner core.

The brand circle can be completed out of current consumer knowledge and the results of any "ideas sessions" on brand extension opportunities.

5. **Brand development worksheet.** Lastly, the brand development worksheet is a checklist to guide you toward setting priorities for brand improvement. The worksheet outlines main levers of brand development that differ by industry and rates your relative position versus the competition with columns for improvement, priorities, and steps. In general, improvement activity should be concentrated on the more important levers, where your company's position is parity with or inferior to competition. Examples of elements generic to all industries to be prioritized and plotted are customer service, quality, value, pricing, range, innovation in meeting needs, and differentiation. Key levers that may be identified could include design, color selection, quality and comfort, customization or personalization, availability, and online capabilities.

PROCESS FLOW FOR OFFENSIVE BRAND DEVELOPMENT

The seven-step brand development process flow is summarized in Table 10-13, which utilizes the principles and tools already covered by this chapter. The summary indicates which of the brand development tools can be used at each step of the process.

The process starts with brand stakeholders and finishes with detailed brand input to meet long-term objectives. It is not essential to follow all seven steps and, you may, for example, start at Step 3—defining 3–5 year objectives by segment—if work has already been done on brand stakeholder needs and alignment.

Table 10-13 Seven-Step Offensive Brand Development Process

Process:	Optional tools to use:
1. **Define, prioritize brand stakeholders**	• Brand Stakeholder Alignment (BSA)
2. **Identify stakeholder needs, check alignment**	• BSA • Segmentation
3. **Define 3–5 year objectives by segment**	• Segmentation
4. **Categorize brands by type (e.g. 'Power')**	• Quantified portfolio analysis • Brand continuum • Brand scorecards • Power brand definition • Brand positioning statement
5. **Determine core and extendibility of brands**	• Brand development worksheet • Brand circle • 1-minute test • Brand Staircase • Brand Iceberg • Brand opportunity tree • Brand conversion model • IDQV
6. **Identify gap v. strategic objectives**	
7. **New brands, acquisitions, licenses**	• Same tools as for Step 5

The Offensive Brand Development process is strategic in nature and long-term in focus. It is about determining future direction, not about numbers or tactics. Time-scale covered should be at least 18 months in the nearer term to three to five years, and output from this process can be fed into each yearly plan during the strategic planning process and into yearly budgeting.

CONCLUSION

The importance of Offensive Brand Development cannot be ignored in today's competitive marketplace. The impact on the significance of brand management has been pushed to the fore of corporate strategy and the rigors of "Effective Execution"—the "E" of POISE.

Despite the era of mega-mergers, which over the past years have seen the disappearance of Chemical Bank, McDonnell Douglas, Shearson, and Nynex Corp., among many others, millions of dollars across industries are being spent on building and extending brands.

Understanding how strong brands are distinctive business systems, not just names, why master branding is gaining ground in this global market influenced by successful Internet companies, and recognizing that stakeholder alignment and effective segmentation are requisites for accomplished brand development, are key take-away points from this chapter. These understandings lead one to the conclusions that brands need to be strategically developed, not exploited, that brand core ideas need to be understood so brand development and extensions do not alienate the brand's strengths, and that brands must produce incremental sales for the company as well as utilize operational efficiencies to be most productive.

For these benefits to fully materialize, it is important to understand that brand development is a process that begins with defining and prioritizing brand stakeholders and ends with a strategy for building new brands, making acquisitions, and decommissioning less profitable brands that have become undifferentiated and weak.

11 Offensive Approach: New Product and Service Development

INTRODUCTION

The previous chapters have laid the foundation for success in New Product and Service Development (NPSD), including prioritizing segments and brands and adopting an integrated approach to marketing using rigorous analytical and planning processes and tools.

This chapter will build further on this foundation, and cover the main activities of NPSD: opportunity identification, idea generation, screening, testing and launching.

Nothing is more important then having superior and distinct products and services, and improving them by building core competencies in both innovation and development.

THE FOUNDATION OF NPSD

Some marketers think that lots of bright ideas are the keys to success in NPSD. Articles are replete with techniques for idea generation, such as attribute listing, dissatisfaction studies, and brainstorming.

Good ideas are important but without a solid foundation of effective structure, well-allocated resources, and strong processes, ideas wither and eventually die. The fundamentals, upon which the more visible and glamorous aspects of NPSD need to be built, are presented in Figure 11-1. The internal organization of NPSD—including the level and allocation of resources, evaluation, and best-practice processes, as well as opportunity identification and idea generation—will be the focus of this chapter.

Figure 11-1
The Foundation of New Product and Service Development

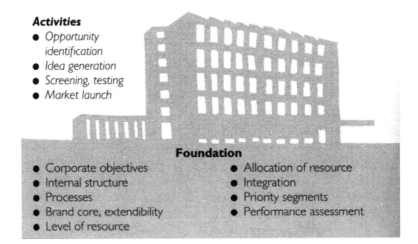

Activities
- *Opportunity identification*
- *Idea generation*
- *Screening, testing*
- *Market launch*

Foundation
- Corporate objectives
- Internal structure
- Processes
- Brand core, extendibility
- Level of resource
- Allocation of resource
- Integration
- Priority segments
- Performance assessment

Corporate Objectives

Once your company has established the desired total revenue and profit for time frames of one year, 18 months, and three to five years, it is important to calculate the gap between the desired total revenue and current revenue figures. "Gap analysis" is concerned with the disparity between revenue and profits generated from new and improved products (or distribution channels) over the next few years, and the desired total revenue and profit. Figure 11-2 illustrates a profit gap analysis.

Figure 11-2
Profit Gap Analysis

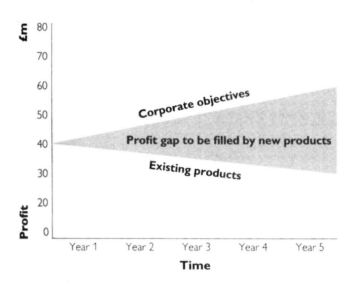

Closing the gap is not as tough as it looks. In practice, your firm will already have a number of new products and line extensions planned, tested, and ready to launch. Improvements to existing products and plans for new distribution channels may also be in the pipeline. Most of these new initiatives will utilize existing brands but some may require new ones.

Priority Segments for Focus

New product ideas should be generated in areas relevant to the future business strategy. To develop and launch ideas in unattractive segments where your company lacks competencies is asking for trouble. The Marketing Alignment Process (see Chapter 2) aligns markets and competencies, whereas market segmentation (see Chapter 9) forms the basis for prioritizing market and channel segments.

271

Integration

NPSD should be led by the Marketing Department; however, more than any other operational activity, this is a team task. Strong integration is essential among Marketing, R&D, Operations, Sales, Finance, and IT. R&D and Manufacturing, in the pursuit of new products, and IT, in the pursuit of new services, become the cornerstones. Finance is also of special importance in accurately predicting future costs.

Please refer to Chapter 4 for a detailed analysis of the Integrated Marketing Approach.

Priority Brands Give Focus

In the previous chapter, your company has been given the opportunity to establish core and extension areas for each brand. Understanding the new market and channel segments that you have prioritized for the future, new product or service ideas can now be efficiently allocated to existing or new brands.

KEY PRINCIPLES OF NEW PRODUCT AND SERVICE DEVELOPMENT

There are seven key principles of NPSD. Let's take one at a time.

1. **NPSD and innovation—Keystones of Offensive Marketing.** How does NPSD fit within the five elements of POISE: Profitable, Offensive, Integrated, Strategic, and Effectively Executed?

   Any company that has clear future objectives and vision successfully identifies the segments and brands to focus on—and that implements through innovation and cost-effective operations—is likely to be highly successful in NPSD.

   The effective development of new products and services is essential to the delivery of "superior customer experiences." Unless your company's prices are below average, your company must be focused on generating and sustaining product or service superiority as compared to the competition. Many companies deceive themselves on this score. They assume that their products or services are better, and often consider it heresy for constituencies to suggest otherwise. Assumptions such as these are dangerous. It is essential to prove beyond dispute, through objective product and service testing with target customers, that the company's offering is superior when compared to competition. The stamp of superiority must be more than technically "confirmed" in the laboratory; it must be further acknowledged by consumers and customers in their interactions with the product or service.

Product and service development is the single most important corporate activity. Every company believes that top product quality is essential, however, few actually take action with respect to this belief. Instead, executives mount aggressive acquisition programs or create corporate objectives that link to innovation goals but are never successfully implemented.

Product or service superiority can be achieved and sustained in any category, even those regarded as price-driven commodities. Your company does not need a dramatic lead. In most markets, a 5 percent or 10 percent difference will be a winning strategy if it is in a performance area important to the consumer and is communicated effectively. Grocery retailers have gained long-term market share by exploiting small differences on a consistent basis. Marketers of bottled water have flourished by creating strong product images and differentiated positioning.

Surrounding products with superior services can also create differentiation in so-called "commodity markets." Take fast food and hamburgers as an example. While it is debatable whether McDonald's has a better hamburger product than its competitors, its package of convenience, speed, friendliness, and consistent reliability add enormous value to a rather pedestrian product, and combine to produce a strong customer proposition. Interestingly, Burger King's challenge to McDonald's, "Have It Your Way," was a response to the perceived loss of customization arising out of McDonald's more standardized, "high-tech" approach. The difficulty that McDonald's has experienced in updating this proposition to make it more relevant to changing customer needs, including lower fat content and a wider selection, should not detract from the successful differentiated proposition it had originally established.

2. **Product life cycle can kill brands or sustain them.** There is a product life cycle but no brand life cycle. The product life cycle can be envisioned as a truncated version of the human development process. It consists of growth, maturity, saturation, and decline, as shown in Figure 11-3.

Figure 11-3
The Product Life Cycle[a]

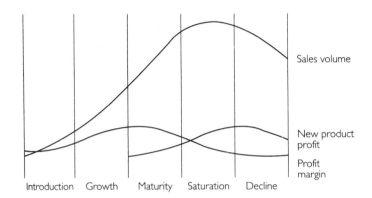

According to this concept, sales volume peaks soon after maturity but is sustained during saturation by product or service improvements, line extensions, and so on. Profits are meager during the early stages when heavy investment must be made, but are maintained even during decline, when additional operating efficiencies are achieved and marketing support is reduced. In the end, though, the product is no longer a viable market offering.

The product life cycle is not an accurate representation of marketplace reality, but more an indication of what can happen to companies that neglect NPSD. In practice, well-marketed brands defeat the product life cycle by continually renewing and extending their product ranges. Consequently, some products within a brand portfolio may be at a late stage of the product life cycle, while others will be in the introductory or growth stage.

---

[a] Booz Allen & Hamilton, *New Product Management for the 1980s*, Internal Publication.

Computers, software, consumer durables, and many business-to-business products have quite short life cycles. They need to be reinvigorated regularly with new products and improvements to existing ones both to meet competition and growing customer expectations.

Intel Corporation is a prime example of a company that regularly innovates and propels new products with heightened capabilities into the market. These products are designed to meet newly created demands growing out of new technology applications and increasing computing and networking speed. As the world's biggest and richest chipmaker, Intel's history of chip innovation has proven its founder's Gordon E. Moore seminal insight—known as Moore's Law—correct. Moore's Law states that the microchip power will double every 18 months while prices plummet. As quality is newly defined with constant shifts in technology, Intel must innovate quickly to stay ahead of its competitors.

Other markets like food, alcohol, and many services change more slowly. However, even in these categories, continuous improvement is now becoming the norm. Individual innovations may often be quite small but over the years they drive cumulative change and more efficient use of resources. For instance, the use of kiosks in public spaces was an innovation and adjunct to the successful introduction of the ATM in the banking industry. Based on increasing accessibility, personalization, and consumers' growing confidence with interacting with technology, kiosks have grown to link online information and service with brick and mortar conveniences.

Charles Schwab is among those companies that continuously redefine themselves, transforming their products and services. Beginning with helping to define the discount brokerage industry by undercutting the steep fees charged by traditional brokers like Merrill Lynch and PaineWebber, Schwab then morphed into a mutual fund powerhouse bringing customers new benefits. By transforming itself a third time into an online full-service broker, its Web offerings complemented its network of branches, allowing it to grow a successful "clicks and mortar" customer experience for those who never had a broker before. With these innovations, Schwab was able to grow its market capitalization, surpassing that of Merrill Lynch for the first time in 1998 as the democratization of investing hit new heights.[1]

Coca-Cola Classic is among the least changed of products over time—indeed, the formula (claimed to be a closely guarded secret known only by a few) was changed only once over the past century: according to sources, the company's original formula contained cocaine. Yet the product continues to grow through broader distribution, new country entry, packaging innovation, and imaginative marketing support. The broader Coca-Cola brand has also been expanded over the years through sub-brands, like the very successful Diet Coke and the newer vanilla-flavored Coke and Diet Coke.

Coca-Cola, however, is the exception. In most markets, quality and innovation, often driven by technological change, are propelling rapid product change at greater speed, as competition intensifies and consumers become increasingly demanding. The product life cycle is alive and well, ruthlessly killing products and services that ignore it.

3. **The principles of product and service development are similar, but applications differ.** Examples of new service developments include e-tickets for airline travel; online self-help often backed by centralized call centers for after-purchase service, product inquiries, or warranty registration; new designs and layouts for restaurant and self-service food bars; loyalty cards or gift cards issued by Tower Records, The Gap, or Walden Books, to name a few of the many retailers now offering this convenience.

Many new service developments center on physical improvements to reflect new uses or meet changing needs, or on innovations driven by people, digitized processes, IT systems or software capabilities, for instance, in customer relationship management (CRM). Service innovations, like product introductions, arise out of innovative business concepts that are competing in the competitive marketplace for customer attention and, ultimately, loyalty.

Obviously consumers—their objectives, attitudes, skills, and training—are an important element of any service proposition. By contrast, historically, consumers of products have been unlikely to meet the people who develop, make, market, or sell them. This is changing as companies seek to establish relationships

---

[1] Gary Hamel, *Leading the Revolution*, Harvard Business School Press, 2000, Chapter 7.

with their best customers. However, differences still exist between product and service development in lead-times, cost, and risk. Managing lead-times in speed to market gains, lowering costs through the application of supply-chain technology, and assessing risk continue to be among the most important business design strategies heading into the twenty-first century.

4. **Testing to reduce risk is an essential part of successful NPSD.** Market research and testing are the main ways to reduce the risk of NPSD, and to increase the chance of success. Testing can range from informal trials with key customers to a full-scale launch of a new global brand in a "lead" country or region. Companies that pride themselves on speed-to-market development time-scales are often measured in weeks or months, not years. Customers have become an instrumental part of the equation by providing real-time input and feedback in cycles of experimentation where the business objective is to load, aim, fire, then load again. This type of experimentation and testing builds market confidence and a culture where innovation is central to market leadership.

There are four main stages of formal testing, which can be combined with the more speed-to-market approach described above.

- **Concept testing.** This is quick and low cost. At its simplest, it involves summarizing new product or service propositions in a few lines, individually on a card and getting consumers or customers to rank them. It can be conducted with individuals or in groups, with either simple or elaborate props. The major purpose is to screen out weak ideas and to find ways to strengthen promising ones.
- **Testing individual stimuli.** The purpose of this stage is to test all the individual elements in the new product or service proposition individually, before combining them at the next stage. Every significant element in the proposition may be individually tested and ranked versus competition or alternative elements. This would cover product (e.g., new airline menu), packaging, advertising (e.g., rough print layout or TV or banner ad), direct marketing literature, or new credit card layout, to name a few examples. Once you are satisfied with the performance of each individual element, you can then move to testing the totality.
- **Test of total proposition.** For business-to-business products, testing is done with one or two leading customers or by

direct contact with a small number of heavy users, early adopters, or industry experts. In consumer goods and services, simulated test markets (STMs) are often used for this purpose. Techniques vary and companies can tailor them to their needs. However, most incorporate a consumer test of the new product or service versus the leading competitor; a test of advertising impact, relevance, and persuasion; or a simulated shopping or use situation.

From the test market results, volume forecast is developed partly from data obtained during the test and partly from estimates made by the brand manager. The test situation generates product preference, response to advertising, and purchase intent. The brand manager, as Offensive Marketer, is responsible for providing an estimate of retailer distribution of the new product, a year-one marketing spending plan, and likely competitor response. All this input is synthesized and provides the basis for estimates of the new product's prospects. (From this description, you would be fully justified in assuming that this "synthesis" or "black box" technique could not possibly forecast likely future volume accurately at all. Surprisingly, though, the accuracy of this method has been shown to be quite impressive—within 10–15 percent of subsequent marketplace results when the final test plan is faithfully followed.)

What is more, the STM techniques can answer "What if?" questions satisfactorily, such as, "What will happen to my volume and market share if I double advertising and raise my price by 10 percent?" Or, "If I increase product acceptance by 20 percent, and hold the price, what will happen to my volume?"

The main limitation of STMs is that they do not measure retailer acceptance or reaction, and therefore, do not truly represent real life market conditions. Competitor reaction is likewise left out of the equation.

- **Market test of full proposition.** This involves launching the whole new proposition commercially in the marketplace. Location can vary from a single test market to a small country test market or a whole regional rollout, such as Europe or Southeast Asia. The main disadvantages of full market tests are cost and time. And, unlike simulated test markets, which are conducted confidentially, market tests reveal your company's hand to the competition.

These four methods or stages of testing are not obligatory. Whether your company undertakes the full gamut will depend on the importance of the project, cost and risk involved, accessibility and relationship with customers, and predicted speed of competitor response. Tests one, two, and three would usually be advisable for any significant new product. Market test of the full proposition would probably only be undertaken if a company felt the proposition was protectable in the medium term because of technology, distinctive competencies, or the need to invest in major future capital to fully realize the concept.

Why test at all? Testing enables your firm to discard potential failures at each of the four stages; to translate good ideas into excellent ones through constant interaction with the consumer or customer; to try out alternative propositions, prices, and marketing support levels; and to forecast sales more accurately so that the launch is handled efficiently with the most appropriate implementation strategy.

It should be noted that there can often be a trade-off between testing and speed to market. While this needs to be seriously considered, the advantages of timely and effective testing are frequently clear. Lack of testing is attributable both to poor planning and to limited assessment of possible competitive reaction.

5. **Superior product or service benefits can always be developed.** In certain markets—for instance, some industrial goods, cars, and consumer durables—it is easier to see how, with skillful marketing and R&D, superior products can be developed. But, in many markets, companies struggle with creating salient and meaningful product benefits. In the consumer products market where capacity is no longer an issue, companies like Kellogg and P&G are adept at creating marketing stories that distinguish their products from competitors in an attempt to have the consumer purchase *their* offerings. This is marketing innovation, which creates the perception of needs instead of product innovation, which answers the call from customers' unaddressed or un-envisioned needs.

One can either accept the difficulties as inherent in the marketplace or follow a basic belief that product superiority can always be developed and that human creativity will spur superior visioning and product offerings that are meaningful. Cancer-fighting drugs, ethanol-based fuel and hydrogen-powered vehicles, fiber optics, real-time satellite data feeds, low-frequency radio broadcast, genetic coding and cloning—all have the potential to create not only new wealth but to add to the human experience.

6. **The 5 percent factor—small differences matter.** Even minor differences in product or service performance can be significant to the consumer, especially in product categories with high purchase frequency. When so many markets are oversupplied with almost identical offerings, being 5 percent better in the mind of the consumer can be a winning margin. Whether it is a product or service offering, the difference between 98 percent reliability and 93 percent can be very significant to a satisfying customer experience. Indeed, having a consistent corporate offering across customer touch-points is a major challenge for today's companies and a major opportunity area for companies seeking the 5 percent factor.

7. **Products—pathways to consumer benefits.** A technical success may be of no interest to the consumer or may in fact spur a negative emotional response. For example, irradiation of food at low and safe levels lengthens product life, but is likely, in this age of greater customer expertise, to create problems for the product out of a growing emotional resistance of consumers to technologically altered foods. The same may be true for genetically engineered foods. Technical performance is certainly important, since every consumer wants a product to fulfill its purpose, but technical advantages should not be viewed in isolation of the product's whole experience. A product that is regarded by scientists as being at technical parity with its competition may nevertheless be regarded by consumers as superior for non-technical reasons. The end result? Consumers are emotional as well as logical beings and may be influenced by the derivation of a product.

WHY MOST NEW PRODUCTS AND SERVICES FAIL

While estimates vary widely, both overall and by market type, there is strong evidence that most newly advertised products and many new services fail. A look at the recent carnage in dot.com companies provides numerous examples of product and services failures. In fact, it is estimated that between 75 and 80 percent of all new products fail.

In order to ensure success, a clear definition of success is essential. So, what is success? Success may be defined in terms of market share, stability of that share over time, payback in a set period of years, or operating profit of a certain percentage. Guidelines for defining success should be delineated up front by the firm.

One of the most comprehensive studies of new product failure was conducted across 84 grocery product classes over a ten-year period in the United Kingdom and United States, using demanding but reasonable criteria of minimum sales levels. This study indicated a 3 percent new product success rate.[2]

Fifty-eight of the 84 categories did not have a single new product success in the ten-year period. The very high failure rate of new products tends to be taken for granted by marketers. High product-failure rate is not an immutable law of nature, and certain companies like 3M, Procter & Gamble, Unilever, and Gillette have quite high success rates, bucking the general trend.

What are the main reasons for the high failure rates of new products? Most lie in the foundation of NPSD—companies bolt new product activities and initiatives on to a quicksand foundation of inadequate commitment, structure, and priority.

The following are some of the more specific reasons for new product and service failure.

1. **Lack of company commitment.** The trouble with new product development and launch, from the view-point of many Boards of Directors, is that they are expensive, will probably lose money the current fiscal year, and are, by most standards, quite likely to fail. This rather unattractive financial and bonus scenario accounts for lukewarm attitudes on the part of senior management even though it is recognized that new product and service development is one of the only sustained routes to real growth.

   What is commitment? It is a conviction by senior management, following thorough analysis, that a new project can be successfully accomplished, together with the willingness to pursue it without reservation and the determination to ride out obstacles when they occur.

---

[2] Bill Ramsey, "The New Product Dilemma," *Nielsen Marketing Trends*, January 1982.

Over 30 years ago, Procter & Gamble committed itself to entering the paper market. Success was slow in coming and involved many setbacks:

Procter & Gamble investigated the market for consumer paper products (toilet and facial tissues) and liked what it saw. The market had reached a good size, was expanding fast, and offered sufficient margins to permit heavy advertising and promotion spending.

What is more, the criteria by which consumers judged the performance of paper products—notably softness, absorbency, and wet strength—could be assessed objectively just like the whiteness result of a clothes washing powder.

There were only two snags—Procter & Gamble knew nothing about paper technology, and the two entrenched competitors, Scott Paper and Kimberley Clark (Kleenex), were well-managed companies.

Procter & Gamble bought a small regional paper firm called the Charmin Company, and used that as a base for learning about the business. It spent some years developing a better tissue. Eventually, a method of adding perfume was worked out and on a consumer blind test, Procter & Gamble's perfumed product beat the competition by two to one.

A test market was opened, supported by heavy advertising and full-size free samples delivered to consumers' homes. The brand quickly gained a high share. However, when the launch activity was over, market share plummeted. The perfume had novelty appeal, but when this wore off, consumers went back to their regular brands.

Procter & Gamble did not give up. Senior management continued to feel that the company had the technical and marketing skills to succeed in this paper market. They were convinced that the strategy was right and that a flawed execution should not deter them.

More R&D work was done and eventually a product was developed with superior softness and wet strength. This was tested and launched nationally. It ultimately achieved brand leadership in toilet paper and paper tissues.

Subsequently, Procter & Gamble entered the disposable diaper (Pampers) and feminine hygiene markets (Always),

> capitalizing on their competencies in paper. Global profits from paper have averaged approximately 25 percent of total P&G profits.

In today's competitive marketplace, it is incumbent upon companies and their leadership to have a strong commitment to market innovation even if their new products cannibalize previously successful products and initiatives. Microsoft is a prime example of this type of "hypercompetitive"[3] firm. Microsoft's commitment to the DOS operating system was supplanted by its newer commitment to Windows—including Windows CE, Internet Explorer, Microsoft Office, which all use a common architecture—and, which may, themselves, in the near future, be upstaged by NT or other software.

These companies use the wealth created by their successes to reach toward their next basis for market leadership. As the boundaries and demands of the personal computing environment shift, Microsoft will need to continue to explore software integration, Internet-based services and strategies, digital home appliance interfacing, open source code and handheld technologies (to name a few of the more obvious) to maintain its leadership. Depending on the future shape of the market and customer demand, any of these technologies or groups of technologies may upstage Microsoft's present PC Windows-based monopoly. Microsoft's commitment to innovation is that it will bring the newer technology to market first.

2. **Lack of balance between enthusiasm and objectivity.** People involved in a new products operating team must be concurrently enthusiastic yet realistic. Senior management should be committed to new products, yet objective in assessing proposals put forward for approval. These contrasting requirements are difficult to balance effectively.

3. **Conflict between speed and quality.** Speed between starting and completing NPSD projects is increasing every year. Companies are getting faster to market in the first country, and either launching globally in one move, as with the latest version

---

[3] See, Richard A. D'Aveni, *Hyper-Competition, Managing the Dynamics of Strategic Maneuvering,* The Free Press, a division of Simon & Schuster, 1994.

of Microsoft Windows, or Gillette's Mach 3, or rapidly expanding to new countries or regions within months or a year of the initial launch. Companies are therefore under pressure to increase speed, both to preempt competition and to save cost. In general, the longer an NPSD project takes, the higher the fixed overhead cost of R&D and origination.

Because many new products and services involve discovery, uncertainty, and unpredictable competitor activity, speed may affect the quality of an initiative and may contribute to its failure. This risk is intensified if supporting budgets are also cut to achieve short-term corporate profit targets.

4. **Lack of rigorous process.** Does your company have an NPSD process? Is it flawed, or not properly observed? Superficial business analysis, weak project management, changes in the NPSD team, poorly planned consumer research, lack of cross-departmental cooperation, and failure to conduct proper testing before launch are often responsible for a new product's failure. Combined, the new offering has little chance of success.

5. **Product or service does not deliver sufficient extra value.** Unless a new offering is distinctive or achieves a superior mix of performance and price, it is unlikely to either succeed or be sustainable. In this day and age where differentiation itself is a competitive advantage, getting a successful message about an undifferentiated offering to a highly besieged audience is highly unlikely.

6. **Underestimated costs.** Future costs are often difficult to estimate, and it is tempting to take a "best circumstance" view of them. Consequently, new product costs are often well above estimate, and since cost overruns are not a relevant justification for increasing prices, profits prove disappointing.

One caveat here: Even having addressed these issues, a product or service offering may not be well timed in the market or accepted by prospective consumers. Witness Global Crossing, Ltd., which filed the largest bankruptcy in telecommunications history in January 2002. Global Crossing never posted an annual profit since it was created to extend its only resource—a fiber optic cable traversing the Atlantic—into a 100,000 mile network connecting 27 countries in the Americas, Europe, and Asia. The company had lost, from its operations, an estimated $7 billion in the last five years. As a spokesperson for Gary Winnick, Global Crossing's Chairman, said, "Sometimes it takes the markets time to catch up to visionary ideas." Ultimately, the company could not create a market from selling capacity directly to telephone and Internet service providers and large companies.[4]

FOUR KEY ISSUES TO RESOLVE ON NPSD

Having discussed the key principles of NPSD, let's now look at some key issues to resolve with the process.

How to Establish the Total NPSD Resource

The first thing to determine is how to define a NPSD resource. This goes well beyond R&D spending, much of which is spent on cost-reduction and process engineering projects unrelated to NPSD. A sensible definition of NPSD resource would be any cost primarily associated with NPSD origination or launch, across every department. Primary NPSD cost areas would be R&D, IT, Operations, Sales, and Marketing. Among the largest items would be those listed in Table 11-1.

Table 11-1   Main NPSD Cost Areas for Products and Services

Function	Products	Services

Marketing development	Personnel
	Market research
	External agencies
	Packaging development
	Other origination costs
		Same as for products,
		  but presentation
		  development rather
		  than packaging

Marketing launch	Advertising Promotion PR Event marketing Direct and e-marketing	Same as for products but add Display Marketing literature Staff training
R&D	Technology research Development and testing Translation to plant	Much of R&D is IT and technology based

Sales	Sales department resource
	Planning
	Retail testing, incentive and
	  advertising costs
		Sales department resource
		Planning, staff training
		Trade literature and incentives
		  (if distributor involved)

IT	Incorporate new product on data systems	New on-line data Management, control systems

Operations	Fit product on to existing lines, modify
	  or build extra plant capacity.
		Adjust operations to new
		  product

---

[4] Simon Romero, "5 Years and $15 Billion Later, A Fiber Optic Venture Fails," *The New York Times*, January 29, 2002.

The next step is to use this definition to analyze NPSD spending.

Spending can then be broken down both by cost area, as in Table 11-1, and by type of activity, such as product improvements, new products or services, line extensions, or totally new brands. What is the overall trend in recent years, both in absolute terms and as a percent of sales? Which activities have been least, and most, effective? What benefit and value is each cost area providing, and how can these be improved? How effectively are NPSD funds being spent compared with the competition?

A straightforward piece of Offensive Business Analysis like this will provide a powerful perspective on how effective your firm's NPSD spending is, how it can be improved, and strong clues as to what future resources should be allocated. In practice, it is rarely carried out, because responsibility for NPSD is so widely spread across departments.

Having analyzed the past, how should future NPSD resource levels be established?

Five methods listed below are in use. These are similar in principle to the approach for setting advertising budgets.

1. **Historical approach.** This method uses history as a base and makes adjustments up or down from this base for the future. Its weakness is that historical spend levels may have been wrong then or may be wrong going forward.
2. **Residual approach.** This system, if it can be called such, is to leave the decision on NPSD spending until the end of the budgeting process, and to allocate "what we can afford" after profit requirements and all other costs have been allocated. The result is almost always too low an allocation.
3. **Match competition.** This approach is to estimate what competitors are spending in absolute terms and as a percent of sales, and to relate your own company's spending to this. The method may not be relevant, since competitors may have more or less ambitious NPSD needs than your company and may be pursuing them more or less effectively. Furthermore, it is both speculative and defensive in nature.
4. **Percent of sales.** This is an important measure, especially trended over time and broken down by type of activity or cost. It is best to use NPSD spending as a percent of new product sales as the measure. Relating NPSD spending to total sales is less useful, because in any one year, total sales may consist

of unchanged products. NPSD spending as percent of new product sales is more useful as a measure than as a system of allocation.

5. **Task approach.** This is by far the best method. To be effective, though, it requires Offensive Business Analysis of past NPSD spending, gap analysis to establish future revenue, profits needed from new products, and a breakdown of the gap figure by major type of project. These pieces of information will enable you to establish the task and to estimate future NPSD resources needed on a basis strong enough to resist any rational attempts to cut.

How to Organize NPSD

This question is often asked in too narrow a context—that of the Marketing Department. Should NPSD be an additional task of existing Marketing Line Managers, or the sole purpose of a dedicated new products group? The drawbacks of both are well known. Managers of existing brands tend to be so busy running them that they have no time for NPSD. A new products group may lack feel for the hurly-burly of the marketplace, and run into "not invented here" attitudes when they hand over new products to existing line management to run.

This narrow question is becoming less relevant, as new development projects become increasingly international and cross-departmental, led by Offensive Marketers. Their success depends less on traditional Marketing Department structure and more on corporate commitment, allocation of resources, clear objectives, and integration and alignment. These factors will drive the type of NPSD organization appropriate to each company. The organizational structure itself will differ depending on the company's size, aspirations, and culture.

It is not therefore meaningful to talk about "right" or "wrong" structures for NPSD. But it is often worthwhile to handle "housekeeping" types of NPSD—where products or services are being improved or extended—differently from major new projects. Straightforward product or service improvements, and conventional line extensions are, in general, best handled by existing line management, with the involvement of an extended brand group.

Significant new initiatives involving high cost, long lead-times, and unusual challenges are often most effectively managed by cross-departmental project teams. They can be part time or full time as set forth in an organizational matrix, depending on their role and on the importance of the project. Basic requirements for such a project team, which should be led by an Offensive Marketer as well as selected others, are to:

- Establish a project leader and team members
- Set clear and measurable objectives for the team and for individual members that are broken down by month or quarter
- Communicate frequently, (at least monthly), and evaluate performance against agreed milestones
- Appoint a member of senior management as project sponsor to link up with the team, provide advice, remove barriers, and assist with internal politics

Project teams may be local, international, or a combination of the two. Video-conferences, and Web-based tools like e-mail, fax, and phone enable effective communication even when spread across continents.

The ultimate approach to NPSD is to develop the three- or five-year corporate plans, identify the half-dozen future initiatives that are critical to their success, and appoint full-time project teams to run them. Each member would be contracted to the project team for two to three years, or whatever the project length was, and provided with heavy incentives at project completion if objectives have been achieved. The major benefits of this approach are:

- High-priority marketing development projects get handled with the discipline and dedication of new production requirements.
- Integration and alignment exist across departments.
- Continuity within the team is present until project completion.
- Everyone in the project team has accelerated learning about other functions necessary to the NPSD process. This learning then becomes transferable across functions.
- Team leadership is excellent preparation for becoming a general manager.

How to Allocate R&D Resources

This relates primarily to product development but similar issues apply to allocation of scarce and expensive IT resources for service development. The setting of clear R&D priorities concentrates effort and reduces waste.

R&D allocations need to be taken at both the macro level, "top down" and at the micro level or "bottom up." Macro allocations relate to types of technology and activities. Strategies for these should be decided at the Board of Directors' and senior staff level. They need to be adjusted to reality through exposure to "bottom up" initiatives developed by people close to the marketplace. At the macro level, investment by technology area is addressed along with product R&D, long-term basic research direction, mid-term development research commitments, and what could be called "innovative" versus maintenance R&D. At the micro-level, individual new product R&D proposals based on identified opportunities are addressed.

How to Evaluate NPSD Performance

How should this be assessed? By whom? And, how often?

At the corporate level, quantitative innovation targets in annual reports are valuable because they are public and measurable. They send a strong message throughout the organization and influence vision, values, and culture. Both 3M and Gillette use these public statements successfully by targeting large percentages of current annual sales to be met by new product launches. Both regularly achieve their set targets. Hewlett-Packard publishes "vintage" charts annually, showing the breakdown of today's sales by year of product introduction, covering each of the past four years individually, with Year 3 and beyond as a single total.[5]

On a more detailed and operational level, NPSD output and success rate can be evaluated. A practical point at which to start measuring output is at the time when a concept idea has been successfully consumer-tested.

Table 11-2 assumes there are four more stages after the validation of a concept. These are: product or service development, testing

---

[5] David Packard, *The HP Way*, Harper Business, 1995.

Table 11-2 Toy Manufacturer: New Product Output, Success Rate (*read across*)

Stage	Output	Success	Success Rate %	Cumulative %
Validated concept	–	**300**	–	
Development	300	200	67	67
Proposition test	200	100	50	33
Test market	30	15	50	–
Launch	70	**40**	57	**13**

of the over-all proposition, test marketing, and launch. Table 11-2 summarizes output and success rate through the four stages for a toy manufacturer over a two-year period.

Here, "Output" measures level of NSPD effort and "Success Rate" evaluates the effectiveness of that effort. As shown by Table 11-2, of 300 initially validated concepts, 40, or 13 percent, have succeeded nationally. Output is therefore 300, success rate 13 percent. About 100 fell out at the development stage due to either feasibility difficulties or cost. Another 100 failed to pass muster at the final proposition hurdle. A hundred reached the marketplace, 30 in test markets, and 70 nationally without market testing.

It is recommended that the Board see a new product output and success rate table at least quarterly. All company development projects merit a monthly priority review by the Marketing Department and interdisciplinary senior staff since priorities can change rapidly.

SUGGESTED NPSD PROCESS

The seven-step NPSD process summarized in Table 11-3 (over page) is structured as a general purpose design for NPSD, and can be modified to fit particular situations. It may be used for total businesses or for brands. To simplify the explanation, the process has largely been applied to a brand.

Step 1: Opportunity Identification

Identify Areas for Collecting Ideas

Opportunity identification and idea generation need to be focused on market segments, channels, brands, and competencies already earmarked as future priorities. This ensures that good ideas with consumer appeal have a fair chance of commercial success. This prioritization can be brought to life by preparing a

Table 11-3   General Purpose NPSD Process—Seven Steps for a Brand

Step Process	Key Elements
1 Opportunity identification	• Identify areas for collecting ideas • Establish criteria for evaluation • List ideas already developed • Generate new ones
2 Initial idea screening	• Apply criteria and screen • Write up best ideas into concepts • Test out with users qualitatively
3 Develop technical briefs	• Discuss with R & D and/or IT • Write brief, for product or service • Get approval and priority for development
4 Develop products, services	• Technical development of concept • Develop outline Marketing plan
5 Develop support elements, validate	• Progress advertising, presentation, packaging • Research overall proposition and main elements with consumers, customers • This may include a simulated test market
6 Final plan	• Operations, Sales, Finance involvement • Marketing plan • Operations plan and action, including capital investment • Sales and trade or distributor marketing plan • Finalize packaging, advertising, customer literature, direct marketing, PR, sales promotion, trade activity • Communicate internally, train staff
7 Launch and one step ahead (test market or national)	• Implement test, roll-out, or national launch plan • Develop next initiatives, for Year 2, to keep one step ahead. • Monitor results, prepare for Year 2 or 3 relaunch.

one- or two-page opportunity development brief to guide the process. It should include future brand objectives, priority market segments that have been identified, the brand core proposition, brand extendibility ideas, distribution channel identification, and a summary of current ideas under development and the timing of these ideas to market. This opportunity development brief is clearly a confidential document and should be circulated internally together with the latest Brand Positioning Statement. A shorter and less confidential version could be used when wider internal or external groups are involved.

Establish Criteria for Evaluating Ideas

These need to be formally established and communicated in order to ensure consistent treatment over time, and overriding changes in internal management. People submitting ideas are entitled to know how these will be assessed, and to be confident they will be treated objectively and fairly. It is usually possible and sensible to agree on company-wide criteria, applicable to all businesses. Possible criteria for evaluating ideas include: strategic relevance to identified priority areas; results to exceed some stated minimum volume level (volume being incremental to existing business); fitting or exploiting existing company competencies; and, whether the idea can be protected, in other words will the idea sustain itself into the future.

List Ideas Already Developed

Your firm will already have built up a sound inventory of ideas and hypotheses conducting the Offensive Business Analysis, SWOT analysis, and by checking past marketing plans. Other ideas may also be culled from internal or external sources and should be reviewed.

Generate New Ideas

There are numerous ways to develop new product or service ideas, but it is difficult to forecast in advance which ones will produce the best results for a given company. The secret is to start by identifying them all and then dropping the ones that appear least fruitful. The most important single rule about new idea generation is to ensure that it is systematic and continuous, not ad hoc and spasmodic. Table 11-4 comprises a checklist of the main sources of ideas, with action steps on how to manage each one.

Customers, consumers, and employees are often the most productive sources of new ideas:

Customers are always a major source, since they either use the products or services themselves or are close to the user. You and your competitor have a theoretical equal opportunity to access them. They will usually respond only if they feel their ideas will be taken seriously by someone who is really listening and, where a relationship has been established that provides the basis for an exchange.

Table 11-4 Main New Idea Sources and How to Activate Them

Ideas source	How to activate
(a) Customers	Brief sales force on where ideas needed
	Train sales people in accessing, reporting new ideas from customers
	Establish reward and recognition system
(b) Consumers	Focus on heavy users, early adopters of new ideas
	Use group discussions, dissatisfaction studies
	Expose consumers to new concepts and ask them to rank, then develop
(c) Employees	Brief on needs
	Acknowledge all suggestions, reward best ones
	Use Extended Brand Groups or special cross-departmental project teams to develop ideas, using idea generation techniques
(d) External agencies and suppliers	Ad agencies, consultancies, suppliers are all good sources, but need to be briefed and motivated
(e) R&D or IT technical ideas	Ideas can be generated from technical hypotheses or breakthroughs as well as from consumer needs
	Encourage R&D and IT to come up with technical ideas even if they can see no obvious consumer application
(f) Competitors	Develop an effective competitor analysis system
	Use competition as a basis for improvement
(g) Overseas sources	Data sources
	Personal visits
(h) Patents	Search recently registered and expiring patents
(i) Previous new ideas on file	Old ideas may have been wrongly assessed
	Times and markets change

Consumers are valuable in reacting to specific ideas, and ranking them. They can also be useful when mixed in groups with creative people, engineers, and R&D, especially if they are heavy users or, in the case of industrial goods, at the leading edge of use.

Employees of successful companies have been encouraged to seek new ideas for improving the company's production, products, and services. Toyota claims that its employees submit two million ideas annually, about 35 suggestions per employee, and over 85 percent of them are implemented. Kodak and some American firms give monetary and recognition awards to their employees who submit the best ideas during the year.[6]

So, how does one use these idea-generating techniques? In addition to the regular flow of new ideas from a variety of sources, formal

---

[6] Philip Kotler, *Marketing Management*, Prentice-Hall, Millennium Edition, 2000, pg. 336.

idea-generation projects are also essential. These need to be well prepared and skillfully managed. The key steps are to identify specific areas for idea generation, select a cross-departmental team, brief the team, and then run an ideas session using a range of techniques.

There are many techniques for generating new ideas from groups of people. The best-known is the brainstorming or idea-generation group, the typical size of which is from three to ten people, usually from varied backgrounds. Possible members are a heavy user, a customer, a sales representative, a technology specialist from a different product field, a marketing person, an advertising agency creative person, an engineer, and a telesales or customer service person. The focus is on generating as many ideas as possible. No evaluation of quality occurs during the group session as this would inhibit the flow of creativity. The leader of the group is usually the key to its success, and he or she needs to be well prepared.

It will be evident that many imaginative idea techniques are available and others can be developed. The result is that you have a long list of promising ideas that now need to be pruned and screened into a strong short list for testing.

Step 2: Initial Idea Screening

Step 2 is the first stage of formal screening. It should be pointed out that screening is a continuous process and should formally occur at each of the seven steps in the process.

Initial idea screening will probably be done by a Brand Manager, or a group facilitated by the Brand Manager, and should involve most of the following elements:

Apply Criteria and Screen

Criteria will already have been established, as part of Step 1. If these have been quantified, the better ideas can be scored. Alternatively, simple judgment, taking the criteria as a guide, may be used.

Write Up the Best Ideas into Concepts

This is an art in itself, and very important. It is rarely given enough priority. Good ideas can fail in consumer testing through poor conversion into concepts. Concept statements should be brief (no more than 50 words), clear, describe the proposition, and express a consumer benefit. They should consist of short sentences, using everyday consumer language, not advertising jargon, and be simple to understand without further explanation.

This concept statement would be consumer tested against others, and ranked. The interviewer or questioner would aim not only to understand the consumer appeal of the total proposition, but also the relative contribution of each benefit. In this way, individual concepts can be strengthened by removing weak benefits, replacing them with stronger ones taken from other concepts.

Test Out Concepts with Users Qualitatively, in Small Groups

At this point, concepts are still being checked, refined and developed, probably with groups of target consumers in discussion with a trained moderator. The strongest concepts may be improved, rewritten, and retested a number of times. The interviewer should go through them phrase by phrase, checking reaction to each element, and the specific wording, as well as the totality. Special groups of interviewees, such as doctors, technicians, retailers, and distributors can be added as the concept demands, in addition to consumer groups.

Procter & Gamble exhibits "best practice" in concept development by using the Concept Laboratory. This is structured as follows:

It is often a two- to three-day exercise, typically involving an advertising agency person, R&D group head, and Brand Manager responsible for the program. There will be an interview room for consumer discussion groups led by a moderator, and a meeting room from which executives can view the discussions unseen.

The Brand Manager will have prepared a number of concepts for the moderator to use, and six to eight groups of consumers will have been booked to appear at specified times. The first consumer group will be exposed to a number of concepts over a one-hour period by the moderator. They will discuss each one, dissect it, and rank it compared to the others. The executives will view this activity through a one-way mirror, analyze the learning, and consider paradoxes (apparent contradictions) and paradigms (ideal requirements). They will then adjust and strengthen the concepts.

These adjusted concepts would then be exposed to the next group of consumers, the results reviewed, the concepts retested and so on. The process would continue until the winning concept(s) have been identified and refined.

Check Concept Winners Quantitatively

Quantification is important in order to validate the relative strength of each concept, to compare it against previous norms, and to make final improvements. Concepts doing well at the qualitative stage may not reach the required standard when quantified measures are applied and should be dropped.

It is worthwhile keeping a summary of quantitative concept test results for at least five years, both to avoid retesting losing concepts and to provide a bank of scores against which to rank new concepts.

Step 3: Develop Technical Briefs

This is the stage at which significant development costs will start to be incurred. At Steps 1 and 2, costs have been modest. A management decision now has to be made whether to allocate scarce R&D or IT resources to developing the concept to final product or service format. As the idea moves up the cost gradient, the screening levels become more demanding.

Working with R&D and Finance, the group led by the Brand Manager would complete a development brief for the winning concept, and submit it for approval to the senior VP of Marketing or an interdisciplinary team, who with other senior staff across the organization, would approve the concept. It will then become a development project within R&D, with its progress monitored at least monthly.

The development brief would summarize previous concept research; outline the benefits and characteristics to be built into the product or service; set a target cost, pricing, and launch date, and very succinctly provide a commercial justification. It should include a projected brand name, describe the market, its size and trend, and outline the consumer target and consumer benefit. The development brief should also outline the competitive advantage offered by the product or service—how it is better or different from the competition and, substantiate the appeal of the proposed benefit.

Step 4: Develop Products/Services

You now have a potentially winning concept and a development brief.

Technical development can be extensive. Offensive Marketers should use this time concurrently to structure an outline of the business plan. It will comprise outline strategies and economics. Strategies would cover the standard areas of product, presentation, customer service, advertising, pricing, and trade channel. Economics would include rough revenue, market share, costs, marketing spending and profits, culminating in a profit and loss plan for the first three years.

At this stage, when technical development is not yet proven, it is not usually worth investing in the cost of advertising or packaging origination. You would only risk such concurrent activity if speed is of the essence.

Once technical development is complete, the product would be consumer blind-tested against competitor products. Success would be defined as a preferred or differentiated product.

New services can be more difficult to consumer-test directly against competitors. However, for example, elements like new menu items in a restaurant, a new seat type for an airline, or a new financial services offering outlined for would-be users can easily be consumer blind-tested.

Of course, demonstrating that the proposed offering is technically feasible at the planned cost, and can deliver the competitive advantage targeted in the brief, is required before progressing further.

Step 5: Develop Support Elements—Validate

Step 5 involves validating all the individual elements in the marketing plan, and evaluating the totality of the proposition. At this level, advertising, packaging, and, in the case of services, consumer presentation will be developed. Elements may be consumer-tested individually, versus competition, and then in totality.

Meanwhile, the marketing plan will be further developed and refined.

Step 6: Develop Final Plan

Using consumer research results from Step 5 and the latest costs, detailed marketing plans can now be finalized in close consultation with Operations and Sales, who will be primarily responsible for implementation.

At this stage, a Board decision has to be made as to whether to conduct a limited market test next, or whether to move immediately to national, regional, or multi-country launch. These alternatives will have been addressed earlier in the process.

Step 7: Launch and One Step Ahead

This is the final level, and is likely to be costly. Even as the new product or service is being launched nationally or regionally, your team should be planning your company's next moves, so that your firm can keep one step ahead of the competition with product improvements or service upgrades in the months ahead. You may also, as part of your national launch, be testing a more offensive variant of your plan in one area, such as upweighted advertising, house-to-house product sampling, or extra direct marketing activity. Your firm may be testing an e-mail program targeting specific users, a Web movie to tie together the broader multimedia campaign, and, with respect to product variation, a wider product range or even an extra-strength product.

Although the launch is the final step in the development process, it is only the start of the life of the new product or service. The first year is the most critical period, when customers will form views. If these are unfavorable, they will be difficult and expensive to change. You can be almost certain that competition will react, and allowance and response for this needs to be built into your plan. You should have considered various competitor response scenarios before you launch, and determined how best to counter, so that your firm can act quickly if and when competitor scenarios occur. On a continuing basis, your company needs to rigorously evaluate each element of the offering's plan in the face of marketplace demands, ruthlessly searching for ways to strengthen the proposition. Elements of the NPSD process get repeated as the offering meets and seeks to exceed the changing and growing expectations of its users.

CONCLUSION

New product and service development is a foundation of Offensive Marketing. Together with low-cost operations, strategic intent, and rigorous analysis and planning, creating and sustaining superior and distinctive products and services are competitive competencies that must be honed and built upon as the marketplace demands change.

In this chapter, four important issues affecting new product and service success have been analyzed. They are: how to establish the total NPSD resource needed; how to organize NPSD; how to allocate R&D and IT resources and prioritize projects; and, lastly, how to evaluate corporate NPSD performance.

A seven-step NPSD process has been presented with a focus on opportunity identification and idea generation utilizing creative thinking from a variety of stakeholders. Screening levels were discussed that incorporate cross-disciplinary input and qualitative and quantitative criteria. Issues arising in the development of detailed technical briefs to support the prospective offering, the final plan and launching decisions were highlighted.

Moving through the NPSD process in a logical and timely manner will increase the likelihood that the new product or service proposition will truly create a meaningful consumer benefit, and will have the resources and company-wide commitment that are the necessary foundation for success.

12 Offensive Communications

INTRODUCTION

Communications is a much broader word than *advertising*, which is often used synonymously with broadcast media. It covers any visual, audio, or interactive medium that creates brand awareness or attitude changes. Sponsorships, event marketing, infomercials, "buzz" or word-of-mouth campaigns, direct marketing, banner and pop-up ads, and the use of sales personnel as influencers, all qualify as "communications." Indeed, one should extend the definition of communications to the packaging of products, inter-active Internet-based games tied to entertainment or movie intro-ductions, as well as to publicity arising from legal cases or breaking news stories—sometimes by design, often not. However, because of the importance of advertising to the marketing industry, it receives the primary focus in this chapter.

With the proliferation in types of media and the ability to target audiences down to a single individual, choice of media and the communication tool have become important decisions. The older scenario of major branders using the mass-market appeal and ease of TV, in conjunction with magazines and posters, is long gone. With the ability of most of American homes to receive hun-dreds of television channels (including specialty channels catering to individual special interests), targeted e-mail, and personalized communications to wireless users, important questions with respect to communications remain unchanged, although some of the possible answers have become more complex.

The first part of the chapter discusses key principles in com-munications and addresses questions that continue to be relevant in this changing communications environment. The second part of the chapter succinctly outlines a process for Offensive Communications Development, which builds on the key principles and translates them into action.

KEY PRINCIPLES OF COMMUNICATIONS

There are a number of key points that have remained relevant over the years, outlined as follows:

How Communications Works

Communication creates awareness of the existence and advantages of goods and services. It is a form of personal salesmanship designed to make consumers *see a brand or organization in a more favorable light.*

With a familiar brand, consumers will have formed a number of different impressions, both favorable and unfavorable, based on previous usage, recollections of past advertising, attitude to packag-ing and price, and opinions of friends and others. Communication will add to this set of impressions by attempting to reinforce favor-able attitudes and to loosen or eliminate unfavorable ones.

The communication devices used are: information, reason, and emotion; and the objective may be informative, persuasive, or to act as a reminder. Communication objectives and methods of appeal should be arrived at through an analysis of the current market situation of the brand, product, or service. Communication interacts with all the other elements that make up the image of a brand and contribute to its performance. These interactions make evaluating effectiveness of communications difficult but not impossible.

The chart on the mechanism of branding from Chapter 10 on Offensive Brand Development (see Figure 10-1) is repeated below as Figure 12-1. It illustrates that communication is only one of the many company inputs to customers. These inputs create awareness, usage, attitudes, and image, all of which are stored in the consumer's mental inventory. This process is continuous, with further inputs of communication, performance experience, and service creating new consumer reactions. These result in modifications to a continuously revised mental picture of the offering and value proposition.

Figure 12-1
The Mechanism of Branding— A Continuous Process

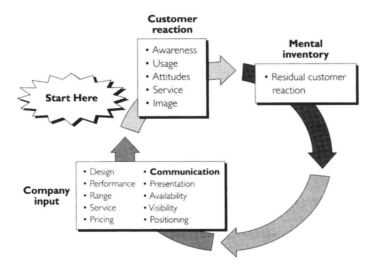

The ideal communications scenario is to spend heavily against the right target audience, with a powerful and well-executed strategy, backed by a preferred product or service that is widely available and visible.

To design effective communications, the Offensive Marketer should start by identifying the target market and buyer motives. A specific advertising objective should be clearly arrived at and stated. This advertising objective is reflective of a communications goal that is tied to an overall marketing strategy, and a quantifiable achievement level to be accomplished with a target audience over a specified time period.

Why Run Mediocre Advertising?

Very good and very bad advertising both cost the same to run. If you insist on top quality in products and services, why accept less from your advertising?

Advertising using a weak communications strategy or poor execution is unlikely to deliver value for the firm, or be effective with respect to the target audience. Most companies have insufficient funds to finance all their communication tasks and, therefore, have to prioritize spending. The question is why waste any of these scarce resources on less than outstanding communication? Whatever the competitive pressure, it is usually best to delay spending until your firm has a strong communications campaign linked to a broad overall marketing strategy.

Only strong messages get noticed by consumers, whose attention is becoming increasingly difficult to attract. In light of the fragmentation of media and the overwhelming amount of advertising information bombarding consumers, selecting the best media mix and messages is not an easy proposition even for the best professional communicators.

Consumer selection of media from which to cull information has been changing and will continue to change as new communication and information technologies become more widespread, accepted, and proven. It remains an open issue, for example, as to how effective wireless advertising or e-mail targeted promotions are for certain product sectors. It is even an open question as to how advertisers best use these new technologies to reach certain targeted consumers. Experience and good analysis of campaigns over time will lead the way in setting the course for effective communications in the future.

Advertising Communications: Limitations and Opportunities

Advertising, in its traditional forms, is not the all-powerful persuader as it was in the mass merchandizing economy. Today, fewer communications are aimed at mass markets, and are instead focusing on niche or specialty viewers or readers. These communications are capitalizing on the variegated changes in American society in the last decade, including two-income households, households with Asian or Latin ancestry, and more households where individuals identify themselves as gay or lesbian. Much of this niche communication seeks a direct connection with the consumer and is often aimed at building and maintaining a relationship instead of luring potential customers to switch brands.

The average consumer in the United States is bombarded with an increasing number of network TV commercials, infomercials, print ads, billboards, unsolicited e-mail or spam, coupons, and daily unsolicited phone calls. This data glut creates difficulty for even the most experienced Offensive Marketer in establishing a presence in the minds of consumers, as each consumer has only a finite mental storage space. Advertising communications have had to work increasingly hard to get noticed amid the noisy clutter.

Yet, despite this ad clutter, e-mail marketing revenues, for example, are expected to hit $1.5 billion by 2005. Although direct mail may have reached its peak and will account for less than 50 percent of mail received by U.S. households by 2005, down from 65 percent in 2001, e-mail may take its place as a communications leader because of its efficiency, compressed response times, and its significantly less cost as compared to traditional direct mail campaigns. E-mail costs range from $5 to $7 per thousand, while direct mail costs range from $500 to $700 per thousand.[1]

Internet users have been assailed over the past year and a half with intrusive pop-up ads. The introduction of the format coincided with the bottom falling out of the online ad industry in early 2000. To date, limitations in ad serving software make it difficult to curtail pop-ups across sites. However, recent decisions by, for example, Netscape to include pop-up blocking options in its Netscape Navigator, or ISP EarthLink's decision to bundle a pop-up blocker in its software, give the Internet user more protection against such intrusions. Yet, NYTimes.com raised its pop-up rates for 2003 in light of the fact that ad format sales were strong.[2]

---

[1] CyberAtlas and internet.com online communication, April 24, 2002. ClickZ E-Mail Strategies sponsored by Double Click.

[2] Brian Morrissey, *Are Pop-Ups Doomed?*, www.internetnews.com/IAR/article.php/1558231, December 17, 2002.

Marketers are focused on using the mobile Internet to extend their marketing affinity programs. Affinity programs are distinguished from unsolicited spam as the user signs up for it. It is also called "permission" marketing.[3] Many marketers today believe that the "m" in mobile stands for marketing. It remains to be seen whether delivering marketing messages where consumers will find them—on their wireless phones and PDAs—and in "real" time, that is, when they can use them, will be a new and effective medium for communications.

Linking mobile devices and Internet access is just part of the larger push into what has been termed "contextual" marketing where marketers link real-life situations to virtual information and offerings. The goal here is not to bring the customer to a site, but to bring the message directly to the customer at the point of need.[4] Some of the firms exploring the contextual possibilities include: Federal Express with its focus on using mobile technology to allow customers to track shipments or to create shipping labels; Mobil's Speedpass that permits customers to pay for gas as well as other purchases; and, Johnson and Johnson with the placement of product offerings in digital contexts where people would be most amenable to accepting these communications—for example, pre-existing online teen communities where teens can make friend-to-friend referrals.[5]

Similar contextual opportunities exist with the convergence of broadband connectivity with the Internet and with TV in the home environment, opening up new opportunities to integrate entertainment and commercial communications to a targeted audience.

Communications: Measures of Effectiveness Are Changing

Communications expenditures are unusual. Although they are an investment with long-term impact, they cannot be depreciated. It is often difficult to confirm, in a given scenario, how much or how little is best to spend. Communications quality cannot be evaluated

---

[3] See Seth Godin, *Permission Marketing, Turning Strangers into Friends, and Friends into Customers*, Simon & Schuster, 1999.

[4] David Kenny and John F. Marshall, "Contextual Marketing, The Real Business of the Internet," *Harvard Business Review*, November–December, 2000.

[5] "Contextual Marketing," Id.

apart from looking at a host of results across many mediums where the communications has been offered.

However, looking at communications expenditures from the competitive positioning perspective, it is an area of business where companies are best informed about competitor activity, because levels of competitor spending can be measured by brand and by geographical area. Share of spending can be compared with share of market by company and brand. Effectiveness of competitive communications can be checked through awareness and attitude surveys or advertising tracking studies. Communications-effect and sales-effect research are generally ongoing. No other area of business can be so precisely monitored. Yet, in no other area of business is value for money more difficult to measure.

For instance, with the recognition that online offerings, product information, and personalized communications in the form of e-mail can drive purchases in other channels, including offline stores,[6] as well as build brand advertising in conjunction with other efforts across media, evaluation of communications expenditures must include both direct and indirect response metrics. Early reliance, for example, on click-throughs as a metric of online campaign performance has been shown to underestimate campaign performance by nearly half.[7]

Because of the consumer growing ability to be in control of where they gain information prior to a purchase, businesses can improve the effectiveness of both their e-mail as well as print, banner, and broadcast campaigns by integrating across media, data, and channels.[8] For example, the tone and presentation of e-mail should reflect the look and feel of other communications.[9] In addition, auto-response acknowledgment of inquiries should be a customer service standard in assessing the effectiveness of online relationship building communications, although many businesses fail in this basic online tool.[10] Because of growing expectations on

---

[6] Christopher Saunders, *E-Mail Works for Direct Marketing*, at http://cyberatlas.internet.com/markets/advertising/print/0,5941_1488681,00.html.

[7] Christopher Saunders, *Studies Point to Branding Effects of Online Media*, at www.internet-news.com/IAR/print/O,12_799971,00.html, July 11, 2001.

[8] *E-Mail Marketing Delivering the Message*, at http://cyberatlas.internet.com/markets/advertising/print/0,1323,5941_356791,00.html, May 9, 2000.

[9] Id.

[10] Robyn Greenspan, *E-Mail Response Time Lags*, at http://cyberatlas.internet.com/big_picture/applications/print/0,1301_14877891,00.html October 24, 2002.

the part of consumers, permission communications across media are being held to higher and higher standards. Measuring communications effectiveness must begin with an understanding of these growing expectations.

In a study conducted by IMT Strategies and sponsored by the Direct Marketing Association and its subsidiary, The Association of Interactive Media, 22 percent of firms studied described their permission marketing e-mail management as "out-of-control," with the average large organization using four independent e-mail databases and only 12 percent using enterprise-wide customer databases.[11] This lack of integrated data across the organization creates the situation where managing the relevancy and therefore the effectiveness of e-mail to customers becomes problematic. Communications relevancy for not only e-mail campaigns—but across channels, media, and data—must be a basic denominator in measuring effectiveness of campaigns. Further thoughts on measuring effectiveness are discussed later on in this chapter.

Creating Integrated Marketing Communications

Marketers spend far too much time with advertising agencies, and too little with internal colleagues in Operations and Finance, or with customers to determine the most effective marketing communications campaign with respect to either message or media choice. In smaller organizations, Sales or Marketing people work with an advertising agency. In a larger firm, a separate Advertising Department may propose a budget, develop advertising strategy, approve campaigns and handle direct communications and advertising. In either event, companies generally use the expertise of an outside agency to assist in creating campaigns and choosing and purchasing media.

If a campaign's vision is created internally, the organization as a whole "owns it" and can align themselves around the message in their different roles and capacities, whether they have direct contact with customers or consumers, or provide the backbone and structure for such communications.

---

[11] Christopher Saunders, *E-Mail Use by Top Firms Highly Inefficient*, Reprinted from internet.com's Internet Advertising Report, September 21, 2001. See, http://cyberatlas.internet.com/markets/advertising/print/0,5941_882821,00.html.

Integrated Marketing Communications has itself become a buzz-word. Stepping back for a moment from the digitized, online world, this propounds the less than revolutionary view that all forms of communication should conform to a consistent strategy and plan, and be managed as a totality rather than as a series of loosely related activities. In response to this, some advertising agencies have attempted to build a one-stop total communications shop, although few have been totally successful, as most clients still prefer to deal with a number of different specialists. These specialists often include advertising, media, event marketing, sponsorship, PR, sales promotion, and direct marketing. Achieving an integrated communications result through such a diffused structure requires considerable client skills in project planning and management.

For a single major brand, the communicated result should be a clear and consistent message to the consumer, even though it may be fashioned by different external agencies working on advertising, media, event marketing, PR, sales promotion, and direct marketing, all in conjunction with the marketing function. From an Offensive Marketing perspective, the integrating force behind the clear and consistent message needs to be the Offensive Marketing team. It has to coalesce the various programs into a consistent message about the offering, as well as bring consistent assessment tools and quality standards to the communication creations. Whether it is the firm that creates the communications message or an outside agency, the ultimate responsibility for integrating and aligning the message lies with the Offensive Marketer.

In the likely event that a communications plan will ultimately involve many diverse media, which oftentimes are handled by several external agencies, within this mix, *how can your company meet the specific information needs of each consumer target group and also communicate a consistent message?*

The answer is for the Offensive Marketer to develop an overall communications plan, brief each agency on its role within this plan, and offer guidelines with respect to implementation, quality, assessment, and controls. It is essential to identify the consumer targets for each medium and the key benefits to be emphasized so that, to state the obvious, you are not communicating space and reliability to car owners on broadcast TV and dynamic performance in magazines to the same potential purchasers.

By taking advantage of direct marketing via e-mail or more traditional techniques to customized segments of high-profit customers, marketers can talk in a way that is most relevant to them but does not confuse the message to a wider audience.[12]

How Much to Spend on Communications?

"I know that half of my advertising budget is wasted, but I'm not sure which half" is a comment that was made many years ago and has now passed into advertising folklore.[13]

Setting communications budgets and assessing their effectiveness remains an art of approximation. The evaluation of communications still relies heavily on the personal judgment of experienced senior staff. A number of different factors influence advertising effectiveness, making it difficult to evaluate. Table 12-1 states ten factors influencing advertising effectiveness.

Table 12-1 Ten Factors Influencing Advertising Effectiveness

• Absolute media weight	• Relative product or service quality
• Weight vs. competition	• Choice of media
• Strength of strategy	• Efficiency of media buying
• Strength of execution	• Campaign wear-out
• Level of brand availability	• Relative pricing

Because advertising is only one of the numerous variables that affect sales, many of the tools for evaluating communications use intermediate measurements. The assumption is made that increases in things like brand awareness and favorable attitudes will feed through into increased sales. In addition, advertising has a carryover effect that lasts beyond the present fiscal period. Therefore, although advertising and communications costs are treated as a current expense, a good deal of it may go into building up brand equity, an intangible asset.

The most difficult types of communication to assess are in markets where a number of major brands are heavily advertised and major spending is needed to maintain market share; "slow-burn" activity, like sponsorship or certain public relations activities, whose effect is difficult to separate from other communications expenditures.

---

[12] Garth Hallberg, *All Consumers Are Not Created Equal*, John Wiley & Sons, 1995.
[13] Most frequently attributed to Lord Leverhulme.

Some companies may use either arbitrary or subjective methods for deciding how much to spend on communications. Often a product's life cycle stage will influence spending as will product substitute availability, competition, and market share. For instance, brands with high market share may require less advertising expenditures, as a percentage of sales, than new introductions or brand extensions. Several marketing scientists have created advertising-expenditure models that take a variety of factors into account including sales-response functions, untapped sales potential, and the sales-decay rate (the rate at which consumers forget the advertising message and brand).[14]

The main approaches to setting advertising expenditures have similarities with those used to fix new product and service budgets. They are set forth in Table 12-2 and discussed individually here:

Table 12-2   Six Main Approaches for Setting Communications Budgets

• Task	• Share of market
• Historical	• Match competition
• % of sales	• Residual

The Task Approach

This involves setting certain marketing objectives. These objectives are derived from the tasks the external communications function is designed to accomplish, and the budget should be allocated accordingly. The objectives may be set in terms of revenue and profit, in which case the translation to a communications budget will necessarily be rather vague. Or, the objectives may be more sophisticated and spelled out as in the number of advertising messages necessary to achieve desired levels of awareness or changes in attitude. Tasks should also cover launches of new and improved products and line extensions.

The task approach can be useful if it is based on detailed analysis of past results, but should not be used in isolation from other methods.

---

[14] Gary L. Lilien, Philip Kotler, and K. Sridhar Moorthy, *Marketing Models*, Prentice Hall, 1992. See Chapter 6.

Historical

This method relates next year's communications budget to spending in previous years.

% of Sales

This allocates a fixed percentage of a brand's sales to communications. When the brand's volume grows, spending will increase, and vice versa. Although this method needs to be used with discretion, its strength is that it feeds success and starves problem areas. Its weakness is that the percentage is often determined arbitrarily. In addition, there may be cases where it is wise to allocate a greater percentage to offerings with lower revenue for periods of time.

Share of Market

This involves estimating the amount of future advertising spending for the category and relating a brand's share of this to its target share of the market. For example: for a product with an estimated total category advertising spending of $25 million and a target brand share of 10 percent, simple mathematics indicates the planned advertising budget for this offering next year would be $2.5 million.

This method is not ideal, because the figures are estimated and there is no definitive evidence brought into the equation on the most profitable relationship between share of category advertising and share of market sales.

Match Competition

This is the second worst method. It is both speculative and defensive.

Residual

This is the worst method of all, but surprisingly used by some quite sophisticated companies. The system, if it can be called such, is to leave the communications budget until last in the budgeting process and allocate whatever is left after costs and profit requirements have been calculated.

In total, none of these approaches are ideal. A combination of task, percentage of sales, and share of market is generally the most useful. However, the truth is that deep and pragmatic analysis, using a variety of information sources and tests, is more valuable than any mechanical system. Considering how much is spent on communication, and how difficult it is to determine value for money spent, it is surprising how little is invested on researching effectiveness—usually less than 1 percent of the total advertising budget.

A Suggested Approach

The following, set forth in Table 12-3, is a suggested approach to setting brand communications budgets that combines both a systems approach and real world pragmatism.

Table 12-3   Setting Brand Communications Budgets

- Classify the brand
- Set the communications task
- Analyse past brand responsiveness
- Establish minimum effective spend by media type
- Ensure advertising quality is high
- Estimate theoretical budget needed, using task and share of spend methods
- Pragmatically adjust theoretical budget by applying other criteria above

First, classify the brand. Is it a "power brand," a "secondary" brand, or a brand that falls into the "other" category? (A brand's classification is determined by its score and position on the quantified portfolio analysis, QPA, in Chapter 7.) Many of the criteria for power brands or for measuring brand strength such as relative value, differentiation, demonstrated growth potential, and future prospects are also indications of likely response to advertising support.

Second, set the communications task. Customer loyalty, awareness, attitudes, and product launches are all likely to feature in this. Answer the question: Is the purpose of the communications to inform, persuade, or to remind? If its purpose is to persuade, is it best to use comparative advertising where claims of, for example, superiority can be proven or, if the advertising's purpose is to remind, does reinforcement of well-made decisions help to move those still deciding to a purchase?

Analyze past brand responsiveness. Below, in Table 12-4, are some ways in which responsiveness to past communications expenditure can be assessed.

Table 12-4 Brand Responsiveness Overall and by Media Type

Type of Analysis	Key Elements
1. Profitability of sales gains vs. cost	Evaluate gain in sales or brand share during and after advertising period, compare with base period.
2. Advertising tracking studies	Use consumer research to track changes in brand awareness, usage, and image during and after advertising and vs. competition.
3. Market testing	Test in limited geographical area higher levels of spending vs. no spending at all. Compare differences vs. rest of the market.
4. Anecdotal	Talk to sales people, distributors, retailers, and colleagues, and get their feedback.

Econometric analysis takes this process of evaluation further and is becoming more widely used. Its purpose is to isolate the effect of advertising from other possible influences on brand share and the purchasing decision and then, using multiple regression analysis, model the effect of such things as:

- The price differential between analyzed brand and leading competitors
- Share of category advertising
- Distribution levels and trends

The model, depending on how it is configured, will help identify the effect of each of these or other variables on brand share.

Besides looking at sales effect, it is important to look at the communication effect to determine whether a specific communication or campaign message is communicating what it was intended to. Consumers may be asked to recall the ad and its content and answer questions relating to the ad's appeal, its effectiveness, and the clarity of its message, as well as its ability to catch and maintain a viewer's attention.

In addition, post-testing is an important technique for evaluating the effectiveness of advertising campaigns. Post-testing occurs after the advertisement has been made, the campaign is up and running, and significantly large amounts of money have been spent. Some would argue that testing at this stage is too late. But for those who see advertising as a continuous and long-term investment, post-testing can check the strength of a strategy, pinpoint whether the communication is effective, and even provide genuine clues about the effect on sales.

Several techniques of post-testing exist. Recall and playback involves interviews where the recollection of elements are recorded and compared. However, this technique is limited as recall does not equate with persuasiveness. Awareness and attitude studies call for more extensive customer interviews and enable comparisons between brands, both before and after the start of the new advertising campaign. Here, studies may be repeated at regular intervals to establish trends in awareness, usage, and product attitudes. Econometric analysis is also very relevant at this post-campaign stage.

Establish minimum effective spend by media type. In certain media—like TV, Internet, wireless, radio, newspapers, or magazines—the minimum spend level necessary to break through the threshold of consumer communication can be roughly estimated. The theory is that advertising levels below this threshold will be too low to make any impression on consumers.

A great many brands advertise at levels below this threshold and waste vast amounts of money. Why? Because in marketing there is a natural trend to diffuse, rather than concentrate resources based on strategic insight and marketing planning.

Ensure advertising quality is high. Run only outstanding advertising proven by pre-testing and tie it to a strong marketing strategy. A proposed campaign can be tested in one or several cities and its impact evaluated before a national rollout.

Estimate the theoretical budget needed by using task and share of spending methods. This theoretical calculation should be modified by the other strategic and pragmatic criteria outlined above.

It should be noted that for a power brand, where the intention is to build position, the brand's share of future total market spending should exceed its present market share, with other brand spending adjusted accordingly.

Identifying and Selecting Key Targets

In selecting targets for a marketing communications campaign, the first task is to decide on the target market and on buyers' motives in addition to deciding the relative priority between acquiring new customers and retaining or developing existing ones. For a new brand, the former would be the prime priority, but for a well-established brand, existing customers would be the main target.

The second task is to identify the heavier users among your company's existing customers, and to determine the most effective way to reach them. In most fast-moving consumer goods categories, about one-third of households account for two-thirds of brand volume, and even in widely purchased mass market categories, like coffee, a very small number of households account for a high proportion of revenue.

Targeting often involves hard and difficult choices. The decisions involved are important, since they form the basis for creatively addressing the campaign's objectives, media planning, and results evaluation.

Determining What to Say: The Communications Strategy

The communications strategy will derive from a brand's marketing objectives and overall strategies. It is one of the means for achieving brand objectives.

The Brand Positioning Statement (BPS) (see Chapter 8) is therefore the starting point for developing the communications strategy. The strategy should be totally consistent with the brand positioning statement. Optimally, the product's "benefit" message should have been designed as part of product development. Sometimes the Offensive Marketer may want to modify this original benefit statement; for example, if consumers are seeking new or different benefits from the product.

A clear and distinctive communications strategy, even if only moderately executed, is more likely to increase sales than an exciting campaign with no strategy.

The communications strategy should cover four main headings.

1. **Target audience.** The communications factual text, emotional draw, and overall message should be strategically directed to the chosen audience. Does the audience need to be educated with respect to the offering? Do they need to be re-introduced to the product, or does the communicated message need to speak to a changing image of a maturing audience?
2. **Key consumer benefits.** The communicated benefits should be in performance areas that are of importance to the target audience. A major cause of weak communications is the inclusion of too many benefits in a single communication. One is best, two is a challenge. Complex or unclear benefits are not absorbed by the consumer.
3. **Support for benefits.** This section will cover facts that support and justify the key benefits. Of course, "believability" is an important ingredient in any persuasive communication. It can also list claims about performance or use, which have been cleared by the R&D and Legal Departments.
4. **Tone of communication.** This will reflect the desired brand personality established in the brand positioning statement.

Increasingly, much TV advertising, or large campaigns supported by large dollars that use a mix of mass communications channels, appears to lack any clear strategy. It has been said that, "too much of it is pretentious nonsense, highbrow and incomprehensible. Copywriters and art directors … regard advertising as entertainment or an art form we sell…." This is not a comment by an advertising client: it is a statement by David Ogilvy, one of the most brilliant copy writers of all time.[15]

The art of persuasion may be captured best in a large, glitzy campaign designed to tap people's emotions or gain attention or through the more recent "buzz" or "word of mouth" campaigns that target a handful of carefully chosen trend leaders in identified communities, and subtly push them to start talking about your brand to their friends and associates.[16] These campaigns have been successful for the Harry Potter book series, Razor kick scooters, and the Ford Focus. In any event, whatever the chosen course of communications,

---

[15] Speech by David Ogilvy to ANA as reported in *Advertising Age*, November 25, 1991.
[16] Special Report: "Buzz Marketing," *Business Week*, July 30, 2001.

the point is that the campaign should not stray far from its intended strategy and proposed results of its objective.

Run Successful Campaigns for Decades

Once your company has developed a clear strategy and strong execution, stick with it. By all means, refine and update a winning campaign, just as you would a successful product. Do not change without cast-iron evidence, based on convincing research that change is required.

Finally, while you should never make change for change's sake, never be satisfied with your advertising. Successful communications through multiple media is an art rather than a science. As pointed out in this chapter, a successfully integrated approach is based on rigorous analysis and systematic marketing planning and design that will have varying inputs and outcomes over time.

EIGHT-STEP PROCESS FOR OFFENSIVE COMMUNICATIONS DEVELOPMENT

This section briefly translates the key principles of Offensive Communications into a succinct, eight-step process using a number of the tools already described. Table 12-5 sets out this process.

Step 1: Determine Objectives, Task, Budget

In Step 1, you are checking and confirming marketing objectives, strategies, and plans. The Offensive Marketing team is establishing communications objectives and tasks and using tools outlined in this chapter to set a total communications budget by campaign element as well as obtaining internal agreement on budgeted items. You are working out a preliminary split by type of media and getting buy-in on operating procedures and performance measurements, both with respect to outside agency and internal input. Agreeing at this time how different agencies will communicate among themselves and with you, with a goal of integrated communications, is a key objective. Instrumental at this stage is the

Table 12-5   Eight-Step Process for Offensive Communications Development

STEP 1 **Determine objectives, task, budget**	• Relate to marketing objectives, plans • Define task • Agree budget
STEP 2 **Develop communications strategy**	• Relate to Brand Positioning Statement • Use strategy format
STEP 3 **Develop media strategy**	• Determine criteria for selection • Select media • Write strategy
STEP 4 **Communications development**	• Agency task • Client interaction
STEP 5 **Subjective client evaluation**	• Client response • Approval for researching
STEP 6 **Objective consumer evaluation**	• Pre-test • Evaluate • Improve
STEP 7 **Produce and run communication**	• Produce • Implement plan
STEP 8 **Evaluate, improve**	• Post-testing • Analysis • Improvement

development of an initial list of product or service claims agreed by your Legal Department and R&D.

Step 2: Develop Communications Strategy

Step 2 calls for the confirming of the Brand Positioning Statement (BPS) and the development of an overall communications strategy consistent with the BPS. Marketing leads this process. You need to translate overall strategy to any sub-brands or special target groups, but ensure the consistency of the message. It is a good idea to consumer concept-test alternative strategies and to use the results to strengthen the overall strategy. All communication strategies need to be agreed upon internally.

Step 3: Develop Media Strategy

This step should be handled concurrently with Step 2. You should determine impact, coverage, and frequency objectives versus target consumers and groups, and review the full range of potential media choices with external agencies. For each medium, evaluate the fit with the target audience, image, impact, cost-effectiveness, fit, or overlap with other media, and the potential role in a total media strategy. Ensure consistency of message again. Here, you write the media strategy, specifying the planned media mix, rationale, and cost impact. Obtain media strategy agreement internally with the overall communications strategy.

Step 4: Communications Development

Conduct a final communications and media strategy briefing with all external agencies and include input from all internal departments, including IT, Finance, Operations, R&D, and Legal. Agree with each agency how creative work will be evaluated, including customer research and market testing.

Step 5: Client Evaluation of External and Internal Work Product

Ongoing evaluation of external and internal work product is the main element of this stage. Approval for consumer pre-testing takes place here as well and includes any new communication claims that need Legal Department and R&D approval.

Sample questions to be asked at this stage include:

- Whether the work product appeals rationally or emotionally to the target consumer's mind and in doing so is it on strategy?

- How well will the communication wear—that is, does it represent a campaign idea that can be run for an extended period of time?
- Does the communication strike the right tone; is it patronizing, or esoteric?
- Is the content interesting to the target audience—that is, will they remember not only the message, but also the brand?

Step 6: Objective Consumer Evaluation

Pre-testing of storyboards or other low-cost visuals with consumers is conducted at this stage. Evaluate the interest level, communication of key benefits, persuasiveness, believability, and brand-name recall. It is at this stage that if testing goes well, you can decide to proceed. Otherwise, it is here that you may decide to go back to the drawing board. If tests are positive, final approval is given, internal and external commitments and buy-in are obtained, as is any necessary regulatory authorization.

Step 7: Produce Creative Work and Run It

With all the effort and energy that has gone into developing effective communications strategy, it is just as important to execute creative work with utmost professionalism and quality. In order for the end result to translate its intended message, quality production and timely implementation are integral to effective execution.

Step 8: Evaluate Results and Improve

Business impact evaluation is conducted at this last stage. Sales and market share changes versus costs are assessed. Econometric analysis is done as is post-advertising consumer research. Future communications spending plans are adjusted. Further improvements are made to the communications campaign program to keep abreast of any changes that may be needed in the communications strategy to meet competitors' response or address changing consumers' needs or expectations.

CONCLUSION

Offensive Communications is an integral part of the daily execution of Offensive Marketing strategy. It requires strong and disciplined execution following a process that addresses the key principles outlined in this chapter. Certainly, creativity and imagination are instrumental to effective communications, including advertising; however, as we have seen, informed judgment and analysis, both of a qualitative and quantitative character, must be applied.

With the proliferation and fragmentation of media, the growing ability to target consumers down to an audience of one, and the effect of communications on one channel—such as e-mail and online advertising impacting consumer decision-making in other channels—integration of communications across media has grown in importance. Offensive Marketers must design and implement communications strategy to address consumers' growing expectations of relevancy and personalization. Ultimately, Offensive Marketing planning and execution should never be "offensive" in the pejorative sense. Instead, the goal of Offensive Communications is to use new technologies to reach consumers with an offer that contains value for *that* consumer, adds positive information or awareness of the product or brand, and moves the consumer toward a purchase decision.

13

Offensive Market Research

INTRODUCTION

All is not well in the realm of market research. Every marketer is familiar with the old saying: "I know half of my advertising budget is wasted, but I'm not sure which half." This can be transmuted to the market research function as, "I know half my market research budget is wasted, yet I also know I'm under-spending." Too little is spent, often on the wrong type of research, and then insufficient action is taken.

A new piece of consumer research should be an exciting voyage of discovery, opening new perspectives for innovation and improvement. Marketers should anticipate the outcome with a sense of excitement. What new perspectives will emerge, what fresh opportunities for action? Will expectations be confirmed, exceeded, or completely confounded?

Too often, research pursues a disappointing and predictable journey, through old and familiar scenery, too tactical in its design, defensive and confirmatory in its purpose, with too little driving it toward new frontiers of customer understanding.

Ask senior marketing staff of well-run companies questions like these:

- Does your company have a really deep understanding of the consumer or customer needs?
- Do you have a distinctive way of segmenting your market, which differs from your competitors?
- Have you got a clear idea how consumer needs in your markets will change in the next 18 months, three or five years?

The honest answer will often be, "no." Why?

This chapter begins with some of the reasons why, and then explores the main principles of Offensive Market Research.

MARKET RESEARCH IS INOFFENSIVE BY DESIGN

Market Research is often too tactical with little strategic research.

Tactical research, which answers short-term questions, fails to build the big picture. Strategic research, like Market Segmentation or Usage and Attitude studies, is a long-term investment in consumer understanding. Often because of time and cost constraints, a company may spend quite heavily on tactical research yet know little about its customers' needs looking into the future.

Poor Planning

Research is often commissioned in a hurry, with insufficient strategic thought by marketers. Why are we conducting this research? What is it that we are seeking to understand? How will this understanding, once obtained, be used and monitored? In light of these questions, objectives may be not clearly stated, action standards not established in advance, and expected use of results not spelled out beforehand.

Weak Knowledge of Research Techniques by Marketers

With the disappearance of many in-house market researchers, and the removal of marketing middle management in the past several years through corporate downsizing, many of today's marketers are less well trained in the basics of market research. In order to brief research agencies and to evaluate their proposals, or to conduct research in-house (research that is often informal in nature and conducted through direct perception or dialogue), it is necessary to understand, among other things, the strengths and weaknesses of different research techniques, the fundamentals of sample sizes, the importance of developing a research plan, and the realities of interviewing and questionnaires.

Undifferentiated Research

The purpose of investing in market research is to gain competitive advantage. Yet many companies buy the same continuous research—advertising tracking studies, consumer panels, retail audits, service monitors—as their competitors do. It is true that a smart company can often exploit this identical data better by integrating it with in-house databases and data-mining techniques to differentiate standard research results.

Smart organizations organize for intelligence gathering and analysis. These firms systematize the collection and dissemination of strategic information and synthesize the information for those needing it to best perform their jobs. In these "knowledge-driven" organizations, information has moved from a support tool, to information as a wealth generating strategic asset. Many industries are fast becoming information intensive. AT&T, IBM, Merrill Lynch, Citicorp, and others, compete in a "super-industry" that is a combination of telecommunications, financial services, computing, and retail, where value added is not necessarily product oriented, but is information based and surrounds the entire customer transaction.[1]

With Michael Porter's influential work on competitive strategy and the increasing global competitiveness of the marketplace and

---

[1] See, Warren J. Keegan, *Global Marketing Management*, 6th Ed., Prentice-Hall Series in Marketing, Prentice-Hall, 1999. Chapter 6.

loss of dominance of many American firms, the focus of much market research has tended to be on competitive intelligence instead of on broader environmental scanning.[2] Both are important. Differentiated research as a strategic asset must address the competitive landscape as well as focus on the customer and his or her changing needs and expectations. As an objective of the research process, Offensive Marketers must bring this information into corporate strategic and marketing planning.

Lack of Integration of New with Existing Research

Many marketing personnel have had the experience of asking for past market research results. Often they encounter a mountain of undigested reports commissioned by a range of people, conducted by a variety of research companies, many using different techniques. They discover that no one has attempted to stitch this patchwork of data into an integrated design. Each new piece of research was conducted and assessed in isolation, sometimes duplicating data already available, with much of this data never being shared with those who could use it for the benefit of the overall offering. Often the credibility of the results and its relevance for users across the organization remains unaddressed.

This scenario frequently occurs, fueled by the rapid turnover of Marketing people and their preference for starting with a clean sheet—a convenient way of saying they haven't got time or the interest in examining the past. However, organized intelligence is rapidly becoming a key issue for most firms. The purpose of a Marketing Information System (MIS) is to provide managers and decision-makers with the most relevant, up-to-date, reliable, and continuous flow of information about markets, competitors, regulations, customers, strategic partners, and operations. Electronic data interchange (EDI) is most often used by companies having regional, national, and global operations to implement critical, daily intracompany information sharing.

Even smaller firms need to become adept at gathering and integrating marketing intelligence. Much of this information is free or can be obtained for a minimal cost. For companies with field sales or merchandizing forces, sales analysis can be productive: reviewing trends

---

[2] Id.

in daily call rates, sales per call, distribution gains and losses, and display levels. A great deal of useful anecdotal data can also be collected.

There has been an explosion in the amount of low-priced "off the shelf" reports about companies and markets. These range from government statistics and syndicated reports to trade journals. The variety is such that one can often initially screen the potential of a possible new market without spending more than $1,000. Much of this data is now available online.

Opportunities for direct customer contact are also escalating and provide rich sources of information, through consumer hot lines, discount cards, chat rooms, information services, and consumer complaints.

Marketers attend stockholder meetings, talk to employees across the organization, distributors, dealers, or leading customers. They may set up advisory customer panels, made up of their most outspoken, large or sophisticated customers and discuss product use, service issues, or strategic requirements heading into the future. Becoming adept at cultivating sources of information and relationships are key competitive advantages for responsive, information-driven corporate cultures.

THE FUNDAMENTALS OF MARKET RESEARCH

Market research is about facts and impressions extracted from customers. It leads to better business decisions. It helps a company to keep in touch with what consumers think of its products or services and those of its competitors, and it monitors their actions in the marketplace. Of course, research is not a way of guaranteeing success, but its effective use makes success more likely.

The key questions that market research, with respect to customer intelligence, can answer are:

- How do consumers evaluate our products or services against those of competitors?
- What are they looking for in this market and are we providing this effectively?
- How are consumer tastes and expectations changing?
- What are consumers buying, from whom and why?
- How do consumers react to new ideas we have thought up and incorporated in our value proposition and current offerings?

- What is our level of customer loyalty, retention, and why?

Market research is a complex industry. At the risk of over-simplification, it takes three forms:

1. **What consumers buy.** The word *consumer* is used broadly, since it covers retail buyers, shoppers, and industrial purchasing agents. We are all consumers.
2. **What consumers know and think, and why.** The raw material for this is consumer awareness, needs, attitudes, images, and reactions, all usually based in emotion, some based in rational thought.
3. **How consumers react in a simulated situation.** What is consumer reaction to possible future marketing initiatives like new advertising mediums such as wireless or the use of permission direct marketing such as e-mail and instant messaging, or online pop-up or banner ads?

Table 13-1 elaborates on these three categories of research. This table is organized in the rough order of the reliability of the research. What people are buying is a fact and therefore quite easily ascertained. What they think about existing products or markets is also a fact, but opinions are volatile. There is both art and discipline in choosing whom to interview and in creative interviewing techniques.

THE EIGHT PRINCIPLES OF OFFENSIVE MARKET RESEARCH

These principles, eight in all, will assist the Offensive Marketer in conducting the most appropriate and effective research:

1. **Offensive market research is a major source of competitive advantage.** As alluded to in the discussion above, if one had to nominate the single most important opportunity for competitive advantage, for most companies it would be superior understanding of consumers, customers, markets, and employees.

   This understanding enables companies to develop distinctive and relevant products and services, to target the most attractive markets, to focus costs on areas of greatest consumer

Table 13-1 Main Types of Market Research

Type	Purpose	Most typical method(s)
What people buy or do		
Retail audits (e.g. Nielsen)	Measure market position	Checkout scanning data
Consumer panels	Measure market position, consumer activity, and responsiveness	Panel discussions and responsive testing
Activity studies	Measure shopping trips, leisure pursuits, and service levels	Face-to-face or telephone interviews; questionnaires
What people think and why		
Usage and attitude studies	Profile of products/services	Telephone or face-to-face
Market segmentation studies	Identify market sub-segments	Telephone or face-to-face
Continuing advertising/usage studies	Trend data on awareness and attitudes	Telephone or mail
Opinion-leaders studies	Get views of opinion leaders	Personal interviews
Product tests	Compare products	Mall or in-home testing
Advertising studies	Measure advertising impact	Telephone
Buyer/distributor studies	Get buyer attitudes	Telephone or face-to-face
Employee attitude studies	Measure employee attitudes	Personal interviews
Exploratory research	Probe consumer motivations	Focus groups
Simulated situations		
Simulated test markets	Test new products or services, estimate volume	Simulated retail store
Advertising tests	Persuasiveness of advertising	Various
Concept tests	Test advertising, product, packaging, or promotion ideas	Focus groups with concepts, pictures, or words
Loyalty research	Forecast consumer behavior	Personal interviews

value, and to motivate employees because they are tied into a mission that is customer-driven and meaningful. Of course, there is a world of difference between understanding an opportunity and actively exploiting it.[3] But understanding is the crucial first step toward Offensive Marketing—"involving every employee in building superior customer value very efficiently for above average profits."

Effective use of market research is one of the primary means to achieve this understanding. Having regular first-hand contact with customers, consumers, employees, and strategic

---

[3] An excellent book exploring the issues surrounding execution (not only with respect to marketing planning) is Larry Bossidy and Ram Charan, *Execution: The Discipline of Getting Things Done*, Crown Business, 2002.

partners is certainly a method of informal qualitative market research, although the results from these dialogues are often not incorporated in a systematic, marketing intelligence effort.

Few companies use market research effectively. Where there is an internal Market Research Department, its focus is often too narrow. It frequently defines its internal customers as members of the Marketing Department, not as every employee. It rarely builds up the totality of research results into a big, moving picture summary that the average employee can access and understand. It may underemphasize customer, as opposed to consumer, research, and it is often overly defensive and confirmatory, rather than creative and provocative.

Where there is no internal Market Research Department, responsibility for research is usually devolved to individual business units or brand groups. The result can be diffusion of activity, lack of consistency in approach, and over-reliance on outside agencies and information sources.

Offensive Market Research has a unique capability to build lasting competitive advantage, yet few professional market researchers inside and outside companies do enough to *market* this fact. Marketers are often insufficiently forceful in accessing top management, and in driving their corporate customers to plan, manage, and act on research in the most effective way. Many of their industry publications and deliberations focus on details rather than important fundamentals of market research.

2. **Develop a real market research strategy.** Most companies have market research budgets. Few have market research strategies linked to corporate or brand strategic plans. A market research strategy will spell out how to achieve the objective of gaining superior consumer understanding as a route to major competitive advantage.

   Here are some of the strategically important questions a market research strategy should aim to answer:
   - **What is the role of market research in the company?** Why do we spend money on it? What benefits do we expect to gain? How can it be used to build long-term advantage?
   - **Who are the main objects of our research?** Customers, consumers, competitors, employees, other stakeholders? Broadly, how will research efforts be allocated?

- **What is the broad priority to be given to various categories of research?** Continuous research or something less? Strategic versus tactical? Should there be a policy on minimum frequency of product comparison tests, major market studies, or consumer-focused inquiries?
- **How will the company's research inventory be disseminated internally and to strategic partners?** How can relevant information on key topics be summarized in easy-to-use format, and delivered on a tailored basis to all internal customers? For example, everyone in the company should be interested in total market trends, company and brand shares, and performance of new products. However, more specific information with respect to individual products, geographical regions, or warranty or after-purchase service levels, for example, should be synthesized and disseminated only to those whose responsibilities are tied to the performance or execution of that offering.
- **How will effectiveness of research spending be monitored?** First, is the right kind of research being done? Is actual spending by type in line with market planning or corporate strategy? Second, is anyone really analyzing it and synthesizing it into their thinking and planning? Do these analyses spell out possible action steps for review? Third, and most importantly, what action has actually been taken as a result of research? And, have the results of this action been looped back into further research as feedback?
- **What is our strategy for achieving differentiation in research?** What is "best practice" in management of market research, and how can we surpass it? What are the opportunities for integrating internal sales and profit data, continuous measurement numbers, and sales figures from key customers? Are we at the forefront of practice or not? What new innovative approaches can be taken for research? How do we make these proprietary to us?
- **What is our external supplier and delivery channels strategy?** Have we built long-term partnerships with a number of key suppliers or distributors? If so, what advantages in cost, continuity, and innovation do they provide? How do we keep our proprietary approaches confidential? What is our rationale for this strategy?

- **How disciplined and creative are we in the market research process?** Are we creative and disciplined in identifying the research problem and developing a research plan? Are we collecting data that is most relevant to highlighting the defined problem? Have we analyzed the research data with the most relevant and most advanced analysis tools? And lastly, have we presented the findings in a way most suitable for managers and the decision making process?
- **What is the strategy for ensuring consistency of research technique?** Consistency of research technique is relevant over time and across countries and regions. Consistency of research technique and quality is important for comparison—to be comparing apples with apples—as well as improving research results over time through global learning and research skills transfer.

3. **Use research as a torch not a crutch.** Research lights the way forward. It only illuminates the areas you point it at and never provides a complete picture. It produces data and insights, not decisions.

   Research is a device for improving the quality of the information on which decisions are based. Market research is sometimes wrongly regarded by executives as a kind of "answer machine" into which they can drop any questions or problems that bother them, in the hope that it will make judgment unnecessary. Applied in this way, research is doomed to misuse and will be stretched beyond its capabilities.

   The sight of timid decision-makers using research as a crutch leads some executives to make statements like, "people with a feel for their markets don't need research" or, "most entrepreneurs have no time for research." They are right to the extent that all business people should be close to their customers. However, they are wrong in implying that "gut feel" is a substitute for good-quality research. Both are necessary and complementary. Even marketers with a strong instinct for their customers are sometimes surprised by the results of new research. Understanding the consumer is an art that is never totally mastered. It requires constant relearning.

4. **See the people behind the numbers.** A well-crafted research report can be fully appreciated and understood only by Offensive Marketers with up-to-date and first-hand knowledge of their company's customers. It is important to get out

"where the rubber meets the road," to talk frequently to consumers, employees with customer contact, strategic partners, and the trade, if only to gain a background understanding of the market. Bringing a sense of the up-to-the-minute market is important in interpreting formal research. To this end, professionally conducted research and informal customer contacts should be run in tandem, since each has limited value in isolation.

Senior management also needs to retain access to the raw data that backs up the research report. In large organizations, research results often reach senior staff in predigested reports, which have been filtered through layers of management. These reports will gain a much richer texture if Offensive Marketers can have access to raw information—unedited videotapes of group discussions, direct access to research fieldworkers, or computer tabulations and inputs with respect to income elasticity measures, for example, or inputs used for comparative analysis of market potential and performance.

5. **Look for the action.** Every market raises questions that would be interesting to research. But unless the research is likely to lead to action, it is not worth doing. Some research, such as continuous retail or consumer panels, is useful as background. Many smaller companies do well without detailed information on market size or brand share.

However, for companies able to afford it, detailed information on market size or brand share is important as it indicates how your firm is performing in the market place, how well the competition is doing, and what your position is by account, service or product, and geographical area. It also holds clues as to why brand shares are changing. Is your share rising because of distribution gains, extra advertising weight, pricing changes, sales promotion, or all of these, and what are the relationships between and among the initiatives that are being taken or are being investigated?

All this is quite basic. However, so-called continuous panel data can become part of the "wallpaper" of a company culture and therefore be taken for granted. The danger here is that comfort with numbers or results can lead to inaction and therefore opportunities for competitors to move in to your company's market space. Non-continuous research, or "ad-hoc" research, is carried out to answer specifically identified questions and should also lead to concrete action. In addition, non-continuous research should shed light and perhaps a new interpretative twist on continuously probed data.

6. **Good research requires imagination.** The objective of most market research is to uncover consumer attitudes and feelings both toward a company's offering and as to possible future value propositions. Although the quantitative means of measuring these are well established, the thinking behind the technique and the questioning must be imaginative. Consumers rarely analyze their real reasons for buying even major commitments like insurance policies and houses, never mind instant coffee and yogurt. For example, if you ask consumers a direct question about why they buy a particular brand, you are likely to get the kind of nonactionable feedback shown in Table 13-2.

Table 13-2   Nonactionable Consumer Playback

Reason for using last brand:

Always used	20
Relative used/recommended	15
Saw advertising	10
Recommended by friend/neighbor	14
Bought on special price offer	12
No particular reason	21
No answer or don't know	8
Total	100

Finding out what consumers really think involves more than throwing a broadly directed question at them. In order to bring out real, as opposed to surface, motivations, the interviewer has to stimulate stronger interest and a motivation to think and make connections. This requires a more creative approach.

The need for imagination in research is often overlooked by Marketing people, who reserve almost all their creativity for advertising, promotions, and packaging. Research should not only be imaginative but also empathetic, since the researcher may, in the early stages of a product's life cycle, be working with a product that only half solves the problem faced by consumers. In addition, most users of a product or service have difficulty envisaging how they would use the same product or service, or one slightly modified or even modified a great deal, if it were to be different in ways they themselves envision. Giving words to future use scenarios on the consumers' part, with respect to changes in products or services, is one of the many challenges market research creativity addresses.

7. **Integrate all data and keep on asking "Why?"** Data zooms in at marketers daily from every direction, from many different media, and more is always available. Companies have been using increasingly powerful databases to collect, store, and ultimately integrate vast amounts of information about their customers and their purchasing practices. The technology has come to a point of maturity where information can be manipulated for real-time use as well as for long-term planning. Through the use of business intelligence software, managers and decision-makers attempt to make the wisest decisions possible by extracting information from computer systems by running data through sophisticated, mathematical software. These software tools are helping companies to make better sense of the massive amounts of information they have collected over the years.

   With more sophisticated data mining and retrieval tools that make it possible for formerly incompatible computer systems to speak to one another, companies are able to conduct market research and obtain actionable results at a level not possible in the past.[4] For example, by working with integrated data, Harrah's in Las Vegas, was able to extract names of gamblers who lived within driving distance of its hotels and casino, and filled its empty rooms after the attacks of September 11th. In another example, Coty, Inc., based in New York, had more than a dozen computer systems and a difficult time retrieving meaningful information from the sales data they had been collecting. Coty's core business was makeup and it had been spending little on toiletries such as shaving cream and shampoo. With the use of business intelligence software, the company realized that it had been missing significant profits in the toiletries sector. With this information, the company boosted its R&D and aims to have a broader range of products in this category in the near future.[5]

---

[4] "Information Is Power," *Business Week*, June 24, 2002.
[5] Id.

Marketing databases usually fall into four categories, and each needs to be integrated with the others into a logical whole. Table 13-3 shows the four main types of marketing data that need to be integrated.

Table 13-3 Four Main Types of Marketing Data Requiring Integration

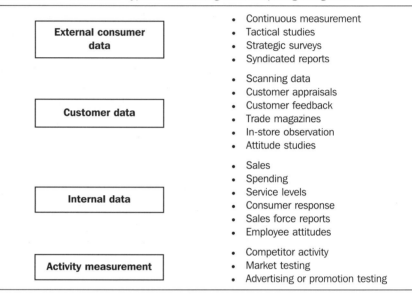

External consumer data	• Continuous measurement • Tactical studies • Strategic surveys • Syndicated reports
Customer data	• Scanning data • Customer appraisals • Customer feedback • Trade magazines • In-store observation • Attitude studies
Internal data	• Sales • Spending • Service levels • Consumer response • Sales force reports • Employee attitudes
Activity measurement	• Competitor activity • Market testing • Advertising or promotion testing

Each of the four boxes in Table 13-3 is interrelated, and taken together helps build a total picture for superior understanding of customers, consumers, and competitors.

Supposing you have just taken over a brand whose market share has declined over the past six months. What steps do you take to understand why? First you check the facts. Do other relevant sources of data point to the same trend?

Checking the facts involves cross-sourcing three of the four main boxes in Table 13-3, that is, external consumer data, customer data, and internal data. If the original facts appear true, then develop hypotheses as to why brand share has declined, and finally access all four boxes to check out the validity of your hypotheses.

8. **Select excellent external research companies and build partnerships.** Unlike advertising, where the best and the worst usually cost the same, outstanding research and external researchers

sometimes cost more, and may be worth it. Once you have found excellent research companies, it pays to build long-term partnerships in the same way as with advertising agencies. They get to know your business well, provide consistency of approach, and should come to you first with new ideas. To ensure competitive cost and continued freshness of thinking, it is advisable to occasionally put projects out for bid, while retaining the overall objective of building long-term working relationships.

What should you look for in identifying excellent research agencies? Let's take a situation where you have provided a written brief for a research study to three outside companies. Table 13-4 lists some criteria for selecting the best firm.

Table 13-4   Main Criteria for Selecting a Research Agency

1. Has the agency fully understood your brief?
2. Does the proposal meet the requirements of your brief?
3. Has the agency questioned aspects of your brief and improved it?
4. What is the quality of the agency people working on your business?
5. What is the likely quality of the fieldwork? How will it be checked?
6. Does the agency have imaginative approaches and techniques?
7. How practical and businesslike is the agency?
8. Has the agency considered a number of research structures, and selected the most cost effective one?
9. What is cost per interview? How competitive? If more expensive, why?
10. What other clients has the agency worked for in this research field? Check references for client satisfaction levels

EIGHT-STEP PROCESS FOR IMPLEMENTING OFFENSIVE MARKETING RESEARCH

The remainder of this chapter will describe the process to implement the principles of Offensive Market Research. From the viewpoint of an Offensive Marketer, it is an eight-step process as outlined in Table 13-5.

Step 1: Analyze Past Research Spending Deployment

Past research spending should be broken down by type, separating continuous from ad hoc, and strategic from tactical.

Table 13-5   Eight-Step Process for Offensive Market Research

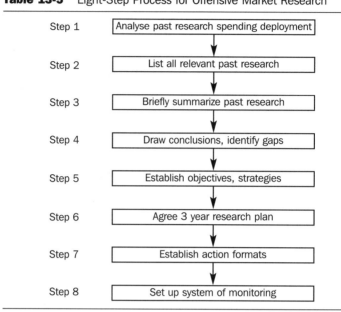

Step 1	Analyse past research spending deployment
Step 2	List all relevant past research
Step 3	Briefly summarize past research
Step 4	Draw conclusions, identify gaps
Step 5	Establish objectives, strategies
Step 6	Agree 3 year research plan
Step 7	Establish action formats
Step 8	Set up system of monitoring

"Strategic" research has lasting value and pushes forward your frontiers of understanding. Market segmentation or attitude and usage studies are examples. "Tactical" research is designed to answer a particular question and its contribution to knowledge is usually *short* term. A test of alternative varieties for a given product offering or a comparison of two different web page presentations for a financial services product are examples. The main criterion for differentiating between strategic and tactical research is whether the information will have future value in 12 to 18 months. Table 13-6 gives an example of a past research analysis for a consumer products company.

What do you conclude from this table? Market research spending has been cut back heavily from 1.5 percent of total revenue to 1.0 percent. The vast majority of this cut has come from strategic ad hoc research, which this year only accounted for 8 percent of total spending compared with 40 percent the year before. This may be acceptable, since you don't necessarily need to run major attitude and usage studies every year, but the size of the change does raise questions. Was the cutback part of greater cuts across the

Table 13-6   Analysis of Past Research

| Research type | % of total research spend | | Value to company |
	Last year	This year	
Market measurement	35	47	High
Advertising tracking	15	20	Medium
Total continuous	50	67	Medium
Usage and attitude	10	–	High
Market segmentation	8	–	High
Consumer usage videos	7	–	Very high
Strategic product testing	5	5	Medium
Quantified concept tests	10	3	High
Strategic ad hoc	40	8	High
Tactical product testing	3	1	Low
Advertising testing	3	1	Medium
Group discussions	4	8	Medium
Promotion tests	–	10	Low
Packaging tests	–	5	Medium
Tactical ad hoc	10	25	Medium
Total	100%	100%	–
Research spending as % of revenue	1.5	1.0	–

organization in response to a recessionary economy or, was there some more specific reason? If the cuts were a response to less projected growth, is cutting back on research the best strategy under the economic circumstances? In this scenario, it's probably worth going back another two years to analyze past spending trends further.

Is continuous research strategic or tactical? It can be either. The answer depends on how effectively it is used. The final column in the table is Value to Company. This is your subjective view based on action taken related to cost. This will help prepare your approach to future research allocation in Step 6. The most valuable research recently carried out by this company was the Consumer Usage Videos that targeted specific use of the firm's product and generated a number of promising new product and packaging ideas.

Step 2: List All Relevant Past Research

Most companies have a list of research conducted over the past five years or more. It will usually specify the title of each study, date, and location, and may include sample size.

Marketers should be familiar with every research study relevant to their brand over the past few years. When taking over a new marketing job, a good starting-point is to scan the past research list and review all studies of possible interest.

Step 3: Briefly Summarize Relevant Past Research Studies

Any research study that you have noted in Step 2 as relevant and useful should be briefly summarized, in 50 to 100 words. Included should be the title and date of the study; the structure of the study (e.g., 4,000 self-completed questionnaires), the key findings of the study including a ranking of items seen as most important, and lastly, comments as to the persuasiveness of findings, applicability of the study, and actions noted as being taken as well as any limitations of the research itself, such as relevant findings in earlier research not being included.

Step 4: Draw Conclusions, Identify Knowledge Gaps

What are your overall conclusions about this inventory of research? What are your key areas of understanding summarized in two to three pages? Does this add up to a superior understanding of consumers, customers, and other relevant stakeholders? If not, what steps do you need to take to achieve this, and what is the likely cost and time frame? Are there any major knowledge gaps that need to be filled? This analysis would include taking stock of the robustness of each piece of research.

You may well find conflicts between different pieces of research, and need to take a view as to which is most reliable.

Step 5: Establish Objectives and Strategies for Offensive Market Research

Here, in Table 13-7, is an example of a set of Offensive Market Research objectives and strategies. These apply to a company with a Market Research Department, albeit a small one. However, most of the strategies are equally feasible for companies without one.

Table 13-7   Example of Offensive Market Research Objectives and Strategies

Objectives:
To disseminate throughout the company a superior understanding of present and future consumer, customer and employee needs, in order to deliver superior experiences, with very efficient use of marketing resources.

Key strategies for achieving objectives:
 1. Focus primarily on consumers, but also cover customers and employees.
 2. Gain a much deeper understanding of consumer habits, needs, attitudes and future aspirations than competitors.
 3. Develop distinctive and proprietary approaches to segmenting markets, channels and customers.
 4. Objectively monitor product and service performance and value, constantly identifying opportunities for improvement.
 5. Develop superior techniques for new concept development, screening and test Marketing, so that future winners reach their full potential, and losers are spotted early.
 6. Constantly strive to discover new research approaches, and gain exclusive use of these for the company in its major markets.
 7. Objectively evaluate value for money gained by each major type of marketing spend, and identify opportunities for improvement.
 8. Ensure that research data is integrated and disseminated throughout the company in usable formats, tailored to specific departments or job holders.
 9. Develop superior internal competencies and processes, so that market research is well planned, implemented, and effective action taken.
 10. Wherever possible, build long-term partnerships with the best research agencies.

Step 6: Agree on a Three-Year Research Plan

The three-year plan would execute the agreed upon objectives and strategies and then be translated into next year's budget. It should be quite brief and cover issues such as:

- **How much should be spent on market research, both in absolute terms and as a percentage of sales?** This is a much better question to ask than the normal one, which is: "How little can we get away with spending on market research?" The principles for setting market research budgets are similar to those for setting advertising appropriations. The budget should be determined by the objectives and strategies agreed upon and the activities necessary to execute these.
- **What are the main types of research to concentrate on in future?** Your analysis of past research, and view on value for

money, at Step 1, is a useful starting-point here. What balance between continuous, strategic, and tactical work should be aimed for? Of course, the amount of tactical research needed will depend on future marketing plans and conditions, and cannot be mandated precisely ahead. Yet all too often a total market research budget is set, tactical research requirements given priority, and the strategic studies are cut to accommodate them. This is not the most advantageous strategic thinking. Strategic research should be given priority, and, if necessary, tactical research cut in order to finance it.

- **How will we reach and stay at the leading edge of market research?** What promising new techniques, technologies, or approaches are being tested? What contributions are our research suppliers making to this thinking? How much of the budget should be allocated to experimental research?
- **Over the next three years, what percent of research should be contracted out?** Clearly objectives and strategies should be set internally. In addition, any research areas where core competencies or competitive advantage can be acquired or built should be handled internally. For example, your firm may have developed distinctive skills or software for integrating internal and external data or mining that data to get leading-edge results. In the alternative, your company may have special skill in developing and testing concepts. In such a case, you would only contract out parts of this work on a secure basis.

    While addressing this question, you also need to decide how market research will be organized internally. Is a Market Research Manager or Marketing Services Department required? If not, how can marketers develop the necessary research skills, and how are budgets and processes to be coordinated in a consistent way?
- **What is your firm's three-year plan for external research?** Will you develop long-term partnerships, with some guarantees of minimum revenue in return for competitive pricing and a top-notch team? Or will your company put most research out to bid? Who are your preferred suppliers? What arrangements have been made for confidentiality? Will your preferred suppliers come to you first with new ideas, technologies, and approaches?
- **Who are your main internal research customers, and how will you meet their needs?** How will your success in doing this be measured?

- **Are there internal processes for planning and acting upon research results?** How satisfactory are they, and what further improvements can be made?
- **How will the available body of company research be integrated and disseminated to your internal customers?** In what format? What delivery system will be used? Do different employees require different formats or delivery systems to make the research most accessible?
- **How will the implementation of the three-year plan be monitored?** Quarterly milestones and review are desirable.

Step 7: Establish Action Formats

Consistent formats are used by Offensive Marketers in best-practice companies for planning, implementation, and action steps.

Planning

A one-page plan should precede the approval of any research. The most important elements are the objectives, and anticipated practical applications. Set forth in Table 13-8 are the elements of a market research proposal.

Table 13-8 Market Research Proposal

Country:

Brand or category:

Title of study:

Background: [List any previous research done on this topic, giving dates and study titles. What was the main finding?]

Objectives: [Why is this research needed? What opportunities is it likely to generate? What problems is it designed to solve?]

Anticipated applications: [What possible action steps can be taken as a result of this research? If the research involves quantification versus competitors, action standards should be set within the proposal, to prevent 'fudging' later. For instance, in a blind test of a new product, the proposal might specify that a 60:40 win is required for a 'Go' decision.]

Competitive advantage: [What advantage is this research expected to generate? In what way is the research innovative or different?]

Technical issues: [What methodology is to be used? What is sample size? What breakouts are needed?]

Research company:

Estimated cost:

Timetable: [Planned start. Fieldwork completed. Results available.]

Implementation

It is desirable to have a standard company technique for conducting recurring types of research like product tests, attitude and usage studies, and concept tests. In this way, you can compare results of different tests over time and across countries.

Action Steps

Every piece of one-time research should be briefly summarized and future planned action specified. This summary should be written by the person responsible for carrying out the action. It is essential for marketers to write these action summaries because:

- This guarantees that they read and think about the research they have commissioned.
- Marketers are best placed to weigh the commercial implications of possible actions.
- Marketers should be accountable for making effective use of research they have authorized.

Step 8: Set Up Monitoring System

This system would monitor achievement of planned market research objectives, strategies, and plans; regularly review value for money being delivered; and, most importantly, check what actions are planned as a result of each research study completed in the past quarter.

CONCLUSION

New technology is changing the face of market research as well as its impact. Market research is one of the more exciting aspects of marketing, but it is often ill served by marketers. To be effective, market research should be positioned as a fulcrum for corporate action. To date, there is an overemphasis on tactical, defensive, and confirmatory research that fails to drive the organization forward to new frontiers of consumer understanding.

The main principles of Offensive Market Research can be summarized in the following five points:

1. Superior consumer understanding generates major competitive advantage. Market intelligence systems and competencies in integrating, mining, manipulating, retrieval, and use of data are competitive assets.
2. Superior customer, consumer, employee, and competitor understanding grows out of a strong market research strategy supported by a thoughtful market research budget.
3. Research should be used as a torch and not as a crutch. It is a device for improving the quality of decision-making.
4. It is important to look for the prospective action in the research proposal and to bring imagination and creativity to research design and implementation.
5. Integrate data and keep asking "why" as consumers' needs and expectations continue to evolve. Integrating internal and external data from multiple sources has the capacity to provide a total picture of consumers and customers for ongoing research as well as new customer-driven initiatives. However, note that good customer relationships and loyalty do not stem from computer applications or software alone, but are based on a full understanding of the customer—and effective execution, the "E" of POISE, of all customer-facing initiatives.

Lastly, following the eight-step process for Offensive Market Research creates the opportunity that your company's research budget will be well spent and relevant to delivering a superior customer experience.

14 Offensive Pricing

INTRODUCTION

Advertising and communications of all types and design play their part in influencing the consumer. However, for most brands the benefits of a product or service versus the price of that product or service is what matters most in the purchasing decision.

Pricing is one of the most difficult areas of marketing in which to make decisions because so many variables are involved. The reaction of consumers, distributors, or retailers as well as competitors has to be considered. Indeed their responses and interactions may be hard to project or read.

Pricing decisions often have to be made quickly, without testing, as they are left to the last minute and are often a compromise between the goal of volume and market share versus profitability and financial return. What is more, pricing is different from the other elements in the marketing mix in one important respect. As one marketer put it:

"Pricing is the only element of the marketing mix that directly generates revenue; all the others add costs."[1]

Producers are not the only group to find pricing difficult. Consumers today have to work harder than ever before to understand where real value lies. Twenty years ago, they had a much easier time. There were more limited choices, and products or services had a "regular price" that was reduced on a disciplined basis by short-term promotions. Now many brands are portrayed with almost continuous promotions, whether they be first-time buyer discounts or special payment options, so much so that consumers can be confused as to where real value lies. Is there a catch somewhere in "the lowest prices anywhere!" claim or will the same product be available online at a significantly reduced price? On top of all of this, the Internet is facilitating price transparency across all pricing categories.

The result of this growing complexity and variety is that consumers seek brands they can trust, as well as simplicity, clarity, and honest advice.

ELEMENTS AND TOOLS OF OFFENSIVE PRICING

Offensive pricing demands strong analysis, a deep understanding of customers and costs, and a mindset that allows for the review of differing pricing scenarios prior to decision dates. In order to do these tasks most effectively, the Offensive Marketer must have a firm grasp of key concepts that drive pricing decisions.

Price: One of Two Key Elements in Value

Price is the concrete expression of the value consumers attach to your company's products and services in the marketplace. If you believe your firm's product or service is superior to the competition, you should either price at parity and grow market share, or price at a premium and sustain market share. Failure to achieve either result would be a clear indication that end users did not share your beliefs in the competitiveness of your product.

---

[1] Peter Doyle, *Marketing Management and Strategy*, Prentice-Hall, 1994.

Price has no relevance in isolation. Let's say the price of a car is $28,000. This information in itself is useless. You cannot convert it into a *value* judgment unless you know the age, model, and manufacturer of the car. For a new Honda Accord $28,000 is very expensive. For a two-year-old BMW, it would be very attractive. Price translates products or services into propositions that can be valued.

Value is an equation relating quality to price (see Chapter 3). It is:

Actual or Perceived Quality × Price = Value

This brand equation can be detailed in a Value Map, which compares various quality/price alternatives. Quality is defined as "the consumer judgment on product/service proposition *relative* to competition." In the Value Map shown in Figure 14-1, both quality and price are compared to competition. The rankings in the boxes are value rankings.

Figure 14-1
Value Map[2]

PRICE

	Higher	Parity	Lower
Superior	Good value	Very good	Excellent
Parity	Poor value	Acceptable	Very good
Worse	Terrible value	Poor	May be acceptable

Quality

Having completed a Value Map, which establishes your firm's value delivery, you can use it to check the robustness of your overall strategy. If, for example, you are pursuing a share-growth or penetration strategy, your company must offer increased value, which translates into increased price sensitivity, or a reduction in the price. Texas Instruments, for example, practices a market-penetration pricing strategy where it sets its price as low as possible to win a large market share. As it experiences falling costs in light of increased volumes and production experience, it reduces pricing further, which stimulates additional market growth. Low pricing additionally inhibits competition from entering the market.

[2] Adapted from Figure 19-1 in Philip Kotler, *Marketing Management*, Prentice-Hall, 1994.

On the other hand, if your firm is pursuing a skimming strategy for the brand, then you would want to reduce the price sensitivity of the offering, in other words, increase the price. Intel is an example of a company with such a pricing strategy. Another pricing strategy includes being the product-quality leader in the industry. Having this position enables the product-quality leader to charge a premium price based on differentiating features.

Often measures of price sensitivity are different with respect to various segments of the market and to various market conditions. Market conditions include planned versus impulse buying or purchasing for oneself or as a gift. Depending on overall market strategy, pricing should depend on the economic value to the purchaser. Accordingly, effective pricing should vary according to the customer's price sensitivity. Measuring price elasticity and the comparative profitability of various pricing schemes is becoming more and more important to strategic pricing as the more traditional model of "one-price fits-all" of the mass merchandizing economy goes by the wayside. Figure 14-2 summarizes the broad market share implications of the Value Map.

Figure 14-2
*Strategic
Implication
of Value Map*

	PRICE		
	Higher	**Parity**	**Lower**
Superior	Hold or gain market share	Grow	Super growth
Parity	Decline	Hold share	Grow
Worse	Exit	Decline	Hold or lose share

Quality (vertical axis)

The Value Map should be regularly updated as your firm's own and competitors' propositions change.

The future expectation of most consumers is that quality will improve and prices reduce in real terms. Offensive Marketers will respond to this desire for continuously improving value by tying economic value to corporate and operational competencies.

Cost-plus and Demand Pricing

The most favored approaches to pricing are cost-plus and demand pricing.

Cost-plus involves taking your costs and adding on a fixed percentage for profits. The advantages are simplicity and less price competition between companies. But the drawbacks are overwhelming for manufacturers in highly competitive markets, since "cost-plus" does not take into account competitive reaction. Cost-plus fails to take into consideration the consumer side of the equation: just what is the consumer willing to spend for the offering in comparison to substitute products or services in the market.

The other problem with cost-plus is that it ignores experience theory for the product. Experience theory, which was introduced to strategic marketing by Bruce Henderson and the Boston Consulting Group is based on the empirical observation that as accumulated experience in production grows, costs decline. What has been observed is that with every doubling of accumulated production volume (total volume from the first unit of production; e.g., from 1 to 2 to 4 to 8 to 16 to 32 to 64 and so on) there is a percentage decline in average unit cost of production that ranges from 5 to more than 15 percent. The most startling conclusion of experience theory is that costs go down forever! Their decline is hidden because as accumulated volume grows the amount of time required to double accumulated volume also grows.

The implications of experience theory for cost based pricing are that if you can increase volume, you can lower costs. If you can lower costs, you should incorporate projected costs into your pricing decision. This means that you must look forward, not backward, for cost data for pricing decisions. In new product categories, experience based pricing can lead to competitive advantage and cost leadership in a rapidly growing market and industry.

Conversely, a rise in price due to cost pressure resulting from declining volume will reduce market share and profits if sales decline.

Demand pricing is important because it takes market response into account. The only justification for a price increase is that it will increase profit and, unless a company is badly strapped for cash or is deliberately milking a product or service, profits should be looked at from a long-term viewpoint, that is, building customer loyalty and future revenues.

With this method of pricing, you want to know what would happen to the sales revenue trend if prices were increased by, for example, 10 percent—whether it would grow or fall so heavily that a price increase would reduce profit.

If a price increase could be expected to deflate profit, it should obviously not be pursued. And if rising costs are a big problem, the solution should be found through cutting costs or increasing volume.

In essence, demand pricing ignores cost. If an increase in price looks likely to raise long-term profit, it should be considered, even though costs remain stable or decline. Whether or not you increase price in this situation depends on your market share objectives. Value rather than cost is what determines pricing.

Key Tools for Decision-making on Pricing

A number of key tools and concepts can be used to guide the decision-making on pricing, among them price elasticity, econometrics, and market research.

Price Elasticity

Price elasticity is the "ratio of sales change to price change."[3] A brand whose volume responds sharply to price changes has high elasticity and the reverse is true. Consumers who are very price conscious have highly elastic demand—their willingness to buy is *greatly* affected by price. The Table in Figure 14-3 illustrates

Figure 14-3
Price Elasticity: Detergent[4]

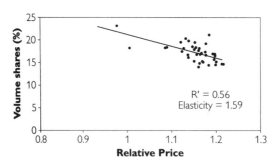

---

[3] Will Hamilton, "How Manufacturers Can Stay Ahead of the Game," *Admap*, March 1996.
[4] Id.

price elasticity for a detergent. Its elasticity is moderate at 1.6, indicating that for every 10 percent cut in price, sales will increase by 16 percent.

Most studies on consumer goods suggest a price elasticity in the 1.5 to 2.5 range. So, for every 10 percent reduction in price, sales grow by 15 to 25 percent. Information Resources Inc.[5] studies revealed a mean elasticity of −2.0. (The minus sign confirms the inverse relationship between price and demand: where the price is increased, demand will fall.) This study identified that the price effect could be greatly enhanced by advertising features and product displays. Where both were used, the average sales effect was much greater, illustrating yet again that the various elements of the marketing mix work best in strategic combination.

Price elasticity can be established by historical analysis of market share versus price *relative* to competition. Relative price is always a more important measure than absolute price. It is usually worthwhile to go back at least three years, on a monthly basis, so that you have 36 individual observations on which to base your line of "best fit." This is relatively straightforward if you have sound continuing data on market share and price (although you need to take into account other factors, such as new product launches, quality changes and levels of advertising). If you do not have market share data, you may still be able to construct a rough but useful elasticity model using your own sales figures, allowing for any major channel inventory changes and tracking your product's relative price versus major competitors.

However, as anyone in the airlines or telecom industry will tell you, it is essential to work out price elasticity *by user type.* In the passenger travel industry, business customers have historically had much lower price elasticity than leisure customers, for the obvious reason that they don't foot the bill.

Elasticity may also vary by distribution channel, and by time or occasion of use. Restaurants always charge less for lunch than dinner, even though the offer may be reasonably similar.

Econometrics

Econometrics is a statistical technique for analyzing a range of variables over time, identifying their impact on sales, as well as

---

[5] Gian M. Fulgoni, Chief Executive Officer, Information Resources, Inc.

their interrelationships. It is sometimes used to sort out the relative effect of changes in advertising, pricing, and sales promotion on sales. Researchers can analyze historical data on all these independent variables, and work out a "best fit," estimating the effect of each factor on sales. Such a model can be regularly updated and used as a guide on future pricing or marketing mix decisions.

Market Research[6]

A study by Clancy and Shulman showed that only 12 percent of American companies did any pricing research. A survey of 300 North American companies by McKinsey produced a similar result—only 15 percent of companies had done any research to measure or predict price elasticity in the past year.[7]

So is it a waste of time to research pricing options? It can be. Some companies still ask consumers how much they would be prepared to pay for given products or services, and then attempt to incorporate the results into price elasticity and profit models. This facile type of questioning can produce misleading answers, since consumers are being asked to predict their response to a speculative future purchase situation. Trade-off or conjoint analysis, covered below, is a much better, though more expensive, way to tackle this kind of question.

Market research can provide valuable insights on pricing, and is relatively inexpensive in relation to the likely profit improvement generated. Here are some examples:

- **Price testing.** Higher or lower price levels can often be tested in panels of stores, in discrete geographical areas, or in business-to-business markets, with specific groups of customers or industry types.
- **Simulated test markets (STMs).** As part of STM, the volume impact of alternative price levels can be estimated with a reasonable level of confidence (see Chapter 11 for greater detail).
- **Trade-off or conjoint analysis.** These are two different names for the same technique.

    In this type of statistical analysis, a respondent's ranked preferences for different offerings can be decomposed to determine

---

[6] This entire section draws heavily from K. Clancy and R. Shulman, *The Marketing Revolution: A Radical Manifesto for Dominating the Marketplace*, Harper Business, 1991.

[7] Clancy and Shulman. Id.

the individual's preferred utility function for each attribute tested, and the relative importance of each attribute in the total offering. In effect, conjoint analysis "enables a researcher to evaluate many different concepts using approaches borrowed from experimental psychology. Essentially, the researcher designs an experiment to test multiple factors—name, key features, key benefits, price—by showing different combinations to different people. By analyzing these results, a company can capture the main effects of, say, seven factors, by exposing consumers to a relatively small set of concepts."[8]

- **Activity-based costing.** Every cost is an estimate, and some estimates are more accurate than others. Accountants need costs primarily for control and to meet statutory and senior management requirements.

  However, marketers need costs for different reasons: to make decisions on brands, channels, products, and services. However, the ritual procedure of allocating costs such as warehousing, sales, engineering and general management across brands, based on share of revenue or volume, can give a misleading picture of brand profitability. For example, large brands, especially if heavily promoted, often absorb a disproportionate amount of sales-force time. And small brands, particularly those with unique raw materials or service problems, can take up a larger amount of manufacturing expense, operations, and supply chain time. Most sets of accounts conceal this reality by relatively arbitrary cost allocation.

  Activity-based costing confronts this issue, and involves delving into those key activities that determine cost. It would, for example, highlight brands that take up disproportionate amounts of sales-force time due to service or warranty problems, and establish the real cost of warehousing large versus small brands. Because activity-based costing involves special exercises, which can be time-consuming and expensive, it is best applied to large cost areas where allocation by brand or channel has been arbitrarily estimated. In this way, previously "allocated costs" can be adjusted to reflect reality, and over time, a series of such exercises will enable a company to build up more accurate principles for cost allocation.

---

[8] Clancy and Shulman, Id.

- **Sensitivity analysis.** This involves working out in advance the answers to relevant "What if?" questions on pricing in order to facilitate quick and accurate decisions when decision time comes. As decision-making time continues to shrink with ever more rapid marketplace changes, having performed sensitivity analysis and therefore having more information about issues relevant to your competitive situation puts your company more effectively in the driver's seat.

  Of these issues, the most important ones to understand are the effect of price changes of, for example, 5 percent, 10 percent, and 20 percent on your firm's costs and profits. It is probably reasonably straightforward for you to estimate the effect of these changes on volume. Your accountants, possibly using activity-based costing, can then calculate the cost and profit implications. Their figures will be influenced most by the ratio between fixed and variable costs and the possible need to invest in new operational capacity in the future. A simplified sensitivity analysis, which estimates the effect of ±10 percent in price, is illustrated in Table 14-1 for a consumer durables brand.

Table 14-1   Sensitivity Analysis: A Consumer Durables Brand

	Price now	+10% price	−10% price
Sales ('000 units)	1,000	900	1,200
Sales ($m)	100	99	108
Fixed cost of goods	20	20	20
Variable costs	50	45	60
Gross margin ($m)	30	34	28
Fixed operating exp.	6	6	6
Variable operating exp.	14	13	17
Total expenses ($m)	20	19	23
Operating profit ($m)	10	15	5

In this example, you calculate that a 10 percent price increase will reduce your volume by 10 percent from 1,000K units to 900K. This means that your sales revenue only drops marginally from $100 million to $99 million. Your fixed costs do not change, but your variable costs fall, reflecting lower volume. The estimate of operating profit at $5 million, a 50 percent increase, looks good.

The 10 percent price cut looks much less attractive, even though it drives volume up by 20 percent and revenue up to

$108 million. It is unattractive because variable costs rise 20 percent in line with volume increases, and profits could be halved if your estimates are right.

- **Competitor analysis.** Making price changes in a competitive market is analogous to playing poker. All prices are relative, and correctly calculating competitive reaction is an important factor in successful pricing strategy. Will your main competitors match your price change? Will they match the price change across their whole brand range or only a part of the product range? How quickly? How consistent are they likely to be in their response?

  You can make reasonable estimates of competitors' reactions by studying their past behavior and competitive moves. You need to understand your competitors' economics, past reactions, attitudes, management, and strategy. Is the competitor a high-cost operator who would fear to lose a sustained price war? Where does this brand stand on the competitor's portfolio analysis—is it a priority global brand or a local one being harvested for investment? What is the price elasticity of competitor brands? Have there been any recent management changes that would change their course of action as you have come to understand it?

  Because pricing decisions often have to be made quickly, the Offensive Marketer should use these tools to achieve a deep understanding of pricing options, so that when decision time arrives, their organizations will be well prepared to act decisively and win.

PRINCIPLES OF OFFENSIVE PRICING

There are several key principles of Offensive Pricing:

1. **Know the price dynamics of your markets.** Even before doing any detailed analysis, you can quickly develop a feel for the price dynamics of your company's markets by being aware of the following:
   - **Frequency of purchase.** This has a major influence on the sensitivity of individual products or services to price changes. Those in markets where frequency of purchase is high—like babyfoods, fast foods, gasoline, bread, and commuter trains—tend to be very price-sensitive.

- **Degree of necessity.** This affects markets rather than products within them. If a product category is very necessary to its users, changes in the prices of all products are less likely to affect its size. Cigarettes have been a prime example in the past, but with increasing price escalations during recent years, price as well as a growing health consciousness has had an impact on market size. However, generally discretionary products—like consumer credit, clothing, or cars—are more adversely affected by general price increases.
- **Unit price.** This is another factor. High-priced items like vacation packages, cars, furniture, and consumer electronics tend to be subject to long deliberation and considerable price-consciousness, although status and styling may also affect the outcome of the purchase.
- **Degree of comparability.** This also influences the price-sensitivity of brands—consumers are less price conscious about their IRA accounts than about grocery products, because they are more difficult to compare.
- **Degree of fashion or status.** This affects pricing, but sometimes in reverse; fashion, cosmetic brands, or exclusive drinks may use high pricing as a way of establishing quality.

The operation of these general principles is illustrated in a number of markets shown in Table 14-2. By applying these broad principles, you can quickly draw some general conclusions about the likely price sensitivity of certain products/services and markets. With this information, you can then analyze price/volume relationships in your specific market.

Two studies in consumer goods markets provide valuable clues about price elasticity related to brand size and age.

Table 14-2   Factors Influencing Price Sensitivity by Market

Criteria	Baby foods	Clothing	Motor insurance	New cars
Purchase frequency	Very high	Low	Low	Low
Necessity	High	Medium	High	Medium
Unit price	Low	Medium	High	High
Comparability	High	Medium	Medium	Medium
Fashion	Low	High	Low	High
Effect of pricing:				
on market	Medium	Medium	Low	High
on brand	High	Medium	High	Medium

In one study, regression analysis of 500 brands over a three-year period used continuous consumer panel data, and another, reviewing 300 brands in 50 markets, again over a three-year period, showed the following:[9]

- **Brand leaders are less price-sensitive than smaller brands**. This is because consumer loyalty to large brands is usually above average and advertising is relatively more effective with respect to larger brands.
- **New brands have above-average price elasticity**. This is no surprise as consumers take time to form an opinion of the relative value of a new brand and to make decisions on trial or loyalty. During the formative period, pricing and promotion can be powerful weapons.
- **Short-term price and value promotions show diminishing returns.** Unless price and value promotions are tied into a longer-term strategy, their effect is very often short-term with varying short-lived impact on returns.

2. **Choose your price segments.** Every market is segmented by price brackets. In general, stronger brands occupy the upper pricing half, while commodity products and weaker brands are in the lower half.

It is important to set a price sector strategy. Is your strategy like that of Seiko Watches, to compete at every price point and to blanket the market with your firm's products? Or is it to focus on the top 20% of selected market sectors, like BMW or Nike?

Perhaps your strategy is to concentrate on the lowest price sector, like Kmart or Kohl's Stores, exploiting efficient low-cost operation. Or, like many Japanese global marketers and store private label brands, your company may use low price as an initial entry point, and once established, widen your coverage of price segments by moving upwards.

There are many alternative strategies for pricing. What matters is having a clear, well thought-out strategy, rather than one that drifts across price segments in response to market conditions. Obvious considerations are:

- **Profitability.** Some price sectors are much more profitable than others. For example, in the car market, the top 10 to

---

[9] Justin Sargent, "Strategies for Brand Success," *Admap*, March 1996.

15 percent of the pricing band is quite profitable, while the bottom 20 percent is overcrowded and generally, produces meager returns.

- **Fit with your company's image and strengths.** What price sectors best capitalize on your company's strengths? Are you a sophisticated marketer with strong brands and heavy R&D backing? Or does your firm's expertise lie in low-cost operations, speed-to-market, and a limited range of high-volume products?

    Companies that have been successful in one price sector often have difficulty moving into new ones. In general, though, it is easier to move up than down. Companies attempting to move down price sectors often lose out to high overheads and suffer sales contraction in the absence of large marketing budgets.

- **Competitive intentions.** Watch out for this strategy well known to be used by Japanese firms. For example, when the Japanese entered the motorcycle market with small machines, Harley Davidson, with its 750–1000 cc superbikes, hardly noticed. It is well known that Harley Davidson worked hard to confront Honda in the marketplace to ultimately gain back the exalted price sector it once owned.

3. **Achieve clarity of pricing.** If consumers do not understand your pricing system or consider it confusing or illogical, there are two likely implications. First, they will trust your brand or company less, and secondly they will probably overestimate your actual prices.

    AT&T's long-distance business may be a prime example of this to an extreme. Adding to its many woes in the marketplace, including successful market invasions by the baby Bells (a loss of 30 million customers in five years, from 80 million to 50 million in 2002), AT&T's billing practices have led to customer anger and frustration. These have included the illegal use of "slamming," which is the practice of changing a consumer's phone service without authorization, and adding monthly $1 and $2 "connectivity charges" and "monthly usage minimum charges" never authorized by the user.[10] Certainly, this company cannot afford the PR taint of illegal activity. But more

---

[10] Edward Robinson, "Will AT&T Ever Put the Customer First?" *Business 2.0 Daily Insight*, May 1, 2001 (copyright Imagine Media 2000).

importantly for our purposes, manipulating pricing, refusing to be upfront with the customer on all charges, and failing to make amends quickly to consumers who have identified problems in their billing or accounts creates immense opportunity for competitors and newer products, such as DSL and wireless, to attract new customers from AT&T's traditional customer base.

4. **Always consider the alternatives.** Pricing is often regarded as a somewhat mechanical aspect of marketing, but in fact it provides plenty of opportunity for creativity. For a start, price is only one part of the marketing mix, and the profitability of a change in price should be compared with all the other viable alternatives. It is important to remember that the marketing mix is truly in fact a mix of factors that adds up to the value perceived by the customer.

Suppose, for example, that a 10 percent increase in price was being considered and expected to bring in $1 million extra sales revenue and $400,000 additional net profit. Before recommending such an increase, it would make sense to consider whether various other possible combinations would raise profit by more than $400,000. Alternatives to be considered could include:

- Increase the price by 5 percent and run an extra promotion.
- Hold the price and reduce advertising by $300,000.
- Raise prices 15 percent and adopt a major product or service improvement.
- Alter payment or delivery arrangements, change the conditions of free maintenance or technical assistance, or increase guarantee/warranty periods to change the value side of the equation.

5. **Target your price changes.** Price elasticity varies by type of consumer, shopping environment, and occasion of use. Loyal customers, by definition, are less price-elastic than occasional users. Someone shopping for fun in a leisure context or on holiday is likely to be less price-focused than an unsalaried head of household doing the weekly grocery shopping.

The Offensive Marketer needs to have sound knowledge of the differing price elasticities of her customers, and to understand the role pricing plays in the value equation. Pricing is a means for linking supply and demand in the most advantageous way. The objective of the Offensive Marketer is to get as many consumers as possible to the point where they acknowledge their brand experience as "superior" and become regular users. Price should be targeted to reach this objective.

Who are the best target prospects? Those you have most chance of moving up to the "superior brand experience" camp. The majority of pricing resources should be targeted at the occasional user where price can be used to convert occasional use to regular use. Rewarding loyal customers who are the core of your business with pricing initiatives is also a strong strategy. With regard to those who have used your product in the past and who are neutral on that experience, targeting more of the heavy users from this group makes sense along with strengthening your offering. Pricing becomes irrelevant for the hostile rejector group and a low priority for the "promotion junkies" group.

"Promotion junkies" are consumers who tend to switch from brand to brand, depending on which offers the best deal today. In the value equation, pricing for this group is the predominant factor. In the detergent market, for instance, 16 percent of shoppers actively seek out price promotions, and account for 64 percent of promotion expenditure.[11]

6. **Avoid profit cannibalization when pricing new products.** A company needs to guard against profit cannibalism. Profit cannibalization occurs where a marketing initiative by one product or service severely damages the profits of other products in the *same* company.

Chapters 9 and 11 emphasized the importance of thinking incrementally about new products. Incremental gains for a company will be maximized when new products are well targeted to take business from competitors, and profit per unit is above the existing average. When Mercedes launched the "C" class, it successfully followed these principles while targeting the mid-sized luxury car market held by BMW, Audi, and Ford among others.

Previously, Mercedes had marketed large cars in two series, the "E" and "S." Clearly, there was the possible risk of trading down Mercedes owners to a smaller car or damaging the company's premium-quality image. The Mercedes C series

---

[11] John Millen, Procter & Gamble Vice-President of Sales, quoted in *EuroMarketing*, October 1996.

was targeted at the high-quality end of the mid-sized market and priced accordingly, at a premium to BMW and Audi and well above other competitors. Worldwide, the C series was very successful. It accounted for 40 percent of Mercedes car sales and, more importantly, there was little trading down. Fifty percent of C series purchasers had never owned a Mercedes before.

7. **Use pricing to optimize your return on capacity, especially with perishable products.** If you have a long-life product, effective management of your firm's production capacity—one of your main assets—should not be too difficult. The key principle is to ensure that your assets and capacity are used efficiently to generate output, in the form of products, which has high value to customers. There is little point in using valuable assets to churn out undifferentiated commodity products.

If, however, your company's product or service is perishable, pricing and capacity management become more challenging. The definition of "perishable," however, has broadened in recent years. Certain types of food have always been perishable, in the sense of having a limited shelf life. Many fashion goods are equally perishable—burnt ochre may be "the color" in autumn, but just try selling it in January. Seasonal goods like Easter bunnies or Christmas lights are perishable—they could be kept until next year but inventory carrying costs are high. Many consumer services are perishable: whenever a train slides out of Grand Central Station, or an aircraft takes off from O'Hare, the empty seats still exist but are not saleable—their time is past. Hotel rooms are also perishable. And, in other markets, prices fall so fast that time is of the essence. In such cases, like personal computing products, or handhelds, the product is not perishable, but its value is in light of rapid changes in technology.

Here are some guidelines for pricing perishable products:

- **Use all available demand forecasting tools.** This includes econometrics, market research, and economic analysis. Having developed the best possible forecast of future demand, take a slightly conservative view. At the margin, it is better to have run out of fully priced product than to be giving them away a short time later. However, do not fool yourself that running out of product will not have a PR effect on your firm.

- **Understand and act upon the price elasticities of different customer types.** Railways know that students and senior citizens are frequent leisure travelers and have high price elasticity. In some regions of the world, they target them by means of special travel cards, whereby they pay a small fixed fee and gain low-price travel for the year.
- **Analyze capacity utilization and use price to maximize it.** The key to pricing perishable products and services is to utilize full capacity at the highest possible price. The ideal for an airline is to take off with a full load at full prices, and no unhappy passengers on the ground. In practice, this almost never happens, and the skillful use of discounting is inevitable. Offensive airline Marketers will have excellent historical analyses of load factors and prices for every flight, fast and accurate information systems providing exact booking status, and quick local decision making on pricing, following well-established and published guidelines.
- **Ensure your firm's cost allocations are first class.** Correct pricing of perishable products and services requires a deep understanding of real costs especially the true split between fixed and variable costs.

8. **If you make a mistake on pricing, admit it and remedy fast.** Anyone can make a mistake on pricing, and the important thing is to face up to it and correct it—fast. There is usually no practical reason why this cannot be done. But it is difficult to put into effect, because neither people nor companies like to admit they have made mistakes.

A note on e-commerce models, here. The use of business models made prevalent by the commercial Internet, such as Priceline.com's "name your own price," works well for both perishable goods and items in oversupply.[12] Because of the nature of a product's sales cycle, and the nature of its fixed costs—for example, filling a hotel room, a rental car, or an airline seat uses capacity that has already been paid for—the cost of additional sales is negligible. Accordingly, almost any sales price is reasonable and profitable. This makes sense where sellers such as airlines or hotels treat their products as commodities, varying their pricing according to supply and

---

[12] "Name Your Own Price—For Everything?" *Business Week*, April 17, 2000.

demand, even though their advertising is based in brand management. This also makes sense where sellers can treat purchasers differently based on differing needs. For example, purchasers willing to travel at the last minute or be booked at a hotel that may not be their first pick, have expectations that differ from the first-class business traveler.[13]

However, Priceline's model has not worked as well for products that do not fit into these categories. Priceline's recent move away from expanded offerings such as groceries and gasoline (privately held WebHouse Club, which had licensed Priceline.com's name-your-own-price business model, shut down in October 2000), and its increasing losses, may be indicative that its model works well for one set of offerings, but not for others.

E-Bay's very successful person-to-person auction community appears to be well suited to the transactional exchange of the Internet. The company estimates that its revenue will hit $3 billion in 2005. This platform and business has given rise to one of the newer cottage industries, online liquidation, which has provided retailers a new way to liquidate merchandise and process product returns. It is projected that in three years, Internet liquidators will handle 60 percent of the retail industry's returned and obsolete product.[14]

What is interesting about e-Bay's business model, platform, and set of evolving tools, is that it is so diffuse that liquid markets appear where there were none previously, and lowered transaction costs create new ways of conducting business.[15] In 2001, sales of discounted products skyrocketed as more and more well-known brand names joined the roster of companies turning to e-Bay to unload excess product. These companies have included IBM, Sears-Roebuck, and Walt Disney. In addition, the online division of Ritz Camera, for example, is using e-Bay technology to run its own Web site, Ritz Interactive. With moves like these, e-Bay is moving its online system outside the borders of its own Web site and influencing

---

[13] This paragraph draws heavily from Raman Muralidharan and Rhonda Germany, "The Priceline Problem," *Strategy+Business Briefs*, at http://www.strategy-business.com/briefs/01119/page1.html.

[14] Bob Tedeschi, "E-Commerce Report, The Success of eBay Is Spawning a Number of Online Liquidation Houses," *The New York Times*, April 29, 2002.

[15] Robert D. Hof, "The People's Company," *Business Week*, December 3, 2001.

business and pricing models.[16] However, as e-Bay's model picks up momentum, it runs up against "consumer-savvy behemoths" such as AOL Time Warner, Amazon, Microsoft, and Yahoo!, and their own brands of online malls.[17]

Internet based business models will continue to affect pricing elements into the future as the application of Web transactions continues to impact ways of conducting business, expand access to the consumer as well as create markets where none existed before.

FIVE-STEP PROCESS FOR OFFENSIVE PRICING

A five-step process is recommended. The first two steps involve customer and channel analysis; the next two cover cost, capacity, and competitor analysis; and the final one generates objectives and strategies built from the analysis of the previous four steps.

Offensive Pricing requires high-quality analysis, and it is no coincidence that four of the five steps are analytical ones.

The five-step process is summarized in Table 14-3

Step 1: Consumer or End-User Analysis

Start by standing back and looking at the general price dynamics of your company's markets and brands—see Table 14-1. Then analyze past price promotions and volume effect of changes in your relative price versus competition, and construct a price elasticity chart, like the dishwashing detergent one shown in Figure 14-3. With respect to your larger brands, identify the main influences on sales through econometrics—this can be done either in-house or by an outside agency. Scan your existing inventory of market research for any useful information on consumer attitude to price or value in your markets.

Bigger brands and companies should consider investing in specific price and value research, like conjoint analysis.

---

[16] Id.
[17] Id.

Table 14-3   Five-Step Process for Offensive Pricing

Step 1	**Consumer or end-user analysis**	• Price elasticity • Market research • Perceived product or service quality • Consumer value
Step 2	**Channel or distributor analysis**	• Channel or account price strategy • Channel margins, discounts • Channel value delivered
Step 3	**Competitor pricing analysis**	• Elasticity • Perceived performance and value • Current price/value strategy • Future strategy
Step 4	**Economic and capacity analysis**	• Quality cost breakdowns • Sensitivity analyses • Value improvement opportunities • Alternate scenarios review
Step 5	**Develop pricing objectives and strategies**	• Relate to overall marketing strategy • Value and profit improvement

If your products or services have a number of identifiable user types, or different user occasions, develop a view of the relative price elasticity of each.

Next, check the perceived quality of your product or service proposition versus competition. Again, review past consumer research. Talk to customers. Is your relative quality better, equal, or worse?

You can now combine the above elements to make a value judgment, comparing the relative quality of your firm's proposition with your relative price. Complete the Value Map, Figure 14-1. Then examine the Strategic Implications Map, Figure 14-2, and check the fit with your current strategy.

Step 2: Channel or Distributor Analysis

Identify the margin, discount, and consumer pricing strategies of each channel and major account. How might these change in future?

What are their margin aspirations, and how do they evaluate them—percent gross margin, or some more sophisticated measure? How well are your brands meeting these aspirations? If your firm were to raise its price, how quickly will the channel or major account react, and will it, in turn, attempt to raise its percent margin? What value for money is the channel providing in return for the margin, discounts, and services that you are providing? Can this be improved to the consumers' advantage?

Step 3: Competitor Pricing Analysis

Put your firm's major competitors through the same processes as you applied to your own brands in Step 1. Establish price elasticity, relative quality, and relative value. Then analyze each competitor's past behavior. What is their growth and profit strategy, overall, and in this market? Are they seeking to grow share or hold on and raise profit margins? What is their cost base—have they recently reduced it, and if so, will they use the savings to improve customer value, perhaps cut price, or will they build profit margin instead?

Next, evaluate how competitors handle price changes. Which business endeavor initiates or leads price changes in each market? Usually it is the brand leader, but not always. There may be an ambitious No. 2 brand, which suddenly cuts price, or an eccentric No. 3 brand, which, desperate for extra profit this year, leads with a price increase. For competitors who do not initiate price increases, what is their "following" strategy? Do they follow immediately? Do they hold off for a few months and build extra short-term volume? Or do they pretend to follow with a list-price increase, but in reality hold their prices by promoting heavily?

Step 4: Economics and Capacity Analysis

Identify the kind of cost breakdowns your company needs, and lay out a charted schedule of these. Explain to Finance why they are necessary, and how, from an Offensive Marketing perspective, you will use the results. Check on how accurately overheads and fixed costs are allocated by brand or major account and, where the numbers are large, insist on activity-based costing exercises.

Armed with this data, and working closely with Finance, develop a number of Sensitivity Analyses (see Table 14-1), indicating profit effect of various price or value changes. Discuss your results with Finance and seek their input as they are likely to provide valuable insights.

Use Sensitivity Analysis to consider "What if?" questions and possible improvement opportunities. What if we improve product quality by 10 percent, increase warranty from two to three years, and raise prices by 5 percent? The aim is to relate every cost to its consumer value. Eliminate high-cost elements that have low value to the consumer. Seek low-cost benefits with high consumer value. This is the Offensive Marketer's job—making every cost your company incurs work hard on behalf of the consumer. This will enable your company to use price to highlight your superior value.

Step 5: Develop Pricing Objectives and Strategies

This step capitalizes on the analysis done in the four previous steps, and converts them into action. It is here that the Offensive Marketer leads the organization toward a holistic strategy, focused on the customer: one that creates alignment throughout the organization as to departmental and functional goals and objectives. Changes may require reducing costs in operations from manufacturing to distribution, modifying product design or functionality, or modifying the marketing mix, to name a few scenarios. Some actions may be taken for the short term to protect profit, while others may be taken in the longer term with an extended view toward sustained profitability and competitive position. The goal of all these interrelated actions is value and profit improvement. Developing pricing objectives and strategies is integral to that goal.

CONCLUSION

Together with product and service performance, pricing is the main determinant of a brand's value to its consumers or users. However, price has no relevance in isolation. It acts to translate products and services into propositions that can be valued. The value equation is instrumental to assessing value in that it links relative quality to relative price and can be modified by any change to the marketing mix.

Offensive Pricing requires a high quality of analysis and research, a deep understanding of external customers and internal costs, and a commitment to structured thinking to develop alternative pricing scenarios well ahead of decision dates. Offensive Marketers need to have a strong understanding of key concepts that facilitate pricing decisions. These include: price elasticity, trade-off or conjoint analysis, econometrics, activity-based costing, sensitivity analysis, and competitor analysis. The Offensive Marketer also needs to understand the applicability of the eight key principles of Offensive Pricing.

Knowing the price dynamics of your markets will allow you to draw general conclusions about the likely price sensitivity of your products and services, which can enable you to analyze price/volume relationships. Selecting price segments to compete in should be a matter not only of profitability but fit with your company's strengths as well as the competitive marketplace. Achieving clarity with pricing from the consumer perspective, targeting price changes as well as assessing the pricing alternatives, will create the most optimum pricing package and value option. Pricing should create incremental sales and avoid cannibalizing your firm's other revenues and should optimize your return on capacity, especially on perishable products because of inherent product or fast-changing technologies. Consideration of online business models should be assessed to move excess inventory or increase sales.

Lastly, following the five-step process briefly outlined at the end of the chapter will permit you to incorporate the principles and strategic design of Offensive Pricing.

15

Offensive Channel Marketing

INTRODUCTION

This is the last of the seven chapters on Offensive Execution, the "E" of POISE.

This chapter discusses the fundamental and key principles of Offensive Channel Marketing. Understanding the role of marketing channels—how they serve customers and add value to brands—is important to strategic decision-making with respect to channel selection and management. Who actually "owns" the consumer is key to channel profitability. Exercising influence over channels and developing new channels are key ingredients to ongoing market success.

As an Offensive Marketer, it is critical to align market and channel plans and to manage brands consistently across channels, particularly as channels change or as channel influence grows. Channel decisions relate directly to building competencies and partnerships and managing resources out of long-term commitments and relationships. As market dynamics and technology changes, market success and sustained profitability are often positively or negatively impacted by channel decisions. Modifying channel partnerships or operational elements is sometimes called for and may be more easily done than the creation of distinctly new products to meet profitability and growth requirements.

CHANNEL MARKETING: ITS ROLE AND FUNCTION

Channels exist to serve customers, and like building brands, channels exist to "build superior customer value very efficiently for above-average profits." Channel analysis and selection as well as the ongoing management of channel relationships are vital roles for the Offensive Marketer.

The Role of Marketing Channels

Marketing channels exist to link producers to consumers. They vary greatly in complexity and efficiency. The channel for electricity is simple and almost ideal: the producer has mass distribution and the consumer has instant availability, literally at the flick of a switch. By contrast, the channel for manmade fibers is extremely complex: the chain runs through producers, spinners, dyers, weavers or knitters, garment manufacturers, and retailers until it finally reaches the consumer.

This chapter will concentrate on channel steps from the finished product to the consumer. Marketing channels are generally described as "sets of interdependent organizations involved in the process of making a product or service available for use or consumption."[1]

---

[1] Philip Kotler, *Marketing Management, the Millennium Edition*, Prentice-Hall, 2000.

These "sets of interdependent organizations," or networks, represent steps in the distribution process that account for between 15 percent and 40 percent of retail price in product and service markets.[2]

Why are channels necessary? Channels are necessary because the producer is sometimes a long distance from the consumer and because skills differ by channel type. Many producers are not skilled in channel efficiency, nor do they have the financial resources to market directly to the consumer. Despite direct to consumer initiatives, including the Web, dealerships in the automobile industry, for example, continue to be integral to sales. Manufacturers would be hard-pressed to take over the myriad of dealership functions even if they had the financial wherewithal to do so. In other industries, channel intermediaries have skills and competencies to create efficiencies in distributing goods, which are not often available to producers. Further, producers may not reap the accustomed financial rewards by directing their investment toward channel requirements. Channel profit stems from managing efficient and intermediary relationships, usually not strong competencies of producers.

Marketing channels have five major roles.

1. **Consumer access.** The primary role of channels is to provide consumers with convenient access to products and services. Channels often gather information on current and potential customers and on competitor initiatives.
2. **Presentation.** The final channel should present products and services in good condition in an appropriate purchase environment.
3. **Endorsement.** The very fact of stocking a product or service implies a degree of endorsement by the channel. This may add luster if the channel is a prestigious one, like Tiffany's or Balducci's, but have negative effects if the channel is a low-price discounter that does not match with the product's image. In addition, the level of endorsement for the producer/manufacturer can vary, from simply stocking the item, to promoting it, and to using the channel brand name. The channel gives its highest level of endorsement to a producer/manufacturer whose goods it brands with its own name. However, here the

---

[2] C. Bucklin, S. DeFalco, and Trip Levis, "Are You Tough Enough to Manage Your Own Channels?" *McKinsey Quarterly*, vol. 1, 1996.

producer pays a heavy price in loss of consumer influence, interface, and potential relationship with the end user.

4. **Additional services.** The channel may provide additional services that add to the producer's proposition. These may include breaking bulk quantities into redistributable amounts, providing the opportunity for customer trial and customer advice, offering customer guarantees in the form of warranties, after-sales services, or opportunities to return goods, and providing financial packages in the form of credit or installment purchases.

5. **Money.** Channels collect money from consumers or other channel members, take ownership of goods and services, pay producers, and assume risks associated with channel functions.

Types of Marketing Channels

Most products or services reach the consumer by more than one type of outlet. Airline tickets, clothes, and financial products all have expanded points of sale direct to the consumer. In the past, brick and mortar stores and outlets were the predominant channel. In the airline industry, for example, these were supplemented by phone sales, travel agents, internal travel departments of large companies, or at the airport. Clothes have been sold at a variety of outlets, including department stores, sport shops, and boutiques, as well as by mail order. Financial services have been sold direct over the phone, in-home from a salesperson, and from independent advisers, banks, or other financial institutions. With the growth of the Internet and e-commerce, companies in all industries have even more access to the consumer and new intermediaries have emerged.

For the majority of markets, one type of channel may be predominant, even though others of less significance may exist and may in fact lend support to the purchasing decision. As online channels become more efficient, secure, and user-friendly, people are increasingly looking across channels to glean the information needed to make a final purchasing decision. For example, in home appliance, automobile, or financial services, consumers often use online sources to select possible sellers, and identify those in closest proximity with the most competitive pricing or most attractive value proposition, prior to actually visiting an on-site location.

Channels Exist to Serve Consumers

The purpose of channels is similar to that of brands. Both exist to "build superior customer value very efficiently for above-average profits." Producers, intermediaries, and retailers all have different roles and objectives, but their primary purpose is to serve the end user.

What are the fundamental needs consumers or users expect to be satisfied by marketing channels? These will vary by type of market and consumer, but are likely to include the following eight factors.

1. **Clarity.** Consumers look to the channel for a clear product statement, which will address their needs.
2. **Convenience.** Consumers look for convenience in location and accessibility including 24/7 hours; well-qualified staff; and a con-ducive, secure shopping experience, whether it be online or off.
3. **Range.** Purchasers look for choice and selection of relevant products and services.
4. **Price.** Consumers look for a range of price points, payment methods, and good value.
5. **Quality.** Purchasers seek quality as it relates to price and value. Making quality transparent is one of the main objectives of the channel.
6. **Service.** Purchasers seek helpful attitudes, speedy transaction time, and relevant services surrounding the purchasing decision.
7. **Environment.** Consumers look to easy to use, clean, and "fit for the purpose" purchasing environments, whether it be virtual or in tangible space. Cleanliness not only relates to the physical environment but also to the virtual presentation of a purchas-ing interaction whether it is experienced in dialogue with a real person or constructed purely from digitized response.
8. **Image.** Consumers look to see whether the image portrayed by the channel fits with the product or service category and expe-rience as well as the buying occasion.

Customer Needs Often Require a Multi-Channel Strategy

Companies in the past often sold through only one channel to a single market. With the ability to segment and target markets, companies seek out channel alternatives to gain more customized selling opportunities, to lower channel costs where it is strategic to do so, and to increase market accessibility and coverage. Often retailers segment markets to meet the requirements of their target consumers by developing propositions that combine the eight needs in different ways. For example, Neiman Marcus, a high-end clothing and accessory department store does this through style, range, quality, and service. Kohl's, on the other hand, achieves this via a more narrow range of product, a basic environment, reasonable quality, low pricing, and service. Both retailers have a clear and differentiated proposition, and offer good value to their consumers.

Consistent with their product's image and branding, producers exploit a range of distribution channels. This is called a multi-channel strategy, which can optimize market coverage, provide customization, and minimize cost. Companies often select channels based on customer size or sales; a direct sales force may be used for large customers, telemarketing, e-mail, or targeted advertising in specialty magazines to reach mid-sized firms and distributors to reach small customers. For instance, a producer of a high-end home-building tool may sell to large-scale commercial builders through specialty distributors. Simultaneously, it may sell to residential builders through a contractor supply distributor and to small-scale home improvement companies or individuals through a home improvement center such as Lowe's or Home Depot.

Channels Add Value to a Brand's Consumer Proposition

Every retailer has the potential to offer the producer access and visibility to the consumer. For most mass-market brands, especially those relying on impulse purchase, maximum availability is an essential element of brand building. Many of these brands, from chocolate bars to pharmaceuticals, distribute their products through extensive networks of privately operated and owned distribution enterprises. Brands ultimately are purchased by the consumer in grocery store chains and local drugstores. Coca-Cola has, from its beginning, pursued a policy of placing its products "within an arm's length of desire." By contrast, for high-image brands like Chanel or Tiffany, restricted availability may be a key strategy, and the channels selected will reinforce that exclusivity.

Some retail channels move well beyond the basic function of availability, and greatly enhance a brand's image or proposition: entertainment stores such as Disney target young children and their parents, providing the informal browsing atmosphere required prior to a purchasing decision with demonstration units, spotlighting, interactive opportunities and fixtures, video clips, and music, which match the product's personality and image and help to further build the brand. The Sharper Image, historically a catalogue company, provides retailing experiences where customers can touch, feel, and experience the products, as well as get expert advice from well-trained staff, prior to a purchase.

The eight main consumer needs targeted by marketing channels are the areas where channels can add value to brands. These areas often involve important trade-offs, like availability versus image, price versus range, and price versus service levels. Producers and manufacturers need to make decisions with respect to these trade-offs in determining their channel strategy.

Customer Influence Affects Channel Profitability

Not so long ago, retailers were passive channels that received goods from producers and resold them to the public. The producer was very much in control and the channel played, at best, second fiddle because private labeling was undeveloped and producer brands were all that were available. However, with the growing concentration of retail and its buying power, increasing trade marketing sophistication, the erosion of media channels for reaching mass audiences, and the growth of private labeling in the form of well-received, often lower-priced brands that compete with manufacturers' brands, the situation has drastically changed. The division between the producer and the retailer is becoming blurred.

Retailers like Sears, Kmart, and Wal-Mart specifically brand and market their own products, using manufacturers as subcontractors. Retailers regard the producer's "ultimate consumer" as their own customer and have become "the customer's buying agent, not the producer's selling agent." In many cases they own the consumer, and are seen as the category authority.

In fact, the use of private labels has become a strong tool of large discounters to increase customer loyalty and pull them away from more traditional brands and producers. Private label brands can also bring down prices of the more traditional brands. For instance, Wal-Mart—the Bentonville, Arkansas, retailer that is the largest in the world, three times bigger than its nearest competitor—is increasingly focused on developing and promoting its in-house, or private label, brands across many categories.[3] These categories have included snack foods, soft drinks, cat food, and batteries as well as health and beauty aids, toilet paper, and detergent. Besides private labels, in-house brands also include exclusive licenses and, more recently, other companies' brands that have been acquired. The beauty of private labeling from Wal-Mart's perspective is that there are no intermediaries, the producers are often the same companies that produce brand-name products, and there is often very little advertising expenditure.[4]

Wal-Mart's goal is to attract more cost-conscious customers as it continues to look for opportunities where over-priced, branded consumer products create the opportunity for successful private-labels that cost less and don't skimp on quality. From the brand-name producer's perspective, Wal-Mart's move into private labels will negatively impact its pricing as it forces prices down. In addition, although their intention must be to work with Wal-Mart and other retailers as integral channel partners, their strategy must be to balance channel partnering with building brand awareness and loyalty in order to be able to continue to exert influence over a strong retail sector.

As the private-label initiative shows, the issue of "who owns the consumer" is not an academic one, since it fundamentally affects the division of industry profitability between producers and other participants in the marketing channel. In practice, of course, no one "owns" consumers, who are free agents. However, share of industry profitability is affected by consumer influence. How is this influence achieved, and by whom? Table 15-1 summarizes the main weapons in this battleground.

Branded producers hold two good weapons in this battle for consumer influence: strong brands and advertising. They can also

---

[3] Constance L. Hays, "The Heavyweight Goes In-House, Wal-Mart Bulks Up on Private Labels," *The New York Times*, July 8, 2001.
[4] Id.

Table 15-1 How Consumers Are Influenced and By Whom

Key influence areas	Main wielders of influence areas		
	Branded producers	Retailers or distributors	Intermediaries
Strong branded product or service	✓✓	✓	
Brand advertising	✓✓	✓	
Direct Marketing	✓	✓✓	
Direct contact		✓✓	
Availability	✓	✓✓	✓✓
Presentation	✓	✓✓	
Customer service	✓	✓✓	
Pricing	✓	✓	

market direct to customers by conventional phone, wireless messaging, e-mail, direct mail, or personal contact. And they can influence availability, presentation, and pricing by exploiting the strength of their consumer and brand franchise with channel owners. Additionally, producers have operational tools that create opportunities for competitive advantage. Electronic data interchange (EDI) has become an important tool for manufacturers to manage inventory, shipments, and related costs in working with strong retailers. EDI, along with Continuous Replenishment Programs (CRP), which permit replenishment of product on the basis of actual or forecasted sales and other integrated systems, comprise what is called Efficient Consumer Response (ECR). These systems allow a producer to build stronger ties with retail customers and, in practicality, enter into partnership arrangements with them to build efficiency into their delivery systems.

Intermediaries have conventionally had little direct influence on the consumer, since their primary role is to provide services for producers or retailers. Intermediaries have a difficult position with respect to directly influencing the consumer and will continue to be squeezed both for profitability and consumer access by retailers and distributors.

The primary determinant of how industry profitability is allocated is the relative brand strength of producer versus retailer or distributor. Strong-branded producers, like Microsoft, Nike, and American Express tend to have above-average industry margins, even though they market via strong channels, with a powerful influence over consumers.

Weak-branded producers struggle even to achieve availability, and usually have to pay heavily for it.

Branders Have Channel Ownership Options

There are at least five alternative channel ownership options open to branders, whether they are producers/retailers or distributors.

1. **Own all brands, no channels.** This is the traditional route for branders of consumer goods. Estée Lauder, Goodyear, and Procter & Gamble are examples.
2. **Own all brands and all channels.** Ikea is an example of a producer/retailer that owns the branding of all products marketed in its stores. Others include The Gap, The Body Shop, and John Deere.
3. **Own channels and some of the brands marketed through them.** J.C. Penny and Wal-Mart control their channels and market a range of brands, including their own.
4. **Own no brands and only part of channel.** This is an unattractive strategy, providing minimum influence over the consumer. Small retailers usually lack the scale or resources to develop their own brands; neither do they have much influence over their marketing channels, since they typically source from powerful wholesalers or distributors.
5. **Own brands and some marketing channels.** American Express has its own travel and exchange outlets, but relies mainly on non-owned channels in marketing its cards. McDonald's owns most of its stores, but franchises others. Levi Strauss has developed its own Original Levi Stores, but these are a minority of its channels. It has recently moved online to strengthen its marketing and channel outreach as have many retailer/producers in industries such as clothing, wine, vacation/entertainment packages, furniture, financial services, and automobiles. In fact, the automotive giants have partnered with dealerships, their traditional channel providers, to offer purchasing opportunities on the Web. The same holds true for many other industries that are being creative in combining conventional customer outreach channels with Web initiatives.

With respect to channel strategy, the important question is what changes are your firm or competitors likely to make in the next decade? Has a channel strategy been articulated and acted-upon? With technology changing and new channels of distribution and marketing becoming more viable, distribution decisions have a long-term impact on corporate competitiveness and need to be reviewed periodically. New approaches to distribution are often easier to develop than superior products, and they can lead to equally large breakthroughs in profitability. Changes in customer purchasing patterns, new competition, or products moving into later product life cycle stages, can all trigger needed channel modifications. Failure to take advantage of new channel arrangements, or modifications, can lead to less future profitability.

Producers and Distributors Compete Within and Across Channels

In their efforts to raise influence with the consumer and improve the presentation of their products and services, branded producers are increasing investment in direct consumer marketing. They are also establishing direct-selling channels with consumers, opening up telephone help and advice lines, online chat communities, wireless messaging, and even investing in retail or wholesale marketing channels.

Retailers and distributors in turn are strengthening their consumer brand images, exploiting their own branded products and services, capitalizing on their improving consumer databases and ability to mine that data and add new consumer-facing services.

The result is a broadening of the competitive field. Tomorrow's competitive scenario within marketing channels will be very different from that of today. Table 15-2 shows some of those changes.

In this increasingly competitive environment, where the dividing lines between branded producers and marketing channels are becoming blurred, and companies are simultaneously competing and cooperating with each other, there has been a trend toward partnerships between producers and distributors.

These partnerships usually involve a joint effort to identify cost reductions in the supply chain, and to increase efficiency of consumer presentation and promotion. ECR, as discussed above, in the consumer goods category, is an example of activity that can offer branders the opportunity to gain competitive advantage over

Table 15-2   Changes in Competitive Scenario Within and Across Channels

Issue	Yesterday	Tomorrow
Private label growth	Branded producer dominates premium price sectors, private label confined to low end	Private label competes in all price sectors, increasingly targets profitable top end
Cross-industry competition	Supermarkets compete with other supermarkets	Supermarkets compete with bars, fast food, restaurants, gas station food marts
Branded producers' isolation from consumer	Branded producer markets mainly via third party channels	Branded producers go direct, buy into part of distribution channels, consumer service lines
Growth of direct and Internet marketing	Limited use except for high ticket items	Increasing use by branded producers and retailers at all price points

their smaller rivals as well as share the cost benefits of greater efficiency with retailers.

In the past, supply chain management and logistics were seen solely from the perspective of physical distribution and a source of expense. With the expanded use of technology, specifically IT, excellence in supply chain management and logistics are seen as sources of competitive advantage. With this understanding, "supply chains" are seen in competition with one another rather than single companies.[5] Accordingly, "the route to competitive advantage lies in leveraging the combined capabilities of supply chain partners."[6] However, such close integration across diverse companies' functions requires a strong degree of cooperation, openness, and information sharing for shared decision-making not often seen in the more adversarial market positioning of many companies. Despite these impediments, companies in many industries are using newer operational models in seeking out both superior customer satisfaction and company profitability by using strategic, digital supply chain designs and building relationships where none had previously existed.[7]

---

[5] For example, see Professor Martin Christopher's comments in an interview conducted by Management Centre Europe, Brussels in an excerpt from *The Executive Issue*, "Why Supply Chains Compete, Not Companies," edited by Liliane Van Cauwenbergh, at http://www.mce.be/news/article20.htm.
[6] Id.
[7] A good source describing the supply chain revolution is David Bovet and Joseph Martha, *Value Nets, Breaking the Supply Chain to Unlock Hidden Profits*, Mercer Management Consulting and John Wiley & Sons, 2000.

Channel Marketing: The Need for Strong Business-to-Business Marketing Skills

While meeting the needs of consumers or users is always the ultimate target of most marketers, channels guard the gate. Offensive Marketers need to access and motivate channels in order to reach users.

In the marketplace, this requires two-stage marketing involving both marketing to channel opportunities and retailers, as well as marketing to consumers or end users. Some companies are good at mass marketing and target marketing but weak at Channel Marketing.

Marketing to channels requires skills needed for successful business-to-business marketing, as opposed to marketing to the mass consumer or targeted consumer audience. Some of these skills include among others: a clear understanding of the customer's needs and strategy; a compelling positioning of the advantages of your firm's product; knowledge of competitors' offers; an understanding of the economics of your product from the customer's perspective; an ability to tailor products to customer requirements and operating and fulfillment systems; an ability to fit a new product within an existing product range; and after-sales support.

KEY PRINCIPLES OF OFFENSIVE CHANNEL MARKETING

There are seven key principles to emphasize when it comes to Offensive Channel Marketing:

1. **Establish clear channel requirements for your brands.** In selecting marketing channels for new products or services, or in reviewing channel arrangements, producers need to consider six key factors: exposure to target customers, performance requirements, influence, flexibility, producer profit, and distributor needs. Each one is assessed below:
   - **Exposure to target consumers.** From the producer's perspective, the primary purpose is to make products or services

available and visible to *target* consumers. A good product may fail because it is in the wrong channel or not exposed to the people most likely to buy it.

- **Performance requirements.** Producers want products to reach the consumer in high-quality condition. In addition, they may wish the channel to provide certain skills, which are a necessary part of the sale. Insurance companies operating through insurance brokers, banks, or accountants will expect a high level of know-how about their products, as well as high ethical standards. Pharmaceutical companies marketing their products through medical doctors similarly seek quality control.
- **Influence.** A producer's influence over its channels depends upon degree of ownership, the number of links in the channel, and the consumer appeal of its products or services. Large and powerful companies like BMW, Honda, or Coca-Cola have a lot of influence over their independent distributors or franchisees, because their strong consumer appeal provides the channel with a large profit opportunity. At minimum, producers need enough bargaining power to achieve their aims of exposure to the right consumers, maintenance of product quality, and profitability.
- **Flexibility.** Channel decisions are often long term in effect. Even so, it is desirable to retain maximum flexibility to alter channel flows and focus.
- **Producer profit.** Offensive Marketers seek the type and mix of distribution channels that gives them maximum revenue at minimum cost over the long term.
- **Channel needs.** Owners of distribution channels usually have clear marketing and profit strategies. They will not bother with products or services which fail to fit these strategies. As retailing strength has grown, being number one or two in your market means the difference between getting shelf space and not. The growth of private labels has also made it more difficult for smaller brands to compete for visibility and access to the consumer.

2. **Use Quantified Portfolio Analysis (QPA) to determine channel strategies.** It is as important to segment channels in the same way that it is important to segment markets. Offensive Marketers reap success by using a five-step market segmentation process described more fully in Chapter 9. The criteria for

assessing channel attractiveness are similar to those used for evaluating market sector attractiveness.

As with other QPAs, the Offensive Marketer builds a list of criteria representing the ideal channel with criteria totaling 100 percent. She then scores each possible channel on each criterion. Figure 15-1 shows a typical channel evaluation portfolio analysis.

3. **Ensure alignment between channel and market strategies and plans.** Channel and customer promotions are usually developed by Sales people; market and brand plans by Marketing people. It is fatal to build these plans in isolation. Sales and Marketing executives need to discuss channel and market goals early in the planning process, and to iron out any inconsistencies in vision and objectives.

Figure 15-1
Typical Channel Evaluation Portfolio Analysis

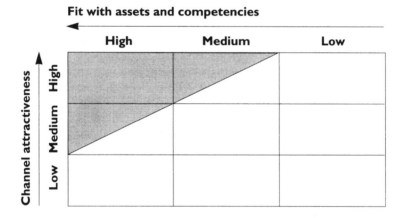

For instance, in the example shown in Figure 15-2, suppose that the product is a category of frozen food. The Marketing Department sees a big opportunity to increase sales in small, single-serve packages. As it happens, the majority of the small-pack market is sold by small independent stores, served by wholesalers. And wholesalers are the lowest channel priority for the Sales Department. This issue would need to be identified and resolved before time was wasted on drawing up detailed brand plans for building a small-pack business.

4. **Find ways to exercise influence over your channels.** Influence translates into bargaining power, and this enables producers to achieve their marketing objectives through channels at minimum cost. The most powerful bargaining chip any producer

Figure 15-2
*Major German
frozen foods
company: channel
portfolio analysis*

Fit with assets and competencies

	High	Medium	Low
High	Multiple A Multiple B	Home delivery	
Medium		Multiple C	Freezer centres
Low	Large independents		Wholesalers

Channel attractiveness (vertical axis, top to bottom: High, Medium, Low)

can have is a strong franchise with the channel's customers. Improving a brand's consumer value creates a virtuous trigger, where increasing consumer strength converts into greater channel influence for the producer.

Another way to enhance your company's position in channels is to help build the channel's total business through new product innovation and greater marketing impact.

5. **Tailor your products and services to channel needs.** Many producers market to a number of distribution channels, often with different requirements. Skillful Channel Marketers identify the needs of channels for different products, packages, sizes, services, and supply arrangements, and match the potential revenue benefits of providing these against the extra cost. The Offensive Channel Marketer faces similar issues to global branders, who try to balance efficiencies of standard international propositions against the need to meet specific local requirements.

Table 15-3 summarizes the type of issues Channel Marketers need to resolve.

Channels offer outstanding opportunities for the Offensive Marketer who sets clear strategies, innovates in response to change, and executes with strength and resolution. The keys to success are a deep understanding of customer and consumer needs, and skill in meeting these needs *efficiently*. It is easy, but ineffective, when managing channel relationships, to respond fully to every conceivable channel need and, in doing so, to destroy the operational economics of your business. You should always look hard for tailoring opportunities that are highly

Table 15-3 Key Issues for Channel Marketers

Strategic areas	Issues
Product or service range	• What type of range best fits the consumer demographics of the channel or individual store? • How wide a range can the channel handle and merchandise?
Packaging or presentation	• What product sizes does the channel need? • What case configurations do intermediaries prefer? • What information do intermediaries need to pass on to their customers?
Pricing	• How does the channel or account pricing strategy fit with the producer's strategy? • How can any pricing conflicts across channels be resolved?
Consumer service levels	• What services does the channel offer to its consumers? • How can the producer enhance these?
Channel service levels	• Do products fit channel's handling systems and space availability? • What frequency of delivery is needed? • How far ahead are new products or services planned? • How can producer and channel co-operate to maximize efficiency of supply chain and sell-out to consumer?
Branding strategy	• What role do producer's brands play in channel's overall branding strategy, which may include private label? • Is the channel seeking high end, niche, mass market or discount brands?
Channel and category development	• What can producers do to build the channel, or the categories in which they compete?

valued by channels and that will increase your firm's channel influence, but involve your company in little added cost.

6. **Ensure consistent presentation of your core brand proposition across channels.** Tailoring brands to channels should be done without compromising your firm's core value proposition. Consumers shop across channels and will be confused by major inconsistencies. They will understand that they can buy your brand more cheaply in a discounter than in a full-service specialty shop, but they will be puzzled if they are buying a product and there is a significant difference in price without corresponding value. Purchasing prices over the Internet or from a hard-copy catalog should not be significantly different.

If you have a major point of difference, ensure that it is exploited through every channel. For instance, Coca-Cola's glass waistline bottle had been a distinctive icon for over half a century, but for many years was abandoned when translated to commodity plastic bottles for supermarkets. This error has now been corrected with the offering of the traditional glass bottle in many market sectors.

7. **Seek to develop new channels.** Companies entering new markets may find that existing channels do not meet their needs. They therefore innovate their own. McDonald's and Avon have done this successfully. McDonald's can now be found along major arteries within the confines of a multiple vendor facility, smaller service stations, bowling alleys, ferries, and airports. Avon's door-to-door sales system had to be adapted to changes in women's working habits. It now achieves significant U.S. revenues outside the home, mainly in offices. Similarly, IBM's exclusive reliance on a well-trained sales force to sell to corporate accounts had to be modified with the introduction of personal computing and its lower-priced hardware and software.

Companies operating in established channels may also innovate new ones to extend their product reach, improve its presentation, or reach a particular target group. Dell Computers innovated the direct-to-consumer approach using the Internet and telephone as sales channels supported by express mail services and well-trained local repair personnel. Another classic example of developing new market channels is Starbucks, discussed in an earlier chapter. Starbucks has established a new model of coffee delivery to community-based coffee shops where comfortable seating, premium products including specialty coffee, and baked goods have redefined the experience of coffee delivery.

SEVEN-STEP PROCESS FOR OFFENSIVE CHANNEL MARKETING

This section will outline how to translate the principles of Offensive Channel Marketing into action by using a seven-step process. The Offensive Marketer would seek to partner with Sales in moving through the process.

Step 1: Review and Analyze Existing Channels

This step involves defining channels, identifying total channel revenue and estimating your company's channel share, sales, and profit margins. Channel definitions should be precise and indicate how different channels interact and support each other. It usually makes sense to define any individual outlet accounting for more than 10 percent of your firm's total revenue as a channel.

Channel profitability also needs to be studied carefully. In many companies, quality of channel profit data is poor, with major costs allocated by some arbitrary measure like channel share of total company revenue. Activity-based costing is necessary to determine the real cost of selling, supply chain, and materials specifically produced for individual channels. Unless you fully understand your channel profitability, you cannot sensibly determine how to allocate investment between or among them.

Analyzing profitability by trade channel enables your firm to get the right balance between profit levels and volume growth. All too often, the fastest-growing channels are the least profitable because they attract so much competition. A well-run company will review its profitability by channel at least every six-month period and make decisions on future modifications as a result.

Table 15-4 is an example of an analysis of profitability by trade channel. The allocation of selling and distribution costs has been done through activity-based costing.

In Table 15-4, differences in margin by channel are very wide. As a result of this analysis, a number of decisions have been made by this firm:

- With respect to Channel A, promotion spending was reduced as a percentage of sales, since it was expensive and not particularly effective.
- With respect to Channel B, priority was increased, new account targets set, and frequency of sales calls raised. Because of its declining trend, this channel had been somewhat neglected.

Table 15-4 Analysis of Profitability by Trade Channel

| | Distribution channel | | | |
	A	B	C	D
Channel volume trend	Flat	Down	Up	Up
Cases per delivery	203	175	1125	37
Gross margin (%)	31.7	40.2	26.4	25.4
Operating expenses (%)	19.7	13.4	7.8	23.0
Operating profit (%)	12.0	26.8	18.6	2.4

- With respect to Channel D, delivery arrangements were renegotiated to achieve larger drops and a target was set to expand stocked product range and to increase cases per drop. A hard line was to be taken on discount arrangements, and selling costs were to be reduced by changing to telesales and e-mail messaging.

Having collected relevant channel data, it is important to draw up a channel map. This summarizes by channel total channel sales, your company's revenue, market share, share trend, and profit margin.

The final stages of Step 1 are to summarize key needs for each channel, identify how well your company meets these needs, highlight current and potential channel conflicts, and evaluate how channels add value to your firm's brands.

Step 2: Project Future Trends

Look to the long term, two to five years ahead. Evaluate each major channel individually, covering the following issues:

- How will company sales change over time and how does this impact channel sales increases over time?
- How will company market-share increases change channel requirements and profit pictures?
- What are your company's channel strategies and how will they change over time? Are changes in channel structure and availability reflected in your company's channel strategies moving forward?
- What channel conflicts are likely to appear over the long term and how can they be resolved?
- How do the key channels add value from the perspective of the customer? How will this value change over time?

Major future marketing trends in most channels include:

- Growth of mass retail distribution.
- Reduction in number of channel steps, driven by need for greater speed and lower cost. Intermediaries are especially at risk. Some will secure their future position by buying retailers or entering into long-term partnerships with producers.

- Growth in direct selling to consumers, stimulated by desire of producers to increase their influence in order to gain a higher share of total channel profit margin.
- Technology development accelerates channel evolution. Data networks are already enabling end users to bypass traditional channels and deal directly with manufacturers and service providers.
- Regulation or de-regulation of channels to spur competition. This has been of particular importance in the pharmaceutical industry, utilities and the financial/insurance sectors as well as the telecom markets.
- Regional and global channel development by retailers. Channel creation and decisions are often more complex in the global context in light of the variation in channel structures from country to country or region to region. In addition, transportation and physical distribution become more onerous because of geographical distances between production facilities and the ultimate end user. The use of electronic linkages between customers, supply/partners, and producers has become key to efficient channel management.
- More automated consumer access including interactive kiosks and Web-based self-help initiatives.
- Greater concentration of ownership within given channels, but increasing competition and cooperation *across* channels. Banking and the financial services sectors are examples.

[A note on e-marketplaces as they grow in importance. Business-to-business (b2b) marketplaces or digital exchanges are growing at a rapid pace. They are industry-specific online exchanges that link buyers and suppliers and most often charge a transaction fee for facilitating the exchange. As the demand for a 24/7 economy expands, companies must manage real-time adjustments and improve inter-company information and collaboration. As companies move to e-marketplaces as the information hub for managing networked relationships, they need to improve on expensive enterprise applications for end-to-end channel management, which may include fore-casting models and ongoing point-of-sale transaction data. The term "extended enterprise resource planning" has emerged to describe tools for creating this seamlessly linked channel network. The Offensive Marketer has a strong role to play in influencing the formation and management of these linked enterprises as a growing trend in supply chain and channel selection.]

Step 3: Prioritize Channels

Quantified Portfolio Analysis is the primary tool to use (see discussion of QPA earlier) for prioritizing channels.

Step 4: Develop Three- or Five-Year Channel Plan

Channel plan time-scale should fit with your firm's short- and longer-term corporate business plan. Similar principles and processes apply to channel plans as to market plans, and the two should be developed together (see Chapter 8).

Creating a channel plan involves performing a Business Analysis (Step 1 above); Anticipating the Future (Step 2 above); as well as Opportunity Identification, Setting Objectives, Building Strategies, and Developing Plans.

In the opportunity identification phase, the Offensive Marketer will focus on the means to help build priority channels and to strengthen the firm's position in them.

Setting objectives means establishing short- and long-term revenue, and share and profit objectives by channel, just as you would do by market.

Building strategies involves exploiting opportunities in priority channels and determining how to achieve your firm's channel objectives. You would also develop sub-strategies by channel, for topics like product or service range and availability, presentation, pricing, or consumer service levels.

Developing plans would cover specific plans to support strategies, development projects, as well as the development of quarterly milestones.

The bulk of this work may be done in conjunction with the Sales Department, and with the full knowledge of market plans being developed concurrently. Close cooperation between these departments and constant updating, is essential to ensure that channel and market plans are closely aligned both in time frame and purpose.

Step 5: Synchronize Channel and Market Plans

As mentioned above, market and channel plans should be developed concurrently and in concert. One of the best opportunities to work concertedly is for senior Marketing and Sales people to create an opportunity workshop to share their thinking and visions and coordinate activity. For example, if a soft-drinks brand plans to greatly strengthen its position in the single-serve impulse sector, the Sales Department will need to take this into account in developing its channel plans for convenience stores and service stations. Equally, if the Sales Department sees great potential in a new direct channel, the Marketing Department will need to consider which markets to focus on, and what direct products or services to develop and how and where to communicate its benefits.

Once overall objectives and strategies are developed, Marketing and Sales Departments should exchange outline documents and meet for a Strategy and Plans Workshop. Results would be *market* objectives, strategies, and plans—broken down by channel; and channel objectives, strategies, and plans—broken down by market.

Step 6: Convert to Customer Plans

Once channel plans have been agreed to and integrated with market plans, the next step is to develop plans for major customers or accounts. These would be done by national account managers. Senior sales staff would use judgment as to who qualified as a major customer.

As with channel plans, *account* plans should be developed in close cooperation with Marketing, and integrated with *brand* plans. An outline format for a customer plan would be developed by the national account manager, working closely with brand managers, with final approval by the senior executive of sales. Content issues would address the following ten items and issues:

1. Identify the customer.
2. Provide customer facts including total sales, profits and trend, number of outlets by type, if applicable. Major competitors should be identified.
3. Identify customer strategies both overall and by major category including attitudes to suppliers, marketing, and consumer strategies. Key strengths and identified weaknesses should be noted.
4. Discuss customer position in your company's categories: customer sales and share of total category in your firm's main markets.
5. Evaluate your firm's position with the customer: By major market category, what are your company's sales, market share, net profit return, and trends relating to each?

6. Perform a SWOT analysis of your company with respect to the customer.

7. Identify key future priorities and objectives with respect to the customer: what future priority will your firm give this customer? What are your company's future objectives with the customer over the next one, three, and five years in sales, profit, market share, partnership, joint activities, and service levels?

8. Identify key strategies for meeting objectives: these would include but not be limited to sub-strategies for branding, key brand development, product range, supply chain, marketing support, and customer service.

9. Describe next year's plan. This would include total revenue by brand and marketing support spend specific to account and target profit margin. For each brand, the totality of its revenue by channel and major customer would be the same as the brand's revenue budget. (Surprisingly, in many companies, this exercise is either not done at all, or when done, the numbers fail to add up.)

10. Describe next year's activity. Activities by major brand for each customer would be specified, and action milestones set. Joint sales forecasting, entry to a major new category or joint direct marketing initiatives would be included.

Step 7: Monitor Results

Set up a simple monitoring system, measuring progress on the annual and three- or five-year plan. Constructing a scorecard with respect to each strategy would be important. In doing so, it is critical to be creative and identify those elements that are important to measure and which will reflect the information your firm wishes to collect about performance and goals both for feedback as well as target purposes.

CONCLUSION

This chapter has demonstrated that channel analysis, understanding, and selection are pivotal decisions for the Offensive Marketer. With changes happening in technology, channel influence, and retail versus producer power, vigilance and creativity are required to manage channel relationships, efficiency, and effectiveness at creating value for the consumer as well as profitability for the producer.

The fundamentals of Offensive Channel Marketing include the following:

- Channels exist to serve customers and to "build superior customer value very efficiently for above-average profits."
- Channels are segmented just like markets. They segment to achieve differentiation and to serve differing customer needs.
- Channels can add value to a brand's consumer proposition by offering image, services, and point-of-sale impact.
- Influence over the final consumer affects allocation of industry profitability.
- Branders have the option of owning their own channels or participating in channel relationships and networks.
- Producers and distributors compete within and across channels and this competition is quickly broadening.
- Lastly, for producers, channel marketing requires business-to-business marketing relationship building and negotiating skills.

Through the application and use of the key principles of Offensive Marketing, Offensive Marketers align channel and market strategies through coordinated and concerted action between Marketing functions and Sales. They establish clear channel requirements that must be met to efficiently and effectively meet the needs of the brand. Treating channels like markets allows the Offensive Marketer to decide major channel and customer priorities. Understanding that channel influence equals bargaining power in the fight for industry profits, the Offensive Marketer finds ways to increase channel influence and create tailored propositions that are aligned with channel needs. To address continuing channel change, the Offensive Marketer seeks new channels to increase brand availability and profitability.

By following the seven-step process outlined at the end of this chapter, the fundamentals of Offensive Channel Marketing and its key principles become imbedded in corporate analysis and decision-making.

Post-Script
Offensive Marketing:
The Way Ahead

There are a number of enduring truths about the power of the marketing approach, which underpin business success and drive the principles, process, and tools of Offensive Marketing. Here is a brief description of nine of these enduring truths.

1. **Superior customer value is essential to corporate survival and success.** In today's competitive markets, consumers have an ever-widening range of choice. They seek superior and constantly improving value. Companies failing to meet this standard won't survive in the long term because customers won't choose them.

2. **Superior or above-average profit growth is achieved by aligning strengths to opportunities, and by excellent cost management.** You will recall the Marketing Alignment Process (MAP)—which matches strengths (assets and competencies) to market opportunities—and how it creates the possibility of optimizing profits by prioritizing market segments and channels that are best suited to your firm's offering. This is one key to above-average profit growth.

   The other key is low-cost and efficient operation. Your firm cannot deliver superior value if your costs are higher than competitors offering similar products and services. Excellent cost management is often heavily dependent on operations leadership and personnel; however, marketing has a key role to play in cost management, primarily through leading value engineering and relating every cost to the value it adds to a superior customer experience.

3. **Everyone is a marketer and should think like one.** You will recall that Chapter 4 on Integrated Marketing outlined a process for getting everyone across the organization to think like a marketer, through job objectives, appraisals, and incentives geared to two things—serving internal and external customers and managing cost from a customer-driven perspective.

4. **Quality is free.**[1] Quality experts have long held the view that the additional cost necessary to achieve better quality was

---

[1] Philip Crosby, *Quality Is Free*, McGraw-Hill, 1979.

offset by the avoidance of reprocessing, scrap, and returns associated with lower-quality offerings. Superior quality also enhances the effectiveness of marketing spending, not the least of which is through high retention of customers and loyalty factors.

5. **Closeness to customers is a key factor for success in any business.** One of the means for achieving superior value is to understand customer needs today by monitoring how well they are being met by your firm and your competitors, and anticipating how they will change tomorrow. In doing this, there is no substitute for direct face-to-face, phone, or online communications with customers and consumers, not just by Marketing people but also by those in Operations, R&D, Finance, and Engineering. Creative and well-planned customer research is helpful, but it needs to be supplemented with in-house direct contact and dialogue.

6. **Differentiation, enhanced by strong branding, builds sustained competitive advantage.** Marketers seek to deliver superior value in areas important to the customer. However, the ideal is to have a differentiated offering and to exploit this differentiation through strong brand management.

7. **Investment in strong and relevant customer communication usually pays off.** If your company has a distinctive and relevant customer proposition, well executed and effectively monitored, you have a powerful engine for profitable growth worth investing in. Of course, it is possible to overly spend on communications, or to spend the right amount the wrong way. However, to protect the communications opportunity, marketers need to seek agreement across the organization and at the governance level on the best criteria for evaluating communications expenditures, and apply these rigorously across media and over time.

8. **The key decisions with respect to marketing are made by the board of directors and senior management, not by marketers.** The board of directors and senior management make critical decisions with respect to stakeholder priorities, commitment to investment, long- versus short-term outlook, attitude to quality, service, and cost. Board decisions create the environment in which Offensive Marketing can flourish. Marketers can and should influence this decision-making.

9. **Rigorous business analysis and purposeful testing greatly increase the effectiveness of marketing.** Thoughtful business analysis is a critical tool for the Offensive Marketer. By converting information into knowledge and understanding and using this to construct relevant tests, risk can be dramatically reduced and a comparison of options is possible. Marketers should be like laboratory workers, continually checking out hypotheses and pushing forward the frontiers of knowledge through experimentation.

What do marketers need to do in the future to exploit the opportunity that Offensive Marketing poses?

First, you need to apply the full Offensive Marketing approach rather than using bits and pieces because it works best as a totality.

Second, you should adopt a process-driven approach to marketing, using sequential steps for implementing principles and programs set out in this book. Process management in marketing, as in other disciplines, involves thinking through the best way of tackling a task, breaking it down into steps, and applying the learning time after time. Instead of it being rigid, creativity must be actively built into these processes to respond to rapidly changing market conditions and customer expectations. Marketing process management can provide many benefits: freeing more time for long-term development; enhancing both creativity and speed to market; and, spreading the marketing message across the company because so many processes are cross-departmental.

Third, spend more time on development and less on housekeeping. Most marketers spend at least 80 percent of their time on tactics and administration and less than 20 percent on things that build customer franchise. Improvement will occur, for example, by restructuring the Marketing Department to create brand-equity managers and by allocating more of the day-to-day tactical activities to specialists.

Fourth, press for change in the way company performance is evaluated. While most marketers are aware that they need to improve efficiencies, especially in accounting for marketing spending, it is time to question outdated financial measures and press for more relevant indicators of company performance. In addition, financial reporting needs to include those intangible assets and competencies critical to future business success.

And lastly, but perhaps most importantly, sell Offensive Marketing to non-marketers in your company. Historically, marketers have not spent enough time and effort selling the merit of the marketing approach to their colleagues in other departments. If marketing is to be a cross-functional process, and if everyone is to think like a marketer in the future, this thinking is essential. Marketers need to inform, educate, persuade, and enthuse their colleagues about the Offensive Marketing approach. A good starting point is the enduring principles of marketing outlined here in the post-script.

Index